CORE CONCEPTS OF INFORMATION TECHNOLOGY AUDITING

James E. Hunton
Bentley College

Stephanie M. Bryant
University of South Florida

Nancy A. Bagranoff
Old Dominion University

WILEY

www.wiley.com/college/hunton

Executive Editor   *Jay O'Callaghan*
Editorial Assistant   *Brian Kamins*
Marketing Manager   *Steve Herdegen*
Managing Editor   *Lari Bishop*
Associate Production Manager   *Kelly Tavares*
Production Editor   *Sarah Wolfman-Robichaud*
Illustration Editor   *Kris Pauls*
Cover Design   *Jennifer Fisher*
Cover Image   *© Guy Crittenden/Images.com, Inc.*

This book was set in Times by Leyh Publishing LLC and printed and bound by Hamilton Printing. The cover was printed by Phoenix Color Corp.

This book is printed on acid free paper. ∞

Library of Congress Cataloging in Publication Data:
Hunton, James E.
Core concepts of IS audit / James Hunton, Stephanie Bryant.
p. cm.

Includes bibliographical references and index.
ISBN 0-471-22293-3 (pbk. : alk. paper)
1. Electronic data processing departments–Auditing. 2. Information technology–Auditing. 3. Auditing–Data processing. 4. Information storage and retrieval–Accounting. 5. Information storage and retrieval–Auditing. I. Bryant, Stephanie M. II. Title.

HF5548.35.H86 2003
658.4'78–dc21
2003049722

USA ISBN: 0-471-22293-3
WIE ISBN: 0-471-45181-9

Printed in the United States of America

10 9 8 7 6 5 4

Betty and Phoebe—this one's for you!

James E. Hunton

To my husband, Gary, and my daughters, Samantha and Amber, for their unwavering support. And to my parents for always being there. There aren't enough words.

Stephanie M. Bryant

For the kids: Stacia and Nick; Kara, Jeff, and Natalie; Amanda and Chris; and Scott.

Nancy A. Bagranoff

CONTENTS

Chapter 3

INFORMATION TECHNOLOGY RISKS AND CONTROLS   **47**

Chapter 6

IT NETWORKS AND TELECOMMUNICATIONS RISKS   **125**

Chapter 7

E-BUSINESS RISKS   **151**

Chapter 8

USING COMPUTER ASSISTED AUDIT TOOLS AND TECHNIQUES (CAATTS)   177

Chapter 9

CONDUCTING THE IT AUDIT   **207**

Chapter 10

FRAUD AND FORENSIC AUDITING   **229**

PREFACE

We wrote this book for three primary reasons. First, we wanted to provide a concise, non-technical approach to information technology (IT) auditing. Many financial auditing professors we talked with all over the country expressed an urgent desire to integrate IT auditing concepts into their courses. However, they have not done so because they could not find a book that was easy to understand and succinct, yet comprehensive. We believe that our IT auditing book fills this need perfectly, as it can be used as a supplemental resource in undergraduate and graduate financial auditing courses. We designed this book in such a way that auditing professors can "pick and choose" various IT auditing topics from the material to fulfill their own course objectives.

Second, although this book reflects core concepts of IT auditing, the breadth and depth of coverage allows it to be used as a standalone text in an IT auditing class or a supplement to an Accounting Information Systems (AIS) course. The juxtaposition of comprehensiveness and conciseness in our book allows IT auditing and AIS instructors to cover a wide range of relevant topics *and* to complement their courses with guest speakers, hands-on audit software such as ACL (which is included with this text), in-class discussions, and cases. Indeed, we designed and tested our book with these objectives in mind, and the reviews and comments have been overwhelmingly positive!

Third, the accounting profession is undergoing dramatic changes due to Enron, Xerox, Adelphia Communications and other high-profile accounting scandals. Consequently, the profession is faced with a variety of new rules and regulations to follow and enforce. Auditors, in particular, have been and continue to be deeply affected, as indicated by The Sarbanes-Oxley Act, Statement of Auditing Standards 94, and Statement of Auditing Standards 99. Importantly, many of the new rules require auditors to more closely examine risks and controls associated with information technology. In this light, this book incorporates all the new rules and regulations and provides insight and guidance to students as to how auditors are affected by these sweeping changes in the profession.

ABOUT THE AUTHORS

James E. Hunton earned his B.B.A. degree in accounting from West Texas State University. He received his M.B.A. degree in management from Rivier College in Nashua, New Hampshire, and earned his Ph.D. in business administration (majoring in accounting and information systems) from the University of Texas at Arlington. Professor Hunton is also a certified public accountant (Texas). Immediately after high school, Jim served for three years in the U.S. Army. Before beginning a Ph.D. program in 1991, he served another four years in the Army as a finance officer. Afterward, he was an information systems auditor for Arthur Young, financial analyst and plant controller for Mobil Oil Company, and controller and general manager for a publishing company located in southeast Texas. Since earning his Ph.D in 1994, Dr. Hunton has served as assistant professor at Virginia Commonwealth University and associate professor at the University of South Florida, where he held the prestigious Quinn Eminent Scholar professorship. He is currently a professor at Bentley College, holding the esteemed chaired position of "Trustee Professor." He has published numerous articles in accounting, information systems, and psychology journals. Some of the many accounting journals in which he has published are *The Accounting Review, Journal of Accounting Research, Accounting, Organizations & Society, Accounting Horizons, Journal of Management Accounting Research, Auditing: A Journal of Practice and Theory, Behavioral Research in Accounting, Journal of Information Systems, International Journal of Accounting Information Systems, Information Systems Audit and Control Journal,* and *Journal of Accountancy.* Other journals in which he has published include *Journal of Applied Psychology, Organizational Behavior and Human Decision Processes, Journal of Behavioral Decision Making, Management Science, Decision Sciences,* and *MIS Quarterly.* He is a co-author with Professors Bagranoff and Bryant of another book, *Core Concepts of Consulting for Accountants.* Professor Hunton is an active member of the AICPA and the American Accounting Association. He served as president of the Information Systems Section of the American Accounting Association from 2002 to 2003. Additionally, he is a professor of Accounting and Information Systems at the University of Amsterdam and University of Maastricht—both located in the Netherlands.

Stephanie M. Bryant, Ph.D., CPA, is an associate professor of Accounting at the University of South Florida, where she holds the position of Advisory Council Professor of Accounting. She previously taught at James Madison University, in Harrisonburg, Virginia, where she served as the director of the Accounting Information Systems Program. She earned both her B.S. in accounting and Ph.D. in accounting (concentration in information systems) at Louisiana State University. Dr. Bryant teaches graduate and undergraduate classes in consulting, accounting information systems, and information systems audit, and previously worked for KPMG Peat Marwick. Professor Bryant is active in the American Accounting Association Information Systems section. She also serves on the national board of directors of Beta Alpha Psi as director of the Southeast Region. Dr. Bryant has published numerous articles appearing in such journals as *Behavioral Research in Accounting, Advances in Behavioral Research in Accounting, Journal of American Taxation Association, Journal of Accountancy, Issues in Accounting*

Education, International Journal of Accounting, Review of Accounting Information Systems, International Journal of Intelligent Systems in Accounting, Finance, and Management, and *Accounting and Business.* She is a co-author with Professors Bagranoff and Hunton on another book, *Core Concepts of Consulting for Accountants.*

Nancy A. Bagranoff received her A.A. degree from Briarcliff College, B.S. degree from the Ohio State University, and M.S. degree in accounting from Syracuse University. Her D.B.A. degree was conferred by the George Washington University in 1986 (accounting major and information systems minor). From 1973 to 1976, she was employed by General Electric in Syracuse, New York, where she completed the company's Financial Management Training Program. Dr. Bagranoff is a certified public accountant, licensed in the District of Columbia, since 1982. She taught at American University for many years and served as the chair of the Department of Accounting from 1995 to 1998. She spent fall 1994 as Faculty in Residence at Arthur Andersen, where she worked for the Business Systems Consulting and Computer Risk Management groups. Professor Bagranoff has published many articles in such journals as *Journal of Information Systems, Journal of Accounting Literature, Computers and Accounting, The Journal of Accounting Education, Journal of Accountancy, Strategic Finance,* and the *Information Systems Audit and Control Journal.* She is co-author, with S. A. Moscove and M. G. Simkin, of *Core Concepts of Accounting Information Systems.* She is also a co-author with Professors Bryant and Hunton on a second book, *Core Concepts of Consulting for Accountants.* Dr. Bagranoff spent several years at Miami University, where she served as director of the Masters in Accountancy program. Currently Dr. Bagranoff is the dean of the College of Business and Public Administration at Old Dominion University.

ACKNOWLEDGEMENTS

We have many people to thank for their efforts in helping us research, write, and edit this book. First, we thank our students, who in some cases "tested" this material for us. Our graduate assistants, including Bin Shen at Miami University, were also helpful in reading our drafts.

We owe a special thanks to Kate Head, audit manager at the University of South Florida's Office of Inspector General. Kate provided the context for the ACL project in Appendix B. She has also spent many tireless hours working with us on ACL issues and serving as a liaison with ACL. Kate is an expert in computer assisted auditing tools and techniques (CAATTs) and provided the table in Chapter 8 showing CAATTs by functional area. Finally, Kate served as a reviewer for several chapters in the book.

Several accounting professionals helped us as well. Kevin Cash of Ernst and Young LLP was very supportive of this project, reviewing several chapters for us and providing insightful comments that helped improve the readability and quality of the book. He also provided the SAS 70 examples in Chapter 9. Tracy Stromberg and Kirk Khan of Ernst and Young LLP also helped provide the framework for much of Chapter 9 based on current IT audit practices. John Hayes, also of Ernst and Young LLP, reviewed Chapters 6 and 7 for technical accuracy.

We would also like to thank our colleagues who reviewed this text and provided invaluable critiques. They are: Walter Baggett, Manhattan College; Alan Friedberg, Florida Atlantic University; Venkat Iyer, University of North Carolina–Greensboro; Louis Jacoby, Saginaw Valley State University; Robert Nehmer, Berry College; and Jerry Turner, University of Memphis.

To the others who graciously gave us permission to use or cite their materials, thank you so much. These include the Association of Certified Fraud Examiners, the City of Toronto, the Information Systems Audit and Control Association, Mike Deyo of JANUS Associates, Tom Buckhoff (professor of Forensic Accounting at North Dakota State University), and the Better Business Bureau of Mainland British Columbia.

We would also like to thank our universities and colleagues for their patience in allowing us the time and space to complete this project.

Finally, we would like to thank Jay O'Callaghan of John Wiley & Sons for his wisdom, patience, and dedication to this book. Jay, we owe you a great debt of gratitude for shepherding us through this project.

CHAPTER 1

IT AUDIT OVERVIEW

CHAPTER CONTENTS

INTRODUCTION

> The need for information technology auditors far outstrips the supply of qualified candidates.[1]

These should be encouraging words if you're thinking about a career in IT auditing. Advances in technology and its pervasiveness, coupled with a heightened appreciation of the need for auditing, are likely to make this statement ring true for some time to come.

Not only are information technology (IT) auditors in demand, but their work is interesting and challenging. IT auditors evaluate an organizational entity's information system, which includes information technologies, data and information, and systems of communication. This evaluation is likely to entail poring over documents and interviewing people as well as entering or manipulating data in a computer. IT auditors need to do this both because business processes use IT to function and because IT is likely to be integral to an enterprise's viability.

This chapter provides an overview of the IT audit function, describing the work of IT auditors and the skills they need, explaining how to become an IT auditor, describing the structure of IT audits, and discussing IT audit's relationship with accounting and financial audit. The last section of the chapter provides an overview of the rest of the book.

THE IMPACT OF IT ON ORGANIZATIONS

You probably don't need convincing that IT is important in all kinds of organizations—but what you may not realize is the influence IT has on organizational risks and controls. IT creates opportunities, but these opportunities bring with them many kinds of risks. For instance, the ability to transmit documents electronically to customers and vendors presents an opportunity to improve efficiency in the supply chain. However, the potential failure of these electronic communications systems poses a new risk. This section of the chapter introduces IT governance, an important concept for IT auditors that relates to risks and controls in the IT process. It also explains the influence of IT on the transactions that business information systems process.

IT Governance

IT governance is the process for controlling an organization's information technology resources, where these resources are defined to include information and communications systems as well as technology. An organization's management and owners (represented by the board of directors) share responsibility for governing both the enterprise and IT. Enterprise governance is the process of setting and implementing corporate strategy, making sure the organization achieves its objectives efficiently, and manage risks. IT governance is an increasingly important part of enterprise governance because of organizational dependency on information and communication, the scale of IT investment, potential for IT to create strategic opportunities, and the level of IT risk. IT governance also requires controlling the IT process to ensure that it complies with regulatory, legal, and contractual requirements.[2]

The objectives of IT governance are to set strategies for IT so that it is closely aligned with organizational goals and to use IT for maximum opportunity but minimum risk. Therefore there are two parts to IT governance. The first part concerns the use of IT to promote an organization's objectives and enable business processes. The second part involves managing and controlling IT-related risks.

IT governance begins with the development of an IT governance plan. Such a plan will help set the strategic course of IT acquisition and deployment or use. IT governance is an ongoing process, and management needs to regularly evaluate and update plans. The IT governance plan should include performance measures against which progress can be evaluated.

In 1998, the Information Systems Audit and Control Association (ISACA) established the IT Governance Institute. The increasing reliance on technology and technology's growing value as an asset to business enterprises created the need for such a group. The IT Governance Institute "exists to clarify and provide guidance on current and future issues pertaining to IT governance, control and assurance."[3] It engages in many projects, including the development of Control Objectives of Information and Related Technology, third edition (CobiT), and Control Objectives for Enterprise Governance (COEG). CobiT provides guidance on IT governance by providing "the structure that links IT processes, IT resources and information to enterprise strategies and objectives."[4] While CobiT was once a tool primarily for auditors to use, the increasing criticality of IT governance has caused it to evolve into a management resource.

The third edition of CobiT includes an IT Governance Management Guideline, which identifies critical success factors, key goal and performance indicators, and a maturity model for IT governance. This guideline is for management to use in evaluating performance relative to IT. Specifically, the guideline states:

> Governance over information technology and its processes with the business goal of adding value, while balancing risk versus return, ensures delivery of information to the business that addresses the required **Information Criteria** and is measured by **Key Goal Indicators,** is enabled by creating and maintaining a system of process and control excellence appropriate for the business that directs and monitors the business value delivery of IT, considers **Critical Success Factors** that leverage all **IT Resources** and is measured by **Key Performance Indicators.**[5]

CobiT defines each of the terms shown in bold type. Of note is the emphasis on accountability through goal indicators and performance measures.

Figure 1-1 shows the IT governance framework. This framework emphasizes that an organization first sets its IT objectives, and then follows a continual process in which performance is measured and compared against those objectives. This process provides direction for increasing IT resources, decreasing costs, and managing risks.

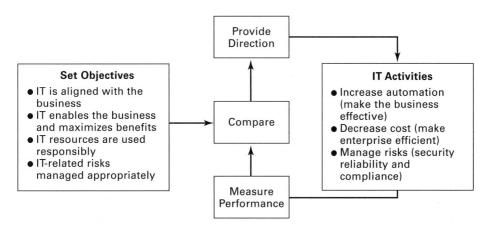

FIGURE 1-1 The IT Governance Framework
Source: www.itgovernance.org. Reprinted with permission from the Information Systems Audit and Control Association, Rolling Meadows, IL, USA 60008.

While IT governance is just plain good business practice, it's also a possible source of competitive advantage. Organizations that leverage IT effectively are likely to create more value for customers and other stakeholders. Horror stories about lack of return on IT investments and security failures are also reasons why organizations should invest in developing IT governance plans and policies.

IT and Transaction Processing

Part of IT governance concerns controlling IT risk. This is important in enterprises because management uses IT to process data about ongoing transactions or events. Businesses and other organizational entities are involved in and affected by many events. As these events occur, the information system collects data about them. For example, when a customer purchases a product, the information system collects data about the product, the customer, the salesperson, quantity, and so on. Eventually these data become information, perhaps in a financial report. The information systems in an organization are involved in a continual process of collecting data about transactions and turning it into information, which it reports to various stakeholders.

A computerized information system for transaction processing may increase some risks and decrease others. In the sales example, a sales clerk who manually records the data surrounding the sale may make a data entry error, perhaps transposing the inventory code. On the other hand, a computer system that scans an inventory bar code will not make that mistake. This is an example where the use of IT can reduce risk. However, if the database administrator has accidentally made a mismatch of inventory item description and item number, then every sale of that inventory item will be recorded incorrectly. The use of IT can reduce risks due to human error, but it can also increase them. Human errors that come from repetitive data entry might be replaced by programming errors. Computers are reliable in that they do the same thing over and over the same way. Unfortunately, if that same thing is incorrect one time, it's likely to be wrong all the time.

THE WORK OF AN IT AUDITOR

The previous example of entering sales data illustrates how risks change with a computerized transaction processing system. This change in risk dictates changes in how an auditor needs to work. For example, an auditor may need to look at a computer program to make sure the system logic is correct.

IT auditors have been around as long as IT itself. They ensure IT governance and, in doing so, assess IT risks and implement or monitor the controls over those risks. The roles of IT auditors vary with their position within or outside an organization and with each individual project. The level of expertise needed for an engagement also varies from the very technical to a need for plain old common sense and good communications skills.

An IT auditor works as either an internal or external auditor. We'll discuss some of these roles throughout this chapter. Regardless of the inside or outside view, these auditors are likely to be assessing IT risks and controls. Sometimes this is done as supporting work for the financial audit (discussed later in this chapter), and at other times the objective of the evaluation of IT risks and controls is done for its own sake. Basically an IT auditor can provide assurance or give comfort over just about anything related to information systems, but some of the specific types of engagements an IT auditor might perform include:

- Evaluating controls over specific applications. This would entail analyzing the risks and controls over applications such as e-business, enterprise resource planning (ERP) systems, or other software.

- Providing assurance over specific processes. This may be an "agreed upon procedures" audit in which the client and the IT auditor determine the scope of the assurance.

- Providing third-party assurance. IT auditors often must evaluate the risks and controls over a third party's information systems and provide assurance to others.

- Penetration testing. This involves trying to gain access to information resources in order to discover security weaknesses.

- Supporting the financial audit. This encompasses evaluating IT risks and controls that may affect the reliability of the financial reporting system.

- Searching for IT-based fraud. IT auditors may be called upon to help investigate computer records in fraud investigations.

THE RELATIONSHIP BETWEEN FINANCIAL AND IT AUDITS

The objective of a financial statement audit is to ensure that an organization's public financial statements are presented in accordance with generally accepted accounting principles (GAAP). Financial statement auditors, in the course of an audit engagement, analyze an organization's internal control system to assess the degree to which it appears to be operating effectively. For example, an internal control system might call for the separation of duties with respect to processing accounts receivable. The financial auditor might inspect job descriptions to be sure that the separation of duties exists. The degree to which an organization has an effective internal control system influences the scope of work the auditor must do. This work includes substantive testing or verification of transactions and account balances.

As organizations have increased their reliance on computer technology in processing transactions and reporting information, it has become increasingly difficult for financial auditors to ignore IT in their audits. When computer systems were relatively simple and computer processing in one system was not integrated with that in another system, it was possible for auditors to audit "around" the computer. This process entailed inspecting inputs and outputs and assuming that the reasonableness of reports based on data input ensured that the computer processing was appropriate. Today's complex IT environments call for an evaluation of the information system as part of the financial audit. Not only does such an assessment better ensure that financial auditors have considered all risks and controls, but the audit of an organization's IT controls also can reduce the scope of the audit.

Figure 1-2 shows the financial statement auditing process and identifies the recommended activities of the IT auditor at each phase. Note that the IT auditor may work hand-in-hand with the financial auditor through each step in the engagement, from planning through delivery of the audit report. The amount of work the IT auditor does may depend on the support the financial auditor requests. For example, the financial auditors may do all the substantive testing themselves. Alternatively, they might ask the IT auditor to assist them by using computer assisted audit tools (CAATs). Specifically, the IT auditor could perform a data analysis routine on accounts receivable files to re-age the data or to perform a computerized data analysis to recalculate asset depreciation.

Several professional standards and frameworks recognize the importance of auditing the information system in the course of a financial audit. For example, in 2001, the Auditing Standards Board (ASB) of the American Institute of Certified Public Accountants (AICPA) issued Statement on Auditing Standards (SAS) No. 94, *The Effect of Information Technology on the Auditor's Consideration of Internal Control in a Financial Statement Audit.* This standard, which we will discuss more deeply in Chapter 3, requires auditors to

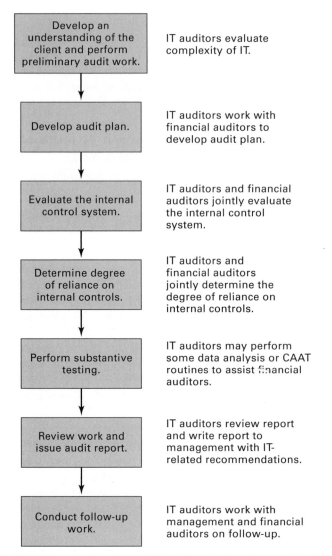

FIGURE 1-2 The Role of IT Auditors in the Financial Audit Process

understand both manual and computerized processes for financial statement preparation and to recognize the additional risks and benefits of IT relative to internal control. The standard also cautions auditors that IT use in an organization may be so pervasive that the quality of audit evidence may depend on IT controls. Finally, SAS No. 94 notes that auditors need specialized skills in order to be able to understand IT controls and the impact of IT on a financial statement audit. Auditors are to acquire those skills themselves or obtain assistance from a specialized IT auditor.

New regulations for audits, such as the Sarbanes-Oxley Act of 2002, have also influenced the relationship between financial and IT audits. This act, which was created to restore confidence in financial reports, mandates that management assess and make representations about internal controls. Auditors will need to test those controls and provide assurance about management's representations. Since many internal controls involve IT, it is likely that these requirements will increase the involvement of an IT auditor in a financial audit engagement. As a result of SAS No. 94 and the Sarbanes-Oxley Act, the portion of the financial audit budget devoted to IT on a typical engagement could increase from zero percent to 10 percent to 20 percent or more, depending on the complexity of the information system and the industry. For example, the IT portion of the financial audit is particularly significant in the financial services industry.

IT AUDIT SKILLS

In order to do their work, IT auditors need training and education. IT auditors are likely to hold at least a bachelor's degree. The graduate might have majored in most anything, but commonly education will be in information systems, computer science, and/or accounting. In addition to a basic undergraduate education, many IT auditors have graduate degrees and special certifications or licenses. The certifications can be fairly general, such as a Certified Public Accountant (CPA), Certified Fraud Examiner (CFE), Certified Internal Auditor (CIA), or Certified Information Systems Auditor (CISA) license. (We'll discuss some of these in detail later in the chapter.) There are also specific certifications for hardware, software, and procedures, such as a Microsoft Certified Systems Engineer for Microsoft Windows 2000 or certification as a business continuity professional.

Another potential certification is the Certified Information Systems Security Professional (CISSP) designation. Trust is particularly important in the computer security industry. After all, how do you know that the security specialist you've hired isn't a hacker? As a result, the International Information Systems Security Certification Consortium (ISC)[2], a not-for-profit security association, created the CISSP. Certification requires three years of practical work experience and candidates must pass an exam that covers topics such as cryptography, access control systems, security architectures, operations security, and legal and ethical issues.

Technical Skills

IT auditors acquire specialized technology skills as they work with different platforms (operating systems) and software applications. The auditors typically have a guide describing specific features of the operating system and steps to follow in extracting data and testing controls. Case-in-Point 1-1 describes how this might work.

Case-in-Point 1-1

A test IT auditors perform in evaluating IBM's Application System 400 (AS/400) is to check user profiles. The AS/400 ships with seven preconfigured user profiles and default passwords for each of them. These profiles grant special privileges to users who will work with the system, such as the system operator and the security officer. The default password is the same name as the user name—i.e., for system operator both are QSYSOPR. One of the tests the IT auditor will want to do is to make sure management has changed the default passwords. To test this, the auditor tries to sign on using QSYSOPR as the sign-on and password. If it works, then obviously the defaults are still operational and any user with this knowledge would be able to access most resources in the system. An alternative to trying to log in with defaults is to run the ANALYZE DEFAULT PASSWORDS command.[6]

While new IT auditors with a lot of knowledge about computer hardware and software, such as enterprise resource planning (ERP) systems, operating systems, e-business, and network security are highly desirable, it's probably most important that an individual planning a career in IT audit just genuinely "like" computers and technology. An interest in learning about technical topics is probably the best asset. After all, information technology changes constantly and IT auditors should recognize that this career entails learning something new every day.

General Personal and Business Skills

While technical computer skills are important to an IT auditor, general communication and business skills probably matter even more. IT auditors, like all auditors, write up their work. They also frequently make presentations to internal or external clients. As a result, written and oral communication skills are keys to success in the profession.

Another important skill area for auditors is interpersonal skills and teamwork. Rarely do IT auditors work in isolation. They generally need the support of other auditors and the cooperation of those whom they are auditing. "The auditor is coming on Monday," is a dreaded phrase. An auditor needs some really good interpersonal skills to overcome the negative bias towards auditors of people whose work is under their scrutiny.

Business education is also important for IT auditors. The IT that the auditors will evaluate is used by business organizations to support their processes. Therefore the auditor needs to understand these business processes, including financial, distribution, human resources, and manufacturing processes.

Because accountants are so well trained in business processes, particularly in financial processes, accounting is a highly desirable knowledge area for IT auditors. Plus, accountants are educated in auditing in general, which makes them ideal candidates for IT audit jobs. However, other business training is useful too. For instance, IT auditors can use marketing skills in selling services to clients, and even in selling them on accepting the results of their work.

Yet another important skill area is decision sciences, as illustrated in Case-in-Point 1-2.

Case-in-Point 1-2

The sheer volume of data processed by IT often call for statistical analysis tools to investigate patterns that might indicate fraud or processing errors. Benford's Law is a mathematical model that analyzes the frequency of numbers in databases against naturally occurring numbers patterns to detect possible data manipulation or falsified data. The law, which was discovered in the 19th century, notes that most numbers begin with low digits, i.e., one, two, or three, and that number distributions are not random. Patterns in these nonrandom distributions suggest manipulation.

PROFESSIONAL IT AUDITOR ORGANIZATIONS AND CERTIFICATIONS

There are a number of professional organizations to which IT auditors may choose to belong. These groups issue certifications to members who meet various service and knowledge requirements. The groups include the Information Systems Audit and Control Association (ISACA), the Institute of Internal Auditors (IIA), the Association of Certified Fraud Examiners (ACFE), and the American Institute of Certified Public Accountants (AICPA).

The Information Systems Audit and Control Association (ISACA)

The Information Systems Audit and Control Association (ISACA), founded in 1969, is the largest professional organization of IT auditors.[7] This group has more than twenty-five thousand members in over one hundred countries and has certified more than twenty-nine thousand IT auditors. ISACA has a research arm, the Information Systems Audit and Control Foundation, which conducts research and issues publications that guide IT audit professionals. ISACA also established the IT Governance Institute, which was discussed earlier in the chapter. The ISACA's Web site hosts K-Net, a knowledge network repository of information about IT governance, control, and assurance; it is available to ISACA members.

The Certified Information Systems Auditor (CISA) designation is the most highly valued global credential for IT auditors. ISACA began offering CISA certification in 1978. A CISA must successfully complete an examination that is administered annually, meet professional experience requirements, abide by the group's Code of Professional Ethics, and meet continuing education requirements.

The CISA examination tests knowledge in seven technical areas. Figure 1-3 lists these topics and the approximate weight given to them on the examination. ISACA offers study guides, and many local chapters sponsor review classes to help members pass the exam.

Certification generally requires a minimum of five years' experience in IT auditing, control, or security, although there are several options available that will waive part of this requirement. For example, a professional can substitute one year of financial auditing experience for one year of IT audit practice. The experience must be within ten years prior to the certification application date or within five years of passing the exam. CISA professionals must also agree to a code of professional ethics designed to guide them in their conduct (described in Chapter 2) and to abide by ISACA's Information Systems Auditing Standards (discussed throughout this book). Because IT auditing careers require continuous learning, a CISA must complete twenty contact hours of continuing education each year and 120 contact hours in a three-year period in order to maintain certification.

In addition to the CISA, ISACA recently created a new credential, the Certified Information Security Manager (CISM), for non–audit security professionals.

The Institute of Internal Auditors (IIA)

The Institute of Internal Auditors (IIA), established in 1941, is an international organization of internal auditing professionals. The organization produces a journal, hosts professional meetings and educational seminars, conducts research through the IIA Research Foundation, and issues the Certified Internal Auditor (CIA) credential, along with certifications in control self-assessment, government auditing, and financial services auditing. The organization also promotes the practice of internal auditing through quality assurance and the issuance of standards, guidelines, and best practices. The IIA is one of the primary professional organizations that serve accountants in their various roles. The IIA's membership is made up of

---

The IS Audit Process (10%)

Management, Planning, and Organization of IS (11%)

Technical Infrastructure and Operational Practices (13%)

Protection of Information Assets (25%)

Disaster Recovery and Business Continuity (10%)

Business Application System Development, Acquisition, Implementation, and Maintenance (16%)

Business Process Evaluation and Risk Management (15%)

FIGURE 1-3   Topical Coverage on the Certified Information Systems Auditor Examination

internal auditors; the American Institute of Certified Public Accountants (AICPA) represents public accountants; and the Institute of Management Accounting (IMA) promotes the practice of management accounting and corporate finance.

An IT auditor may be either an external auditor or a member of an organization's internal audit staff. Many large corporations employ fairly large internal audit staffs, which include a number of IT auditors. Interestingly, some public accounting firms also employ internal auditors, if they engage in provide outsourced internal audit services to organizations that cannot justify maintaining a sufficiently large internal audit staff. The internal auditors working for public accounting firms may have more specialized IT skills than a true internal auditor may be able to maintain because they have the opportunity to work with many business, government, and not-for-profit organizations and with multiple technologies.

An internal auditor may choose to become certified as a CISA or a CPA. In addition, such professionals may seek to become a Certified Internal Auditor, which carries with it the designation of CIA (which means that internal auditors are at risk to be mistaken for spies or chefs). To be a CIA, a candidate must have a bachelor's degree or meet international equivalency standards, provide a character reference, have twenty-four months of internal audit or equivalent experience, and pass the CIA examination. The internal auditor, upon obtaining certification, must agree to abide by a professional code of ethics and also complete eighty hours of continuing professional education (CPE) in every two-year period.

The CIA examination, given twice each year, covers, in addition to the Professional Practices Framework, four main knowledge areas: (1) the internal audit process, (2) internal audit skills, (3) management control and information technology, and (4) the audit environment. Questions on information technology comprise about half of the section on management control and information technology. IT topics include: (1) IS strategies, policies, and procedures; (2) hardware, platforms, networks, and telecommunications; (3) data processing; (4) systems development, acquisition, and maintenance; and (5) IS security and contingency planning. As a result, the CIA designation ensures a level of competency with respect to IT audit areas.

Internal auditors are frequently involved in assessing their organization's IT risks and controls. Audit committees of the corporate Board of Directors often wish to be apprised of the security risks associated with such technologies as the Internet. While most large businesses employ an information systems security officer and maintain a security administration function, the internal auditor can provide oversight for security activities and can ensure that the appropriate resources are directed toward controlling IT risks.

The Association of Certified Fraud Examiners (ACFE)

The Association of Certified Fraud Examiners (ACFE), as its name implies, issues the Certified Fraud Examiner (CFE) credential to professionals who specialize in auditing for fraud. Many frauds are enabled by technology or use IT in some way. As a result, an IT auditor may wish to seek a credential demonstrating expertise in this area. Chapter 10 discusses fraud auditing in depth.

CFE candidate eligibility is based on a point system. Points are awarded for higher education and professional experience. Professional experience must be either directly in fraud examination, or in related areas that include accounting and auditing, criminology or sociology, fraud investigation, loss prevention, and certain legal fields. Applicants must pass an examination administered by the ACFE and agree to abide by the organization's Code of Ethics and Bylaws.

The CFE examination is made up of five hundred objective questions and is given by computer. Areas of coverage are: fraudulent financial transactions, fraud investigation, legal elements of fraud, and criminology and ethics. Interestingly, the exam does not cover IT explicitly, and IT is not a focus.

The American Institute of Certified Public Accountants (AICPA)

The AICPA is the professional organization that confers the Certified Public Accountant (CPA) license. The organization has a membership of about 350,000 accounting professionals. In 1934, the Securities and Exchange Commission (SEC) began requiring public companies to have their financial statements audited by CPAs. CPAs engage in all aspects of accounting, including tax, consulting, and IT auditing. The CPA provides a good foundation for an IT auditor, because it ensures that the auditor will have a thorough understanding of financial processes and reporting.

In 2000, the AICPA introduced a new credential that is an "add-on" to the CPA license. This is the Certified Information Technology Professional (CITP) certification. The purpose of this credential is to demonstrate that a CPA has specialized expertise in IT. The topical areas covered by the examination required for CITP certification, and their relative weights are shown in Figure 1-4.

While the CITP is *not* a credential directly intended for IT auditors, many of the areas of knowledge tested on the qualifying examination do overlap those covered by the CISA examination. CPAs who engage in IT consulting work, which may include some aspects of IT audit, security, or control, may benefit from obtaining the CITP credential. The credential would demonstrate some level of expertise and knowledge about IT beyond that of a traditional financial auditor. The AICPA also maintains an IT Membership Section for professionals with an interest in IT-related work.

STRUCTURING IT AUDITS

So how do you do complete an IT audit engagement? The procedures vary with the many types of IT audits. These include: (1) attestations or agreed upon procedures audits, (2) Statement on Auditing Standards #70 audits, (3) IT audits in support of external financial audits, and (4) findings and recommendations reviews. Each of these is discussed in some detail in Chapter 9. In this section of our introductory chapter, we will briefly discuss some of the standards and guidelines IT auditors use in their work.

AICPA Audit Standards and Guidelines

The Auditing Standards Board (ASB) of the AICPA has traditionally issued auditing standards, opinions, and other guidance for public accountants to follow in conducting

---

Information Technology Strategic Planning (18%)
Information Systems Management (15%)
Systems Architecture (11%)
Business Applications and E-Business (16%)
Security, Privacy, and Contingency Planning (11%)
System Development, Acquisition, and Project Management (13%)
Systems Auditing and Internal Control (8%)
Databases and Database Management (8%)

FIGURE 1-4   Topical Coverage on the Certified Information Technology Professional Examination
Source: citp.aicpa.org/content.htm, March 13, 2003.

financial statement audits and other types of engagements.[8] The AICPA first issued the ten generally accepted auditing standards (GAAS) in 1947. These standards, falling into the categories of general, field work, and reporting standards, provide a framework for more specific guidance. Statements on Auditing Standards (SAS) are interpretations of GAAS with which a CPA must comply in financial statement audits of public companies. Several of these SAS concern IT risk, control, and audit, and Chapter 3 of this book discusses them in some detail.

Another set of AICPA audit standards is Statements on Standards for Attestation Engagements (SSAE). While IT auditors often do work to support financial statement audits, they may also be engaged by clients to perform an attestation. These are assignments where the auditor issues a report stating a conclusion about the reliability of subject matter that is the responsibility of someone else. For example, an auditor may be asked to make assertions about an organization's compliance with the Health Insurance Portability and Accountability Act (HIPAA), which created national privacy and security standards over health-related data.

In 2001, the ASB issued SSAE No. 10, *Attestation Standards: Revision and Recodification,* which superseded all previous attestation engagement statements. The new standards recognized that auditors are increasingly involved in providing assurance over nonfinancial information and so broadened the areas in which the standards would apply. Much of the new assurance that auditors are asked to provide concerns IT. For example, an auditor might be asked to attest to the number of "hits" at a Web site or the security of the Web server.

Attestation standards now concern any engagement where a CPA is to issue an examination, review, or agreed-upon procedures report. One objective of the new standard is to clarify the distinction between consulting services and attestation engagements. SSAE No. 10 explains that a consulting engagement is one in which advice is sought, whereas an attestation engagement results in a report that provides assurance over a specified area.

International Federation of Accountants (IFAC) Guidelines

The International Federation of Accountants (IFAC) is an international umbrella organization of national professional accountancy groups. These groups represent accountants in a variety of roles, including management, auditing, education, and tax. Member organizations are classified as full members, associate members and affiliate members. Full members in the United States are the AICPA, Institute of Management Accountants (IMA), and the National Association of State Boards of Accountancy (NASBA). ISACA and the IIA are affiliate members, and, like full members, they support the objectives and work of IFAC and the International Accounting Standards Board (IASB).

The mission of IFAC is to develop harmonized or common international accounting standards and guidelines to assist professionals in their work. They do this, in part, by supporting the work of the IASB.

IFAC has issued several types of guidance of use to IT auditors. The *IFAC Handbook of International IT Guidelines* provides direction concerning IT areas such as security, management of IT, acquisition of IT, IT operations, monitoring, and implementation. In addition, the International Auditing and Assurance Standards Board (IAASB), an IFAC committee, issues two types of auditing pronouncements. The International Standards on Auditing (ISAs) are to be used in financial statement audits and the International Auditing Practice Statements (IAPSs) provide auditors with help in implementing the standards. ISA No. 401, *Auditing in a Computer Information Systems Environment,* provides both financial and IT auditors with guidance in conducting financial statement audits that involve IT. Many of the practice statements provide help for auditing in specific environments or technologies such as e-commerce, database systems, and stand-alone computer systems.

ISACA Standards, Guidelines, and Procedures

Recognizing the complexity of IT auditing, the Standards Board of ISACA issues IT audit standards, guidelines, and procedures. The standards prescribe minimum performance levels required to comply with ISACA's Code of Professional Ethics, and they also communicate to management and others the type of work that an IT audit should encompass. A licensed CISA *must* comply with ISACA standards or face investigation and possible disciplinary actions. Guidelines provide help in applying the standards, and procedures are steps an IT auditor would take during the course of an audit engagement.

Figure 1-5 lists ISACA's IT audit standards. The first three numbers designate a standards category, and the three numbers following the decimal point indicate the actual standard. ISACA's categories of standards mirror many of those of the AICPA. For example, both professional bodies prescribe standards relative to independence, responsibility, competence, and reporting.

ISACA audit guidelines are indicated by a third level of detail in numbering and yet another decimal point and number system describes specific procedures within guidelines. (See Figure 1-6.)

The following provides an example of the hierarchical system (shown in Figures 1-5 and 1-6) for standards, guidelines, and procedures.

> **EXAMPLE** ISACA IS audit standard category *060 Performance of Audit Work* includes two standards. *060.020 Evidence* is the second standard within that category. This standard includes several guidelines. One such guideline is *060.020.070 Use of Computer Assisted Audit Techniques (CAATs) Guideline.*[9] So how should a CISA use CAATs to gather evidence? ISACA provides detailed procedures describing their use. Procedure 3.1.1 within 060.020.070 suggests that auditors reconcile control totals where appropriate. Note that this is a very specific activity that a CISA can include in an audit plan.

CobiT, ISACA's IT governance framework, may be used by auditors in assessing and advising management about internal controls. It includes a set of audit guidelines that provide IT auditors with a structure for internal control evaluation. The audit guidelines can help in audit planning, but they are not intended as a detailed template for the overall audit.

In addition to standards, guidelines, and procedures, ISACA, like most professional organizations, also publishes a variety of materials that practitioners can refer to in their work. These materials are particularly important for IT auditors because the ever-changing nature of IT requires continual learning.

AN OVERVIEW OF THIS BOOK

This book has three sections and two appendices. The first section of the book, which includes this chapter, is an introduction to the concept of IT audit. In addition to an overview, we include a chapter describing the legal and ethical environment surrounding the professional practice of IT auditing. At its core, IT auditing is about controlling risks associated with information systems and technologies. Chapter 3 introduces the concept of

010 Audit Charter

010.010 Responsibility, Authority and Accountability

The responsibility, authority and accountability of the information systems audit function are to be appropriately documented in an audit charter or engagement letter.

020 Independence

020.010 Professional Independence

In all matters related to auditing, the information systems auditor is to be independent of the auditee in attitude and appearance.

020.020 Organisational Relationship

The information systems audit function is to be sufficiently independent of the area being audited to permit objective completion of the audit.

030 Professional Ethics and Standards

030.010 Code of Professional Ethics

The information systems auditor is to adhere to the Code of Professional Ethics of the Information Systems Audit and Control Association.

030.020 Due Professional Care

Due professional care and observance of applicable professional auditing standards are to be exercised in all aspects of the information systems auditor's work.

040 Competence

040.010 Skills and Knowledge

The information systems auditor is to be technically competent, having the skills and knowledge necessary to perform the auditor's work.

040.020 Continuing Professional Education

The information systems auditor is to maintain technical competence through appropriate continuing professional education.

050 Planning

050.010 Audit Planning

The information systems auditor is to plan the information systems audit work to address the audit objectives and to comply with applicable professional auditing standards.

060 Performance of Audit Work

060.010 Supervision

Information systems audit staff are to be appropriately supervised to provide assurance that audit objectives are accomplished and applicable professional auditing standards are met.

060.020 Evidence

During the course of the audit, the information systems auditor is to obtain sufficient, reliable, relevant and useful evidence to achieve the audit objectives effectively. The audit findings and conclusions are to be supported by appropriate analysis and interpretation of this evidence.

070 Reporting

070.010 Report Content and Form

The information systems auditor is to provide a report, in an appropriate form, to intended recipients upon the completion of audit work. The audit report is to state the scope, objectives, period of coverage, and the nature and extent of the audit work performed. The report is to identify the organisation, the intended recipients and any restrictions on circulation. The report is to state the findings, conclusions and recommendations and any reservations or qualifications that the auditor has with respect to the audit.

080 Follow-Up Activities

080.010 Follow-Up

The information systems auditor is to request and evaluate appropriate information on previous relevant findings, conclusions and recommendations to determine whether appropriate actions have been implemented in a timely manner.

Effective Date

These standards are effective for all information systems audits with periods of coverage beginning 25 July 1997.

FIGURE 1-5 ISACA Standards for IS Auditing, Copyright 1997
Reprinted with permission from the Information Systems Audit and Control Association, Rolling Meadows, IL, USA 60008.

010 Audit Charter
    .010 Responsibility, Authority and Accountability
        .010 Audit Charter Effective 1 September 1999
        .020 Outsourcing of IS Activities to Other Organisations
        Effective 1 September 1999
020 Independence
    .010 Professional Independence
        .010 Effect of Nonaudit Role on the IS Auditor's
        Independence Effective 1 July 2002
        Also see 020.020.010 Organisational Relationship and Independence
    .020 Organisational Relationship
        .010 Organisational Relationship and Independence Effective 1 September 2000
        Also see: 020.010.010 Effect of Nonaudit Role on the IS Auditor's Independence
030 Professional Ethics and Standards
    .010 Code of Professional Ethics
        .010 Irregularities and Illegal Acts Effective 1 July 2002
        Also see: 030.020.020 Due Professional Care; 020.020.010 Organisational Relationship
        and Independence
    .020 Due Professional Care
        .010 Audit Considerations for Irregularities Effective 1 March 2000
        .020 Due Professional Care Effective 1 September 1999
        Also see: 060.020.070 Use of Computer Assisted Audit Techniques (CAATs) 030.010.010
        Irregularities and Illegal Acts
040 Competence
    .010 Skills and Knowledge
    .020 Continuing Professional Education
050 Planning
    .010 Audit Planning
        .010 Materiality Concepts for Auditing Information Systems Effective 1 September 1999
        .020 Planning Revised Effective 1 March 2002
        .030 Use of Risk Assessment in Audit Planning Effective 1 September 2000
        .040 Effect of Third Parties on an Organisation's IT Controls Effective 1 March 2002
        Also see: 030.020.010 Audit Considerations for Irregularities; 010.010.020 Outsourcing of
        IS Activities to Other Organisations; 060.020.070 Use of Computer Assisted Audit
        Techniques (CAATs)
060 Performance of Audit Work
    .010 Supervision
    .020 Evidence
        .010 Audit Documentation Effective 1 September 1999
        .020 Application Systems Review Effective 1 November 2001
        .030 Audit Evidence Requirement Effective 1 December 1998
        .040 Audit Sampling Effective 1 March 2000
        .050 IT Governance Effective 1 July 2002
        .060 Effect of Pervasive IS Controls Effective 1 March 2000
        .070 Use of Computer Assisted Audit Techniques (CAATs) Effective 1 December 1998
        .080 Using the Work of Other Auditors and Experts Effective 1 June 1998
        Also see: 030.020.010 Audit Considerations for Irregularities; 010.010.020
        Outsourcing of IS Activities to Other Organisations; 050.010.030
        Use of Risk Assessment in Audit Planning
070 Reporting
    .010 Report Content and Form
        .010 Report Content and Form Effective 1 December 1998—Withdrawn 1 January 2003
        Reporting Effective 1 January 2003
        Also see: 060.020.010 Audit Documentation; 030.020.010 Audit Considerations for Irregularities
080 Follow-Up Activities
    .010 Follow-Up

FIGURE 1-6 ISACA Guidelines for IS Auditing, Copyright 1997
Reprinted with permission from the Information Systems Audit and Control Association,
Rolling Meadows, IL, USA 60008.

risk and control in general. It includes an examination of the primary control frameworks used by IT managers to control risks. IT managers and auditors are becoming increasingly aware of the importance of assessing risk prior to deciding on controls and control levels to implement. Chapter 3 discusses the importance of risk assessment.

The second section of the book examines risks and controls in depth. Chapters 4 through 7 describe risks over specific processes and technologies. Two major processes associated with IT are the deployment or implementation of information systems and the operation of these systems. Earlier in this chapter, we introduced CobiT, a management framework for IT governance that emphasizes control. CobiT is segmented into four domains, paralleling the "life cycle" of an information system. The first three of these domains are (1) Planning and Organization, (2) Acquisition and Implementation, and (3) Delivery and Support. Chapters 4 and 5 describe the risks and controls over these areas. The final domain within CobiT is Monitoring. Because much of IT auditing is the process of monitoring, this domain is addressed throughout the book.

Various individual technologies pose specialized IT risks. We cover many of these within the book, including databases. Two technology areas that are particularly important to securing and controlling an information system are network and telecommunication systems and e-business. These receive detailed attention in Chapters 6 and 7.

The third section of the book is the "how to" portion. Chapter 8 shows how IT auditors use computer assisted auditing tools (CAATs) in performing their work. These are tools like ACL software, which allow you to extract and manipulate data from databases. Chapter 9 takes you step-by-step through an IT audit. The final chapter, recognizing the potential for IT-related fraud, describes fraud auditing.

This book includes two appendices. Because IT auditing requires knowledge of many technical terms, Appendix A provides a glossary for easy reference. Appendix B is a tutorial for using ACL and it includes a case.

SUMMARY

This chapter provided an overview of IT auditing. You now have a clear idea about what IT auditors do, the training and skills they need to do it, the various professional organizations that certify practitioners, and the standards, guidelines, and procedures available to help them in their work.

The chapter began with a discussion of the effect of IT on auditing. That section includes information about IT governance, an important part of overall enterprise governance. The next section described the variety of types of work that IT auditors do, running the gamut from penetration testing to supporting the financial audit. IT auditors need both technical and business skills, which we described in some detail in the next major part of this chapter. Then, because IT auditing is a profession, we described the various certifications or licenses that these professionals may hold and the organizations that grant them. The chapter next describes the various standards and guidelines that IT auditors can use in their work. The chapter ends with a brief overview of the rest of this text.

IT auditing is a growing field. Technology is changing daily and increasingly impacting businesses and other entities. The need for auditing is also increasingly important. The accounting scandals in recent years point to a need for more monitoring and oversight. So if IT is becoming more and more pervasive and complex, and if the need for auditing is on the rise, then IT auditors are going to be in demand.

DISCUSSION QUESTIONS

1-1 Describe the two objectives of IT Governance. Which do you think is more important?

1-2 Describe the various types of transactions that an IS might process in the course of acquiring raw materials for production.

1-3   This chapter described several types of work done by IT auditors. Using the Internet, can you identify any other types of work these auditors might do?

1-4   IT auditors often have technical skills related to specific software. One such software specialization area are enterprise resource planning (ERP) applications. Explain how an IT auditor could acquire and maintain knowledge about one of these software packages.

1-5   CISA is the most common credential obtained by IT auditors. Discuss how this certification would add value for someone practicing IT auditing.

1-6   The AICPA recently created a credential for CPAs who have specialized training and experience in IT. Discuss whether or not you think the CITP is likely to be a sought-after credential by both IT audit practitioners and those contracting with IT audit professionals.

1-7   How do IT audit guidelines, such as those issued by ISACA, help IT auditors to do their work?

1-8   ISACA recently made their standards, guidelines, and procedures "open." This means that they share them at no cost—anyone can download them from the ISACA Web site. Discuss the value of such a strategy.

EXERCISES

1-9   In 2001, the Auditing Standards Board of the AICPA issued Statement on Auditing Standards No. 94, *The Effect of Information Technology on the Auditor's Consideration of Internal Control in a Financial Statement Audit.* This standard is likely to increase the involvement of an IT auditor on a financial audit engagement. The standard requires auditors to consider how an organization's use of IT might affect internal controls. The standard explains that auditors may determine that it is more effective and efficient to assess control risk than to perform detailed testing of account balances and transactions (i.e., substantive testing).

   Required:

   Explain how SAS No. 94 is likely to influence the work of both the financial and IT auditor.

1-10   Many large business, not-for-profit, and government organizations, including the U.S. House of Representatives, have adopted CobiT as a framework for IT governance. IT governance has two primary components: (1) acquisition and deployment of IT to promote an organization's objectives and enable business processes and (2) management and control of IT-related risks.

   Required:

   Assume that you have been asked to consult a Fortune 1000 business enterprise about implementing IT governance. Using the framework shown in Figure 1-1, identify an implementation plan with six or more specific activities you would recommend.

REFERENCES AND RECOMMENDED READINGS

Arens, Alvin A., Mark S. Beasley, and Randy J. Elder. 2002. *Auditing and Assurance Services: An Integrated Approach,* 9th ed. Englewood Cliffs, N.J.: Prentice-Hall.

Bagranoff, Nancy A., and Valaria P. Vendrzyk. 2000. "The Changing Role of IS Audit Among the Big Five US-Based Accounting Firms." *Information Systems Control Journal* 5: 33–37.

Guldentops, Erik. 2001. "Asking the Right Questions for IT Governance." *Information Systems Control Journal* 4: 13–14.

Hasan, Bassam. 2002. "Assessing Data Authenticity with Benford's Law." *Information Systems Control Journal* 6: 41–43.

Lainhart, John W. 2000. "IT Governance Can Help Guide Business eCommerce Initiatives." *Information Systems Control Journal* 6: 23–24.

Mancino, Jane M., and Charles E. Landes. 2001. "A New Look at the Attestation Standards." *Journal of Accountancy*, July: 41–45.

Moscove, Stephen, Mark Simkin, and Nancy Bagranoff. 2003. *Core Concepts of Accounting Information Systems,* 8th ed. New York: John Wiley and Sons.

Quinn, L. R. 2002. "Risky Business." *Journal of Accountancy.* June: 65–70.

Tucker, George H. 2001. "IT and the Audit." *Journal of Accountancy.* September: 41–43.

Web Sites

The Web site for the IT Governance Institute is at www.itgovernance.org. The site has many useful resources, including case studies and links to security, IT, and accounting Web sites.

The following are Web sites for the professional organizations identified in this chapter:

American Institute of Certified Public Accountants—www.aicpa.org and www.cpa2biz.com
Association of Certified Fraud Examiners—www.cfenet.com
Information Systems Audit and Control Association—www.isaca.org
International Federation of Accountants—www.ifac.org
Institute of Internal Auditors—www.theiia.org

NOTES

1. Kenneth P. Laury and John F. Cronin. "Need and Supply Is Unbalanced," *Information Systems Control Journal,* Vol. 5 2000, p. 44.
2. The need to comply with external requirements is specified as *High Level Control Objective, PO8, Planning and Organizations—Ensure Compliance with External Requirements* in *CobiT,* 3rd edition, 2000. IT Governance Institute, p. 54.
3. www.itgovernance.org/sponsor.htm (October 31, 2002).
4. CobiT, 3rd edition, 2000. IT Governance Institute. Executive Summary, p. 3.
5. CobiT, 3rd edition. IT Governance Institute 2000. Executive Summary, Appendix I, p. 14.
6. "A Beginner's Guide to Auditing the AS/400 Operating System." Judith S. Bines, *Information Systems Control Journal,* Vol. 2, 2002, pp. 31–34.
7. The professional designations *IT auditor* and *IS auditor* are virtually interchangeable. We chose IT auditor and IT auditing for this book because we felt it reflected a trend in terminology. Once, these auditors were called EDP auditors, then they were named IS auditors, and today many refer to them as IT auditors. Regardless of the name, the work is the same. Therefore, an IT auditor's most common certification is that of CISA.
8. In 2003, the Public Company Accounting Oversight Board (PCAOB) took over this regulatory authority over public companies from the AICPA. For more information about PCAOB, see www.pcaob.com.
9. CAATs are discussed thoroughly in Chapter 8.

CHAPTER *2*

LEGAL AND ETHICAL ISSUES FOR IT AUDITORS

CHAPTER CONTENTS

INTRODUCTION

News Flash: Save the Oppressed Programs (STOP), a nonprofit organization dedicated to improving the living conditions and lives of software programs and promoting alternatives to brutal software testing, announced today that seven more software companies have been added to the group's "watch list" of companies that regularly practice unethical software testing.

"There is no need for software to be mistreated in this way so that companies like these can market new products," said a spokesperson for STOP. "Alternative methods of testing these products are available." According to STOP, these companies force software programs to undergo lengthy and arduous tests, often without rest for hours or days at a time. Employees are assigned to "break" the programs by any means necessary, and inside sources report that they often joke about "torturing" the software until it confesses.

"It's no joke, innocent programs, from the day they are compiled, are cooped up in tiny rooms and 'crashed' for hours on end. They spend their whole lives on filthy, ill-maintained computers and are unceremoniously deleted when they're not needed anymore. Further, the software programs are kept in unsanitary conditions, crawling with infestations of 'bugs.' It's a dirty little secret of the software industry and a horrible tragedy indeed!"

"We know alternatives to this appalling treatment exist," said a STOP representative, citing industry giant Microsoft Corporation as great example. "Microsoft is extremely successful at treating software programs in a kinder and gentler fashion, as it markets its software applications without any testing at all, thus saving innocent programs around the globe from such unthinkable treatment."

Ethical codes of conduct are vital to the health of professional societies, since members who are asked to conform to societal rules benefit the most from the conformity of others. It is important for IT auditors to understand their ethical obligations toward employers and clients, as well as toward the broader IT audit community and society. In this light, we examine a code of professional ethics aimed at IT auditors in this chapter. IT auditors also need to be aware of their responsibilities with respect to investigating and reporting irregular and illegal acts. Is the IT auditor responsible for detecting, preventing and reporting such acts? If so, how should they search for and prevent irregular and illegal acts, and to whom should they report their suspicions and findings? If IT auditors are not responsible in this regard, who is accountable? Answers to these questions will be examined in this chapter. Finally, IT auditors should have a working knowledge of various regulations and laws applicable to IT engagements. Such guidance can be found by briefly examining relevant audit issues, such as contract law, intellectual property, computer crime, and privacy rights. We begin this chapter by examining IT auditors' ethical obligations.

CODE OF ETHICS

Why do organizations develop ethical codes? Do not people know how to act ethically under all circumstances without a written guidance? Answers to the first question will be articulated in this section. The answer to the second question should be obvious, particularly in light of the recent business atmosphere, which is rife with examples of corporate malfeasance. No, not all people will act ethically under all circumstances, as social, economic, political and other pressures can drive "good" people to do "bad" things. Hence, a formal code of ethical conduct sends a message to all affected parties that the organization will not tolerate unethical acts and that there are consequences for behaving in unacceptable ways. This type of communication fits into the Committee of Sponsoring Organizations of the Treadway Commission (COSO) internal control framework, which emphasizes the importance of setting a clear "tone at the top" regarding acceptable behavior. While written ethical guidelines will not prevent some people from engaging in unethical conduct, it does make clear the organization's stand on such matters. Just like locks on doors, ethical codes will help to keep honest people honest!

There are at least six good reasons for organizations to develop codes of ethical conduct.[1] As outlined here, ethical codes of conduct serve to:

1. Define acceptable behaviors for relevant parties;
2. Promote high standards of practice throughout the organization;
3. Provide a benchmark for organizational members to use for self-evaluation;
4. Establish a framework for professional behavior, obligations, and responsibilities;
5. Offer a vehicle for occupational identity; and
6. Reflect a mark of occupational maturity.

The very exercise of developing a code of ethical conduct is enlightening and refreshing, as it forces the organization and its members to think about their values, rights, and obligations to one another and society at large. Yes, IT auditors, too, need a professional code of ethics to guide them through auditing process, as next discussed.

The Information Systems Audit and Control Association (ISACA) has promulgated a code of professional ethics applicable to ISACA members and those who hold the designation of Certified Information Systems Auditor (CISA). As this is the most relevant and up-to-date source of information regarding IT auditors' ethical obligations, we will use it as a guide.[2] The ten ethical standards set forth the by ISACA are as follow. ISACA members and CISA certified auditors shall:

1. Support the implementation of, and encourage compliance with, appropriate standards, procedures, and controls for information systems.
2. Serve in the interest of relevant parties in a diligent, loyal, and honest manner, and shall not knowingly be a party to any illegal or improper activities.
3. Maintain the privacy and confidentiality of information obtained in the course of their duties unless disclosure is required by legal authority. Such information shall not be used for personal benefit or released to inappropriate parties.
4. Perform their duties in an independent and objective manner and avoid activities that impair, or may appear to impair, their independence or objectivity.
5. Maintain competency in their respective fields of auditing and information systems control.
6. Agree to undertake only those activities that they can reasonably expect to complete with professional competence.
7. Perform their duties with due professional care.
8. Inform the appropriate parties of the results of information systems audit and/or control work performed, revealing all material facts known to them, which, if not revealed, could either distort reports of operations or conceal unlawful practices.
9. Support the education of clients, colleagues, the general public, management, and boards of directors in enhancing their understanding of information systems auditing and control.

10. Maintain high standards of conduct and character and not engage in acts discreditable to the profession.

The code of ethics further stipulates that failure to comply can result in investigation and, ultimately, disciplinary action. Hence, as you can see, the guidelines are quite comprehensive and the ISACA organization takes them very seriously—as should all IT auditors. While each of the ten ethical standards is vitally important in its own right, we shall focus the next section on the seventh and eighth standards, which, in part, require IT auditors to conduct audits with due professional care and to report irregular and illegal acts that come to their attention to appropriate parties.

IRREGULAR AND ILLEGAL ACTS

An irregular act reflects either an intentional violation of corporate policies or regulatory requirements or an unintentional breach of law. An illegal act represents a willful violation of law. What types of behavior constitute irregular and illegal acts? The most obvious act under this umbrella is fraud, which reflects the intentional use of deception to achieve unfair or unlawful personal gain at the expense of another party. Computer crimes, too, would qualify as irregular and possibly illegal acts. Another act within this realm would be nonconformity with agreements and contracts between the organization and third parties. Violations of intellectual property rights would also reflect irregular and illegal acts, as would noncompliance with other applicable regulations and laws. Before discussing these issues, it is important to know the IT auditor's obligations and responsibilities with regard to the prevention, detection, and reporting of irregular and illegal acts. The best way to begin investigating the many issues surrounding irregular and illegal acts is to summarize the ISACA auditing guideline dealing with Irregularities and Illegal Acts (ISACA document #30.01.01).

Professional Guidance

The ISACA guideline to IT auditors on irregular and illegal acts clearly points out that auditors are not qualified to determine whether an irregular, illegal, or simply erroneous act has occurred. Instead, the characterization of an act as irregular, illegal, or erroneous should be made by a qualified expert, such as a lawyer or judge. Additionally, the extent to which the observed unusual act is material to the financial statements taken as a whole is outside the scope of an IT audit; rather, certified public accountants are qualified to make such materiality judgments. However, during the course of an IT audit, the auditor might discover a transaction or situation that appears to be out of the ordinary and suspect that an irregularity or illegality has taken place. If so, what is the auditor to do next?

It is important to point out that management is responsible for the prevention and detection of irregular and illegal acts, not the IT auditor. In discharging their responsibilities in this regard, managers should establish policies and procedures aimed at governing employee conduct; institute appropriate internal controls, such as proper segregation of transaction authorization and execution; and ensure compliance with policies, procedures, and controls. Despite management's best intentions and actions in attempting to prevent and detect irregular and illegal acts, some could nevertheless slip through the system.

An overview of the IT auditor's responsibilities with respect to irregular and illegal acts is as follows:[3]

1. Plan the IT audit engagement based on an assessed level of risk that irregular and illegal acts might occur and that such acts could be material to the subject matter of the IT auditor's report.

2. Design audit procedures that consider the assessed risk level for irregular and illegal acts.

3. Review the results of audit procedures for indications of irregular and illegal acts.

4. Report suspected irregular and illegal acts to one or more of the following parties:

    a. The IT auditor's immediate supervisor and possibly corporate governance bodies, such as the board of directors or audit committee;

    b. Appropriate personnel within the organization, such as a manager who is at least one level above those who are suspected to have engaged in such acts;

    c. If top management is suspected, then refer to corporate governance bodies only; and

    d. Legal counsel or other appropriate external experts.

5. Assume that the act is not isolated.

6. Determine how the act slipped through the internal control system.

7. Broaden audit procedures to consider the possibility of more acts of this nature.

8. Conduct additional audit procedures.

9. Evaluate the results of expanded audit procedures.

10. Consult legal counsel and possibly corporate governance bodies to estimate the potential impact of the irregular and illegal acts, taken as a whole, on the subject matter of the engagement, audit report, and organization.

11. Report all facts and circumstances of the irregular and illegal acts (whether suspected or confirmed) if the acts have a material effect on the subject matter of the engagement and/or the organization.

12. Distribute the report to appropriate internal parties, such as managers who are at least one level above those who are suspected or confirmed to have committed the acts, and/or corporate governance bodies.

IT auditors are obligated to keep such matters confidential with respect to external parties. However, under certain circumstances, IT auditors may be mandated by authorized regulatory, legal or legislative entities to disclose such acts. In these situations, IT auditors should first consult legal counsel before making such disclosures to external parties.

Earlier, it was made clear that IT auditors usually are not qualified to determine the legal status of unusual acts that may come to their attention during the course of an IT audit (unless, of course, the IT auditor is also a lawyer.) However, IT auditors should have a general, albeit very basic notion, regarding whether highlighted "unusual" acts might be in violation of law, as they need to decide if they should refer such matters to legal counsel for further investigation. Hence, IT auditors need to have a working knowledge of relevant regulations and laws that could affect IT audits. In the next section, we briefly discuss some of the more notable issues in this regard.

REGULATORY AND LEGAL ISSUES

The types of regulatory and legal issues that IT auditors might confront during an audit are vast and varied; thus, it is not possible to cover them all in a book of this nature. Instead, we will examine the following more obvious issues: legal contracts, computer crime, intellectual property rights, and privacy issues.

Legal Contracts

What is a legal contract and what essential elements should one look for in a contract? The answers to these questions are important, as IT auditors are likely to run across various contracts the organization holds with external, and sometimes internal, parties.

A contract is an agreement between or among two or more persons or entities (businesses, organizations, or government agencies) to do, or to abstain from doing, something in return for an exchange of consideration. Thus, contracts are essentially promises that are enforceable by law. If the terms of a contract are breached, the law provides remedies, which can include recuperation of losses or specific performance of the contractual terms.

For the most part, contracts are governed by each state, and guidelines concerning the legality of such contracts fall into two general categories: statutory law and common law. Statutory law, which is set by legislative action, may require some contracts to be reduced to writing and executed with specific requirements; else, parties may enter into binding contracts without a written document (e.g., verbal and implied contracts). The Uniform Commercial Code (UCC), a federal statute, has been adopted in some form by nearly every state and represents a body of law that governs the sale of goods. All other types of contracts, such as the purchase and sale of services, are governed by less precise and more varied statutory and common law dealing with commercial transactions. The term "common law" reflects customs and general principles (embodied in case law) that serve as precedents to situations not covered by statutory law. Most principles pertaining to the common law of contracts are outlined in the Restatement (Second) of the Law of Contracts published by the American Law Institute.

IT auditors typically will examine written contracts dealing with purchase and sale of goods (e.g., computer equipment and software applications) and services (e.g., outsourcing arrangements and maintenance agreements). Accordingly, at a minimum, auditors should look to ensure that at least three elements are contained in the contract: offer, consideration, and acceptance.

The offer should identify the nature, or subject matter, of the agreement in clear, unequivocal language. For example, if the contract is for the performance of services, such services should be completely described (e.g., time, place, quality and so on). If the contract is for the sale of goods, the goods should be properly identified (including the quantity, which is a material term of the contract under the UCC). The contract should make obvious whether the promise deals with the sale of services or goods, as this will ensure that correct body of law is applied in the event of a dispute. Also, the person or entity making the offer (the offeror) must be properly identified. With respect to consideration, the contract must state what the offeror expects in return from the other party (the offeree). For example, the offer may be for the purchase of a certain computer hard drive (to be fully described), and the consideration would be stated as a certain sum of money. Regarding acceptance, the agreement should properly identify the offeree and, in the case of a written contract, the offeror and offeree must sign and date the contract.

Reducing the contract to writing and including the three essential elements just mentioned will serve as documented evidence that on a certain date the named contractual parties had a "meeting of the minds" with respect to a promise and related consideration, as well as any other stipulations contained in the contract. We will next look at the types of contracts IT auditors might encounter regarding employees and trading partners.

EMPLOYEE CONTRACTS   What about employment contracts? After all, they reflect a type of service contract—don't they? The answer is yes, but an employment contract reflects a special type of agreement, as it reflects a one-sided promise. In a unilateral contract, the offeror makes a promise and the offeree chooses to accept the offer "at will" as indicated by his/her continued performance. The employee is not bound to a unilateral contract. Only the employer can breach the contract; for instance, if the employer refuses to pay certain compensation as promised, the promise is violated. Yet, a unilateral contract is just as enforceable as a bilateral contract. With an employment contract, neither party suffers a loss if they terminate the contract, unless the employer violates statute or common law in the process. Thus, an employer can abruptly release an employee for good cause and the employee can abruptly terminate the contact by not performing the required work.

Many employees receive written contracts from their employers. Such contracts often stipulate position titles, performance criteria, compensation schemes, relocation expense reimbursements, and so on. What an employment contract cannot include, because it is not enforceable by law, is that the employee *must* work for the employer for a stated period of time, as an employment contract is an "at will" contract for an indefinite period of time. Hence, an employer cannot force an employee to work if the employee chooses not to do so. Many times, employees may be required to sign stipulated agreements during the hiring process, for the employer will insist that certain issues be agreed upon via written contract as a condition of employment, as next discussed.

Confidentiality Agreements   Some employees may be in positions to see confidential employer information, such as payroll records, litigation actions, inimitable processes, and strategic plans. This may be particularly true for IT employees, who often have access to sensitive information of this nature. With respect to such employees, the employer might require a written, signed agreement that the employee promises not to divulge confidential information during employment and for a specified period of time thereafter. Confidentiality agreements should describe the nature of information protected by the agreement, list permissible uses of such information, affirm a duty of confidentiality, identify remedies for noncompliance, and qualify the term of the agreement (a typical time period of enforcement is during employment and up to five years thereafter). Failure to comply with a confidentiality agreement can lead to immediate dismissal and/or a specific remedy; however, the legitimacy of such dismissal and/or remedy depends on state statute and common law, as well as the particular circumstances of the contract and its purported breach. A special case of confidentiality agreement is found with trade secrets.

Trade Secret Agreements   Trade secrets are the lifeblood of many successful organizations. Hence, protecting such secrets from disclosure is essential to the continued economic viability of the company. According to the U.S. Trade Secrets Act, a trade secret is defined as:

> information including a formula, pattern, compilation, program, device, method, technique or process, that: (i) derives independent economic value, actual, or potential, from not being generally known to, and not being readily ascertainable by proper means by other persons who can obtain economic value from its disclosure, and (ii) is the subject of efforts that are reasonable under the circumstance to maintain its secrecy.

Thus, a trade secret reflects a wide array of information that derives independent economic value from not being widely disclosed or readily ascertainable.

Trade secret agreements bring to light an interesting wrinkle in contract law—they are enforceable for an indefinite period of time! Why? Because, according to the law, once a company reveals its trade secret, the secret is no longer protected as intellectual property.

Thus, if a trade secret stipulation were to include an expiration date, the trade secret would lose its protected status after said date. Nondisclosure agreements dealing with trade secrets differ depending on the nature and value of the trade secret; nevertheless, such stipulations should convey the same elements mentioned (confidentiality agreements) except that the term of the agreement may last indefinitely. Enforceability of a trade secret agreement depends on state law (statutory and common), the specifics of the agreement, and the circumstances under which an alleged breach occurs.

Discovery Agreements   Items not covered in original employment contracts fall under the umbrella of common law at the state level. Hence, unless employees are specifically hired to develop certain ideas or inventions, they might own the intellectual rights to such discoveries, depending on the state and circumstances. Plus, if intellectual discoveries incidentally arise out of employment, the rights could belong to the employee of discovery, unless otherwise stipulated in the employment contract. Therefore, employees who are hired to develop ideas and innovations, such as software applications and hardware inventions, often are required to sign employment agreements that transfer the ownership of discovery to the employer. Once again, the legitimacy of a discovery agreement depends on state law (statutory and common) and the specifics contained within the agreement.

Noncompete Agreements   An employee might be required to sign a noncompete agreement (also known as a "covenant not to compete") as a condition of employment. For instance, an IT employee might learn how a company's particular business model is built and what makes it more successful than competitors. Armed with such knowledge, and perhaps key client contacts, the employee might decide to quit employment and establish her own business down the street—directly competing with her prior employer. To preclude this from happening, the employee might be asked to sign a noncompete agreement. A sample noncompete agreement is shown in Figure 2-1. Note the following elements of such a contract: offer (employment), consideration (employment), period of time (years), geographic radius (miles), and agreement (signature).

Noncompete agreements are enforced by the courts using common law principles if legitimate business interests of the employer justify the restraint of the employee's lawful economic interests, and if the agreement restriction is reasonable with regard to time (which can not be indefinite) and geographic scope. If a noncompete agreement is signed before or immediately after employment, the usual contract element of "consideration" is not required, as the employment itself reflects consideration. However, if an employer requests an employee to sign a noncompete agreement during or upon termination of employment, additional consideration on the part of the employer may be required.

TRADING PARTNER CONTRACTS   It is common business practice to ratify agreements between companies and their trading partners (e.g., customers and vendors) via written contracts. The same type of agreements as just described (confidentiality, trade secrets, discovery, and noncompete) can apply to trading partners as well. More commonly, IT auditors will be dealing with trading partner contracts pertaining to the sale (customers) and purchase (vendors) of goods and services.

As discussed earlier, a contract must contain the following three elements if it is to be legally binding: an offer (e.g., a company offers to sell or purchase goods/services), an acceptance (e.g., a customer agrees to purchase or a vendor agrees to sell goods/services for a certain price), and consideration (e.g., the customer or company agrees to exchange money for the goods/services). In addition to these basic elements, additional terms can

EMPLOYEE NONCOMPETE AGREEMENT

For good consideration and as an inducement for _____ (Company) to employ _____ (Employee), the undersigned Employee hereby agrees not to directly or indirectly compete with the business of the Company and its successors and assigns during the period of employment and for a period of _____ years following termination of employment and notwithstanding the cause or reason for termination.

The term "not compete" as used herein shall mean that the Employee shall not own, manage, operate, consult, or to be employed in a business substantially similar to, or competitive with, the present business of the Company or such other business activity in which the Company may substantially engage during the term of employment.

The Employee acknowledges that the Company shall or may in reliance of this agreement provide Employee access to trade secrets, customers, and other confidential data and good will. Employee agrees to retain said information as confidential and not to use said information on his or her own behalf or disclose same to any third party.

This noncompete agreement shall extend only for a radius of _____ miles from the present location of the Company and shall be in full force and effect for _____ years, commencing with the date of employment termination.

This agreement shall be binding upon and inure to the benefit of the parties, their successors, assigns, and personal representatives.

Signed this _____ day of _____ 20____.

_____
Company Representative

_____
Employee

FIGURE 2-1   Sample Noncompete Agreement

and should be written into a contract to further clarify the nature and extent of the agreement; however, these terms cannot be deemed "unreasonable" in the eyes of the law. Legislation dealing with additional contractual terms is covered by the Unfair Contract Terms Act 1977 and the Unfair Terms in Consumer Contracts Regulations 1994. These laws are designed to stop traders from putting unfair terms in contracts.

While statutory and common law differs with respect to the purchase and sale of goods versus services, there are nevertheless common contractual terms that apply to both situations. While we could examine hundreds of variations of such contracts, we offer a contract template (see Figure 2-2) that is indicative of the types of contractual elements an IT auditor should look for when reviewing trading partner agreements between the company (client) and outside parties. The template is self-explanatory, so there is no need to duplicate the discussion here, but you should carefully read through each section in the template to gain an appreciation of the salient aspects that comprise a sound business contract. We next turn our attention to a fascinating and rapidly developing area of law—computer crime.

COMPUTER CRIME AND INTELLECTUAL PROPERTY

As an unregulated medley of corporations, individuals, governments, educational institutions, and other organizations that have agreed in principle to use a standard set of communication protocols, the Internet is wide open to exploitation. There are no sheriffs on the Information Superhighway waiting to zap potential offenders with a radar gun or search for weapons if someone looks suspicious. By almost all accounts, this lack of "law enforcement" leaves net users to regulate each other according to the reigning norms of

Document Title

The title should state the overall purpose of the document in short form. Some examples of titles are "Sale Agreement," "Equipment Transfer," or "Outsourcing Agreement." The document title should be placed at the top of the document for easy referencing.

Unique Number

A number should be used to identify the particular document. Whether the number is a tracking number or an identification number, it should be prominently displayed on the document for reference and verification purposes.

Effective Date

A contract should always have a date defined as to when the contract becomes effective and legally binding.

Expiration Date

In contrast to the effective date, the expiration date defines the date that the agreement expires.

With respect to goods, this date should be far enough ahead to easily accommodate preparation and transfer time.

Regarding services, the expiration date sets an upper bound on the agreement; meaning, the agreement begins with the effective date (lower bound) and ends on a certain future date (upper bound).

Seller and Buyer Names/Addresses

This section of the document identifies the contractual parties and provides contact information about each party involved in the agreement. In this section, legal names should be used along with contact information for each, including (but not limited to) addresses, phone numbers, and e-mail addresses.

Document Purpose

In this portion is a statement describing the transaction; that is, this portion defines what and why the contract is being drawn up, whether it is a sale or transfer of goods or services.

Authorized Signatures

In order for both parties to publicly acknowledge the terms of acceptance for this document, they must sign the document. This portion should contain both parties' signatures, printed names, titles (e.g., president), and the date the document is signed.

Goods/Services Description, Quantity, and Price

Goods should be as specifically identified as possible, such as model number, description, serial number, and other defining characteristics.

Services should be thoroughly described herein. For example, outsourcing agreements typically stipulate dozens, and sometimes hundreds, of agreed-upon terms and conditions, such as service quality, uptime demands, backup strategies, and so on.

Also, in this section, the quantity (if goods) and selling price should be listed.

Payment Terms

As in the prior section, the selling price should be placed here also. However, this is a more in-depth description of how, when and to whom the invoice(s) will be paid.

Delivery and Shipping

All information about how and when goods will be shipped belongs here. A detailed description of timing, criteria, and title/risk transfer is needed to explain the terms of shipping. Also, any packaging, transportation, or insurance costs associated with the shipping should go here to disclose any additional costs for the delivery. This would be the proper place to put which party, the buyer or the seller, should pay for these costs.

If the contract is for the delivery of services, this portion of the contract should clearly spell out the "who, when, what, where, and how" of such delivery. For example, say that the company signs an agreement with a vendor who is supposed to service the building's alarm system. In this section, the contract should state who will perform the service, when and where the service will be rendered, what the service entails, and how the service will be delivered.

(continued)

FIGURE 2-2 Contract Template (1 of 2)
This template is adapted from a contract format suggested by an industry trade group called Surplus Equipment Consortium Network, Inc. (www.secninc.com).

Disclosures

Full disclosure of properties pertaining to the goods should be revealed here. This may include (but is not limited to) software, title, known history, and/or any problems the equipment has experienced in the past.

Regarding services, the selling party should disclose any and all qualifications to the agreed upon service, such as what the service does not cover, the estimated response time in case of emergency calls, the vendor's responsibility in the event that the service target (say, and alarm system or satellite dish) has been tampered with, and so on.

Intended Use

This is a description of how the goods should be used.

This section does not apply to services.

Warranty

The warranty on goods is very important since it informs the buyer of the conditions under which the transfer is taking place (e.g., "new," "as is," or "refurbished"), the period of time during which the seller will warranty the goods, the specific terms of warranty claims (e.g., labor, materials, on-site), disclaimers of warranties if the goods have not been used as suggested in the "Intended Use" section (above), and so on.

Liability

A statement should be included defining which party is to be held responsible for each aspect of the transaction and what recourse will be taken if that party should lapse in their agreed-upon duties.

Compliance with Laws

This portion of the contract should identify applicable laws and regulations pertinent to the transfer of goods or delivery of services (national, state, and local). By disclosing such in the contract, both parties are well aware of the laws and regulations and can agree to them. For instance, if the purchase/sale takes place in the state of Florida, this section should state that the agreement is under the jurisdiction of that state's uniform commercial contract law dealing with goods or services.

Export Control

Not only are there laws and regulations on the shipping of goods, there are also export laws that must be abided by. These should be defined in the document so that both parties can understand and comply with applicable export laws.

This section may also apply to services if, for instance, the provider operates from one country and the service is performed in another country.

Information Confidentiality

This area of the document defines any confidentiality requirements that may go along with the sale of goods or delivery of services. By having these requirements written into the signed document, both parties are stating that they agree to the confidentiality terms and will not break them. For instance, a vendor who services manufacturing equipment might learn about the trade secret of how a company makes a certain product. In this event, this section of the contract should include a confidentiality agreement related to the nondisclosure of said trade secret or other confidential information of which the vendor might become aware.

Force Majeure

To prepare for unforeseen or uncontrollable situations, it is helpful to have something in the contract that would explain what should happen in regard to the agreement. For instance, if a piece of equipment was being shipped by air freight and the plane crashes, does the buyer still have to pay or is the sale then null and void? If a service provider, who owns the company and is the only one in the company who is qualified to provide the service, suddenly dies, can the purchaser place legal claim against the provider's estate for the breached contract?

Penalty/Cancellation Terms; Resolution Remedy

In order to preclude any one party canceling their part of the sale or breaking contract, an arbitration clause should define what would happen to that party. Also, this section should be used to define any resolutions that are appropriate for the party that abided by the contract. These resolutions may be financial or any other options that both parties deem fit, as long as they are deemed reasonable by state law.

FIGURE 2-2 Contract Template (2 of 2)

the moment. Community standards in cyberspace appear to be vastly different from the standards found at the corner of Main Street and Elm in Any City, USA. Unfortunately, cyberspace is also a virtual tourist trap where faceless, nameless con artists can work the crowds. (Natalie D. Voss at www.digitalcentury.com/encyclo/update/crime.html)

But wait! Marshals and sheriffs are headed for Any City, USA, at this very moment because computer crimes have pervaded every aspect of society and presently threaten our national security. Since every state has myriad regulations and laws governing computer crime and intellectual property, it would be impossible to cover them all here. Instead, in order to focus this discussion, we will examine the U.S. government's response to computer crime and intellectual property, as each state follows similar guidelines.

Computer Crime

What is computer crime anyway? The term "computer crime" or "cybercrime" refers to the direct or indirect use of computer and communication technologies to perpetrate a criminal act. The acts covered under this broad umbrella include any behaviors that are deemed by states or nations to be illegal, such as hacking into an entity's network, stealing intellectual property, sabotaging a company's database, denying service to others who wish to use a Web site, harassing or blackmailing someone, violating privacy rights, engaging in industrial espionage, pirating computer software, perpetrating fraud, and so on. Even an illegal narcotics trafficker who uses the Internet to coordinate sales and logistics has committed a cybercrime, as the use of a computer and the Internet was incidental, yet instrumental, to the crime.

Intellectual Property

Intellectual property is encapsulated into the cybercrime domain, as a great deal of computer crime involves the theft or misuse of such property.[4] Intellectual property refers to valuable creations of the human mind, such as inventions, literary and artistic works, symbols, images, and designs. Intellectual property is subdivided into two general categories: industrial property (e.g., patents and trademarks) and individual property (e.g., copyrights of literary and artistic works, such as novels, poems and plays, films, music, drawings, paintings, photographs, sculptures, and architectural designs). The use of computer and communication technologies in violating intellectual property rights constitutes cybercrime.

Patents grant an inventor the right to exclude others from producing or using the inventor's discovery or invention for a limited period of time. The main body of law concerning patents is found in Title 35 of the U.S. Code (U.S.C.). In order to be patented, an invention must be novel, useful, and not of an obvious nature. Four general types of intellectual discoveries covered under patent law are: machines, human-made products, compositions of matter, and processing methods. The protection offered by a patent lasts for a nonrenewable period of twenty years from the date of application (www.law.cornell.edu/topics/patent.html).

Trademarks reflect distinctive images (e.g., symbols and pictures) or words that sellers affix to distinguish and identify the origin of their products. Trademark status may also be granted to distinctive and unique packaging, color combinations, building designs, product styles, and overall presentations. It is also possible to receive trademark status for identification that is not on its face distinct or unique but that has developed a secondary meaning over time that identifies it with the product or seller. The owner of a trademark has exclusive right to use it on the product for which it was intended to identify and on related products. Service marks receive the same legal protection as trademarks but are meant to distinguish services rather than products. Trademark protection is offered under Title 15 of the USC (www.law.cornell.edu/topics/trademark.html).

A copyright protects creative works from being reproduced, performed, or disseminated by others without permission. The owner of copyright has the exclusive right to reproduce a protected work; to prepare derivative works that only slightly change the protected work; to sell or lend copies of the protected work to the public; to perform protected works in public for profit; and to display copyrighted works publicly. Limited exceptions to this exclusivity exist for types of "fair use," such as book reviews. The life of a copyright begins the moment the work is created and lasts for the author's life plus an additional fifty years. Copyright status is protected under Title 17 of the USC (www.law.cornell.edu/topics/copyright.html).

Efforts to Thwart Cybercrime

The federal government is serious about combating computer crime! For instance, in 1991 the Justice Department established the Computer Crime and Intellectual Property Section (CCIPS).[5] As stated on the Justice Department's Web site:

> The Computer Crime and Intellectual Property Section (CCIPS) attorney staff consists of about two dozen lawyers who focus exclusively on the issues raised by computer and intellectual property crime. Section attorneys advise federal prosecutors and law enforcement agents; comment upon and propose legislation; coordinate international efforts to combat computer crime; litigate cases; and train all law enforcement groups. Other areas of expertise possessed by CCIPS attorneys include encryption, electronic privacy laws, search and seizure of computers, e-commerce, hacker investigations, and intellectual property crimes. (www.usdoj.gov/criminal/cybercrime /ccips.html)

Further, the Justice Department sponsors a program called Computer Hacking and Intellectual Property (CHIP). The threefold purpose of the program is to provide legal resources to local prosecutors, offer regional prevention and outreach, and provide regional training in the area of cybercrime. The international community too is deeply concerned about cybercrime, and joint efforts to establish international laws and guidelines in this regard are ongoing, as indicated by the Council of Europe's attempt to enact a global cybercrime treaty and the recent Group of 8 meeting on transborder intellectual property crime.

A handful of key Congressional legislative actions guide state and federal investigators and prosecutors with alleged cybercrime violations. For instance, the Computer Fraud and Abuse Act (1986) clarified definitions of criminal fraud and abuse for federal computer crimes and removed legal ambiguities and obstacles to prosecuting these crimes. The Electronic Communications Privacy Act (ECPA) of 1986 was enacted to address legal privacy issues surrounding use of computers (other privacy legislation will be addressed in the following section). The National Information Infrastructure Protection Act (1996) amended the 1986 Computer Fraud and Abuse Act. The Digital Millennium Copyright (1998) is designed to protect electronic intellectual property rights. The most encompassing legal guidance from the federal government is found in Title 18 of the USC, "Crimes and Criminal Procedure." The following sections of Title 18 are most pertinent to cybercrime:

1029—Fraud and Related Activity in Connection with Access Devices. This section applies to any persons who knowingly and with intent to defraud, produce, use, or traffic in one or more counterfeit access devices. The term "access device" means any card, plate, code, account number, electronic serial number, mobile identification number, personal identification number, or other telecommunications service, equipment, or instrument identifier, or other means of account access that can be used, alone or in conjunction with another access device, to obtain money, goods, services, or any other thing of value, or that can be used to initiate a transfer of funds (other than a transfer originated solely by paper instrument). The term "counterfeit access device" means any access device that is fictitious, altered, or forged. The term "unauthorized access device" means any access device that is lost, stolen, expired, revoked, canceled, or obtained with intent to defraud.

1030—Fraud and Related Activity in Connection with Computers. This section applies to any persons who knowingly access a computer without authorization or exceed authorized access and thereby obtain information contained in a financial record of a financial institution, information from any department or agency of the United States, or information from any protected computer if the conduct involves an interstate or foreign communication. Additionally, this section covers any persons who access a protected computer without authorization or exceed authorized access, engage in fraudulent behavior, and obtain anything of value. Other acts covered by this section pertain to persons who:

1. Knowingly cause the transmission of a program, information, code, or command, and, as a result of such conduct, intentionally cause damage without authorization to a protected computer; or

2. Intentionally access a protected computer without authorization, and, as a result of such conduct, cause damage.

1362—Communication Lines, Stations, or Systems. Crimes included under this section pertain to any persons who willfully or maliciously:

1. Injure or destroy, or attempt to injure or destroy, any of the works, property, or material of any radio, telegraph, telephone or cable, line, station, or system, or other means of communication, operated or controlled by the United States; or

2. Willfully or maliciously interfere in any way with the working or use of any such line or system, or obstruct, hinder, or delay the transmission of any communication over any such line or system.

2511—Interception and Disclosure of Wire, Oral, or Electronic Communications. Acts that fall under this section include those designed to:

1. Intentionally intercept, endeavor to intercept, or procure any other person to intercept or endeavor to intercept, any wire, oral, or electronic communication; or

2. Intentionally use, endeavor to use, or procure any other person to use or endeavor to use any electronic, mechanical, or other device to intercept any oral communication when:

    a. Such device is affixed to, or otherwise transmits a signal through, a wire, cable, or other like connection used in wire communication; or

    b. Such device transmits communications by radio or interferes with the transmission of such communication.

2701—Unlawful Access to Stored Communications. Prohibited acts falling under this section concern any persons who:

1. Intentionally access without authorization a facility through which an electronic communication service is provided; or

2. Intentionally exceed an authorization to access that facility; and thereby obtain, alter, or prevent authorized access to a wire or electronic communication while it is in electronic storage in such system.

2702—Disclosure of Contents. This section specifies the following:

1. A person or entity providing an electronic communication service to the public shall not knowingly divulge to any other person or entity the contents of a communication while in electronic storage by that service; or

2. A person or entity providing remote computing service to the public shall not knowingly divulge to any other person or entity the contents of any communication that is carried or maintained on that service.

2703—Requirements for Governmental Access. This section of the USC provides that a governmental entity may require the disclosure by a provider of electronic communication service of the contents of an electronic communication for 180 days or less, only pursuant to a properly issued warrant. However, under certain circumstances, the 180-day maximum can be extended to a longer period.

Last, but not least, the U.S. Patriot Act (2001) gave sweeping powers to law enforcement agencies with respect to their ability to monitor and arrest suspected terrorists by making it much easier and faster to obtain wiretaps and warrants for e-mail messages and library, bookstore, and banking records. There is considerable debate surrounding the U.S. Patriot Act's effect on civil liberties, particularly on individual privacy. As one can see, initiatives to prevent, detect, and prosecute cybercrime are expansive and the body of law in this area is rapidly evolving.

Cyber Information Crimes

When electronic information is compromised, the ramifications of such crime fall into three broad categories:[6]

- **Confidentiality.** A breach of confidentiality occurs when a person knowingly accesses a computer without authorization or when a person exceeds his authorized access. Confidentiality is also compromised when hackers view or copy proprietary or private information, such as social security numbers, credit card numbers, and medical files.

- **Integrity.** A breach of integrity occurs when a system or data has been accidentally or maliciously modified, altered, or destroyed without authorization. For example, viruses and worms alter source code in order to allow a hacker to gain unauthorized access to a computer reflect integrity breaches.

- **Availability.** A breach of availability occurs when an authorized user is prevented from timely, reliable access to data or a system, such as a denial of service attack.

Figure 2-3 illustrates the types of cybercrime that have been investigated and prosecuted under various sections of Title 18 of the U.S.C. As you can see, the nature and extent of the crimes vary considerably. It is important for IT auditors to obtain a working knowledge of the types of acts that constitute cybercrime so they can gain a general feel for when suspicious or unusual activities encountered during an audit should be referred to legal experts for a more in-depth analysis.

Cybercrime and IT Auditors

What types of cybercrime activities or issues might auditors encounter? While the answer to this question could fill an entire book, the illustrations presented in Figure 2-4 offer insight into how and why IT auditors need to have a general knowledge of cybercrime law, as they are likely to run across suspicious activities in this regard or they might be able to

Computer Crimes Case Chart — Case Name (District) Press Release Date	Interest Harmed — Confidentiality (C) Integrity (I) Availability (A)	Est. Dollar Loss	Target — Private or Public Safety Issue	Geography — International	Sentence & Punishment — Sentence in Months (TBD = To Be Determined)	Sentence & Punishment — Fine Forfeiture Restitution (TBD = To Be Determined)	Other
U.S. v. Cazenave (C.D. Cal.) August 2, 2002	CIA		Private		TBD	TBD	Company insiders deleted software project
U.S. v. McDaniel (C.D. Cal.) June 25, 2002	CIA		Private, Public		TBD	TBD	Disgruntled former employee
U.S. v. Zezov (S.D. N.Y.) May 21, 2002	CI		Private	X	TBD	TBD	Hackers from Kazakhstan
U.S. v. Blum (S.D. N.Y.) May 16, 2002	CI		Private		TBD	TBD	Former Chief IT Officer of Askit.com
U.S. v. Smith (D. N.J.) May 2, 2002	IA	80M	Private, Public	X	20	5K	"Melissa" virus creator
U.S. v. Sandusky (D. Nev.) April 17, 2002	CIA		Private		TBD	TBD	Former employee of computer consulting business
U.S. v. Lloyd (D. N.J.) February 26, 2002	IA	10M	Private		41	2M	Disgruntled former employee
U.S. v. Diekman I (C.D. Cal.) February 4, 2002	CI	23M	Public		TBD	TBD	Hacked into NASA computers

FIGURE 2-3 Recent Cybercrime Cases (1 of 3)

This table was reproduced, in part, from www.usdoj.gov/criminal/cybercrime/cccases.html.

(continued)

Computer Crimes Case Chart

Case Name (District) Press Release Date	Interest Harmed — Confidentiality (C) Integrity (I) Availability (A)	Est. Dollar Loss	Target — Private or Public Safety Issue	Geography — International	Sentence & Punishment — Sentence in Months (TBD = To Be Determined)	Sentence & Punishment — Fine Forfeiture Restitution (TBD = To Be Determined)	Other
U.S. v. Farrai (S.D. N.Y.) January 30, 2002	CI		Private		18		Paralegal's scheme to sell trial plan
U.S. v. Osowski (N.D. Cal.) November 26, 2001	C	6.3M	Private		34	7.8M	Cisco accountant stole stock from company
U.S. v. Gorshkov (W.D. Wash.) October 10, 2001	CIA		Private	X	TBD	TBD	Russian hacker
U.S. v. Carpenter (D. Md.) July 24, 2001	CIA		Private		TBD	TBD	IRS computer sabotage
U.S. v. McKenna (D. N.H.) June 18, 2001	CIA	13K	Private		6	13K	Disgruntled former employee
U.S. v. Sullivan (W.D. N.C.) April 13, 2001	IA	100K	Private		24	194K	Disgruntled former employee
U.S. v. Ventimiglia (M.D. Fl.) March 20, 2001	IA	209K	Private		60 prob.	233K	Disgruntled GTE employee
U.S. v. Dennis (D. Alaska) January 22, 2001	A		Public		6	5K	Denial of service attack

FIGURE 2-3 Recent Cybercrime Cases (2 of 3)

(continued)

Computer Crimes Case Chart — Case Name (District) Press Release Date	Interest Harmed — Confidentiality (C) Integrity (I) Availability (A)	Est. Dollar Loss	Target — Private or Public Safety Issue	Geography — International	Sentence & Punishment — Sentence in Months (TBD = To Be Determined)	Sentence & Punishment — Fine Forfeiture Restitution (TBD = To Be Determined)	Other
U.S. v. Sanford (N.D. Tx.) December 26, 2000	CIA	45K	Private, Public	X	60 prob.	45K	"HV2K" hacking group member
U.S. v. "cOmrade" (S.D. Fl.) September 21, 2000	CA	41K	Public		6	0	First juvenile hacker to receive prison sentence
U.S. v. Gregory (N.D. Tx.) September 6, 2000	C	1.5M	Private		26	154K	"Global Hell" hacking group member
U.S. v. Iffih (D. Mass.) February 23, 2000	CA		Public		TBD	TBD	Hacked into federal government computers
U.S. v. Burns (E.D. Va.) November 19, 1999	CIA	40K	Private, Public	X	15	36K	Designed "Web Bandit" program
U.S. v. Mitnick (C.D. Cal.) August 9, 1999	CI	1M	Private		68	4K	Notorious hacker
U.S. v. An Unnamed Juvenile (D. Mass.) March 18, 1998	CA		Public		TBD	TBD	FAA control tower disabled

FIGURE 2-3   Recent Cybercrime Cases (3 of 3)

United States Code	Examples of cybercrime and related issues IT auditors might encounter during the course of an IT audit
Patents (Title 35, U.S.C., all sections)	If the IT auditor observes that the client appears to use some distinctive techniques within its IT infrastructure, such as novel processes of encrypting data or unique methods of thwarting denial of service attacks, the auditor should investigate whether such processes are already patented by other entities. If so, the auditor should ensure that the client has legally procured the right to use such patents. If the IT auditor learns that the client owns one or more patents pertaining to the IT infrastructure, such as those mentioned above, the IT auditor should investigate whether and how the company continually scans the environment to ensure that other persons or entities are not infringing on the client's patent(s). If the company has no policies or activities aimed at protecting its patent(s) in this regard, the IT auditor could add value to the engagement by suggesting several scanning methods. If the IT auditor discovers that the client has developed unique and novel components of the digital IT infrastructure that give competitive advantage to the company, such as those mentioned above, the IT auditor could suggest that the client consider the possibility of applying for patents, if it has not already done so. If successful, the client will be able to legally protect its intellectual property rights.
Trademarks (Title 15 U.S.C., all sections)	If the IT auditor observes that the client appears to use the trademarks of other entities in its digital communications, the auditor should ensure that client is not illegally using such trademarks. For example, if the company were to attach the Nike "Swoosh" logo (which represents the wing of the Greek goddess Nike) on its digital communications, they might be in violation of Nike's trademark rights. If the client places its own unique logo on its digital communications, the IT auditor should investigate whether and how the company continually scans the environment to ensure that other persons or entities are not using the company logo. If the company has no policies or activities aimed at protecting its logo, the IT auditor could add value to the engagement by suggesting several scanning methods. If the client places a unique logo on its digital communications but has not properly registered it with the U.S. Patent and Trademark Office, the IT auditor should suggest that the client do so as a way to protect the marketing value ascribed to the logo.
Copyrights (Title 17 U.S.C., all sections)	If the IT auditor observes that the client appears to use copyrighted creative works belonging to external parties, such as software applications, the auditor should investigate whether the rights to use such copyrighted works have been properly procured. With regard to software applications, which reflect the most likely type of infringements an IT auditor will encounter, the client should possess properly executed software licensing agreements. For instance, if the company has loaded Microsoft Office on all computers yet has not purchased such software through legal channels, a copyright infringement may exist.

(continued)

FIGURE 2-4   IT Auditors and Cybercrime (1 of 4)

United States Code	Examples of cybercrime and related issues IT auditors might encounter during the course of an IT audit
Copyrights (continued)	If the IT auditor learns that the client owns one or more copyrights, such as software applications that the company has developed, the auditor should investigate whether and how the company continually scans the environment to ensure that other persons or entities are not infringing on the client's copyrights. If the company has no policies or activities aimed at protecting its copyrights in this regard, the IT auditor could add value to the engagement by suggesting several scanning methods. If the IT auditor discovers that the client has developed its own creative works, such as software applications, and the company has not copyrighted its material, the IT auditor could suggest that the client consider the possibility of registering for such copyrights, if it has not already done so. Under current law, works are covered whether or not a copyright notice is attached and whether or not the work is registered. Nevertheless, the client still should register its creative works as a way to put the public on notice that it considers its works to be protected as intellectual property.
Fraud and Related Activity in Connection with Access Devices (Title 18 U.S.C., section	The IT auditor should ensure that the client's system of internal controls prevents or detects unauthorized persons or entities access to sensitive information belonging to another party. Examples of such information would be digital signatures, access cards, passwords, social security numbers, bank account numbers, credit card numbers, and IP addresses. In this regard, the IT auditor should ensure that the company's access devices (e.g., access cards, digital signatures, and passwords) are properly secured from misuse by internal or external parties. Also, the IT auditor should check to see that access information belonging to trading partners (such as social security numbers, bank account numbers, credit card numbers, and IP addresses) are not misused by internal or external parties.
Fraud and Related Activity in Connection with Computers (Title 18 U.S.C., section 1030)	This broad area of cybercrime includes such acts as hacking into computer systems, producing and distributing viruses, stealing employer information, damaging corporate databases, attacking Web sites to deny service and so on. The key issue for IT auditors is that if they run across situations where computers have been accessed without proper authorization or where authorized users have exceeded their bounds and thereby engage in fraudulent or malicious behaviors, a "red flag" should go up signaling the possibility that cybercrimes may have been committed. As just mentioned, denial of service attacks might also fall under this umbrella, particularly if the denial does not affect public use of the Internet. However, if the denial of service attack is so pervasive that it degrades considerably Internet communications, it could fall under the next category of cybercrime (below).
Communication Lines, Stations, or Systems (Title 18 U.S.C., section 1362)	A key factor in the tremendous growth and acceptance of e-commerce has been the collaborative support of the government in developing, implementing, and supporting the Internet. In the U.S. culture, less regulation of business is typically preferred to more.

(continued)

FIGURE 2-4 IT Auditors and Cybercrime (2 of 4)

United States Code	Examples of cybercrime and related issues IT auditors might encounter during the course of an IT audit
	Hence, the government has had a "hands off" policy with respect to how businesses use the Internet. However, use of the Internet for e-commerce is now so pervasive that, were the Internet to be disrupted, the economic well-being of the United States could be at stake. As a result, Critical Infrastructure Assurance Office, a government office, is playing an active role in seeking to influence both public and private sector policy and practices with respect to how to best protect the Internet from disruption and destruction. A partnership is needed between the government and the private sector in this regard for the following reasons:

- To establish the level of assurance needed to support reliable interchange between organizations involved in e-commerce;
- To assure the continuing availability of the services provided by critical infrastructure industries; and
- To enable the establishment of a set of "ground rules" that can assure protection of both the critical information assets and those who depend on their integrity, availability, and confidentiality.

To the extent that IT auditors run across incidences involving interference with communication lines, stations, or systems, it will most likely be in the realm of widespread "denial of service attacks" whereby perpetrators attempt to obstruct, hinder, or delay the transmission of communication over the Internet. If a denial of service attack has hit the auditor's client, the IT auditor should determine the origin, which could be an internal or external party, and extent.

It is important for the IT auditor to understand that a denial of service attack can appear to emanate from the client's site, yet the attack's origin may have begun somewhere else by someone else. This can occur when the perpetrator misrepresents the client's IP addresses as the source of the attack. Thus, as a preventive measure against such attacks, the IT auditor must ensure that effective internal controls aimed at stopping malicious behaviors, such as hacking and IP spoofing, are in place and operating at the client site.

United States Code	Examples
Interception and Disclosure of Wire, Oral, or Electronic Communications (Title 18 U.S.C., section 2511)	If during the course of an IT audit the auditor suspects that parties internal to the client are intercepting corporate communications, say over the company's intranet or local area network, cybercrimes may have been committed. For instance, if an IT auditor is checking the security of the client's e-mail system and learns that someone has planted a program that copies all e-mail correspondence as it traverses the communication system and routes the copies to another location, this would constitute a crime under this section of the U.S.C.

Additionally, IT auditors should check to see if the client uses techniques designed to thwart external parties from intercepting electronic communications (e.g., cyber espionage), such as encrypted messages and digital communication lines. If not, the IT auditor can add value to the audit by suggesting ways to prevent such criminal acts against the company.

(continued)

FIGURE 2-4 IT Auditors and Cybercrime (3 of 4)

United States Code	Examples of cybercrime and related issues IT auditors might encounter during the course of an IT audit
Unlawful Access to Stored Communication (Title 18 U.S.C., section 2701)	The same issues as just discussed apply to unlawful access to stored communication. The difference is that this section of the U.S.C. deals with communications (such as e-mail) that have already traveled over communication lines and are stored somewhere, whereas the prior discussion involved the interception of electronic communications during transit. Additionally, this section covers attempts to prevent authorized access to stored digital communications. The IT auditor's primary role in this respect is to ensure that corporate computers, networks, and storage devices are secured from unauthorized access.
Disclosure of Contents (Title 18 U.S.C., section 2702)	This category of cybercrime deals with persons or entities providing electronic communication services or remote computing services to the public. If IT auditors work for a company or client that fits into this definition, the auditors must review the existence and effectiveness of policies and internal controls designed to maintain confidentiality over the contents of electronic communications while in transit over communication lines or stored in computers. Failure on the part of an organization to maintain and operate such internal controls could place it in legal jeopardy.
Requirements for Government Access (Title 18 U.S.C., section 2703)	This category of cybercrime also concerns persons or entities electronic communication services or remote computing services to the public. The law basically says that the government can require the content disclosure of electronic communications for a period of up to 180 days, and perhaps longer under special circumstances. If IT auditors work for a company or client that fits this description, they should ensure that the organization securely retains all digital communications for at least 180 days. IMPORTANT! Even if the company or client does not fit into the aforementioned category (meaning all for-profit, not-for-profit, and governmental entities), it would behoove every organization that offers e-mail capability to employees to retain copies of electronic communications for a period of at least 180 days, if not for one year. The reason for this is rooted in the U.S. Patriots Act, which gives expansive powers of search and seizure to the government when and where terrorist activity is suspected, which could take place within any organization.

FIGURE 2-4   IT Auditors and Cybercrime (4 of 4)

help their companies/clients ward off potential acts of cybercrime. Some of the issues highlighted in Figure 2-4, such as viruses, hacking, and denial of services attacks, will be covered in more depth in subsequent chapters of this book.

The digitization of personal information has dramatically increased in the past few years, thus, it is becoming progressively easier for persons and organizations to illegally obtain private information on individuals. In the next section, we examine efforts designed to protect individual privacy and explain how and why IT auditors should be concerned about privacy rights.

PRIVACY ISSUES

Interestingly, the word "privacy" is not used in the text of the U.S. Constitution. However, the Supreme Court has found the concept of privacy to be protected by a number of amendments. Thus, privacy is known as a "penumbra right." Privacy is the essence of the Bill of Rights and, thus, a guaranteed right to all U.S. citizens. The major federal laws and regulations dealing with privacy rights are shown in Figure 2-5. There are a plethora of state laws and regulations dealing with privacy issues, as well as hundreds of legislative efforts at the state and federal levels aimed at further protecting private information. Existing laws and regulations, however, are still quite narrow in scope, as laws are typically made in response to a specific perceived problem, thus, they usually offer narrow protections in specific instances. However, the body of law dealing with privacy issues is rapidly expanding, as privacy is becoming a serious problem in the digital world. The European Union, however, is attempting to set forth a comprehensive framework pertaining to privacy rights.

The international community is also working hard to protect individual privacy rights, as reflected by the European Union's broad-based approach to protect confidential personal information. The U.S. Department of Commerce explains the European Union's effort in this regard as follows:

> The European Commission's Directive on Data Protection went into effect in October, 1998, and would prohibit the transfer of personal data to non-European Union nations that do not meet the European "adequacy" standard for privacy protection. While the United States and the European Union share the goal of enhancing privacy protection for their citizens, the United States takes a different approach to privacy from that taken by the European Union. The United States uses a sectoral approach that relies on a mix of legislation, regulation, and self regulation. The European Union, however, relies on comprehensive legislation that, for example, requires creation of government data protection agencies, registration of data bases with those agencies, and, in some instances, prior approval before personal data processing may begin. As a result of these different privacy approaches, the Directive could have significantly hampered the ability of U.S. companies to engage in many trans-Atlantic transactions.
>
> In order to bridge these different privacy approaches and provide a streamlined means for U.S. organizations to comply with the Directive, the U.S. Department of Commerce, in consultation with the European Commission, developed a "safe harbor" framework. The safe harbor—approved by the EU this year—is an important way for U.S. companies to avoid experiencing interruptions in their business dealings with the EU or facing prosecution by European authorities under European privacy laws. Certifying to the safe harbor will assure that EU organizations know that your company provides "adequate" privacy protection, as defined by the Directive.
>
> The safe harbor framework offers a simpler and cheaper means of complying with the adequacy requirements of the Directive, which should particularly benefit small and medium enterprises. (www.export.gov/safeharbor/sh_overview.html)

As one can see, it is becoming increasingly difficult to coordinate privacy regulation and legislation across the globe. The United States responded to the European Union's privacy criteria by establishing a "safe harbor" provision for U.S. companies, which was

The Privacy Act of 1974

Title 5, United States Code, Section 552(a)

Provides safeguards against an invasion of privacy through the misuse of records by federal agencies.

Right to Financial Privacy Act of 1978

Title12, United States Code, Sections 3401–3413

Prohibits financial institutions from providing copies or access to the information contained in the financial records of any customer to government agencies for law enforcement purposes unless the government has received consent or provided notice and an opportunity for the customer to object.

Federal Trade Commission Act

Title 15, United States Code, Sections 41–58 (as amended)

Empowers the commission to prevent unfair competition methods, and unfair or deceptive acts or practices that may affect commerce, which includes the misuse of private information for such purposes.

Cable Communications Policy Act (CCPA)

Title 15, United States Code, Sections 521–551

Protects cable television subscriber information from unauthorized disclosure to third parties.

Identity Theft Assumption and Deterrence Act

Title 18, United States Code, Section 1028 (note)

Designates the Federal Trade Commission as a clearinghouse for identity theft complaints.

Fair Credit Reporting Act (ECPA)

Title 15, United States Code, Section 1681

Protects the privacy of information collected by consumer reporting agencies such as credit bureaus, medical information companies, and tenant screening services: Requires consumer reporting agencies to develop reasonable measures to store consumers' information in a confidential and accurate manner.

The Children's Online Privacy Protection Act (COPPA)

Title 15, United States Code, Section 6501

Protects children's privacy by giving parents the tools to control what information is collected while children are online.

Gramm-Leach-Bliley Act

To be codified in Title 15, United States Code, Sections 6801–6809

Ensures that financial institutions protect the privacy of consumers' "nonpublic personal financial information."

The Electronic Communications Privacy Act (ECPA)

Title 18, United States Code, Section 2501

Prohibits unlawful access and certain disclosures of communication contents and prevents government entities from requiring disclosure of electronic communications from a provider without proper procedure.

Customer Proprietary Network Information Electronic Communications Privacy Act of 1986

Title 47, United States Code, Section 222

Protects the information telephone companies obtain about customers regarding the quantity, technical configuration, type, destination, and amount of use of a telecommunications service subscribed to by such customers.

The Health Insurance Portability and Accountability Act of 1996 (HIPAA)

Code of Federal Regulations 45, Sections 160 and 164

Prohibits covered entities (health plans, health care clearinghouses, and health care providers who transmit any health information in electronic form in connection with a transaction regulated by the HIPPA) from disclosing protected health information to third parties without the patient's prior consent.

FIGURE 2-5   Privacy Laws and Regulations

approved by the European Union in 2000. Applying for "safe harbor" certification is voluntary for U.S. organizations. Companies that are certified must agree to remain compliant with the seven "safe harbor" rules shown in Figure 2-6.

The American Institute of Certified Public Accountants (AICPA) has begun an initiative aimed at determining the profession's role in the increasingly complicated, yet important, world of individual privacy rights. In this light, the AICPA has formed a committee, called the AICPA Privacy Task Force, to look into privacy related issues. The task force defines privacy as:

> The rights and obligations of individuals and organizations with respect to the collection, use, disclosure, and retention of personally identifiable information.

The link between individual privacy rights and organizations (for-profit, not-for-profit, and governmental) is that managers who are responsible for such organizations are obligated to institute proper internal controls aimed at protecting the confidentiality of personal information that is collected during the normal course of business. The link between organizations and the accounting profession is that the AICPA believes that independent accountants are highly qualified to conduct privacy engagements designed to ensure that privacy-related controls are in place and operating effectively.

What type of private information is protected anyway? Any personally identifiable information, factual or subjective, that is collected by an organization (for-profit, not-for-profit, and governmental) falls into the realm of private information. While exact specification of personally identifiable information covered under privacy laws and regulations varies depending on the circumstances, a sample list of such protected information is as follows:

1. Factual: Age, name, income, ethnicity, blood type, biometric images, DNA, credit card numbers, loan information, and medical records.

Notice: Organizations must notify individuals about the purposes for which they collect and use information about them.

Choice: Organizations must give individuals the opportunity to choose (opt out) whether their personal information will be disclosed to a third party or used for a purpose incompatible with the purpose for which it was originally collected or subsequently authorized by the individual.

Onward Transfer (transfers to third parties): To disclose information to a third party, organizations must apply the notice and choice principles.

Access: Individuals must have access to personal information about them that an organization holds and be able to correct, amend, or delete that information where it is inaccurate, except where the burden or expense of providing access would be disproportionate to the risks to the individual's privacy in the case in question, or where the rights of persons other than the individual would be violated.

Security: Organizations must take reasonable precautions to protect personal information from loss, misuse and unauthorized access, disclosure, alteration, and destruction.

Data integrity: Personal information must be relevant for the purposes for which it is to be used. An organization should take reasonable steps to ensure that data is reliable for its intended use, and is accurate, complete, and current.

Enforcement: In order to ensure compliance with the safe harbor principles, there must be (a) readily available and affordable independent recourse mechanisms; (b) procedures for verifying that the commitments companies make to adhere to the safe harbor principles have been implemented; and (c) obligations to remedy problems arising out of a failure to comply with the principles.

FIGURE 2-6   Safe Harbor Rules
Adapted from the U.S. Department of Commerce Web site at www.export.gov/safeharbor/sh_overview.html.

2.   Subjective: Opinions, evaluations, comments, disciplinary actions, and disputes.

The key is that such information is considered "private" if it can be specifically tied to or identified with an individual.

The IT auditors' role in privacy is to ensure that management develops, implements, and operates sound internal controls aimed at protecting the private information it collects and stores during the normal course of business. Particularly since the explosion of concern and regulation regarding privacy rights centers on digital information, IT auditors are highly qualified to assess the strength and effectiveness of controls designed to protect personally identifiable information in organizations.

SUMMARY

This chapter discusses the importance of creating a positive ethical atmosphere for IT auditors, explains IT auditors' responsibilities with regard to irregular and illegal acts, and provides an overview of various regulatory and legal issues germane to IT audits. It is important for IT auditors to understand proper and expected rules of conduct, such as those as codified in the ISACA Code of Professional Ethics, for such guidelines promote high standards of professional practice, among other benefits. Additionally, it is critical that IT auditors be cognizant of their roles and responsibilities in detecting, preventing, and reporting suspected irregular and illegal acts, as they are likely to encounter such acts during the course of an IT audit. Finally, there are key areas in which various regulations and laws can impact an IT audit, such as contracts, cybercrime, intellectual property, and privacy rights. While IT auditors are not qualified to offer legal advice or render legal opinions, they should have a working knowledge of relevant regulations and laws so they can know when to seek legal counsel, and how to help their companies and clients in compliance efforts.

DISCUSSION QUESTIONS

2-1   Who is responsible for prevention and detection of irregular and illegal acts?

2-2   What types of written contracts do auditors typically examine? What three elements must the auditor ensure a contract contains?

2-3   What cannot be included in an employment contract?

2-4   What stipulation of nondisclosure agreements dealing with trade secrets differs from confidentiality agreements?

2-5   When is the contract element of "consideration" required and not required in a noncompete agreement? Why?

2-6   What does computer or "cyber" crime mean? Give ten examples.

2-7   What are the three requirements of an invention in order to receive a patent?

2-8   What are four general types of intellectual discoveries covered under patent law?

2-9   What does a "breach of availability" mean?

2-10 What is the responsibility of a manager in an organization for individual privacy rights?

EXERCISES

2-11 In September 1997, eBay revolutionized the concept of online marketplace exchanges by holding auctions over the Internet. Competitor online auction sites soon followed, such as Yahoo! and Amazon.com, and a new industry was born. In spring 1999, a related business model emerged—auction aggregators. The auction aggregator model was to search online auction sites and offer listings and price information to users. For example, if a user of an auction aggregator was looking for, say, a particular rare coin, the aggregator would search eBay, Yahoo!, and Amazon.com for the coin and display the description and price to the user. Bidder's Edge was one of the most notable auction aggregators.

The rise of auction aggregators was sparked by a court case that found that "facts" are public property, even if such facts are collected through the "sweat equity" of another entity (*Feist Publications, Inc. vs. Rural Telephone Service Co.,* 499 U.S., 340). eBay decided to sue Bidder's Edge for intellectual property right violations, even though the *Feist* decision weighed heavily in favor of Bidder's Edge. Various consumer groups, on both sides of the argument, rallied to the cause. As a result, H.R. 354 and H.R. 1858 were introduced in Congress in 1999 and remain under deliberation.

H.R. 354 basically asserts the "sweat of brow" doctrine, which states that "facts" collected as a result of substantial investments of time, personnel, and effort are protected intellectual property of the collector. HR 1858, on the other hand, argues that it is in the public interest for Internet users to be able to obtain and compare information from various databases; thus, collected facts are public property.

Required:

> Discuss the pros and cons of H.R. 354 and H.R. 1858. In responding to this question, please consider the positions taken by Coalition Against Database Piracy (CADP) and NetCoalition.com in the debate.

2-12 In 1999, a company called DoubleClick was formed. The business model of DoubleClick was to track click-stream data, stored on cookies, for advertisers. There was little consumer opposition to DoubleClick, as the company did not collect personal information from users or their computers; rather, users were identified only by an ID number. DoubleClick offered an "opt out" policy, although it was difficult to find on its Web site. In 2000, DoubleClick formed Abacus Online, a click-stream database in which users' click-streams were linked to personal information (with an opt-out policy) only when they made catalog purchases, completed online surveys, or participated in drawings. Then, DoubleClick decided to merge the two databases to provide tailored information to advertisers. This strategy was vehemently opposed by Internet privacy rights groups. After much public outcry, DoubleClick abandoned its merger plans, at a sunk cost of $1.7 billion.

Required:

a. How important is "privacy" to the ultimate survival of the Internet as a viable platform for e-commerce?

b. What have the private sector, U.S. federal government, and the European Union done to protect Internet privacy rights?

REFERENCES AND RECOMMENDED READINGS

Casey, E. 2000. *Digital Evidence and Computer Crime.* Academic Press; ISBN: 012162885X.

Hunter, R. 2002. *World Without Secrets: Business, Crime and Privacy in the Age of Ubiquitous Computing.* John Wiley and Sons; ISBN: 0471218162.

Hyatt, M. S. 2001. *Invasion of Privacy: How to Protect Yourself in the Digital Age.* Regnery Publishing; ISBN: 0895262878.

Miller, R. A., and M. H. Davis. 2000. *Intellectual Property: Patents, Trademarks, and Copyright.* West Wadsworth; ISBN: 0314235191.

Richards, J. R. 1998. *Transnational Criminal Organizations, Cybercrime, and Money Laundering: A Handbook for Law Enforcement Officers, Auditors and Financial Investigators.* CRC Press; ISBN: 0849328063.

Salehnia, A. 2002. *Ethical Issues of Information Systems.* Idea Group Publishing; ISBN: 1931777152.

Web Sites

Business Ethics

www.ethics.ubc.ca/resources/business/codes.html

www.whitehouse.org/news/2002/070802.asp

groups.yahoo.com/group/corp-ethics/

Intellectual Property

www.wipo.org/

www.eff.org/IP/

www.intelproplaw.com/

Law and Computer Crime

www.law.cornell.edu/topical.html

www.cybercrime.gov/

www.crime-research.org/eng/

www.epic.org/security/

Privacy

www.ftc.gov/privacy/

www.privacyrights.org/

www.epic.org/default2.html

NOTES

1. The six reasons for developing codes of ethical conduct were adapted from "Life Skills Coaches of British Columbia," which can be found at www.calsca.com/ethics_lscabc.htm#preamble.
2. The official ISACA Code of Professional Ethics code can be found at www.isaca.org/codeofethics.htm.
3. This outline detailing the IT auditor's responsibilities toward irregular and illegal acts is summarized from the IS Auditing Guideline (Document #30.01.01) promulgated by the ISACA. However, since this outline is highly aggregated, readers should obtain a copy of Document #30 from ISACA for more detailed guidance.
4. See www.wipo.org for a thorough analysis of international efforts to protect intellectual property.
5. For more information, visit www.usdoj.gov/criminal/cybercrime.
6. These three categories are adapted from www.usdoj.gov/criminal/cybercrime/cccases.html.

CHAPTER **3**

INFORMATION TECHNOLOGY RISKS AND CONTROLS

CHAPTER CONTENTS

INTRODUCTION

No risk, no reward: In recent years, auditors have shifted their approach to controlling risks. They have moved from a control-based audit model to a risk-based one. The simple exchange of the word "risk" for the word "control" represents a sea change in terms of the usefulness and influence of auditing. Rather than controlling just for the sake of control, auditors today evaluate risks related to an organization's strategy and objectives. They then choose to implement the set of controls that best mitigates those risks in a cost-effective manner.

This chapter discusses risks and controls as they relate to information technology (IT). Figure 3-1 shows the risk management process. It begins with identifying risk and ends with documenting internal controls—except that it never really ends. Risk management is a continuous process. Through monitoring, an organization constantly seeks to find new ways to manage risks.

The first section of this chapter describes the various kinds of IT risks. Next, we discuss ways to assess the extent of risk in a particular case. Only after studying and evaluating risk should auditors and management begin to think about identifying internal controls. This chapter discusses several models for controls, including COSO and CobiT. The chapter next explains how to document controls. Last, because risk management never ends, we discuss the continuous monitoring process. Chapters 4 through 7 will continue our discussion of risks and controls, describing them in detail for a variety of processes and technologies.

IDENTIFYING INFORMATION TECHNOLOGY RISKS

What is risk? Simply put, risks are the chances of negative outcomes. Business enterprises face a variety of risks, including business, audit, security, and continuity risks. Managers and auditors strive to balance risk, rather than eliminate it. It is true that no risk means no reward. It's also true that IT in some cases makes business riskier and in other cases makes it more secure. Classifying risks can be helpful in identifying specific risks.

Business Risk

A business risk is the likelihood that an organization will not achieve its business goals and objectives. Both external and internal factors can contribute to the chances of this occurrence. To understand a particular organization's business risk, an auditor must first become familiar with the enterprise's strategic plan. This plan should outline the organization's mission for the near term (3–5 years), along with the strategies and objectives it will employ to carry out that mission. Risks may emerge from the external environment, such as the risk that a new competitor will enter the market or the risk of a poor economy. Other risks could rise internally. Examples of internal risks are labor disputes, equipment failures, or management fraud.

IT is likely to play a significant role in any organization. Businesses make large investments in these systems, such as in procuring an enterprise information system or developing an

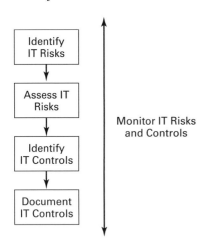

FIGURE 3-1 The Risk Management Process

intranet. The business risks associated with these systems are many. For instance, there is often an IT timing risk associated with acquiring new software and hardware, as the following scenario illustrates.

EXAMPLE   A company operates in a segment of the retail clothing industry. There are four major competitors in this industry. None of the businesses has yet to adopt an enterprise information system. Company A has been thinking about integrating its systems and talks to a major software vendor. The vendor suggests that it would like to gain expertise in adopting its enterprise software to the industry and would be happy to give the company a discount if it will be first adapter and is willing to work with the software vendor in creating Best Practices for the industry. Company A's management is now faced with a difficult decision. They can adopt the software early, take a discount, and possibly because of the early adoption have the chance to outperform their competitors for a few years. Alternatively, they can wait and acquire the software after one of their competitors has done so and the "kinks" have all been ironed out. By being an early adapter, the company may run into difficulties, such as problems in the supply chain, that could delay orders. Thus, the company faces a business risk related to IT timing.

Audit Risk

Audit risk is the likelihood that an organization's external auditor makes a mistake when issuing an opinion attesting to the fairness of its financial statements or that an IT auditor fails to uncover a material error or fraud. For example, an auditor might say things are fine when they are not. While auditors bear business risk of their own associated with audit risk, audit risk is not limited to them alone. The failure of Enron and problems with the financial statements of Fortune 500 companies like Xerox and AOL demonstrate that shareholders, employees, and the economy as a whole can suffer when companies issue financial statements that do not reflect their true financial situation.

Audit risk is actually a combination of risks. It includes inherent risk, control risk, and detection risk, as shown in Figure 3-2. The word "inherent" implies an existing and inescapable characteristic. Inherent risk is the element of risk that exists due to the nature of an enterprise's environment and activities. Every organizational entity has some inherent risk—doing business is risky. However, there are types of organizations and types of activities in which they might engage that are more or less risky. For instance, doing business internationally is likely to carry more risk than maintaining only domestic operations. Control risk is the probability that an organization's internal control system will fail to prevent or detect a

	Inherent Risk (IR)		Control Risk (CR)		Detection Risk (DR)
Audit Risk (AR) =	Likelihood of material errors or fraud *inherent* in the business environment.	X	Likelihood that the internal control system will not prevent or detect material errors or fraud on a timely basis.	X	Likelihood that audit procedures will not detect material errors or fraud on a timely basis.

FIGURE 3-2   The Audit Risk Model

material misstatement in recording transactions or adjustments affecting financial statements. Detection risk is the chance that an auditor will not detect existing control failures.

Figure 3-2 illustrates that inherent, control, and detection risk are not independent. In planning an audit engagement, auditors must assess each of these risks and determine an acceptable level. In no case can auditors reduce risks to zero, so they must choose the set of controls that manages the risks at an acceptable level and in a cost-effective manner. Any risk remaining after implementation of effective internal controls is called residual risk.

Security Risk

IT security risk includes risks associated with data access and integrity. Unauthorized access to data may be physical or logical. Perhaps a user neglects to log off a PC at the end of a workday and the cleaning custodian sits down at the PC and reads confidential e-mails. This would be an example of unauthorized physical access and an associated risk. If the user logged off the machine and it required a password to log on to the company network, the custodian would be denied logical access to the system, even with physical access.

Many risks are associated with both unauthorized physical and logical access. These risks increase with information system integration and remote access capability. In a business that has integrated systems but does not require separate passwords for access to various parts of the system, an unauthorized user not only may be able to access sensitive company data but also perhaps even manipulate it. Allowing users to access the system only on the business premises limits the risk of unauthorized access to employees or visitors. Remote access is a nice feature for employees, but it does create the potential for any hacker to break in to an information system.

There are many potential negative outcomes associated with unauthorized data access. At a minimum, access to data by unauthorized users compromises the confidentiality of data. Hackers sometimes justify their actions by asserting that they didn't "take" anything. However, simply viewing data you do not have a right to see violates the privacy and confidentiality of the data. Of course, at the other extreme, unauthorized users may also help themselves to an organization's information or other assets.

An information system converts raw data by processing it into information. To ensure that the IT produces accurate, complete, timely, and reliable data (i.e., data integrity), an organization must control for risks associated with collecting and processing the data. Many of the risks associated with data integrity are most evident at the data collection point, and they vary with the type of data collection process. For example, in a retail store where sales clerks record sales transactions manually, there are many opportunities for error. A clerk may easily transpose numbers or drop a decimal point. A modern grocery store using electronic scanners to record sales and inventory data faces a smaller risk that the data the systems collect will not be accurate, complete, timely, or reliable.

The negative outcomes associated with a lack of data integrity range from poor decision making to increased business risk. If the information available to managers is unreliable or not timely, decisions may be less than optimal. Business risks can result from having inaccurate information as occurred in a well-known case involving a spreadsheet error. A construction company significantly underbid a project because the formula for costing the project failed to include one of the spreadsheet cells containing a cost item.

Continuity Risk

Continuity risk includes risks associated with an information system's availability and backup and recovery. Availability refers to security that ensures that an information system is always accessible to users. For example, hackers may threaten availability by flooding a system with mail and overloading the servers so as to shut down a company's Intranet or Web site. When a retail Web site is unavailable to consumers, there are not only lost sales for the period the site is unavailable, but also lost consumers who buy elsewhere because of fears about reliability.

Backup and recovery procedures ensure that in the case of interruptions in continuity, procedures are available to restore data and operations. The September 11 disaster brought the issues of backup and recovery to the forefront of security concerns. However, backup and recovery are important in many more instances than extreme emergencies such as terrorist attacks. For example, an employee may open an e-mail attachment containing a virus and wipe out the company's budget stored on the hard drive. Backup and recovery procedures vary widely in complexity and cost. For a small business, the procedure may involve a daily dumping of files onto a diskette that the owner takes home. Larger businesses are likely to schedule frequent full and incremental data backups and to use procedures such as physical or electronic vaulting, formal disaster recovery planning, and redundant systems. We discuss disaster recovery planning and backup procedures in more detail in Chapter 5.

ASSESSING INFORMATION TECHNOLOGY RISKS

Managers and auditors must assess IT risks in order to determine how to apply resources to risk management. In a later section of this chapter we discuss the many models and frameworks available for internal control. While many of these models incorporate risk and risk assessment in them, at this time they do not separate risk from control. Some groups have sought to standardize business risk models.

Risk management attempts to balance risk against the needs of an organization. To balance risk, you must assess it. This requires both identification and measurement. It also requires determining levels of acceptable risk since no organization can afford to expend the resources to control risk to zero levels.

Threats and Vulnerabilities

Figure 3-3 shows one approach to the IT risk assessment process. In this approach, IT risk assessment begins with identifying threats or exposures. These threats are not limited to

---

1. Identify Threats/Exposures
Examples:
    Data Confidentiality
    Data Availability
    Data Integrity
    Data Timeliness
    Data Accuracy
    IT Infrastructure
2. Assess Vulnerabilities to Threats/Exposures
Examples:
    Data Confidentiality
    — Remote access by unauthorized users
    — On-site access by unauthorized personnel
3. Determine Acceptable Risk Levels
    Assess the Probability of Vulnerabilities
Example:
    Chance of remote access by unauthorized users is .05 percent

---

FIGURE 3-3   *An Approach to IT Risk Assessment*

purposeful acts; errors and acts of nature can do as much or more harm than malicious acts. There are many kinds of threats to IT resources. These include threats to data confidentiality, availability, integrity, timeliness, accuracy, and threats to IT infrastructure.

The next step in risk assessment is to evaluate vulnerabilities to risk. Why and how are an organization's IT resources vulnerable to identified threats? For example, in what way could someone accidentally or maliciously impair data confidentiality? The data confidentiality vulnerability would be lower for an organization that does not have an intranet or Internet access versus one that does.

Finally, risk assessment requires determining acceptable risk levels. You may do so conceptually or through what is likely to be "guesstimation." To assign values requires estimating both the likelihood of loss and a dollar amount associated with the loss. These are used to calculate an expected value for a risk as follows:

$$\text{Expected value of risk} = \frac{\text{Estimated Loss}}{\text{from Specific Risk}} \times \frac{\% \text{ Likelihood}}{\text{of Loss}}$$

Theoretically, management would be willing to spend an amount equal to the expected value of the risk in order to control it. Practically, however, that is not likely to be the case. Management must instead decide what is an acceptable risk level and should seek to offset that risk through purchased insurance.

The following example shows how to apply the steps in this risk assessment approach to a specific scenario.

EXAMPLE Almost every IT environment is vulnerable to virus attacks. The threat or exposure associated with a virus attack might include data availability, data integrity, and system hardware performance. The virus attack is the vulnerability. The business consequences range from mild to severe. If the virus simply sends unwanted messages to users in your address book, there may be some inconvenience and embarrassment at worst. A virus that wipes out data files, including back ups, would have fairly severe ramifications. There are controls and patches available to detect and prevent viruses. However, since virus perpetrators seem to be challenged to create new viruses almost daily, it is difficult or impossible to stop viruses completely. Determining for an organization the harm a virus attack might do will help to decide how much to spend on controlling this risk and how much of the risk is acceptable. For most organizations it would make sense to purchase virus protection software and keep it up to date. It probably also makes sense to create firewalls to keep viruses from entering a network. But not everyone can or should spend the resources to regularly scan security reports for new virus reports and to update security patches.

Risk Indicators and Risk Measurement

Another way to assess risk is to identify IT processes and then develop a set of risk indicators relative to these. The risk indicators would point to a need for controls. For example, in acquiring software applications (an IT process), a risk indicator would be failure to map software acquisitions to the strategic plan. The risk indicator is, in a sense, a mirror of an internal control or a control objective. An organization can note the presence or absence of risk indicators for each IT process, and then choose to control them or not, depending on an analysis as to whether or not the risk is acceptable. Chapters 4–7 in this book identify risk indicators associated with several IT processes and specific technologies.

Risk assessment measurement is important because it allows IT auditors to narrow the audit scope and maximize efficiency and effectiveness. There are several ways to measure risk. One way is to calculate expected value of losses as described or to simply assign a value to each risk indicator based on an assessment of its criticality.

Information Systems Audit and Control Association (ISACA) IS Audit Procedure #1, *IS Risk Assessment Measurement,* effective July 1, 2002, recommends a weighted ranking or scoring approach. Applying the ISACA procedure, the IT auditor will collect data about the enterprise and identify "IS auditable units." These are the separate segments of an organization and its IT. The IT auditor rates each of these units relative to risk. The standard provides several different ways to do this. In one example, IS Risk Assessment of Auditable Units, the IT auditor ranks categories of auditable units. The categories include data center operations and software package acquisition. Then, the auditor lists the major risk components within each category and assigns a weight to each risk element. Next the auditor assigns a score to components of the risk element. The weighted average is the product of the score times the weight. The auditor finally sums the scores and prioritizes the risk associated with each auditable unit accordingly.

IDENTIFYING INFORMATION TECHNOLOGY CONTROLS

Once an entity has identified and assessed its particular set of risks, it must set about designing specific controls over those risks. In recent years, various groups have developed internal control frameworks and guidelines to assist auditors and management in developing optimal control systems. In this section, we describe general internal control models, quality control models, and frameworks that specifically address internal control over IT.

COSO and Other Control Models

Professional organizations in several countries have sought to develop generalized internal control models. These include COSO, Cadbury, and CoCo.

THE COSO FRAMEWORK   In 1992, five U.S. accounting and finance professional groups, in an alliance known as the Committee of Sponsoring Organizations of the Treadway Commission (COSO),[1] issued a comprehensive report on internal control. The motivation for the COSO report was concern about a lack of uniform internal control standards. The COSO report is meant for managers and auditors to use in developing and evaluating internal control systems.

The COSO internal control framework consists of a definition of internal control and identification of five components. The definition is as follows.

> Internal control is broadly defined as a process, effected by an entity's
> Board of Directors, management and other personnel, designed to provide
> reasonable assurance regarding the achievement of objectives in the follow-
> ing categories: effectiveness and efficiency of operations, reliability of
> financial reporting, and compliance with laws and regulations.[2]

The COSO definition emphasizes that internal control is a process and that it is the responsibility of an organization's management, employees, and board of directors. Importantly, the definition links internal control to organizational objectives.

Included within the COSO framework are five interrelated components of internal control. The nature of these components may vary from organization to organization in terms of degree, formality, and structure. Each of these components relates to the three objectives of internal control as defined by COSO. The components are: control environment, risk assessment, control activities, information and communication, and monitoring.

An organization's control environment is its "tone at the top." This is the attitude of management toward internal control. Is the organization control conscious of or is it relatively indifferent to internal controls? Often this attitude is relatively easy to evaluate, as Case-in-Point 3-1 illustrates.

Case-in-Point 3-1

An auditor engaged on an IT audit of a large retailer learned that a programmer was regularly scheduled to supervise the computer room, meaning that programmers could access the control panel of the mainframe at any time. When the IT auditor asked the chief information officer about this internal control violation, the manager replied, "If you can't trust your programmers, who can you trust?" Noting that trust is not a sufficient internal control, the auditor quickly concluded that the control environment was not control conscious.

The COSO report recognizes risk assessment as an important component of internal control. In 2001, the Committee of Sponsoring Organizations began a project to provide guidance to organizations on enterprise risk management. The enterprise risk framework will provide organizations with guidance in developing plans to identify, measure, evaluate, and respond to risks. PricewaterhouseCoopers is leading the project, which is to be completed in 2003.

Control activities are specific internal control procedures and policies. Examples are authorizations, approvals, passwords, and segregation of duties. These are the heart of the internal control system.

Information and communication refers to the need for organizations to make sure they obtain and communicate the information needed to carry out management strategies and objectives. The information may be internal to the organization or external. Management must communicate internal control policies and procedures across the organization, and to related parties outside the organization. Additionally, there needs to be upward communication (for example, from an employee to a manager) concerning internal control concerns.

The fifth component of COSO is monitoring. COSO calls for continuous monitoring of an internal control system. This may be accomplished by regular audits and evaluations, as well as by constant attention to internal control violations.

The COSO report provided a framework for internal control. Since its issuance, many organizations have implemented it successfully. Case-in-Point 3-2, involving Boeing, is an example.

Case-in-Point 3-2

Shortly after issuance of the COSO report, Boeing adopted it as a basis for its internal control system. Because the company found it challenging to integrate the standards, it set out to reengineer its audit approach to fit the new framework. Boeing created a form with a matrix of COSO objectives (e.g., reliability of financial reporting) along one axis, and the five internal control components along the other (e.g., control environment). Auditors evaluate each cell in the matrix as satisfactory or unsatisfactory. These evaluations are communicated to management to show the effectiveness of controls within a specific area. Boeing ran into a few snags in adapting COSO, but the effort was ultimately so successful that the company now uses the COSO framework as the foundation for its internal audits.[3]

INTERNATIONAL INTERNAL CONTROL STANDARDS   While Cadbury and CoCo may conjure up images of chocolate, the two are also names of internal control models. The COSO report was a U.S. effort; two international internal control models emerged at about the same time. One was a model issued by the United Kingdom's Cadbury Commission. Like the COSO report, the Cadbury model provided a broad definition of internal control. Also similarly to COSO, the Cadbury model recommends a system of internal control to ensure effective and efficient operations, reliability of financial information and reporting, and legal and regulatory compliance. Cadbury stressed that internal control encompasses both financial and operational controls and that auditors should report on both.

The Canadian Criteria of Control Committee (CoCo) also issued a model for internal control that built on COSO and Cadbury. Its model is similar in definition and elements to the COSO and Cadbury models, although it is a bit less complex than the other two. The CoCo model also includes reliability of internal management reports and addresses risk management and management objectives. However, this framework groups its criteria of control within four categories: purpose criteria that relate to an organization's missions and objectives; commitment criteria that relate to ethics, policies, and corporate identity; capability criteria that relate to the competence of an organization; and monitoring and learning criteria that concern an organization's evolution.

COSO, Cadbury, and CoCo are likely the best known and most widely used internal control models. However, several other countries have also developed their own standards for internal control and corporate governance. Two examples of these are South Africa's King Report and France's Vienot Report.

QUALITY CONTROL STANDARDS   Internal control systems are an essential component of sound corporate governance. In addition to using internal financial and operational controls, many organizations have sought to improve public confidence in their products and processes by adopting quality control standards.

ISO 9000   The International Organization for Standardization (ISO) has been setting technical engineering standards for product quality since 1947. In 1987, the organization introduced ISO 9000, a much broader quality standard that encompasses products, processes, and management. ISO 9000 is actually a family of standards that includes ISO 9001, 9002, and 9003. These are three quality assurance models that organizations can choose among for certification. Each represents a different kind of organization. For instance, ISO 9002 is applicable to organizations that do not carry out product design and development.

ISO 9000 certification does not necessarily ensure the quality of a company's products or processes. It simply means that the organization complies with documented standards that would contribute to high quality. Still, there are many motivations for businesses to seek ISO 9000 certification. First, the standards represent group thinking about the best practices in managing organizations to ensure effective and efficient delivery of products and services to customers. Many organizations, particularly manufacturers, seek standards to provide a systematic process for consistent quality. Secondly, suppliers or customers frequently insist that their business partners obtain ISO 9000 compliance. Third, many countries require product manufacturers in regulated industries to have ISO certification.

Six Sigma   ISO 9000 forces managers to document processes. Doing so may lead to process or product improvement, but that's incidental to certification. Six Sigma, on the other hand, represents a standardized approach to process improvement. The term "Six Sigma" refers to a statistical level, implying that tolerance of defects in quality should be controlled to less than six deviations from customer specifications or to 3.4 defects per million instances. The focus of Six Sigma is on process improvement to the point where management maintains this level of quality.

There are two methodologies for Six Sigma. One, DMAIC, is for established processes, and the other, DMADV, is for new products or processes. Figure 3-4 describes the steps in the DMAIC methodology. What makes Six Sigma so useful is the set of tools that accompanies each step in the methodologies. For example, in defining processes, Six Sigma requires creating SIPOC process maps. SIPOC refers to suppliers, inputs, processes, outputs, and customers and therefore encompasses the supply chain of a process.

Many businesses, primarily manufacturers, have embraced Six Sigma. Perhaps the best-known Six Sigma success story is that of General Electric. GE claims savings of $10 billion during its first five years of implementation. Many other companies have realized benefits as well, and the methodology is being used in many types of companies, including service enterprises. Quality improvements provide many types of financial, organizational, and operational benefits. Financial benefits may include cost avoidance, increased revenue, and lower cost of production.

Statements on Auditing Standards

The Auditing Standards Board (ASB) of the American Institute of Certified Public Accountants (AICPA) issues Statements on Auditing Standards (SAS) as guidelines for external auditors in conducting the financial statement audit. Several of these guidelines are relevant to the issues of risk assessment, IT risk management, and internal control. Figure 3-5 provides a summary of these statements.

In 1988, the ASB issued its first comprehensive statement on internal control, SAS No. 55, *Consideration of Internal Control in a Financial Statement Audit.* Soon after, COSO issued its report on internal control, which required revision of the standard. SAS No. 55 directed auditors to consider internal control in attesting to financial statement reliability.

In 1995, the ASB issued SAS No. 78, *Consideration of Internal Control in a Financial Statement Audit: An Amendment to SAS No. 55.* This standard amended SAS No. 55 to accommodate the new definition of internal control developed by COSO. In addition, SAS No. 78 included the five components of internal control in the COSO report. One difference between SAS No. 78 and the COSO report is the auditing standard's emphasis on the

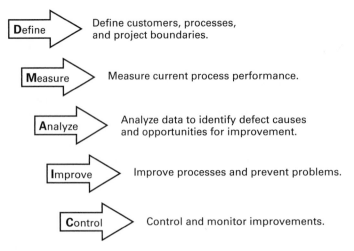

FIGURE 3-4 Steps in the Six Sigma DMAIC Methodology

Statements on Auditing Standards	Summary
SAS No. 55, *Consideration of Internal Control in a Financial Statement Audit.* Issued in 1988.	Was the first auditing standard to address the need for auditors to understand internal control Defined internal control and three components auditors must address
SAS No. 78, *Consideration of Internal Control in a Financial Statement Audit: An Amendment to SAS No. 55.* Issued in 1996.	Revised SAS No. 55 to conform to COSO internal control definition and components Required auditors to obtain a sufficient understanding of internal control
SAS No. 94, *The Effect of Information Technology on the Auditor's Consideration of Internal Control in a Financial Statement Audit.* Issued in 2001.	Recognized the pervasive use of IT and its effect on risk and control Required auditors to consider effect of IT on audit strategy Recognized that significant IT use may mean that audit evidence depends on controls over accuracy and completeness Explained that auditors should understand an organization's manual and automated procedures used to prepare financial statements
SAS No. 95, *Omnibus Statement on Auditing Standards.* Issued in 2002.	Issued in response to report of the Public Oversight Board Panel on Audit Effectiveness Requires greater understanding of enterprise and its environment, including internal control Requires more rigorous risk assessment related to financial statement material misstatements Improves relationship between risk assessment and audit procedures

FIGURE 3-5 A Summary of Audit Statements on Internal Control and Information Systems

reliability of financial reporting. SAS No. 78 requires external auditors to perform procedures sufficient to obtain an understanding of each component of internal control when planning the audit engagement. The standards also require these auditors to report significant internal control weaknesses that might impact the reliability of financial statements to the client's audit committee.

SAS No. 94, *The Effect of Information Technology on the Auditor's Consideration of Internal Control in a Financial Statement Audit,* issued in 2001, further amended SAS No. 55. The new statement provided guidance on the influence of information technology on auditors' understanding of risk and control. SAS No. 94 applies to organizations of all sizes. The standard notes that IT may affect any of the five components of internal control defined in the COSO report and SAS No. 78. It also acknowledges the risks, as well as the benefits, of IT on an entity's internal control system and increases the auditor's responsibility with respect to reporting on internal control. Auditors must now consider how IT influences audit strategy. Therefore, auditors must obtain satisfaction that using substantive testing alone will accomplish control objectives. If the client system supports financial statement assertions with a significant amount of electronic information, auditors will need to gather evidence about controls over IT risks. In the end, SAS No. 94 recognizes the pervasive effects of IT on accounting information systems and requires auditors to consider them.

In 2002, responding to concerns about audit quality and effectiveness, the ASB issued SAS No. 98, containing seven new audit standards that are to replace existing ones related to the audit risk assessment process. The new statements will improve audit practice in several ways. They encourage internal control testing and put increased emphasis on an enterprise's process of risk assessment. The standards proposed in the Exposure Draft also improve the link between risk assessment and auditing procedures.

CobiT

Unlike other internal control models, the Control of Business Information Technology (CobiT), first issued by ISACA in 1996, integrates internal control with information and information technology. Another important feature of CobiT is that it is intended for use by managers and business process owners, along with auditors and information users. ISACA's mission with respect to CobiT is:

> To research, develop, publicise and promote an authoritative, up-to-date, international set of generally accepted information technology control objectives for day-to-day use by business managers and auditors.[4]

The CobiT framework consists of several parts, as illustrated by the CobiT "cube" in Figure 3-6. The three dimensions of the cube are information criteria, IT processes, and IT resources. Organizations must ensure that their information assets satisfy requirements of quality, fiduciary, and security. CobiT further breaks down these three requirements into seven information criteria: effectiveness, efficiency, confidentiality, integrity, availability, compliance, and reliability. Managers must achieve these characteristics while balancing

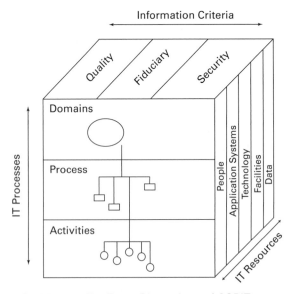

FIGURE 3-6 The Three Dimensions of COBiT
Reprinted with permission from the Information Systems Audit and Control Association, Rolling Meadows, IL, USA 60008.

their use of IT resources, including people, application systems, technology, facilities, and data. The third dimension of the cube identifies IT processes. CobiT groups these processes into four domains: planning and organization, acquisition and implementation, delivery and support, and monitoring. These domains somewhat mirror the major activities in a system development life cycle. Within each domain are processes. These processes are the center of the CobiT framework as the model identifies a control objective for each one. For example, one process within planning and organization is to identify a strategic plan. CobiT describes the control objective over that process in terms of how it satisfies business requirements, what characteristics of the process enable it, and what factors it considers (e.g., enterprise business strategy). Managers and users can develop their IT control policies around each of these control objectives.

In 2000, the CobiT Steering Committee and IT Governance Institute released the third edition of CobiT. As with earlier versions, this report includes an Executive Summary, the Framework, Audit Guidelines, an Implementation Tool Set, and detailed Control Objectives. The new edition adds a set of Management Guidelines to help managers to satisfy their control objectives. These guidelines incorporate Maturity Models that managers can use to gauge where they are today in meeting their control objectives against best practices and where they want to be.

Since its introduction, IT auditors and managers have embraced CobiT as a framework for designing and implementing control over their information technology. Case-in-Point 3-3 describes one use of CobiT in practice.

Case-in-Point 3-3

Fidelity Investments, a privately held investment management company with almost twenty-five thousand employees and total customer assets of almost $1 trillion, used CobiT to manage risk and provide control over and improve IT systems. In 1996, the company reviewed its IT controls using the CobiT framework. A year later, it created a database including the CobiT domains, processes, and control objectives. Auditors mapped the database to the types of audits conducted internally and created a plan to evaluate IT entities and processes systematically. Fidelity's experience with CobiT has been quite positive. The auditors believe it allows them to evaluate risks consistently and allocate controls efficiently. In the future the company plans to use CobiT to conduct control self-assessment reviews and to further improve the control environment.[5]

Because of the importance of CobiT to IT auditors, as noted in Chapter 1, much of this textbook relies on the framework for guidance in its discussion of risk and control over information and information processes.

Systems Reliability Assurance

In recent years, the American Institute of Certified Public Accountants has sought to expand the types of assurance services public accountants offer to its clients. The AICPA, along with the Canadian Institute of Chartered Accountants, developed one such assurance service, SysTrust, which is closely linked to IT auditing. The value of these services to clients is that SysTrust assurance should increase management, customer, supplier, and business partner confidence in the IT. In a SysTrust engagement, an auditor provided independent assurance about the reliability of the client's information system. SysTrust identified four principles for reliability: availability, maintainability, integrity, and security. In addition, SysTrust described three criteria to enable organizations to evaluate reliability. These criteria are policies, procedures, and monitoring.

The AICPA is combining multiple assurance services, including SysTrust, under one "Trust Services" umbrella (discussed in Chapter 7). Auditors offering systems reliability assurance, such as SysTrust, may provide assurance on one or more reliability principles. To do so, they evaluate the principle against the criteria and subcriteria. For example, an IT meeting SysTrust security standards would need to include policies, procedures, and monitoring of security criteria. The policies would need to be identified, documented, and communicated to IT users. The policies should be consistent with those defined in other agreements and regulations, and there should be assigned responsibility and accountability for system security within the organization.

SysTrust has its roots in COSO in that the pillars of reliability are the information qualities of reliable systems as described in the COSO report. The SysTrust model and CobiT also have similarities. First, these two models both are intended for use as governance tools in managing risks associated with information technology. Second, both frameworks include similar sets of information qualities. The SysTrust model contained the four elements of reliability; CobiT is based on efficiency, integrity, effectiveness, availability, confidentiality, reliability, and compliance qualities. The components of IT defined by SysTrust were infrastructure, software, personnel, procedures, and data. These parallel the IT resources outlined in CobiT.

In systems reliability assurance engagements, auditors seek to give comfort that controls over an IT ensure its reliability. They identify the controls over the IT and test the extent to which controls are meeting their objectives for the period covered by the engagement. The AICPA provides guidance and training regarding the specific control activities effective in ensuring each element of information quality. IT auditors may also use CobiT as a foundation for making these assurances. The end product of a systems reliability assurance engagement may be a report to management on IT reliability against specified criteria.

DOCUMENTING INFORMATION TECHNOLOGY CONTROLS

IT auditors use many tools to document their understanding of IT controls. These tools include narrative descriptions, flowcharts, and internal control questionnaires.

Internal Control Narratives

An internal control narrative is simply text describing controls over a particular risk. Narrative descriptions of internal controls should describe the origin and disposition of each document (paper or electronic), list processing steps, and describe internal controls such as approvals and authorizations. The following is an example of such a narrative concerning a program change control process (discussed in depth in Chapter 4):

> **EXAMPLE** Users must complete a sequentially numbered Change Request document when they would like programmers to make a change to an application program. These forms are available in the Security Administration office. The user's supervisor signs the request form and forwards it to the security administrator. The security administrator reviews the approved request and assigns it to an application programmer. The programmer will make the requested changes to the program in a test environment. Once the changes are made, the programmer will

review them with the user. Both the user and the security administrator must sign off on the changes on the Change Request form before introducing the revised program into the production system. The user and the security administrator each retain final signed copies of the Change Request form.

The example included one document, the Change Request. The narrative describes the source and disposition of this document. The narrative also explains each step in the change control process and identifies what each person involved in the process does. The authorizations and separation of responsibilities comprise the internal controls in the narrative.

Flowcharts

Auditors have many graphical tools available to them in documenting internal controls. Pictures are easier to understand and follow than written narratives, and diagrams are likely to be easier to update. The most common diagramming technique for documenting internal controls is the internal control flowchart. Internal control flowcharts are a type of systems flowchart that highlights control points. These tools use symbols and connectors to show documents, data flows, and process steps.

Flowcharts use a variety of symbols. Figure 3-7 shows a set of common flowchart symbols. These are available as templates in popular word processing software or an IT auditor may use specialized flowcharting software to draw them.

Figure 3-8 is an internal control flowchart for the program change control process example described previously. The flowchart clearly shows who does what. The small ovals with numbers in them identify internal controls. Attached to the flowchart is a key that describes each of these controls. An IT auditor may prepare the flowchart or review it to assess the adequacy of the internal controls.

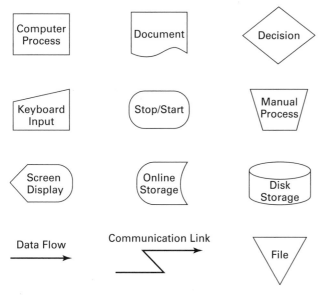

FIGURE 3-7   Common Flowchart Symbols

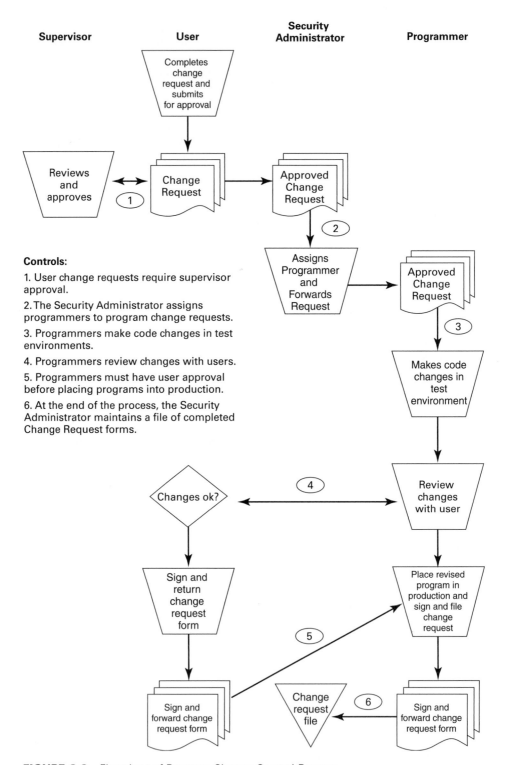

Controls:

1. User change requests require supervisor approval.

2. The Security Administrator assigns programmers to program change requests.

3. Programmers make code changes in test environments.

4. Programmers review changes with users.

5. Programmers must have user approval before placing programs into production.

6. At the end of the process, the Security Administrator maintains a file of completed Change Request forms.

FIGURE 3-8 Flowchart of Program Change Control Process

Flowcharts are easy to read but they can be difficult to create. They take a bit of artistry as there is no one right flowchart to describe a process or function. There are a few guidelines that are helpful. These include:

- The "flow" in the flowchart is top to bottom and left to right.
- The flowchart should use a common set of symbols.
- Each item in the flowchart should describe a similar level of detail.
- Flowcharts shouldn't be too busy. The flowchart designer should use connectors such as circle symbols rather than crossing lines.
- Of course, the most important criteria for a good flowchart is that it is easily understandable.

Internal Control Questionnaires

To gather data for either an internal control narrative or flowchart, an IT auditor may use an internal control questionnaire. This tool allows the auditor to ask questions about internal controls over various applications, processes, or risks, such as application program changes or logical data access. The questionnaire would simply list questions, such as "Does the organization require users to complete a request form for application program changes?" or "Does an application program change request require supervisory approval?" Individuals within the organization who are involved in the process (i.e., users or security administrators) would complete the questionnaire with yes or no answers.

There are several advantages to using internal control questionnaires. First, they ensure that auditors don't overlook any controls when they evaluate various risks. Second, the completed instruments provide auditors with the opportunity to compare notes among several individuals. Finally, the answers may help the auditor in constructing an internal control narrative or flowchart.

MONITORING INFORMATION TECHNOLOGY RISKS AND CONTROLS

Risk management requires constant attention. The risk management process described in this chapter and in Figure 3-1 includes continuous monitoring of risks and controls.

The CobiT model identifies several control objectives associated with monitoring. These include: monitoring the processes, assessing internal control adequacy, obtaining independent assurance, and providing for an independent audit.[6] Monitoring the processes speaks to the continuous nature of monitoring. Organizations should employ performance measurement systems and benchmarking to ensure that their IT meets business objectives. Assessing internal control adequacy involves constant monitoring of the internal control system and may include exception-reporting systems. As Case-in-Point 3-5 all too chillingly illustrates, just because an organization has created an adequate set of internal controls does not mean that these controls are always working. It also points to the fact that sometimes humans do not make use of IT controls.

Case-in-Point 3-5

Following the September 11 attacks, the Immigration and Naturalization Service (INS) received universal criticism for its inability to track tourists and foreign students traveling in the United States. Six months after planes crashed into the World Trade Center, INS sent visas to two of the terrorists who had piloted the aircraft. The INS computer system did contain controls that tracked information regarding the travels in and out of the country by Mohamed Atta and Marwan al-Shehhi. And INS regulations stipulate that if an international traveler seeking student visa status leaves the United States during the application period, the INS should discontinue the application process. The problem, though, was that the controls weren't actually working. The IT appropriately recorded that Atta and al-Shehhi had left the country twice, but the official who granted the visas failed to check the IT. This action prompted the INS to adapt a new information system that will provide real-time information about international students traveling and studying in the United States.[7]

The CobiT model recognizes the value in obtaining independent assurance and audit of an organization's IT controls. The pervasive nature of IT today mandates that auditors evaluate an IT relative to business, audit, security, and continuity risks. An organization may engage an internal and/or external auditor to evaluate its IT as part of the monitoring process. Many entities employ internal auditors with IT expertise who regularly provide assurance to management regarding IT risks. SAS No. 94 requires external auditors to consider the IT in forming an opinion about an organization's financial statements (i.e., in managing audit risk). Additionally, organizations may ask their external auditors to conduct a systems reliability assurance engagement, or to provide other assurance regarding its IT. Yet another type of engagement auditors may perform to provide assurance related to IT risk is penetration testing (discussed in Chapter 7).

SUMMARY

This chapter describes the process of risk management over IT. It begins with the identification of IT risks. There are several types of IT risks, including business, audit, security, and continuity risks. Managers and auditors use a variety of approaches in assessing risk. One way is to identify threats, their associated vulnerabilities, and the probabilities of occurrence. Another is to consider risk indicators associated with specific processes or technologies.

An organization should develop an understanding of its IT risks before determining an appropriate set of internal controls to manage them. There are several internal control models available, some of which are IT specific, and others that are more general in nature. In this chapter we reviewed COSO, Cadbury, CoCo, ISO 9000, Six Sigma, CobiT, several Statements on Auditing Standards, and AICPA Trust principles and criteria. All of these models may provide some assistance in controlling IT risks.

IT auditors may document existing internal controls or they may study the flow of information around a business activity to develop new internal controls. Tools available for documenting internal controls are internal control narratives, flowcharts, and internal control questionnaires.

The IT risk management process is never-ending. Changes in technologies and/or business processes may create new threats. As a result it is important to constantly monitor IT risks and controls. This monitoring includes independent auditing.

DISCUSSION QUESTIONS

3-1   Why is it important to identify and assess IT risk before developing IT internal controls?

3-2 This chapter identified four types of IT risks: business, audit, security, and continuity risks. Discuss the similarities and differences among them.

3-3 One approach to risk assessment is to identify threats, vulnerabilities, and acceptable risk levels. What vulnerabilities might exist for a business organization's intranet?

3-4 Describe three risk indicators that might be associated with a company's intranet.

3-5 Why would an organization accept some level of risk?

3-6 What is the difference between COSO and ISO 9000?

3-7 Discuss each of the five components of COSO. Which do you think is most important to an effective internal control system?

3-8 Go to www.aicpa.org and view the Trust Services Principles and Criteria. How does this new model incorporate SysTrust?

3-9 How might an auditor use an internal control flowchart? Do you agree that a flowchart is a better documentation for internal control than an internal control narrative?

3-10 Discuss the importance of monitoring risks and controls. What components would exist in a structure for monitoring risks and controls in a large, global public corporation?

EXERCISES

3-11 Mi Mexico, Inc., a national fast food restaurant chain, recently hired consultants to build a data mart containing its sales data. The company owns and operates 174 stores, with average annual revenue of $650,000 per store. Mi Mexico has an enterprise information system that integrates its accounting, human resource, and distribution subsystems. Appropriate sales data from the enterprise system is automatically sent to the data mart. The marketing and sales department queries the data mart to learn about sales trends and patterns. Jeff Ewing, the CIO, recently met with Sylvia Rangel, the CFO, and Juan Hernandez from the Internal Audit department, to discuss risks and controls related to the new data mart.

Required:

a. Describe any business, audit, security, or continuity risks that may be associated with the new data mart.

b. How might Mi Mexico go about identifying specific risks and controls introduced by the new data mart?

3-12 Cyber Com is an Internet start-up company that offers business intelligence software and consulting services to help companies with customer relationship management. The business is quite new and has just recently completed a successful initial public offering (IPO). All of management's energies have been consumed with growing the business and going public. As a result, not much time has been devoted to internal control. The company uses state-of-the-art technologies to manage its business. These include an enterprise-wide information system, electronic commerce, an intranet, and a knowledge management system. The CEO has recently issued a directive to Joy Bridges, the CFO, to work with the company's auditor to see how they should proceed in developing an internal control system that manages the company's IT risks.

Required:

a. How might you use COSO, CobiT, ISO 9000, or Six Sigma to help in constructing such an internal control system?

b. After developing an internal control system to manage IT risks, Joy thinks it might be a good idea to have the company's auditor conduct a Systems Reliability Assurance engagement to test the controls. Explain the value this might add.

3-13 Schneider Manufacturing, Inc., employs 236 salaried and hourly workers. All employees are paid weekly. The company's accounting information system includes a payroll module that records payroll expenses, issues checks, and updates the general ledger. The following is an internal control narrative for the payroll system:

Hourly employees clock in and out to record their hours worked. Salaried employees do not report time, but they must complete a form available on the company's intranet to account for vacation and sick days. Each week, departmental supervisors deliver time cards to the payroll office. The supervisors also deliver the completed and authorized vacation and sick-day forms. A payroll clerk checks the cards and forms to see that they are complete and then enters them into the payroll system through a PC. The payroll software checks the entered data against employee files to verify the existence of employees and retrieve pay rates. The software contains several internal controls. For example, it checks to make sure that time worked does not exceed 60 hours a week. The software also makes sure that employees do not exceed allotted vacation and sick days.

The payroll system either issues checks encoded with a digital signature, or makes direct deposits to employee bank accounts for those employees who have chosen this option. The payroll clerk prints the checks and gives them to the appropriate departmental supervisors for distribution to employees. The payroll system also produces a payroll register. The Accounting Department supervisor receives a copy of the payroll register.

Required:

a. Prepare an internal control flowchart for Schneider Manufacturing's payroll system, identifying internal controls as shown in Figure 3-8.

b. Can you identify any internal control weaknesses associated with Schneider Manufacturing's payroll system?

REFERENCES AND RECOMMENDED READINGS

Arens, Alvin A., Randal J. Elder, and Mark S. Beasley. 2003. *Auditing and Assurance Services,* 9th ed. Upper Saddle River, N.J.: Prentice Hall:

Boritz, Efrim, Drin Mackeler, and Doug McPhie. 1999. "Reporting on Systems Reliability." *Journal of Accountancy*. November: 75–87.

Brewer, Peter C., and Tina Y. Mills. 1994. "ISO 9000 Standards: An Emerging CPA Service Area," *Journal of Accountancy*. February: 63–67.

Brown, C. 1999. *IT Management Handbook*. Boca Raton, Fla.: CRC Press-Auerbach Publications.

Burnette, Mark, and Claudia Gomez. 2001. "When Code Red Attacks: Addressing Vulnerabilities Behind Virus Hysteria." *Information Systems Control Journal* 6: 30–32.

Colbert, Janet L., and Paul L. Bowen. 1996. "A Comparison of Internal Controls: COBIT, SAC, COSO, and SAS 55/78," *IT Audit and Control Journal* 4: 26–33.

Frownfelter-Lohrke, Cynthia, and James E. Hunton. 2002. "New Opportunities for Information Systems Auditors: Linking SysTrust to COBIT." *Information Systems Audit and Control Journal* 3: 45–48.

Galloway, Duncan J. 1994. "Control Models in Perspective." *The Internal Auditor* 51 (6): 46–52.

Gerber, J. A., and E. R. Feldman. 2002. "Is Your Business Prepared for the Worst?" *Journal of Accountancy*. April: 61–64.

Hunton, James E. 2002. "Back Up Your Data to Survive a Disaster," *Journal of Accountancy*. April: 65–69.

IT Governance Institute. 2000. *COBIT Management Guidelines* (3rd Edition). Rolling Meadows, Ill.: Information Systems Audit and Control Foundation.

Krause, M., and H. Tipton. 1999. *Information Security Management Handbook*. Boca Raton, Fla.: CRC Press-Auerbach Publications.

McNamee, David, and Georges Selim. 1999. "The Next Step in Risk Management." *Internal Auditor*. June: 35–38.

Messier, W. F. 2000. *Auditing and Assurance Services: A Systematic Approach,* 2nd ed. New York: Irwin McGraw-Hill.

Rittenberg, L. E., and B. J. Schwieger. 2000. *Auditing Concepts for a Changing Environment,* 3rd ed. Fort Worth, Tex.: Harcourt College Publishers.

Tucker, George H. 2001. "IT and the Audit." *Journal of Accountancy.* September: 41–43.

Web Sites

Information about CobiT is available at www.isaca.org.

The Institute of Internal Auditors provides comprehensive guidance and information concerning risk and control at www.theiia.org.

Information about COSO's internal control and risk assessment frameworks are at www.coso.org.

The home page for the International Organization for Standardization (ISO) is at www.iso.ch.

Detailed information on trust services and auditing standards is available at www.aicpa.org.

You can obtain information about Six Sigma at www.sixsigmaforum.com.

NOTES

1. The sponsoring organizations were the American Accounting Association, American Institute of Certified Public Accountants, Institute of Internal Auditors, Institute of Management Accountants, and Financial Executive Institute.
2. *Internal Control—Integrated Framework,* September 1992, Committee of Sponsoring Organizations of the Treadway Commission.
3. Source: Applegate, Dennis, and Ted Wills, "Integrating COSO," *The Internal Auditor,* December 1999: 60–66.
4. CobiT, 3rd ed., July 2000, Executive Summary.
5. This is one of many case examples of CobiT usage available at www.isaca.org./ctcase16.htm.
6. CobiT, 3rd ed., 2000, CobiT Steering Committee and IT Governance Institute (www.ITgovernance.org).
7. Source: Thompson, Cheryl W. 2002. "INS 'Failure' Cited in Visa Case." *Washington Post.* Tuesday, May 21: Page A1.

CHAPTER **4**

IT DEPLOYMENT RISKS

CHAPTER CONTENTS

INTRODUCTION

Planning, changing, and growing—steps along a never-ending journey.

This chapter discusses various risks associated with the deployment of information technology (IT) in organizations and ways in which managers can cope with such risks. We will first examine the strategic planning process, as planning is one of the most effective means of managing risk. Next, we will learn how to reduce generic risks related to systems development and implementation projects. Afterward, we will discuss specific risks associated with acquiring, developing, changing, and implementing IT applications throughout the organization. IT auditors should identify the extent to which the client uses a formalized risk management process.

DEVELOPING STRATEGIC PLANS

Strategic planning is one of the most important responsibilities of management, as this process serves as the primary guideline for allocating scarce resources throughout the firm and keeping the organization headed in a profitable direction. In essence, long-term planning is one of the most effective means of minimizing the risk that organizational resources will be used in ways that are incongruent with the company's overall goals and objectives.

Strategic planning begins with a vision or an image of the future. The vision is translated into a mission, which serves as the guiding light for developing a set of objectives. In turn, objectives help shape the articulation of a formal strategy. Finally, the strategy is used to develop a set of policies. The IT auditor should look for evidence of a prescribed, documented IT strategic planning process, for the existence of an ongoing process of this nature indicates that the company is diligently seeking an optimal "fit" between the information technology infrastructure and the organization's overall goals. Figure 4-1 presents an overview of the planning process.

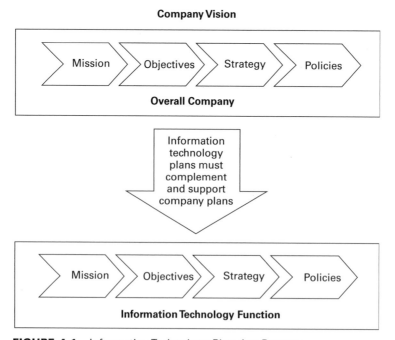

FIGURE 4-1 Information Technology Planning Process

A vision represents what "might be," based on a set of goals and objectives the organization would like to achieve. For the most part, the growth and success of business organizations (as well as individuals) are limited only by their vision of what they believe they can accomplish. A firm's vision is translated into a mission statement, which must be articulated in crisp, understandable language. For instance, Ben & Jerry's mission statement is as follows (see www.benjerry.com/mission.html):

> Ben & Jerry's is dedicated to the creation & demonstration of a new corporate concept of linked prosperity. Our mission consists of three interrelated parts. Underlying the mission is the determination to seek new and creative ways of addressing all three parts while holding a deep respect for individuals inside and outside the company, and for the communities of which they are a part.
>
> **Product:** To make, distribute, and sell the finest quality all natural ice cream and related products in a wide variety of innovative flavors from Vermont dairy products.
>
> **Economic:** To operate the Company on a sound financial basis of profitable growth, increasing value for our shareholders, and creating career opportunities and financial rewards for our employees.
>
> **Social:** To operate the company in a way that actively recognizes the central role that business plays in the structure of society by initiating innovative ways to improve the quality of life of a broad community—local, national, and international.

Notice how clearly and concisely Ben & Jerry's has expressed its vision of the future through its mission statement. The company's mission statement becomes the catalyst for strategic planning within functional areas of the firm, as the goals and objectives of each area must support and promote the overall mission. Here, we will focus only on the long-term planning process of the IT function. Although the mission statement for the IT function of Ben & Jerry's is not publicly disclosed, a mission statement of this nature might translate into the following:

> The Information Technology function intends to offer high-quality, innovative information processing and management services to internal and external information consumers, while providing a reliable, responsive, and leading-edge technology infrastructure throughout the entire organization aimed at supporting new and creative ways of addressing the company's three-part mission statement—composed of product, economic, and social components.

Mission statements guide the establishment of business objectives. For instance, the IT function described might develop the following set of objectives:

1. Create an atmosphere that embraces innovation and change.
2. Apply computer hardware and software technologies to opportunities that promote prosperity.
3. Incorporate an enterprise-wide information system to facilitate the intracompany coordination of business activities.
4. Develop a technology-based communications network capable of linking suppliers, customers, and employees into a seamless, virtual and extended enterprise.

Next, the objectives serve as the foundation for setting an explicit IT strategy, which details *how* the IT function will achieve its objectives through its organizational structure, relationships with others, and IT configurations. For instance, an IT strategy that would support the mission and objectives listed might read as follows:

> The IT function will use a decentralized, organic form of organization that is adaptable and responsive to the dynamic nature of the Company. The IT function will include a chief information officer (CIO) who, in coordination with other executive officers throughout the Company, will determine the precise structure of the IT function, which is expected to change over time depending on Company needs. The CIO, along with his/her delegates, will strive to cooperate and coordinate with all internal information consumers to ensure that the Company's information system is fully integrated, as well as to listen and respond to external constituents to ensure that the Company's business processes and related information technology infrastructure meet the ever-changing needs of the broader community of information consumers.

Finally, the IT strategy is supported by specific policies, which are designed to enact the realization of the strategy. For example, a computer hardware acquisition policy might specify that all computer purchases must be supported by a request for proposal from the IT function, which is sent to at least three outside vendors, and the final vendor selection would be made by an appointed "hardware acquisition" committee composed of three IT personnel. IT policies should cover at least the ten general areas shown in Figure 4-2. Sample policy issues are provided for each of the ten areas to provide insight into the types of concerns and topics that should be covered in IT policy guidelines.

As indicated, a formal IT planning process follows a clearly defined path from vision → mission → objectives → strategy → policies. A coherent planning process of this nature increases the likelihood that the company is making the most efficient use of information technology throughout the organization. Key IT planning risk indicators, which should trigger "red flags" for IT auditors, are listed in Figure 4-3.

Professional Guidance

The CobiT guidelines discuss in depth a variety of issues related to IT planning.[1] The guidelines suggest that eleven processes should be incorporated into IT strategic plans. Notice that each suggested process is integrated throughout the IT policy areas discussed in Figure 4-2. Additionally, the processes, taken as a whole, are designed to manage the key IT risks presented in Figure 4-3. As suggested by CobiT, the IT function should:

1. Develop a strategic IT plan.
2. Articulate the information architecture.
3. Find an optimal fit between IT and the company's strategy.
4. Design the IT function to match the company's needs.
5. Maximize the IT investment.
6. Communicate IT policies to the user community.
7. Manage the IT workforce.
8. Comply with external regulations, laws, and contracts.
9. Conduct IT risk assessments.
10. Maintain a high-quality systems development process.
11. Incorporate sound project management techniques.

The final issue, project management, is critically important to creating an atmosphere of responsibility and accountability over systems development projects. Elaboration of this

1. **Planning Policies**
   a. Responsibility (who is involved with planning?)
   b. Timing (when does planning take place?)
   c. Process (how should planning be conducted?)
   d. Deliverables (what planning documents are produced?)
   e. Priorities (what are the most to least critical planning issues?)

2. **Organizational Policies**
   a. Structure (what is the organizational form of the IT function?)
   b. Information architecture (is the infrastructure aligned with the firm's mission?)
   c. Communication (are the IT strategy and policies known by all affected parties?)
   d. Compliance (are all external regulations and laws being addressed?)
   e. Risk assessment (are IT risks identified, measured, and controlled?)

3. **Human Resource Policies**
   a. Training (what kind of training is provided and to whom?)
   b. Travel (what are the travel guidelines and priorities?)
   c. Hiring (who determines needs and who screens applicants?)
   d. Promotion (what are the guidelines and how does the process work?)
   e. Termination (what are voluntary and involuntary termination guidelines?)

4. **Software Policies**
   a. Acquisition (how is software acquired from outside vendors?)
   b. Standards (what are the software compatibility standards?)
   c. Outside contractors (should contractors be used for software development?)
   d. Changes (how is the software change process monitored and controlled?)
   e. Implementation (how are conversions, interfaces, and users handled?)

5. **Hardware Policies**
   a. Acquisition (how is hardware acquired from outside vendors?)
   b. Standards (what are the hardware compatibility standards?)
   c. Performance (how are computing capabilities tested?)
   d. Configuration (where are client-servers, personal computers, and so on used?)
   e. Service providers (should third-party service bureaus be used?)

(continued)

FIGURE 4-2   Important Policy Areas for IT Functions (1 of 2)

point is provided later in the section "Managing Development Projects." Next, we discuss the importance of measuring salient aspects of IT projects using the balanced scorecard approach.

IT Function Scorecard

The balanced scorecard concept was introduced by Kaplan and Norton (1996). They envisioned organizational performance measures to include traditional financial metrics, as well as additional nonfinancial indicators within three broad areas (i.e., customer satisfaction, internal processes, and organizational learning and growth). Additionally, Kaplan and Norton devised a three-layer structure for each of four perspectives (financial results, customer satisfaction, internal processes, and organizational learning and growth): mission (absolutely, positively, overnight) [Federal Express], objectives (exceed customers' delivery expectations), and measures (percentage of late deliveries). Initially, the balanced scorecard was conceived as a planning, control, and performance measurement system. Over time, companies realized that the balanced scorecard could serve as the cornerstone of a management system designed to facilitate the establishment of long-term strategic goals, the communication of the goals throughout the firm, the alignment of initiatives and incentives to

6. **Network Policies**
   a.   Acquisition (how is network technology acquired from outside vendors?)
   b.   Standards (are local area networks, intranets, extranets, and so on compatible?)
   c.   Performance (how much bandwidth is needed and is the network fast enough?)
   d.   Configuration (how are servers, firewalls, routers, hubs, and other technology used?)
   e.   Adaptability (is there capability to support emerging e-business models?)

7. **Security Policies**
   a.   Testing (how is security tested?)
   b.   Access (who can have access to what information and applications?)
   c.   Monitoring (who monitors security?)
   d.   Firewalls (are they effectively used?)
   e.   Violations (what happens if an employee violates security?)

8. **Operations Policies**
   a.   Structure (how is the operations function structured?)
   b.   Responsibilities (who is responsible for transaction processing?)
   c.   Input (how does data enter the information system?)
   d.   Processing (what processing modes are used?)
   e.   Error Handling (who corrects erroneous input/processing items?)

9. **Contingency Policies**
   a.   Backup (what are the backup procedures?)
   b.   Recovery (what is the recovery process?)
   c.   Disasters (who is in charge and what is the plan?)
   d.   Alternate Sites (what types of sites are available for off-site processing?)

10. **Financial and Accounting Policies**
   a.   Project management (are IT projects prioritized, managed, and monitored?)
   b.   Revenue generation (should services be sold inside or outside the organization?)
   c.   Technology investments (are the investment returns being properly evaluated?)
   d.   Funding priorities (where are resources most effectively allocated?)
   e.   Budgets (are budgets aligned with funding levels and priorities?)

FIGURE 4-2   Important Policy Areas for IT Functions (2 of 2)

1.   A strategic planning process is not used.
2.   Information technology risks are not assessed.
3.   Investment analyses are not performed.
4.   Quality assurance reviews are not conducted.
5.   Plans and goals are not communicated.
6.   Information technology personnel are disgruntled.
7.   Software applications do not support business processes.
8.   The technology infrastructure is inadequate.
9.   The user community is unhappy with the level of support.
10. Management's information needs are not met.

FIGURE 4-3   Key Planning Risk Indicators

the goals, the allocation of resources commensurate with the goals, and the deliverance of feedback and learning about the strategy. In short, the balanced scorecard has become a critical component of management's long-term command and control superstructure.

In an analogous manner, the balanced scorecard concept can be used to plan and monitor the performance of the IT function, resulting in a concept called the IT Function

Scorecard. For instance, financial performance of the IT function can be evaluated with respect to its contribution to the overall company. This perspective, which we call Organizational Contribution, can be measured in myriad ways, such as return on IT investments, discounted cash flow of IT projects, and transaction cost comparisons before and after implementing IT projects. The customer satisfaction perspective of the balanced scorecard is termed User Satisfaction, which could be assessed by periodically surveying users' attitudes toward system reliability, ease of use, and relationship with IT staff, to name a few metrics. The third balanced scorecard perspective, internal processes, is called Operational Performance and can be measured using indicators such as number of security breaches, number of backlogged requests, and percentage of downtime. Finally, the learning and growth perspective of the balanced scorecard is termed Adaptability and Scalability and can be measured by resources expended on developing interfaces from application to application, ease of integrating new technology into the existing computing architecture, and ability to keep pace with IT growth throughout the organization. As with the balanced scorecard, the conceptual IT Function Scorecard shown in Figure 4-4 can be used to align the IT function with the organization's strategic goals, judiciously control the growth of IT resources, and monitor the performance of IT projects.

MANAGING DEVELOPMENT PROJECTS

The acquisition of software from outside vendors, in-house development of applications, and modification of existing computer programs are all examples of IT projects. Regardless of the specifics of each project, there are sound project management techniques that apply to most situations. Using a structured methodology to manage systems development projects minimizes the risk of project failure, which can be defined in various ways. For instance, a project may be deemed to be a failure if it was delivered later than estimated, cost considerably more than budgeted, did not offer the functionality desired, or failed to meet the quality expected. The IT auditor should look for indications that the client is using project management techniques to plan, schedule, monitor, control, and close IT-related projects.

The overall purpose of a project is to solve a problem. It is imperative that each project is properly managed to meet time, cost, and quality objectives. Incorporating sound management techniques into each systems development project will help to ensure a successful outcome, as a solidly planned and executed project reduces the risk of failure. The project life cycle shown in Figure 4-5 depicts a prototypical life cycle.[2] Understanding the fundamentals of a project life cycle will help you know what to look for at the client site.

Once the decision has been made to pursue a particular project, the first order of business is to assign overall responsibility to a project manager. The project manager should have a great deal of experience in the domain area and skill at managing projects. The project manager should work with representatives from senior management, the IT staff, and affected users in planning and executing the project.

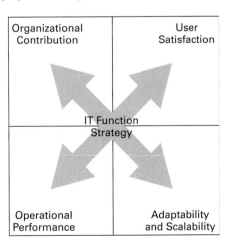

FIGURE 4-4 IT Function Scorecard

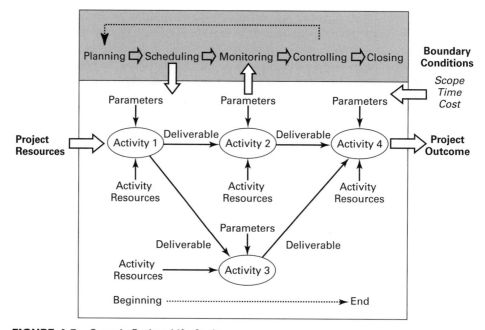

FIGURE 4-5 Generic Project Life Cycle
From *Core Concepts of Consulting for Accountants* by Bagranoff, Bryant, & Hunton (2002), John Wiley & Sons: New York, NY.

The first phase of the project life cycle is to plan the project. This involves setting time, scope, and cost parameters (or boundary conditions) for the entire project. Project resources are identified and the project outcome is clearly articulated. At this point, the project manager should work with area specialists (such as analysts, programmers, and users) to determine a work breakdown structure (WBS), which details specific activities that will take place throughout the project. Additionally, development of the WBS will help define the following for each activity: a) who is responsible, b) what resources are available, c) how the work will proceed, d) what are the deliverables, and e) what are the constraining parameters (scope, time, and cost).

The second phase in managing projects is to schedule the specific sequencing and timing of each activity and associated resources. Several techniques assist in this regard. For instance, Gantt Charts, Critical Path Analysis, and Critical Path Method are three methods one can use when scheduling projects. Also, Microsoft Project is a software application that is quite handy at dealing with the intricacies of project scheduling.

The third phase of the project management life cycle involves monitoring of activities. That is, as the project unfolds, one should use benchmarks, milestones, and deliverables (which includes quality assessments) to track progress. The frequency with which monitoring should take place varies from project to project, depending primarily on how sensitive the project is to deviations. For instance, if the nature of the project is such that a 5 percent deviation from the time schedule would adversely affect upcoming activities, then the project manager should allow no more than 5 percent of the total estimated time to elapse before monitoring any deviations from the time schedule. Ideally, the project manager should monitor the time schedule even more closely, as it would take time to react to a time deviation of this nature. A rule of thumb is to determine the maximum percent deviation allowed (in time or cost) and monitor activities at the halfway point. In the example just provided, assume that the project is estimated to take ten thousand hours. In this case, the project manager should monitor time deviations every 250 hours (2.5 percent of the total elapsed time).

The fourth phase—controlling—concerns the development of specific actions aimed at keeping a project moving forward in the most efficient and effective manner possible, considering unexpected issues, delays, and problems that arise. To the extent that a project is slipping—for instance, the project is off from anticipated time, cost, and/or quality expectations—the project manager must take concrete steps to adjust the project plan accordingly.

Finally, the project manager needs to properly close out the project. The manager should obtain client acceptance (in writing), release and evaluate project personnel, identify and reassign remaining project assets, conduct a post-project evaluation, and chronicle the history of the project so that future project managers can learn from its successes and failures.

This overview of project management techniques can be applied to most of the work performed by the IT function, as the nature of IT work is quite project-centric. As mentioned earlier, the application of project management techniques can minimize project-related risks. Ten key project risk indicators or "red flags" are summarized in Figure 4-6. IT auditors should be concerned about the quality of project management efforts if one or more of these risk indicators are present. While the preceding section dealt with projects in general, the following sections will examine specific risks associated with acquiring, developing, modifying, and implementing software applications.

ACQUIRING SOFTWARE APPLICATIONS

With respect to software applications purchased from outside vendors, the IT auditor should determine how the software fits into the grand scheme of things. Has the client mapped acquired software to its strategic plan? The results of such inquiry can vary considerably. On one end of the spectrum, a client may have no guidance or control over who purchases what software applications, resulting in many individuals throughout the company purchasing all kinds of software from a plethora of vendors. For instance, the purchasing manager might read about and acquire an application for creating purchase orders. Meanwhile, the company's strategic plan calls for the implementation of a new electronic data interchange (EDI) application that will eliminate purchase orders altogether. In this case, the time and money spent on the purchase order application would be incongruent with the strategic plan, resulting in the misallocation of valuable resources.

On the other end of the spectrum, the client might have such tight controls over software purchases that the company is unaware of innovations in the marketplace; hence, profitability-enhancing opportunities are passing by unnoticed. The latter scenario is especially prevalent in situations where the IT function manager would rather develop all

---

1. Management does not use a formal project management methodology.
2. Project leaders are not adequately experienced at managing projects.
3. Project leaders have insufficient domain expertise.
4. Project teams are unqualified to handle the project size or complexity.
5. Project team members are dissatisfied and frustrated.
6. Projects do not have senior-level executive support.
7. Projects do not include input from all affected parties.
8. Project recipients are dissatisfied with project outcomes.
9. Projects are taking longer to develop than planned.
10. Projects are costing more than budgeted.

FIGURE 4-6 Key Project Risk Indicators

applications in-house, possibly due to power and control issues, *and* the manager has total control over the purchase of outside software applications. To ensure that software acquisitions are being made in the best interest of the company, the client should develop and follow a formal software application acquisition policy.

A software acquisition policy should be formulated by first mapping upcoming application needs to the strategic plan. Once needs have been identified, they should be prioritized. Then, IT management, users, and senior management, at a minimum, should determine which application needs are best satisfied via software acquisition rather than in-house development. Once it has been determined which applications should be purchased, then a formal selection process should begin, starting with the highest priority need.

A specific individual should be assigned the overall responsibility for finding and comparing alternative software applications. Depending on the circumstance, the project manager (yes, the software acquisition process is considered a project) might come from the IT function, user community, or upper management. The project manager should be acutely aware of the needs and concerns of all affected parties (such as users, IT technicians, and managers) and be sure to include them in the decision process. For instance, users can offer valuable input regarding ease of use and functionality requirements. Technicians can help ensure that the proposed applications will integrate smoothly with existing software applications and computer technology. Managers can provide input regarding the decision-making information they must have from the application.

The next step is to identify and compare alternative solutions. The specific criteria used to compare software solutions will vary depending on the situation, but the IT auditor should determine if a process of this nature is used and to what extent. The more obvious attributes that can be compared across applications include ease of use, functionality, reporting, and documentation. Other important criteria to consider are the robustness of security features, soundness of built-in internal controls, smoothness with which the applications will integrate with existing systems, and future scalability of the software. The performance of proposed software solutions should also be investigated. For instance, one might obtain benchmarking standards from industry or trade associations and compare the throughput performance of each alternative application to such standards. Additionally, the company might compare the performance of the applications against existing systems (e.g., compare how many payroll records can be processed per hour against current capabilities) or against desired metrics (e.g., the system should be able to process at least 1,000 payroll records per hour).

Finally, the total cost of ownership for each application should be considered. The purchase price of each application is but one component of ownership costs. Sometimes, the initial acquisition price is a fairly small portion of total cost of ownership. One must also consider other cost factors, such as:

1. User training,
2. Multiple licenses,
3. Service and support,
4. Future upgrades, and
5. Software modifications.

Ten salient risk areas surrounding the software acquisition process are listed in Figure 4-7. The presence of one or more risks of this nature should alert the IT auditor that the client's acquisition process could be improved.

---

1. Software acquisitions are not mapped to the strategic plan.
2. There are no documented policies aimed at guiding software acquisitions.
3. There is no process for comparing the "develop versus purchase" option.
4. No one is assigned responsibility for the acquisition process.
5. Affected parties are not involved with assessing requirements and needs.
6. There is insufficient knowledge of software alternatives.
7. Security features and internal controls are not assessed.
8. Benchmarking and performance tests are not carried out.
9. Integration and scalability issues are not taken into account.
10. Total cost of ownership is not fully considered.

FIGURE 4-7   Key Acquisition Risk Indicators

DEVELOPING SOFTWARE APPLICATIONS

As with purchased applications, the first step in developing software is to determine the extent to which proposed systems development projects are aligned with the strategic plan. In this regard, individuals who request such projects must formally document reasons why the project should be considered and explain how the project maps to the strategic plan. The deliverable that arises from this process is called an *information systems development proposal.* Each proposal should be reviewed by a *steering committee* (composed of senior company managers, IT function managers, and other functional area managers). Steering committees are typically permanent in nature, in that the members serve in this capacity over multiple years and guide or steer numerous projects. The committee's objectives are to evaluate submitted proposals, determine which potential projects merit further investigation, prioritize projects in order of their importance, evaluate feasibility studies (upcoming), and oversee the project's progress as it unfolds.

Conducting a Feasibility Study

The steering committee should form a *feasibility group* for each project that makes the initial cut. The feasibility group is temporary in nature; members are assigned for the purpose of evaluating a specific project. Group members are typically interested in, involved with, and knowledgeable about the proposed development project. At a minimum, the group should be composed of representatives from affected functional areas, general management, and IT function management. The group's primary objective is to develop and produce a *feasibility study.* The feasibility study will recommend to the steering committee whether the project should move forward and, if so, provide a preliminary assessment of financial obligations, human resource requirements, and time estimates. Once the feasibility study's recommendations are communicated, the group is typically disbanded.

A feasibility study should assess, at a minimum, *technical feasibility, financial feasibility,* and *cultural feasibility.* For instance, assume that the client company owns and operates thousands of rail cars throughout North and South America. The company spends millions of dollars each year merely keeping track of the cars' location twenty-four hours a day, seven days a week. This is no easy task, considering that rolling stock, such as rail cars, seldom stands still for an inventory count. The feasibility study at hand proposes that the company should install global positioning satellite (GPS) transponders in each car and develop application software designed to tell the company where the rail cars are at all times, rather than having humans keep track of the cars.

The first issue to consider is technical feasibility, which focuses on assessing whether current, affordable, and reliable technology can be reasonably applied to the project. Suppose that after a thorough investigation, the feasibility group determines that the GPS system is available, accurate, and reliable. Also, the group found out that miniaturized transponders of this nature could be built to withstand temperature extremes inside the rail cars, climatic conditions outside the rail cars, and percussive stresses caused by continual starting, stopping, and moving. Accordingly, the feasibility group decides that the proposal meets the technical feasibility criteria.

The next step is to determine if the project can be justified on an economic basis; is the project financially feasibile? While there are many financial modeling techniques available, assume that the group calculates the net present value of the project over a ten-year time frame and finds that the rate of return exceeds 20 percent. Assuming that the company's internal rate of return is something less than 20 percent, the proposed project would meet the financial feasibility hurdle.

The remaining question concerns whether the project is culturally feasible. This aspect of feasibility has several dimensions. First, if the company were to develop and implement the proposed system, the group should question the adequacy of intellectual skills within the company to keep the system operating. If the necessary skills are not available, the company could acquire such skills from the outside or develop the skills using existing employees. If it is not possible to do either, the system might fail. Another dimension of cultural feasibility concerns the extent to which users and other affected parties will embrace the system. If affected parties do not want the system to be successful, perhaps due to power, control, or fear issues, the system is doomed from the outset. A third consideration of cultural feasibility involves legal and regulatory concerns. For example, if use of the GPS system is subject to legal restrictions that can adversely affect the project (say, the military will allow access to only a few restricted GPS channels during times of national crisis, and the restricted channels are incapable of handling the number of rail cars owned by the client), then the project might be subject to costly interruptions. Another legal/regulatory concern could be the existence of a collective bargaining unit or employee union. That is, if the proposed system will result in downsizing a number of employees who currently keep track of rail cars, the feasibility team will have to consider if the company can properly deal with collective bargaining or union rules, restrictions, and remedies in this regard.

If the proposal meets technical, financial, and cultural feasibility criteria, the feasibility group would prepare a *feasibility report* recommending that the project go forward to the development phase. At this point, the steering committee would assign responsibility of the systems development project to a project leader, who should use sound project management techniques to facilitate the project from planning through completion. The project manager would assemble a *project team,* the composition of which would depend on the nature of the project. The project manager should include functional area representatives, information technology specialists, systems analysts, computer programmers, and accountants/auditors. Additionally, it is important to assign at least one senior manager to the project to act as project champion. Without such support from the top echelon of the company, the project could fall into jeopardy somewhere down the road, particularly if things do not run as smoothly as planned (which is not uncommon), and upper management becomes impatient and prematurely pulls the plug on the project. A savvy senior-level project champion can save the project under such circumstances.

Considering Additional Systems Development Issues

The project team should pay close attention to additional key development issues. Insensitivity to these critical areas can lead to project failure. The first issue involves the thorough analysis of business processes related to the systems development project.

BUSINESS PROCESS ANALYSIS   An integral part of the planning phase of project management entails conducting a thorough business process analysis before starting any technical development work. The project team should employ various modeling techniques to identify which business processes are relevant to the current project, determine what resources, events, and agents comprise each process, and understand how the processes relate to one another. The team should next develop and consider alternative business process designs (e.g., modifications of the existing model or radically new models) that could be more efficient and effective. During this exercise, the team should also look to external sources, such as industry groups or consulting firms, to see if "best practice" models exist for the proposed system. Afterward, the team should compare the alternative models and derive the particular business process model they believe is best under the circumstances.

DEVELOPMENT AND TESTING   When technical activities begin (such as writing programs, creating input screens, and developing reports), the project team should execute such tasks in a secured area of the computer called a *development library*. The purpose of this library is to safeguard ongoing work from being unintentionally destroyed or maliciously altered. In this space, programmers develop and store source code (human-readable programming code). Containing such activities in a development library ensures that programmers are not allowed to tamper with live data and applications, which are housed in a secured *production library*. Only authorized users should be allowed in the production library, as it contains real data and production object code (machine-readable code that is used to process transactions). Finally, some project teams use a third library, called the *test library*. Its purpose is to create a secured space where applications can reside while they are being tested, without affecting live data. Both programmers and users are allowed into the test library. Once testing is complete and the users are satisfied, the test object code is transferred into the production library, wherein it becomes production object code. The company should have secure procedures, which are monitored, regarding who is authorized in which library and how program code (both source and object) and data can be safely moved from one library to another. The secured library procedure is depicted in Figure 4-8.

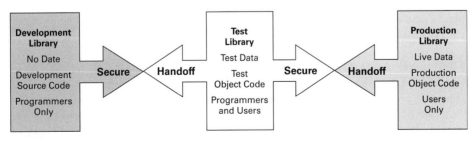

FIGURE 4-8   Development, Test, and Production Libraries

SECURITY AND CONTROLS   While measures should be taken to ensure that development activities are well controlled, the project team also has to consider how the application will be secured and controlled once it is placed into production. In this regard, there should be a concerted effort during developmental activities to incorporate security and control features into the new system. Many times, security and control features are afterthoughts, primarily because development teams do not include auditors and/or accountants. As a result, when weaknesses are eventually noted (sometime after the system is installed and operating), programmers rush around and start "patching" program code to incorporate such features or third-party security packages are laid on top of the software applications. The ultimate goal is to design as many automated security and control features into the system as possible, as system reliability is optimized once this is accomplished.

CONVERSIONS AND INTERFACES   During developmental activities, the team must also pay close attention to data conversion and interface issues. Conversion deals with getting existing data into the appropriate format for the new system. During conversion, it is important to clean, or *scrub,* the data. That is, conversion programs can be written to check for missing information, incorrect formats, duplicate postings, and so on. Such errors and omissions can be corrected before the data are placed into the new system, which increases data integrity. Interfaces represent programs that form bridges from the developed application to related external applications, so that data can be passed back and forth as needed. Developing external linkages is absolutely necessary if the new system is to succeed.

IMPLEMENTATION TESTING   Another important issue for development teams involves fully testing the software before going into live production. Proper testing should take place in three phases. First, individual programs should be tested in isolation. In a structured programming environment, each program represents a relatively small number of code lines that are designed to handle a fairly simple task. For instance, a program might be designed to close the current input form and open a new input form. The process of testing an individual program (or unit of code) is called *unit testing.* Next, related programs are strung together to form a module, which is designed to handle multiple related tasks. For example, a sales order module is designed to handle all tasks that occur during the sales order process, such as open the sales order input screen, check inventory levels, confirm customer credit, and send an e-mail confirmation to the customer. The process of testing a module is called *string testing* or *module testing.* Next, related modules are joined to form the entire application, which is called *system testing.* A final category of testing concerns *stress testing.* That is, the newly developed system is tested under extreme conditions to determine whether it can handle peak loads and to ascertain the point at which the system can no longer handle the load. Too many times, when a project team is running behind on its schedule, it shoves the application into production before rigorous testing has been completed. As a result, applications are often riddled with "bugs," which can create huge productivity losses, not to mention information integrity problems.

TRAINING AND DOCUMENTATION   Yet another critical task for the project team is the establishment of a training schedule for all affected parties, such as users and managers. Training should take place early, be all encompassing, and continue throughout the project life cycle. Training is expensive but absolutely essential—it is not a trivial issue, as the best built system in the world will fail if affected parties are left to figure it out on their own. Last, but certainly not least, every aspect of the systems development project should be completely documented. Documentation for all programs and user manuals should be fully developed.

Figure 4-9 lists ten key project risk indicators to which IT auditors should pay special attention. Deficiencies should be noted and investigated, as they indicate a systems development process that could be better controlled.

The next area of consideration concerns changes or modifications that are made to existing software applications. While many of the issues described in this section also apply to software changes, we will briefly examine the most salient issues.

CHANGING SOFTWARE APPLICATIONS

It seems as though existing software applications are in a perpetual state of change. The reasons for changing applications are many, but for the most part they reflect the volatility of the business environment in which the company operates. Thus, companies that function within highly dynamic industries, such as high tech, are more likely to change their software applications at a faster pace than less dynamic industries, such as petroleum refining. Regardless of the speed, breadth, and depth with which software applications are modified, a structured change procedure should be followed. If not, the company runs the risk that its software applications could mutate into a patchwork of inefficient and ineffective systems that no longer support the overall mission.

The software change process is triggered upon the completion of a *change request* document, either paper-based or electronic. Although the specifics of a change request document will inevitably vary from company to company, such requests should, at a minimum, clearly specify the change to be made to the software application, provide compelling justification for the requested change, and obtain appropriate approval(s) for the request. A change request is typically initiated by a user and approved by his supervisor. Often times, one or more higher-level approvals are also required. The primary reason for requiring multiple layers of approvals is to make sure that all parties agree that the change is necessary and congruent with the strategic plan. Fully approved change requests are sent to the IT function.

Within the IT function, approved change requests are logged in and assigned a unique tracking number. Then, change requests are reviewed by a *software change committee,* which is composed of representatives from senior management, functional areas of the company, and the IT group. The purpose of this committee is similar to the steering committee discussed earlier. That is, the software change committee prioritizes approved change requests and decides whether to form a feasibility group. If the

---

1. Development projects are not aligned with the strategic plan.
2. Feasibility studies do not consider the following areas:
   a. Technical feasibility
   b. Financial feasibility
   c. Cultural feasibility
3. Senior management and users are not involved.
4. Business process analyses are not performed.
5. Alternative designs are not compared.
6. Separate development, test, and production libraries are not used.
7. Security and control features are not designed into the system.
8. Conversion and interface issues are not taken into account.
9. System testing is inadequate.
10. Training and documentation are poor.

FIGURE 4-9 Key Development Risk Indicators

change request is simple, obvious, and critical, the committee might forward the change request immediately to the IT function, where it will be assigned to technicians for quick resolution. For more complex requests, the committee might form a feasibility group, the composition of which depends on the nature and extent of the proposed software change. It is very important that a group of reviewers, like the software change committee, exists in the company. If prioritization of change requests is left up to one person or one function within the company, then self-interest factors (e.g., economic, political, and personal) factors may unduly affect the fair allocation of resources across the company.

As with the feasibility study concept described earlier, the feasibility group's responsibility with respect to investigating software change requests is to determine if the request is technically, financially, and culturally feasible. For relatively simple changes, the feasibility study could be completed in very little time. For more complex change requests, the feasibility study might take much longer. Although the depth and scope of the feasibility study is likely to be less for change requests than for full-blown systems development projects, a similar process is nevertheless followed. As with systems development projects, the feasibility group should consider alternative ways to deal with the requested software change, as the best solution might not be the most obvious. If the feasibility group determines that the change request should move forward, the group approves the request for development and forwards it to the IT function.

The change request is assigned to one or more persons within the IT function, depending on the scope of change. Typically, at least a systems analyst and computer programmer are involved in the technical aspects of the software change process. When designing and programming work begins, the secured procedure of using separate development, test, and production libraries should be followed. The analysts and programmers must be keenly aware of security and control implications. As with newly developed systems, security and control features should be incorporated into the software application to the extent possible. If there are security and control issues involved with the software change but such features cannot be integrated into the affected application, the IT function should quickly notify parties who are responsible for maintaining the company's internal control structure, such as accountants, internal auditors, functional managers, and perhaps senior management. In this manner, alternate procedures can be formulated to deal with compromised security and control issues.

Another possible ramification of the software change could involve integration, or lack thereof, with related programs and applications. Programming change(s) could adversely affect the flow of data to and from related systems. One way to make sure that integration issues have been properly identified and remedied is to thoroughly test the altered software before placing it into production. This would include unit testing, module testing, and system testing. Once the modified application is fully tested, the IT function should obtain written approval from the party who initiated the change that the application is functioning as desired.

When software changes are made, poor documentation is often a problem. IT function management must ensure that all modifications are clearly and thoroughly documented. Otherwise, numerous programming changes made over time could be documented "inside the head" of a few programmers. Upon their eventual departure from the company, valuable institutional knowledge walks out the door with them. Figure 4-10 shows ten key risk indicators dealing with system changes. If one or more of these indicators are brought to light, the IT auditor should be aware that client's software change process could be improved.

1. A structured system change methodology is not in place.
2. A software change request procedure is not used.
3. Change requests are not reviewed/prioritized by a representative group.
4. Feasibility studies are not performed when appropriate.
5. Alternative software change designs are not considered.
6. Separate development, test, and production libraries are not used.
7. Security and controls implications are not considered.
8. Integration issues are not taken into account.
9. Testing is inadequately conducted.
10. Application changes are poorly documented.

FIGURE 4-10 Key System Change Risk Indicators

IMPLEMENTING SOFTWARE APPLICATIONS

Software applications that have been purchased from the outside, fully developed in-house, or changed (externally or internally) are now ready for implementation. Once development and preliminary testing have been accomplished (Figure 4-8), the application is ready for final testing and a secure handoff to the production library. While this may sound relatively simple, the implementation process is complicated indeed. The best system in the world can fall flat on its face if the implementation process is short-circuited.

Implementation Strategies

The first issue to consider is which implementation strategy best fits the situation. One possibility is called *parallel implementation.* With this strategy, the new application is placed into production alongside the existing application and both are used to simultaneously process live data. The upside of this strategy is that the risk of interrupting operations is minimized, since unanticipated problems in the new system can be identified and remedied without affecting current operations. This is the safest, or least risky, of all implementation strategies. The downside is that parallel implementation can consume a great deal of resources, as all affected data are input, processed, and reported in tandem. Plus, the two systems must be reconciled periodically and disagreements resolved. Parallel implementation is best used for very large projects in which the new (or modified) application encompasses a wide scope and has tentacles in many related applications and functional areas. For mission-critical applications, where any downtime can result in disastrous consequences, parallel implementation might be a wise choice.

On the opposite end of the risk spectrum sits the *big-bang implementation* strategy. Using this approach, the company ceases using the old system and immediately begins operating the new system. The upside of this strategy is that all affected personnel are forced to focus on the new system and cannot continue to depend on, or use as a crutch, the old system. The big-bang approach can be efficient, as only one system (the new one) is used to handle incoming data and all resources are focused on perfecting the new system. Under certain circumstances, however, this can be the most risky of all implementation strategies. The downside is that if the new system fails, all affected business processes are interrupted. Big-bang is best used when the scope of the system is fairly contained and the business processes involved can withstand a reasonable degree of disruption. There are exceptions, of course, to this general rule. Specifically, if the old system is no longer capable of functioning properly, the company may have no choice but to use the big-bang strategy.

Another strategy is *partial implementation*. Under this strategy, the system is phased in one piece at a time. For instance, assume that the client just developed a fully integrated human resources system (FIHRS) capable of handling all employee needs from recruiting through outplacing. Rather than plugging in the whole system at once, a company might consider starting with just the recruiting application. The company can then decide if the recruiting application should be implemented using the parallel or big-bang approach. Using parallel implementation, the new recruiting application would run concurrently with the old application until all bugs have been worked out. Using the big-bang technique, the new recruiting application would take over immediately and the old application would be disabled. The upside of partial implementation is that the risk of a critical business inter-ruption is minimized, since any damage can be contained to a specified area. In terms of the overall risk profile of this strategy, it falls between the extremes of the parallel (lowest risk) and big-bang (highest risk) strategies; hence, it is considered a medium risk strategy. The downside of partial implementation is that it could take a fairly long time to fully implement the whole system. If implementation time is not overly critical, however, the partial implementation technique can be a relatively economical and effective choice.

Another medium risk strategy is called *focused implementation*. The company iden-tifies a relatively small group of users (defined perhaps by a single office, plant, or region) to first use the new system before placing it into use throughout the organization. Focused implementation can be used in conjunction with the parallel, big-bang, or partial imple-mentation strategies. For instance, continuing with the FIHRS example, the company might focus implementation efforts on the Chicago office. Within that office, the entire FIHRS could run concurrently with the existing human resource system (parallel) or in place of the existing human resource system (big-bang), or perhaps a partial implementa-tion technique could emerge wherein only the recruiting application is implemented either alongside (parallel) or instead of (big-bang) the existing recruiting application. The upside of the focused strategy is that unexpected problems and delays associated with the new system are contained to a small, focused group of people. The downside is that it could take a relatively long time to complete the implementation. As with the partial implemen-tation strategy, if time is not critical, the focused implementation approach reflects a com-fortable balance between outcome risk and implementation success.

Implementation Planning

Once an implementation strategy has been selected, formal implementation plans should be developed and the implementation process should be handled as a project. As reflected in Figure 4-5, a project includes planning, scheduling, monitoring, controlling, and clos-ing phases. In this section, we will focus not on the project life cycle itself but instead on specific issues that must be considered during the implementation process.

Some implementations will involve only a few people, while other implementations might include huge numbers of individuals. Naturally, the quantity of people involved in the project depends on the nature and scope of the application. At a minimum, the imple-mentation should include at least one representative from the affected user community and one representative from those involved in acquiring, developing, or modifying the appli-cation. Regardless of how many people are involved, the leader of the implementation effort should make every effort to embrace and include as many affected parties as possi-ble (users, managers, technicians, and so on) throughout the process.

As with any project, the specific tasks that must be accomplished should be identified and organized into a work breakdown structure. Organizing tasks in this manner will allow the implementation leader to schedule the work in an orderly fashion. Timing and sequencing of tasks is critical during an implementation, as some tasks can be performed concurrently, while other tasks must follow a designated order of completion. Planning and scheduling of implementation tasks, coupled with obtaining top management approval of the time schedule, will help minimize externally and internally applied pressures to hurry the implementation and risk failure.

It is vitally important to manage change during implementation projects. That is, the implementation of software applications typically means that users and other affected parties face a degree of uncertainty with respect to how their work lives will be affected. Such uncertainty can breed frustration and resistance if not handled professionally and responsibly by the implementation team. In this light, the company should develop a formal change management policy to be followed during every implementation project. Among the most important issues to consider with respect to change management are the establishment of open lines of communication among all affected parties, the development of thorough training and educational programs, and an invitation to all parties to provide instrumental input as the implementation process unfolds.[3]

Other Implementation Issues

Although thorough testing should have been performed during the application acquisition, development, and/or modification processes, there is still more testing to be conducted during implementation. Interface and conversion programs were developed for the new or modified applications, but those programs were tested using only archived or simulated data. Now is the time to see if they work using live data.

The first item on the final testing agenda is to move from the development library to the test library the exact object code to be used in the production library. Next, the implementation team should test the built-in security and control features. The effectiveness of such features should be observed, tested, and approved by qualified overseers, such as company accountants, internal auditors, or external auditors. Once these parties are satisfied, the implementation team should test, one last time, the interface programs to make sure they are passing data correctly.

Next, final data conversion takes place as the implementation team runs the programs that convert live data from the old to the new format (if necessary). The safest way to convert data is to first work with archived data up to, say, a day or so prior to the official date when the new system will be placed in operation. This way, if something goes wrong with the data conversion programs, including data scrubbing, daily operations are uninterrupted. To the extent that problems are encountered, the implementation team can continue to fix the data conversion programs until they work right. Once this is accomplished, only the last day or two of data needs converting, which should occur at a specified time when all other operations on such data are temporarily halted. Typically, the conversion programs run very quickly. If something goes wrong, the implementation team may have to allow the old system to continue processing, so as not to disrupt operations, and fix the programs once again. After the data are converted, the application object code, converted data, and interface object code are moved into the production library.

The application is now live, but the job is not yet finished. The implementation team should work with users and other affected parties for a while, the specific length of time dependent upon the scope of the implementation project, magnitude of problems, and critical nature of the application, to answer questions, fix problems, and monitor performance. Other issues, such as performance tuning and user acceptance, should be handled as well. Finally, a post-implementation report should be compiled so that future teams can learn from the experience of the current team.

Figure 4-11 lists ten key implementation risk indicators or red flags. The IT auditor should determine the extent to which one or more of these indicators are present. If application implementations are not being handled in a methodical and consistent manner, the client is exposed to relatively high risks with respect to potential misuse of resources and loss of business opportunities.

SUMMARY

Information technology (IT) auditors must be acutely aware of the risks associated with purchasing, developing, changing, and implementing information technology in business organizations. The foremost way to deal with such risks is to adopt and follow a formal, strategic information technology planning process. Once the company has articulated its vision and mission, the IT function can develop a congruent mission, which leads to IT objectives, strategies, and policies. Earnest use of a strategic planning process helps ensure that IT resources are properly aligned and allocated in accordance with the overall company vision.

Specific risk areas of concern are project management, software acquisition, application development, system changes, and software implementation. The IT auditor should probe into each of these areas to identify inherent risks, ascertain existing controls, evaluate residual risk, and provide advice regarding how the company might improve its risk management practices. In the final analysis, the IT auditor can add considerable value to the client by identifying weaknesses and suggesting solutions in these areas, as the percentage of dollars spent on information and communication technologies in business organizations is skyrocketing. Hence, seemingly small observations in this regard can yield huge dividends for the client company.

DISCUSSION QUESTIONS

4-1 What could be the consequences if a company's information technology function does not align its strategy with the company's overall company vision?

4-2 Why should the information technology function develop policies?

4-3 What is the purpose of the information systems steering committee?

4-4 Why is it important to understand the boundary conditions (scope, time, and cost) of any information technology project?

4-5 When contemplating the acquisition of application software, how would the company determine if the software can handle the information processing load?

---

1. Alternative implementation strategies are not considered.
   a. Parallel
   b. Big-bang
   c. Partial
   d. Focused
2. Formal implementation plans are not followed.
3. All affected parties are not involved.
4. Implementation teams are uncoordinated.
5. Implementation processes are rushed.
6. Change management procedures are not developed.
7. System users are inadequately trained.
8. Security and control issues are slighted.
9. Final testing is insufficient.
10. Post-implementation reviews are not conducted.

FIGURE 4-11 Key Implementation Risk Indicators

4-6 Why use three libraries (development, test, and production) in the information technology function?

4-7 Why should the steering committee form a separate feasibility group for each potential project?

4-8 What is the objective of a feasibility study?

4-9 Why should the company be concerned with developing formal procedures for changing existing software applications?

4-10 What are the alternative implementation strategies, and which one is best?

EXERCISES

4.11 Archetype Technologies, Inc., (ATI) has grown at a phenomenal rate of over 45 percent per year for the past five years. The legacy information system at ATI is laboring under the heavy processing load. Additionally, ATI managers are frustrated because it is extremely complicated and time consuming for them to get the information they need to make decisions, primarily because the applications are not integrated with one another. The current applications are written in the Cobol programming language and the data are stored in flat files. ATI is contemplating several options for dealing with its information technology problems. At this point, ATI has formed a feasibility group to examine each alternative.

Required:

Develop a checklist of issues that the group should consider for each of the following options:

a. Upgrade the existing applications such that they better integrate with one another.

b. Develop (in-house) an integrated suite of applications using a relational database.

c. Purchase an enterprise resource planning system from a vendor.

4.12 Dogwood Manufacturing, Inc., (DMI) just purchased and implemented a popular and widely used enterprise resource planning (ERP) system. The ERP applications run on a relational database, which is purchased separately. The consultants who installed the ERP system and relational database have advised DMI to incorporate security controls (ID/Password) at the network, database, and application levels. Because DMI employs only a few people in its information technology function whose jobs focus on helping users and keeping the information technology infrastructure operating, DMI feels that it does not have the expertise to maintain three levels of security once the consultants are gone. Thus, DMI has decided to rely on the security features incorporated into the ERP system, which restricts users to authorized applications based on their ID/Password. Furthermore, the person responsible for maintaining the ID/Password security features will be the company controller, since she is the most computer-savvy person of all company managers.

Required:

a. What are the advantages of relying only on the ERP security features?

b. What are the disadvantages of relying only on the ERP security features?

c. What are the risks of assigning the security responsibility to the controller?

REFERENCES AND RECOMMENDED READINGS

Ahituv, N., and S. Neumann. 1990. *Principles of Information Systems for Management*. Dubuque, Iowa: Wm. C. Brown Publishers.

Bagranoff, N., S. Bryant, and J. Hunton. 2001. *Core Concepts of Consulting for Accountants*. New York: John Wiley & Sons.

Brown, C. 1999. *IT Management Handbook*. Boca Raton, Fla.: CRC Press-Auerbach Publications.

Cassidy, A. 1998. *A Practical Guide to Information Systems Strategic Planning*. Boca Raton, Fla.: CRC Press-Auerbach Publications.

Haag, S., M. Cummings, and J. Dawkins. 2000. *Management Information Systems for the Information Age.* New York: Irwin McGraw-Hill.

IT Governance Institute. 2000. *COBIT Management Guidelines,* 3rd ed. Rolling Meadows, Ill.: Information Systems Audit and Control Foundation.

Kaplan, R., and Norton, D. 1996. *The Balanced Scorecard Translating Strategy into Action.* Boston: Harvard Business School Press.

Krause, M., and H. Tipton. 1999. *Information Security Management Handbook.* Boca Raton, Fla.: CRC Press-Auerbach Publications.

Laudon, K., and J. Price Laudon. 1999. *Management Information Systems: Organizations and Technology in the Networked Enterprise.* New York: Prentice Hall.

Sharp, A., and P. McDermott. 2001. *Workflow Modeling: Tools for Process Improvement and Application Development.* Norwood, Mass.: Artech House.

Spewak, S., and S. Hill. 1993. *Enterprise Architecture Planning: Developing a Blueprint for Data, Applications and Technology.* New York: John Wiley & Sons.

NOTES

1. CobiT, 3rd ed., 2000. *CobiT Steering Committee and IT Governance Institute* (www.ITgovernance.org).
2. The project life cycle shown is reproduced from *Core Concepts of Consulting for Accountants* by N. Bagranoff, S. Bryant, and J. Hunton (2002). New York: John Wiley & Sons.
3. To read more about change management, see *Core Concepts of Consulting for Accountants* by N. Bagranoff, S. Bryant, and J. Hunton. 2002. New York: John Wiley & Sons.

CHAPTER 5

MANAGING THE IT FUNCTION

CHAPTER CONTENTS

INTRODUCTION

Facts of life for the IT manager

1. When you get to the point where you really understand the computer system, it's obsolete.
2. When the computer says: "Directory does not exist," it means: "… any more."
3. When you instruct the computer to take an action, there is an equal and opposite malfunction.
4. When looking in the manual for help, you find only one sentence, "Good Luck!"
5. When a complex system does not work, it invariably evolved from a simpler system that did.

Information technology (IT) managers must learn how to simultaneously balance stability and change, which is a difficult juggling act indeed! Managing the IT function day to day is a tough job, as the IT manager must deal with a multitude of divergent and often conflicting users, demands, and priorities. Paradoxically, IT managers who try hard to please everyone can soon be overcome by events, losing sight of long-term value-added goals and thereby harming the very people they are trying to help. Unfortunately, internal controls can also fall by the wayside in an IT department that places undue focus on "fighting fires" each day, as this crisis management mindset can lead to utter disregard for following proper procedures. Even the brightest, best-intentioned IT manager can succumb to the "squeaky wheel gets the grease" mentality and lose sight of the big picture. In such an environment, it is all too easy for IT managers to rationalize why they bypassed procedures and violated internal controls. One way to avoid becoming drawn into the black hole of IT chaos is for managers to follow sound policies and procedures designed to structure IT work such that short-term and long-term goals are met while IT resources are productively deployed and securely employed.

This chapter discusses five general areas in which IT managers can establish sound policies and procedures aimed at controlling key risks associated with running the IT function: organizing, funding, staffing, directing, and controlling. By establishing a methodological approach toward managing the IT function, managers and auditors can increase the likelihood that the function is adding value to the organization, while minimizing *business risks*—composed of *system risks* (availability, security, integrity, and maintainability)[1] and *information risks* (effectiveness, efficiency, confidentiality, integrity, availability, compliance, and reliability)[2]—and *audit risks* (inherent risk, control risk, and detection risk).[3]

ORGANIZING THE IT FUNCTION

Chapter 4's emphasis on aligning the IT function's strategy with the organization's strategy is worth reinforcing here. That is, the IT manager must clearly define the role and articulate the value of the IT function within the greater organization or the IT function will inevitably drift from crisis to crisis with no clear vision of where it is headed or why. If the IT manager allows this situation to occur, the IT function inevitably will be viewed as merely fulfilling a service role within the organization; it will not be recognized as a value-added player in determining the economic viability of the company. Justifying the IT function's worth does not just happen—it requires careful planning.

As discussed by Simons (2000), organizational units must balance many countervailing influences, such as profit, opportunity, growth, and control, juxtaposed against concurrent pressure to achieve short-term and long-term goals (see Figure 5-1). In order to deal with simultaneous and interdependent, yet conflicting, forces, the organization must

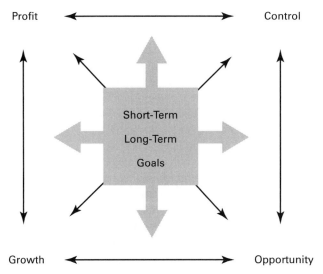

Profit ⟷ Control

Growth ⟷ Opportunity

FIGURE 5-1 Interdependent Conflicting Forces Acting on the IT Function

determine the appropriate location and structure of the IT function. The business risk of improperly locating and structuring the IT function are that organizational resources consumed by the IT function will fail to address that company's strategic initiatives, suboptimizing the company's potential efficiency and effectiveness. The audit risks associated with mislocating and ill-structuring the IT function are that improper segregation of incompatible functions can threaten the integrity and security of enterprise-wide information, as well as the computing infrastructure.

Since there are several approaches to designing the structure of an IT function, there is no "right" way to determine the ultimate structure, nor is there a perfect design. The resulting configuration of an IT function within a company is contingent on a host of external and internal organizational factors. Regardless of the eventual layout of the IT function, one important consideration must be built into any design—the IT function needs to incorporate sound internal controls into the structural framework. The idea is to weave the internal control concept of "segregation of incompatible duties" into the fabric of the IT architecture. In this section, we address where to locate the IT function within an organization, discuss ways to design an IT function, and explain key internal control issues involved in locating and designing an IT function.

Locating the IT Function

To whom should the IT manager report? The answer has important ramifications on the IT manager's ability to acquire resources and prioritize workloads. There is a positive relationship between how high in the organization IT managers report and the political clout they possess. However, when answering this question, one must consider a concept known as segregation of incompatible duties, which requires that the following responsibilities be vested in different people: *authorizing transactions, recording transactions,* and *maintaining custody of assets.* While it is becoming increasingly difficult in today's high-tech computing environments to vest these responsibilities in different people, segregation can nevertheless be accomplished through judicious choices with respect to placing the IT function in the organization and with integrating programmed controls into computing infrastructures and applications (discussed later in this chapter).

Should the IT manager report to whomever manages corporate accounting? After all, most IT applications deal with accounting transactions in one way or another; it appears to make sense for the IT manager to report to someone who has knowledge of and responsibility for corporate accounting. There is a problem with this scenario, however; most corporate controllers can already authorize and record certain transactions, such as accounting adjustments, estimates, and accruals.[4] Hence, they perform two of the three incompatible duties in these instances. If they are also allowed to maintain custody of assets, such as information databases and software applications, all three incompatible duties would be located under one umbrella—not a good idea!

What could go wrong? It would be possible for errant corporate controllers to authorize and record seemingly valid accounting transactions while altering results to achieve fraudulent objectives. To perpetrate such a fraud, the devious controllers could either make data and software changes themselves or instruct their IT function managers to make such changes via allegedly valid requests. While it is nice to think that organizations should trust in the integrity of their controllers, corporate governors and IT auditors should be professionally skeptical when designing internal control structures, regardless of the corporate position being reviewed. Plus, one should keep the following in mind— do not tempt employees beyond their ability to resist! Therefore, it seems unwise to have the IT function manager report directly to the corporate controller.

What about having the IT function manager report to another functional/line manager, such as the marketing, human resources, or operations manager? On the surface, one of these options might make sense, as many software applications deal with each of these functional/line areas. Let's keep in mind, however, that each of these managers has the ability to authorize certain transactions, and giving them further responsibility over the custody of computing assets would vest two of the three incompatible duties in one person. But unlike the corporate controller scenario just presented, at least the other functional/line managers would not have all three duties within their grasp, as the recording responsibility would remain with the corporate accounting function.

While there are some internal control concerns with having the IT manager report to another functional/line manager, such concerns could be dealt with effectively via proper procedures, programmed controls, and diligent oversight. However, there are some pragmatic issues to consider as well. First, it is possible, but unlikely, that other functional/line managers would know enough about computing infrastructures, operating systems, software applications, and related matters to offer effective guidance and support to IT managers. Also, some functional/line managers could be so narrowly focused on their own areas and in their own ideas that they would place undue emphasis and priorities on their computing systems while ignoring other computing needs throughout the organization. Accordingly, while a local subsystem of the company (e.g., marketing or operations) may be optimized, effectiveness of the global system (i.e., the organization itself) likely would be suboptimized in this situation. Finally, if the IT manager reports to another functional/line manager, the IT function might receive inadequate attention from upper management and possess relatively weak power when it comes to acquiring resources.

What about placing the IT function alongside other functional/line managers? Certainly, locating the IT function at least at the same organizational level as other functional/line managers makes good business sense. In this manner, the IT function would be politically strong enough to compete with other functional/line managers for resources, and the IT manager could work directly with upper management with respect to setting strategies, placing priorities, and allocating resources.

From an internal control perspective, in theory, there are incompatible duties involved in this scenario too. At the top of the perch, the CEO has the ultimate responsibility over authorizing transactions, recording transactions, and maintaining custody of assets. Naturally, these responsibilities are rarely performed directly by CEOs; they delegate such duties to others, such as vice presidents and functional/line managers. Even vice presidents rarely perform these duties themselves, for they too delegate them to midlevel managers. Nevertheless, the internal control structure should consider the possibility of opportunistic (perhaps fraudulent) behaviors stemming from upper management brought about by an overlap of incompatible duties by instituting sound procedures and exercising vigilant oversight in this regard. In this manner, the internal control implications of locating the IT function at or above the level of other functional/line managers can be effectively managed.

As discussed, it is optimal for the IT function manager to be located at least at the same organizational level as peer functional/line managers. In come cases, even higher placement might make sense. For instance, as depicted in Figure 5-2, not only is the IT function located directly below the vice president of North American Operations, but there also exists a vice president of IT. This way, the vice president of IT can coordinate strategies, set standards and establish priorities across the entire organization, while the IT managers, who report to the vice president of North American Operations and vice president of Foreign Operations (not shown), can focus on local issues and needs. Notice that with this configuration, the IT manager has a dotted-line relationship with the vice president of IT. It is important to remember that organizational culture, situational circumstances, and conditional constraints and tradeoffs will dictate precisely where the IT function is located in a given organization. Nevertheless, it is imperative that IT auditors consider the internal control ramifications of misplacing the IT function in the organization. Let's next consider how to design the IT function.

Designing the IT Function

A typical approach to organizing an IT function is along lines of specialization, such as systems analysis, software programming, information processing, computer security, and so on. As with determining the precise location of the IT function within the organization, designing the ultimate structure of the IT function is often determined by cultural, political, and economic forces inherent in each organization. While there are myriad blueprints for the layout of an IT function, we will focus on the one shown in Figure 5-3 as point of discussion. The important internal control considerations within

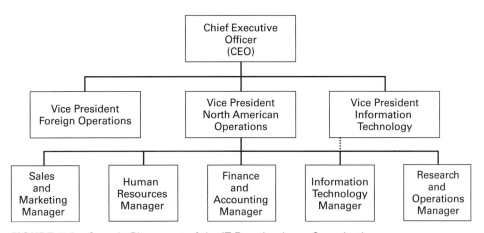

FIGURE 5-2 Sample Placement of the IT Function in an Organization

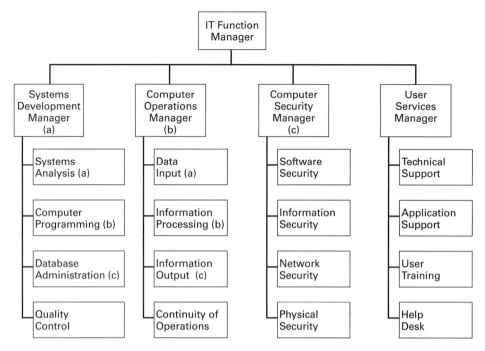

Analogous to the internal control concepts of: (a) 'authorizing transactions'
(b) 'recording transactions' (c) 'maintaining custody over assets'

FIGURE 5-3 Specialization-Focused Design of the IT Function

an IT function are to separate systems development, computer operations, and computer security from one another for the following reasons.

Personnel who work in the systems development specialization have access to operating systems, business applications, and other key software. Upon proper authorization by requesting parties, systems developers can create or change software. While systems developers should not be authorized to make unilateral additions and changes, they are authorized to perform such work once proper requests to do so have been approved. Thus, their responsibility in this regard can be likened to the internal control concept of "authorizing transactions," although it is admittedly a loose analogy. Systems developers are eventually authorized to create and alter software logic, so they should not be allowed to process information (similar to the internal control concept of "recording transactions") nor should they maintain custody of corporate data and business applications (similar to the internal control concept of "maintaining custody of assets"). Rather, segregation of the latter two incompatible duties across the IT function is accomplished by allowing computer operations to process information and computer security to maintain control over data and applications. Notice too that within the systems development specialization, systems analysis "authorizes" the software changes to be made, computer programming "records" or makes the changes, database administration sets a variety of standards to which the analysts and programmers must abide (similar to the internal control concept of "maintaining custody" over valuable assets—data and table standards). Quality control ensures that the appropriate standards have been applied and that the new and altered software applications work as requested before placing them into production; as such, quality control creates an effective check-and-balance environment.

Computer operations personnel are responsible for entering data into the computer system, processing corporate information via software applications and disseminating output, as well as ensuring continuity of operations (discussed later in this chapter). With the recent explosion of end-user computing and transaction-capturing applications (e.g., point-of-sale and stakeholder self-service), the computer operations specialization is performing less and less of the input-process-output type of work depicted in Figure 5-3. Nevertheless, in many large corporations, batch processing of this nature still takes place. Within the computer operations specialization, notice that entering data (similar to the internal control concept of authorizing transactions), processing information (similar to the internal control concept of recording transactions), and disseminating output (similar to the internal control concept of maintaining custody) are segregated.

The computer security specialization is responsible for the safekeeping of valuable corporate resources, which includes ensuring that business software applications are secure. For example, if systems developers are authorized to change an application, they must request the release of affected programs (source or human readable code) from software security. Once the changes are completed and tested, software security will compile the final source code into object code (machine-readable code) and place the altered object code into production. In this manner, systems developers never have access to the operating environment housed within computer operations. Some IT functions control source and object codes within the systems development specialization, while other IT functions handle such control as depicted in Figure 5-3. The important point is that systems analysts and programmers should not have access to the production library (see Chapter 4 for further elaboration of this internal control point). The computer security specialization is also responsible for the safety (custody) of corporate information, communication networks, and physical facilities. The user services specialty will be discussed later in this chapter.

The bottom line for IT auditors when examining the structure of an IT function is to ensure that systems developers and computer operators are segregated. It is also advisable for the IT function to form a separate security specialization to maintain custody of software applications and corporate data. However, control over applications and data can be effectively integrated into the systems development and computer operations specialties if circumstances warrant. The next issue to address is how to fund the IT function's operations and projects.

FINANCING THE IT FUNCTION

It is critically important that the IT function be adequately funded, or else it will be unable to conduct day-to-day operations and fulfill strategic objectives. Lack of proper financing can result in significant business risk for the organization, as the needs and demands of customers, vendors, employees, and other stakeholders will go unfulfilled. In the final analysis, an underfunded IT function can hinder the company. From an audit risk perspective, lack of sufficient funding can trigger IT function employees to bypass internal controls, as they struggle to keep up with day-to-day workloads in the most expeditious manner possible, which can lead to a culture of working around the system of internal controls. One aspect of financing deals with funding ongoing operations, while another aspect focuses on acquiring productive resources.

Funding IT Operations

We will discuss two basic approaches to funding IT operations—treating the IT function as a cost or profit center. Under the cost center approach, the IT manager prepares a budget, along with other functional/line managers, submits it to upper management, and justifies the request for operating funds. Typically, the budget is delineated along the lines of human resources, materials and supplies, and overhead. Remember, the IT manager is competing for scarce resources along with peer managers, so each line item should be well reasoned and economically justified. For instance, an IT manager asking for two additional computer operators should justify her request by showing how the operators will add value to the company using the IT function scorecard approach described in Figure 4-4.

Regarding the "operational performance" aspect of the IT function scorecard, the IT manager can explain how the addition of the operators will increase expenses (financial indicator) yet quicken the turnaround time of getting mission-critical decision-making reports to function/line managers (nonfinancial indicator). Focusing on "user satisfaction," the IT manager can show, via a user survey, how the addition of operators will improve users' perceptions (e.g., customers, employees, and vendors) of the IT function's responsiveness and usefulness (nonfinancial indicators). Looking at "adaptability and scalability," the IT manager might demonstrate how the two new operators will allow the company to keep pace with the rapidly increasing transaction processing load in the next two or three years (nonfinancial indicator). Finally, with respect to "organizational contribution," the IT manager can express how the new operators will contribute to budgeted sales volume increases (financial indicator) by building the capacity to process more sales orders per hour than currently possible (nonfinancial indicator). IT managers should take care to justify each budgeted line item in a similar manner, to ensure that they receive sufficient resources to operate the IT function day to day.

Another approach to financing the IT function is to treat the function as a profit center. This approach requires the same budgeting process just described with respect to expenditures. Additionally, the IT function can charge internal users for IT services, thereby creating intracompany funding of the IT function based on usage. A positive aspect of intracompany billing for IT services is that functional/line managers will be careful not to abuse the IT function by demanding inordinate attention during the year to relatively trivial matters. Accordingly, intracompany billing can foster a sense of "responsible use" throughout the company. The negative side of intracompany billing is that, without some safety valve, the IT function could abuse its billing privilege by irresponsibly building an IT empire that cannot be reasonably justified and setting inordinately high billing rates to absorb the costs.

For instance, say that a given IT function should ideally run on an annual budget of $1 million. Because the IT manager can get away with it, however, he builds an empire that consumes $1.5 million. Why should the IT manager worry about this situation in the absence of countervailing controls? The IT auditor should see whether there are any "reasonableness" checks in place to temper the possibility of such abuse.

For example, an extreme control is to tell functional/line managers that if they can find an equally reliable provider of IT services outside the company at a significant cost savings, they can use it and refuse the company's IT services. This approach would help ensure that IT managers do not charge excessive fees, as there would be significant pressure to stay competitive with the outside market. However, the business risk involved with this strategy is potentially damaging. If different functional/line managers outsource with various providers, service levels could vary considerably across the company and integration of enterprise-wide information would be difficult indeed. Plus, if the relationship with an outsource provider were terminated, there could be substantial disruption of business.

Another control approach is for upper management to ask an independent party within the company—say, the corporate controller or finance officer—to obtain market prices for the delivery of similar IT services from outside providers or other companies in the same industry. This way, IT managers could be held accountable for the reasonableness of the internal billing rates. There are likely other ways to enforce accountability for internal rates, but the internal control concept is the same; that is, the IT auditor should check to see that some sort of reasonableness check is performed, at least annually, to ensure that internal IT billing rates are not excessive.

Acquiring IT Resources

In conjunction with running daily operations, the IT function should engage in long-term planning, which includes developing, purchasing, and implementing various components of the computing infrastructure (e.g., application software, computer hardware, and communication systems) designed to support the company's business strategy. In this regard, the IT manager should justify capital projects/acquisitions using a methodological approach. While it is not the purpose of this book to delve into the "how" of calculating a cost-benefit analysis, it is worthwhile mentioning that when attempting to justify capital projects, the IT manager should determine the net benefit (present value of benefits minus costs) of planned projects/acquisitions via a structured approach. Usually it is quite easy to estimate most costs (e.g., labor, materials, and overhead) associated with projects/acquisitions, but quantifying benefits can be considerably more difficult. It suffices to say that the IT auditor should see if the organization uses a formal net benefit approach to justifying capital projects/acquisitions, as an approach of this nature can reduce the business risk of expending valuable resources on projects that likely will not yield a positive return.

Attempts to quantify net benefit of projects/acquisitions do not always work, as there are nonquantifiable paybacks that defy reasonable calculation. Accordingly, referring once again to the IT function scorecard, the IT manager should list nonfinancial benefits associated with the project/acquisition. For instance, say that a company is contemplating the in-house development of a Web-based customer ordering system. Regarding operational performance, the IT manager could estimate the increased number of sales the system would handle each day and determine the faster speed with which each sale can take place compared to the existing system. With respect to user satisfaction, the IT manager might conduct a customer survey to find out how well such a system would be received, the type of functionality customers want to see in a sales ordering system, and so on. For adaptability and scalability, the manager could forecast the overall increased sales capturing capacity of the system and explain how the new system would integrate with existing accounting and inventory applications. Finally, regarding organizational contribution, the manager would present the net benefit analysis of the project, including estimated financial costs and benefits.

The ultimate goal of formally justifying capital projects/acquisitions is to ensure that company resources are being judiciously allocated across the organization. The IT auditor would ascribe lower business risk in this regard to companies with more formalized procedures. The next concern facing the IT manager is staffing.

STAFFING THE IT FUNCTION

Managing the human resources of an IT function is every bit as important as managing technical and economic resources. In fact, one could argue that human resources are the most valuable of all IT resources! The business risks associated with mismanaging human resources are that IT function employees lack sufficient knowledge and experience and are inefficiently and ineffectively used. The audit risks are that employees are unaware or unconcerned about internal controls and that disgruntled, mischievous, and criminal employees might expose the company to computer security threats, information integrity problems, and asset misappropriation. These risks can be effectively controlled via sound human resource procedures in the areas of hiring, rewarding, and terminating employees.

Hiring

Acquiring and retaining qualified IT personnel is a critical factor in the ultimate success of the IT function. The acquisition phase includes recruiting, verifying, testing, and interviewing prospective employees. The IT auditor should determine if the company has formal procedures in this regard and whether such procedures are duly followed. Additionally, each job should have an up-to-date substantive description of responsibilities and procedures.

RECRUITING   The recruiting phase involves identifying needs, writing a job description, obtaining permission to hire for an open position, advertising the position, accepting applications, reviewing applications, and selecting a pool of qualified candidates. Each of these steps must be carefully planned and executed, as the IT manager must be careful to comply with company, regulatory, and statutory rules. A highly qualified human resources manager can be of valuable assistance in ensuring that no rules are violated. While it is beyond the scope of this book to detail the regulatory and statutory rules involved, the IT manager should be aware that sloppy recruiting can expose the company to business risks in areas such as privacy of information and equal employment opportunity. Hence, the IT auditor should look for clear authoritative guidance in recruiting. Once a qualified set of applicants is chosen, their personal and professional qualifications should be verified by external sources.

VERIFYING   Verifying involves, at a minimum, contacting references (personal and professional) and conducting background checks. Depending on the position, the extent to which reference and background inquiries are performed can vary considerably. However, all candidates selected for a particular job should be subjected to some level of reference checking. As well, if a given position requires, say, a bachelor's degree in computer science, the company should obtain proof that each candidate has indeed received such education. If the position involves security, privacy, and confidentiality, there should be documented evidence that the company has performed background checks for convictions of criminal or civil violations of this nature. The IT auditor should make sure that the company follows and documents written procedures in this regard.

TESTING   Some companies next engage in a testing phase. That is, if the position involves, say programming in the C++ language, candidates might be asked to take a written and oral test regarding their knowledge of the language. While the testing phase is not always necessary, it often makes good sense. The IT auditor should determine whether and when testing is performed and check to see that the company consistently follows testing procedures.

INTERVIEWING   Several steps are involved in interviewing: selecting appropriate interviewers, developing an internal interview schedule, arranging for interviews with interviewees, and conducting the interviews. As with recruiting, the interviewing phase is fraught with the potential danger of violating company, regulatory, and statutory rules. For instance, interviewers must be aware of what they can and cannot discuss with interviewees. Once again, the human resources function can be of great assistance and the IT auditor should see whether the company is following sound interviewing procedures.

Once a final candidate has been selected and has accepted the position, the other candidates should be notified of the results.

As indicated, the hiring process involves compliance with company, state, and federal guidelines and laws. Additionally, unsound hiring procedures can result in the IT function's becoming burdened with inadequately qualified personnel, which can reduce the efficiency and effectiveness of the IT function, not to mention the entire company. To minimize such risks, the IT auditor should ensure that hiring procedures have been formally developed and are judiciously followed.

Rewarding

Once employees are on board, it is important to continually challenge and motivate them in positive ways. Doing so will help to build their sense of self-efficacy and self-esteem, as well as develop loyalty and commitment to the company. While there are many aspects of rewarding employees, the major steps examined herein are evaluating, compensating, promoting, and learning. The business risks of improperly rewarding employees are that they might develop a bad attitude toward the IT manager and the company, which can lead to lower productivity, higher frustration, and greater turnover. The audit risks are that bored and disgruntled employees might engage in mischievous and criminal behaviors, both of which can threaten the availability, accuracy, security, and reliability of corporate information.

EVALUATING   The most common form of employee evaluation is the annual review, where a superior assesses the performance of a subordinate. The superior might compare the subordinate's performance to predetermined objectives, prior period performance, peer employees, a superior's expectations, or a combination thereof. Regardless of how performance is benchmarked, it is vitally important that subordinates fully understand the basis on which they are being evaluated—before, during, and after the evaluation period. It is also imperative that the superior be as fair as possible when evaluating employees.

Misunderstandings and disagreements can lead to employee frustration and resentment. The IT auditor should examine the evaluation process for structure and reasonableness.

COMPENSATING   Compensating employees has several aspects. First, the company should strive to compensate employees at least as well as peer organizations. Otherwise the company runs the risk of losing valuable employees. Such turnover, if excessively high, can place at risk the availability and reliability of computing systems, not to mention the possibility that employees who jump ship might reveal sensitive information. Additionally, high employee turnover involves significant productivity losses and costs a great deal of money, as replacing employees is expensive. The IT auditor can check to see if the IT function periodically assesses comparative wage rates.

The next aspect of compensation is to ensure that the company offers equal pay for equal work. Violations of this concept can lead to expensive economic remedies and harmful legal actions. The issue is that the IT function must not discriminate in appearance or substance among employees based on gender, race, sexual orientation, and so on. The IT auditor can test for compliance by comparing the compensation packages of employees holding similar positions across the IT function and investigating any outliers.

Finally, the IT function must deal effectively with two additional compensation issues known as compression and inversion. Compression occurs when the compensation of newly hired employees gets close to experienced employees in similar positions or the compensation of subordinates is nearly the same as their superiors. This situation happens quite frequently in fast-paced markets, like IT, where salaries rise quickly. As one can imagine, it would be disheartening if you worked hard for a company for five years and found out that new hires with no experience were making nearly what you do. Inversion takes place when the compensation of new hires is greater than more experienced employees in the same position, or the compensation of subordinates exceeds that of superiors. Wow, talk about a demoralizing situation! The IT auditor could compare compensation packages within and across ranks and scrutinize any unusual relationships.

PROMOTING   Promoting employees is intertwined with evaluating and compensating them. That is, promotions should be based on merit, not subjective whims, and compensation should be commensurate with the new role and responsibility. Additionally, the compensation package offered to a promoted employee should be evaluated in light of compression and inversion concerns. The primary risks of failing to establish and follow proper procedures involve promotion discrimination and pay inequity issues, which can lead to economic remedies, civil lawsuits, and morale problems. The IT auditor should see that formal, written policies and procedures exist with regard to promotion and that such guidance is consistently followed.

LEARNING   The last issue under the umbrella of rewarding employees is for organizations to shape a positive culture of learning. One of the most valuable benefits an employee can receive is the opportunity to learn and grow, both personally and professionally. The ultimate payback to the company is enormous, as fostering employee growth, through on-the-job experiences, company-sponsored training courses, and higher education programs, can result in greater productivity, higher job satisfaction, and deeper organizational commitment. The psychological benefits to employees and their families resulting from such learning opportunities are substantial as well, as individuals' self-esteem and self-efficacy rise. Additionally, society as a whole benefits from such corporate-sponsored initiatives. The business risk of failing to foster learning opportunities are the potential loss of competitive positioning due to an uneducated workforce and low employee morale. The audit risks are that employees who are not learning and growing become stagnant and frustrated, which can lead to complacency toward or utter disregard for internal controls.

Terminating

The subject of terminating employees either voluntarily or involuntarily is laden with potential internal control threats. Most notably, a disgruntled employee who works for the IT function can wreak havoc on the company's information systems. Thus, the availability, reliability, and integrity of information, computers, and networks are at risk. If the company is sincerely sensitive to employees' concerns and consistently involves workers in decision processes, the number of destructive incidences arising from disgruntled employees can be minimized. However, despite the best working environment, it is likely that a few employees will be dissatisfied anyway, as the flames of their frustration are often fanned by emotional problems and personal circumstances outside the company. The IT function should be ever vigilant in attempting to identify and deal with unhappy employees. However, it is not always possible to spot disgruntled employees, as some of them harbor their ill feelings deep inside while appearing to be content on the outside. Employees of this ilk can be covertly planning to disrupt the company's systems and controls for psychological benefit or economic gain.

Then there are the usual cases of employees who voluntarily quit the company for family reasons, alternative job offers, and so on. The IT manager cannot let down her guard on seemingly benign cases of voluntary termination, as IT employees have been known to damage computer systems and corrupt information databases. To ward off the threat of internal control violations of this nature, the IT function needs to design and implement countervailing controls, such as backup procedures, checks-and-balances, cross-training, job rotations, and mandated vacations.

Although it sounds rather cruel on the surface, IT employees who have given notice or who have been told they are being terminated should immediately be separated from the computing environment and terminate all computer privileges. What if the employer and employees have agreed to a two-week notice? No problem; offer the employees working space outside of the IT environment. Even this solution could pose too much risk, as savvy technicians who are intent on breaking into the computer system can find ways to do so without any passwords or privileges. Thus, this is a judgment call on the part of IT management. The best advice is to err on the side of conservatism, as a destructive employee can grind the entire business to a halt.

The IT auditor should look for the existence of and compliance with a formal termination policy. As part of their field work, IT auditors should inquire into how many internal control and computer system violations in the past have been of suspicious origin and attempt to find the root cause, if not the perpetrator(s). Using investigative techniques of this nature, the IT auditor can constantly survey the landscape for possible sabotage, theft, and fraud by IT personnel.

We now turn our attention to how IT managers can direct the IT function, with the aim of maximizing productivity and effectiveness while minimizing business and audit risks.

DIRECTING THE IT FUNCTION

IT function managers are principally responsible for administering the workflow, managing the computing environment, handling third-party services, and assisting users. Proper management of each of these responsibilities minimizes business and audit risks.

Administering the Workflow

One aspect of workflow administration is to define the levels of service that the IT function promises to deliver to users. By doing so, the IT function is able to plan its capacity requirements to meet business needs and IT users are able to plan their activities around expected service levels. Effective capacity planning will help ensure that systems and information are available to users when needed. Additionally, aligning the IT function's capacity to user needs helps prevent misunderstandings and fosters an atmosphere of mutual trust. The IT auditor should see if the IT function has a formal capacity plan and workload forecast and that written service level agreements exist between the IT function and each user group.

Another aspect of workflow administration is to schedule and perform the work. It is important to judiciously administer workflow so that IT function resources are efficiently and effectively used at a fairly steady rate. That is, if all work is squeezed into the last two days of the month, the IT function would have to acquire sufficient resources to handle severe peak workloads. The upside is that the system would be available and the work would get done. The downside is that the IT function would have idle resources for most of the month, which leads to inefficient use of such resources. Naturally, it is unlikely that the IT function can schedule and perform all of its work at an even rate and avoid workload peaks and valleys altogether. However, if the peaks are extremely high and short lived, the IT manager should meet with user groups in an attempt to better streamline the workload. Procedurally, the IT manager should develop formal workload schedules, monitor actual performance, denote actual-to-planned workload variances, and continually adjust capacity and schedules to meet business needs of the user community. The IT auditor should map workload peaks and valleys throughout the year, understand how the IT function handles extreme workload variances, and determine the efficacy of the IT function's performance monitoring process.

Managing the Computing Environment

Managing the computing environment involves taking responsibility for the computing infrastructure. The computing infrastructure includes computer hardware, network hardware, communication systems, operating systems, application software, and data files. It is important that the IT manager completely understand how these infrastructure elements work in concert to fulfill the IT function's mission, vision, and strategy. The IT manager should establish policies for acquiring, using, and disposing of inventory items; build and periodically verify an inventory list of configuration items; and maintain accounting records of all inventory transactions. It is not unusual for IT functions to rent and lease configuration items, so the IT manager should keep meticulous track of rented and leased computer equipment and software. Also, the IT manager should comply with all software licensing agreements. The IT auditor needs to verify the inventory of owned and nonowned items, as well as test the extent to which the company complies with software licenses.

Another aspect of managing the computing environment centers on maintaining physical facilities. While the security aspects of physical facilities will be discussed later in this chapter, there still exists a major nonsecurity responsibility—ensuring that the physical environment is safe for humans and computers. In this regard, the IT manager should assess whether the facilities are located in an area that is unlikely to experience severe damage from external environment, such as floods, hurricanes, and tornadoes. There should be effective fire suppression systems, along with a fire evacuation plan, both of which are tested periodically. Also, the interior climate needs to be controlled so that both humans and computer equipment can operate within a tolerable temperature and humidity range. IT facilities should also be inconspicuous both in location and design. This is an important safety issue because criminals and terrorists could harm people and computers by damaging the physical facilities, not to mention bringing business to a halt. Finally, the IT manager must comply with appropriate safety and health regulations, most of which are promulgated by the Occupational Safety and Health Administration (OSHA).[5] The IT auditor should walk through the IT facilities and determine whether they appear to be safe for humans and computers, review the IT function's formal safety plan, determine how well the IT function tracks safety violations, and investigate all safety violations.

Handling Third-Party Services

Many IT managers work with third-party service providers, such as Internet service providers (ISP), communication companies, security firms, and call centers. The recent trend is toward more use of third-party service providers, as many providers offer economies of scale not possible in a single IT function. For instance, the application service provider (ASP) concept is growing in popularity. ASPs allow user companies to, in essence, rent application software, such as enterprise resource planning (ERP) systems, which offer users the benefits of such software without having to worry about installing and maintaining complex systems of this nature. Thus, it is likely that IT managers will be responsible for handling increased numbers of third-party service providers into the foreseeable future. Proper management of third-party service providers involves several key issues.

First, the IT manager should, in concert with upper management, establish policies and procedures regarding the purchase, use, and termination of third-party services. Next, there should be legally binding contracts between the company and service providers articulating the roles and responsibilities of each party, services to be performed, service level agreements, contract duration, service costs, dispute resolution, dissolution arrangements, and so on. Additionally, the IT function must work with the service provider to ensure the security and confidentiality of company information. In this light, the IT auditor should obtain a list of all third-party service providers, verify the existence of legal contracts, inquire about the source and resolution of disputes, and examine the compliance monitoring process. Additionally, a potentially serious business risk the IT auditor must address is how the IT manager plans to deal with an unexpected disruption of mission-critical services. If one or more service providers fail to deliver as promised, the IT manager must have a backup and recovery plan in place, and it should be tested periodically.

Assisting Users

One aspect of assisting users deals with creating a healthy environment of learning and growth through user training and education. This involves identifying training needs, designing training curricula to meet those needs, and delivering training programs. In addition to delivering training in-house, the IT function might also send users to training/education programs offered by vocational-technology schools, colleges and universities, and other outside providers. Given the fast pace with which IT hardware and software evolves, it is imperative that companies offer continual training and education to computer users; those that don't do so run the risk that users cannot or will not use the IT infrastructure to its fullest extent and that productivity and job performance will be suboptimal. The IT auditor should review the nature and extent of user training/education and determine if such learning opportunities appear consistent with the complexity of the IT infrastructure.

Another way to assist users is by providing helpful advice when needed. IT managers often handle requests for advice and assistance through a "help desk" where users can turn when they have questions. The help desk must do precisely that—help! Typically, when users ask for help, they are already frustrated with some aspect of the computer system and they often demand immediate attention. Admittedly, some users need to "chill out" and understand that the help desk personnel have an ongoing priority list and that the users will sometimes have to wait in line. On the other side of the coin, there are plenty of anecdotal stories about help desks with staff members who are not the friendliest people in the world and either cannot or will not deliver meaningful, timely assistance. The truth, as usual, is probably in the middle; there are many users who expect the world to stop when they need help and there are many help desk personnel who need a course or two in human relations. The IT manager needs to design and monitor effective ways to assist users when they request help, or users could get upset with the IT function. That begets a "slippery slope syndrome"—IT personnel resent users, users dislike IT personnel, the downward spiral escalates, and the relationship between the two parties hits a new low. The situation can be quite harmful to the company as a whole. IT auditors need to assess the effectiveness of user assistance processes and recommend any needed changes to create an atmosphere of mutual trust and respect between the IT function and user community.

A related facet of assisting users via a help desk is the effective handling of problems and incidences. Differences among help, problems, and incidences are often blurred. While there are no objective criteria for delineating help from problems and incidences, requests for help generally arise from users' lack of understanding about how applications work. Hence, help desk personnel are typically "super users" who have considerable experience with applications used by the company. Problems and incidences, on the other hand, typically reflect improperly functioning elements of the computing infrastructure (e.g., hardware, networks, and applications) that require the intervention of experienced technicians and programmers. Accordingly, handling problems and incidences requires a formal set of policies and procedures. The IT auditor should determine the extent to which the IT function is effective at logging, tracking, resolving, and reporting problems and incidences. Failure to prudently and expeditiously deal with problems and incidences can reduce the company's productivity and profitability.

CONTROLLING THE IT FUNCTION

The major control categories involved in the IT function are security, input, processing, output, databases, backup, and recovery. Each of these categories is intended to minimize business and audit risk via internal controls, as discussed next. When examining IT function controls, it is vitally important for the IT auditor to assess whether control risk (i.e., the risk that a material misstatement in an assertion will not be prevented or detected promptly by the IT function's internal controls) is within a tolerable range; otherwise, existing controls may have to be strengthened or compensating controls may have to be developed in order to lower control risk to an acceptable level.

Security Controls

The IT manager is responsible for ensuring that the computing infrastructure is secure from internal and external threats. A compromise of the infrastructure can result in significant business risk (e.g., network downtime or database corruption) and audit risk (e.g., material misstatements in accounts due to incomplete or inaccurate data capturing). We will examine security issues along two avenues: physical and logical security.

PHYSICAL SECURITY   Physical security focuses on keeping facilities, computers, communication equipment, and other tangible aspects of the computing infrastructure safe from harm. Regarding facility controls, access security is of paramount concern. Only authorized personnel should be allowed into the facility, and visitors should be accompanied by authorized personnel at all times. Remember, personnel who do not work for the IT function frequently enter the facility, such as vending machine, paper supply, and janitorial supply employees, and these visitors should be carefully screened and constantly monitored. This is a hole in many security systems through which intruders could penetrate. Access restriction can be accomplished in many ways, such as the use of security guards, keys and locks, card readers, and biometric devices (e.g., fingerprint readers or retinal image scanners) at all doors into and out of the facility. Additionally, windows, outside vents, and other possible penetration points should be adequately secured by using bars, safety glass, or other materials.

The next phase in a security system is to install mechanisms for monitoring who is entering, roaming, and leaving the facility. For instance, security guards could walk inside and outside the facility looking for suspicious people and activities. Video cameras should be installed at all access points, as well as throughout sensitive areas of the building. Finally, penetration alarms could be located at access points, some of which could be triggered all day and others of which could be armed after normal business hours.

The company should periodically review access evidence. For example, visitors should sign in and out of the facility. Electronic access systems, such as card readers and biometric devices, automatically create signage logs for authorized personnel. IT management should implement a formal review procedure in which signage logs and monitoring devices are examined and suspicious activities, unauthorized persons, and known violations are investigated.

The precise combination of access, monitor, and review mechanisms employed at a given company is dictated by many situational factors, such as the facility's location, the company's industry, and budgetary restrictions. The IT auditor should assess the effectiveness of such mechanisms by reviewing visitor logs, observing monitoring devices, examining review procedures, and investigating reported violations. Additionally, IT auditors should conduct penetration tests in which they attempt to enter the facility without authorization, break into access points, and gain admission as a visitor but try to leave the authorized party and wander around the facility unescorted. Figure 5-4 shows a sample set of physical security controls and tests.

Communication and power lines coming into the facility are also a concern, for disabling either could shut down the entire operation. The IT manager should monitor the primary communication and power lines via cameras and guards, and install secondary (backup) lines in case the primary lines fail. It would be wise, although somewhat expensive, to have primary and secondary power lines arrive from separate power grids. This way, if the power station and/or transmission facility feeding the primary line are brought down, the secondary line would deliver power from a separate station and transmission facility. The same logic holds for communication systems; ideally the primary and secondary communication systems should be delivered by different communication providers using independent transmission systems. The IT auditor should inquire about

Security Issue	Physical Controls	Logical Controls
Access controls	Security guards Locks and keys Biometric devices	ID and passwords Authorization matrix Firewalls and encryption
Monitor controls	Security guards Video cameras Penetration alarms	Access logs Supervisory oversight Penetration alarms
Review controls	Formal reviews Signage logs Violation investigations	Formal reviews Activity logs Violation investigations
Penetrating tests	Unauthorized attempts to enter IT facilities Attempts to break in through vulnerable points As authorized visitor, attempts to leave authorized personnel and wander around the facility without oversight	Unauthorized attempts to enter servers and networks Attempts to override access controls (hacking) As authorized user, attempts to use unauthorized applications and view unauthorized information

FIGURE 5-4 Physical and Logical Security

the contingency plan with respect to power and communications, then determine whether the plan is effective under the circumstances.

Other computing equipment not housed in the main facility, like local area network equipment, personal computers, and secondary servers, needs to be controlled and monitored as well. The same concepts of accessing, monitoring, and reviewing should be employed to the extent possible. Additionally, the IT manager should design a backup plan that will ensure continuous service should such equipment be disabled. The IT auditor should review and assess the efficacy of security systems surrounding computer hardware components located outside of the main computing facility.

LOGICAL SECURITY   Arguably, the most valuable portion of the computing infrastructure is invisible—corporate data and computer software (e.g., user applications, network systems, communication systems, and operating systems). Data and software of this nature are known as "logical" components of the infrastructure. Part of the security system surrounding logical components is handled via physical controls; that is, most corporate data and software are located on computers, servers, and storage devices housed in the main computing facility and other sites throughout the company. The other part of the logical security system is handled through computer controlled access, monitor, and review systems. One can approach logical security in the same manner as physical security; accordingly, the IT auditor needs to recognize the many access points to logical components, review the access controls, examine the monitoring controls, understand the review procedures, and perform penetration tests (see Figure 5-4 for sample controls and tests for logical components).

The most obvious point of entry into logical components of the computing infrastructure is through a computer terminal. Hence, anyone attempting to use a company computer should supply an authorized identification (ID) and password. Based on the ID/password combination, the user is authorized to execute certain applications and view certain information. As illustrated in Figure 5-5, user #1 is authorized to execute the accounts receivable (A/R) and accounts payable (A/P) applications. Within the A/R application, user #1 can read customer data and add receipts. Within the A/P application, user #1 can read vendor data and add payments. Similar authorizations to applications and information would be ascribed to users #2, #3, and so on.

There are other points of entry into a company's computer systems as well, most notably through the Internet. Once intruders have gained access, they can destroy data files, insert viruses, and steal information. Therefore, it is vital that the IT function surround the computer system's external access points with logical controls. The most common control of this nature is a firewall, which is a security application often located on a stand-alone computer that disallows external parties into the company's computer system without proper authorization. Firewalls can also be used to block authorized users from uploading, downloading, or using illicit materials and files. Similar ID/password authorization matrices are integrated into firewall applications. Additionally, should an intruder happen to compromise the firewall and gain access to the computing environment, databases can be encrypted so that unauthorized persons cannot read the database files.

Next, the IT auditor should assess the effectiveness of monitoring controls. For example, the authorization matrices keep track of when users signed into the system, which applications they used, and what information they added or altered. Additionally, authorization systems, including firewalls, track failed attempts to enter computers and networks. Typically, security applications employ a "three strikes and you're out" procedure; someone attempting to enter the system gets three tries at the ID/password combination. If they fail to authenticate within the three tries, the computer system refuses further attempts. More sophisticated features found on access security systems deny future

User #3 [ID = XXXXX, Password = YYYYY]

User #2 [ID = XXXXX, Password = YYYYY]

User #1 [ID = XXXXX, Password = YYYYY]

Information	Applications	
	A/R	A/P
Customers	Add ☐ Edit ☐ Read ☑ Delete ☐	
Vendors		Add ☐ Edit ☐ Read ☑ Delete ☐
Sales	Add ☐ Edit ☐ Read ☐ Delete ☐	
Purchases		Add ☐ Edit ☐ Read ☐ Delete ☐
Receipts	Add ☑ Edit ☐ Read ☐ Delete ☐	
Payments		Add ☑ Edit ☐ Read ☐ Delete ☐

FIGURE 5-5   Sample Authorization Matrix

attempts for a specified period of time from, say, the same company computer, phone number, IP address, or ID/password.

Additional monitoring controls can involve supervisory oversight; that is, supervisors should frequently walk around and see who is sitting at computer terminals and what applications they are using. If authorized users are using unauthorized applications, the supervisor should investigate. Additionally, any unfamiliar people should be interrogated on the spot.

Another monitoring control is to install penetration alarms, which track usage patterns for unusual activity. For example, say that user #3 is not allowed into the general ledger (G/L), yet somehow the user bypasses the authorization matrix and begins to snoop around in G/L data files. A penetration alarm can be used to frequently scan who is into what applications/information, compare such activity with the authorization matrix, and report all exceptions. Additionally, penetration alarms can immediately report failed attempts to enter the computing environment, such as each time the "three strikes rule" is violated.

Access and monitor systems are quite ineffective if no one is reviewing the security system. Accordingly, there should be a formal review procedure in which activity logs are examined and violations are investigated. The IT auditor should test the effectiveness of the company's set of review controls.

Further, IT auditors can conduct penetration tests of the client's computer system. For instance, an IT auditor could attempt to gain unauthorized access via company terminals, computer modems, or the Internet. Intruders could also find ways to bypass the authentication controls altogether by using "hacking" software, some of which can be found on the Internet. In this regard, IT auditors should become familiar with and learn to use hacking software that is publicly available, because authorized and unauthorized system users can find and try such software on the company's computer system as well. Finally, the IT auditor could ask permission to, say, view certain computer files and then try to use applications and view information for which she is not authorized. IT auditors must be quite knowledgeable in the area of logical risks and controls, particularly with respect to infiltration methods used by hackers and penetration testing techniques.

Information Controls

The process of capturing, processing, and distributing accounting information arising from economic events can be classified into input, process, and output activities. Within each activity, certain controls are needed to ensure the integrity and accuracy of vital decision-making information. Additionally, the company must integrate sound backup controls into the process. The business risk of not properly controlling information is potentially devastating, as corrupt information can grind business to a halt. The audit risk is extremely high, particularly in the presence of weak internal controls, as improper segregation of authorizing and recording transactions throughout the input-process-output cycle leaves the accounting system vulnerable to abuse, which can lead to material misstatements in account assertions.

INPUT CONTROLS   The IT auditor should see whether the company follows written procedures regarding the proper authorization, approval, and input of accounting transactions. These are incompatible functions, so they should be segregated to the extent possible and controlled. Let's examine three typical scenarios.

First, assume that the customer purchases goods at a store counter, a cashier records the sale on the cash register, and an accounting clerk later processes cash register sales in batches. The customer is *authorizing* the sale, as he is voluntarily submitting the goods to the cashier for payment. The cashier is *approving* the sale by either accepting cash or processing a credit card transaction. If credit sales are involved, the cashier has the responsibility to ensure that the customer is using an authorized, valid credit card. At the end of each shift, the cashier balances the cash register drawer with cash and credit sales recorded during the shift. Importantly, cashiers must log into their registers using an ID/password routine or some alternative specific identification scheme (such as swiping an employee ID card), so that each cashier on each shift can be traced to a given register. Then, the accounting clerk *inputs* the sales transactions into the accounting system in batches, checks the initial input against batch totals for accuracy, and makes input corrections if the batch total does not match the initial input total. The latter process of correcting input, called "error handling," should be properly documented in the company's procedure manual.

Second, assume the same scenario except that the cash register automatically records the sale in the accounting system. The customer *authorizes* the sale, and the cashier both *approves* and *inputs* the sale. In this scenario, a compensating control should be in place since two incompatible functions are vested in one person. For example, an accounting clerk might reconcile cash register transactions to related accounting system input before such transactions are processed (similar to the batch technique). Or, if transactions are automatically processed by the cash register in real time, the accounting clerk should, at a minimum, perform random periodic reconciliations of cash register transactions to accounting system inputs. Proper error handling procedures must be designed to fit the transaction input process used.

Third, assume that customers order and pay for goods via the company's Web site. The customer, perhaps named John Smith, once again *authorizes* the sale, but there is no human on the other end of the counter to verify that John Smith actually ordered the goods. This can be problematic if not properly controlled, as John Smith could later repudiate the sale by sending the goods back to the company with no valid reason other than to say that he never authorized the sale in the first place. Thus, the company must integrate nonrepudiation procedures into the Web site. One control in this regard is for prospective customers to complete an authorization form before any sale can take place. This procedure would record such data as the customer's name, address, and phone number; the customer also would be required to create a unique ID and password, which must be used for all upcoming sales transactions. This way, the company can verify that the supposedly unauthorized person who ordered the goods via the Web site just happened to know the customer's ID/password combination—an unlikely scenario! Further, the Web site should capture the IP address of the computer from which the sale took place; in this manner, the point of entry of the sale could be traced back to a specific computer or network (if multiple IP addresses are randomly assigned to computers within a given network) and the company could determine if the customer had access to the IP address at the time of the sale. This combination of controls would provide sufficient evidence in investigating repudiated sales.

Continuing with the third scenario, the customer also *approves* the sale. Typically, this is performed in at least two steps. First, the customer submits a credit card for payment. The company Web site should validate the credit card before accepting the sale and match the cardholder's name with the customer's name in the company database. Immediately before the sale is finalized, the customer should be offered a chance to cancel, change, or accept the sale. The *input* of the transaction into the accounting system could be deferred or immediate. If deferred, an accounting clerk could use batch processing and error handling techniques to check transactions before allowing them to be processed. If sales are immediate (real-time updating), the accounting clerk could periodically reconcile sales transactions to accounting transactions and follow an appropriate error handling process.

PROCESS CONTROLS   The processing stage involves validating, error handling, and updating activities. Processing controls are sometimes performed after transactions are input into the accounting system, but such controls are often integrated into the input procedure.

In some computer systems, especially large legacy systems, accounting transactions are input into the computer system, stored on disks or tape, and processed later. Let's revert to scenario #1, in which cash register transactions are batched and entered into the accounting system by an accounting clerk. The next step, which might be temporally displaced from the input stage, is to validate the transactions. In large computer operations, this would require loading the input transaction media into the computer, loading affected master files into the computer (say, the customer and inventory master files), loading appropriate program files into the computer, and validating the transactions. That is, each transaction would be verified against the master files to ensure that the customer and the inventory item(s) are valid (meaning that each exists on the respective master files). If they do not match, the computer system will reject the transaction, place it in a "suspense file" (the erroneous transactions are held in suspense until corrected), and move on to the next transaction. At the end of this process, the computer operator has a file of valid transactions and a suspense file of rejected transactions. In this scenario, the computer operator is responsible for processing transactions but has no part in authorizing, approving, or recording transactions (segregation of incompatible functions).

Next, an error handling procedure is invoked. Typically, the operator is authorized to continue processing the valid transactions and send the suspense file to an authorized person, say, a designated accounting clerk, for investigation. The operator should maintain a log of who received the suspense file and when it was transferred, for accountability reasons. Also, the computer operator should not investigate and correct errors, as this would be an incompatible function. Sometimes, however, company policy mandates that the operator will not process the valid transaction file until rejected transactions are corrected by an authorized party and revalidated by the operator, or until an authorized person instructs the operator to continue processing the validated transactions. The IT auditor should ensure that the IT function is following proper procedure.

At this point, the validated input transactions, affected master, journal, and ledger files, and updating programs are loaded into the computer, and the updating stage begins. Sometimes multiple programs are involved in the updating process. For instance, the customer and inventory master files might be updated first, then the journal files, and finally the ledger files. In this three-step process, one would expect to see run-to-run control totals, where batch and sometimes hash totals are created at the end of one run and checked at the beginning of the next run. In this manner, missing or corrupt data can be quickly spotted from run-to-run before the next processing step begins. An IT auditor can see if run-to-run controls are effective by using test decks of data and checking the batch/hash totals from one run to the next.

At the end of the processing phase described, all master, journal, and ledger files are properly updated. More often, however, the processing of accounting information is performed immediately with little or no human intervention. This is especially true with newer accounting information system applications that are built on relational databases, where most processing controls are integrated into the input phase.

For instance, in the third scenario, customers ordered goods via the company's Web site. At the time of entry, the sales ordering application would validate the customer, credit card, and inventory item(s). Additionally, the inventory validation routine would determine if the ordered items were in stock, and, if not, ask the customer if she would like to back-order the items. Any errors, such as an invalid customer, credit card, or inventory item, would be noted during the sales entry process and the customer would be given a chance to correct the input. If such corrections were not acceptable to the sales ordering application, the order would not be processed. Accordingly, validating and error handling activities take place simultaneously with the sales input process.

Next, validated sales transactions are used to update relevant files (or tables in a relational database). This can take place instantaneously or later. If the updating is deferred, an authorized person, who could be a computer operator or accounting clerk, typically processes the transactions in batches, and compares batch and hash totals to the updated files (tables). If updating is instantaneous, the operator/clerk periodically checks to see if the updating procedure is working as intended. Either way, when errors are detected the operator/clerk initiates error handling procedures, which involve investigating and correcting problems. The IT auditor should identify the type of processing used at the client site, obtain an understanding of the processing controls, ensure that company personnel are following the control procedures, and test the efficacy of such controls.

In most instances, combined sales ordering/transaction processing scenarios take place automatically in real time. Since there are no sequential, temporally displaced computer runs involved (as with the earlier scenario), there are typically no run-to-run totals to compare. However, most point-of-sale applications are built on a relational database, which involves a unique set of processing controls that serve essentially the same objective of run-to-run totals, which are described next.

DATABASE CONTROLS   Since database processing involves the (near) simultaneous update of multiple tables (called files in nonrelational database environments), a glitch such as a power failure or computer malfunction can corrupt or destroy many data items throughout the database. The damage can quickly ripple throughout the entire database primarily because a) related tables are linked to one another and b) update routines often incorporate one or more of the following processing techniques: multitasking (the computer executes more than one task [program] at a time), multiprocessing (multiple CPUs simultaneously execute interdependent tasks), and multithreading (a computer executes multiple parts of a program [threads] at one time). Thus, multiple tables and data items can be instantaneously corrupted when an interruption occurs. To defend against this threat, the database management system (DBMS) is designed with *roll-back* and *recovery* features.

Databases operate on a transaction principle, in which a logical unit of work is considered a transaction. The processing of a transaction takes the database from an initial state to an altered state. For instance, say that a customer wants to change his phone number in the customer table. This involves locating the block on the computer disk containing the phone number, buffering the block in memory, updating the phone number attribute (or field) in the appropriate tuple (or record), and writing the updated block back to the disk. While these interdependent tasks are being performed, the database is temporarily in an inconsistent or contradictory state. Upon completion of all related tasks, the database has achieved the desired altered state, which becomes the new initial state. Since a transaction is considered an atomic unit of work, all of the steps must be successfully completed; otherwise the database is corrupted.

If an interruption occurs, the transaction is aborted and the DBMS evokes a process designed to restore the database to its initial state. Database restoration can be complicated, particularly when multitasking, multiprocessing, or multithreading techniques are employed, as there can be multiple transactions in various processing states at one time. While there are numerous technical ways in which restoration is accomplished, depending on the particular DBMS in use, the basic premise is as follows: An activity log places a unique identifier on each transaction once it begins to process and tracks or records each step (e.g., buffering the block or updating the attribute) along the way (called checkpoints). Assume that at this point an interruption occurs and processing is abruptly terminated. Once the system is restarted, the DBMS identifies the transaction(s) that was in process during the interruption, performs a *roll-back* procedure in which the uncompleted transaction(s) is placed back into the processing queue, *recovers* the initial state of the database before the interruption occurred (the write procedure had not taken place, so the database on the disk was left unaltered), and reprocesses the affected transaction(s). While IT auditors do not have to fully understand the intricacies of the roll-back and recovery procedures built into each DBMS, they should determine, through documentation, inquiries, or tests, that such procedures are operating effectively.

Another situation that must be adequately dealt with in a relational database environment is termed *concurrency control*. Concurrency problems can occur when, say, multiple users attempt to update the same data item simultaneously or when one user is updating while another user is reading the same data item; in either situation, conflicts can occur and the integrity of database information can be compromised. As with restoration procedures, concurrency controls are also integrated into the DBMS. A common way to prevent concurrency problems is to *lock* a database object while it is in use and release the object upon completion. For instance, say that Joe wants to read a customer's phone number, while Sally wants to change the number. In the event of a tie (meaning, both requests arrive simultaneously), the DBMS will process the change operation before the read operation; this way, Joe will see the most recent number. The DBMS can determine which operation to perform in what order, as it *timestamps* each transaction when the processing request is initiated. While the change operation (transaction) is being processed, the DBMS will lock Joe from reading the phone number. Here, the database administrator is faced with a choice; that is, at what level of *granularity* should the database object be specified.

At a *coarse level* of granularity, the entire database would be locked while the phone number is being updated. Unfortunately, in this circumstance, everyone throughout the entire company who wishes to use the database would be locked out. In most cases, this is an undesirable situation. At *moderate level* of granularity, the database object to lock could be specified at the tuple (record) level. Accordingly, no one else could use the customer tuple until the update has completed. This too may be unacceptable. At a *fine level* of granularity, the database object could be defined at the attribute (field) level. In this manner, no one could access this particular customer's phone number until it has been updated. Naturally, the lowest level of granularity is the most intuitively appealing, but there is a tradeoff. Specifically, there is an inverse relationship between the granularity level and system performance; meaning, a lower level of granular locking equates to slower computer performance. This occurs because low locking levels consume CPU processing time, as the computer must keep track of huge amounts of database objects as they are locked and unlocked. This is a database performance/tuning issue, which may not be included as part of the normal IT audit. However, the IT auditor needs to ensure that concurrency controls are working effectively. Further, as a management advisory service, the IT auditor could assess whether level of granularity is set so that the information system is responsive, yet prevents concurrency problems.

OUTPUT CONTROLS   Access to computer output should be controlled so that proprietary company information is requested and seen only by authorized parties and so that printed reports remain within company premises. A logical control is to ensure that only authorized parties can request certain output, whether it takes the form of a computer screen or printed report. Such logical access control is accomplished via the ID/password authorization matrix procedure described earlier, which should be reviewed periodically.

If the requested output is presented on a computer screen, the screen must be physically secured from unauthorized "eyes" while the output is visible. If the authorized party leaves the area where the screen is located, the output should be removed from the screen and logically locked with an ID/password combination. If the output takes the form of a printed report, other control concerns arise.

In organizations where the IT function is large and reports are printed in a common area, such as a printer room, the space in which reports are printed should be physically controlled via a lock of some sort. Computer reports leaving the secured area should be logged out, requiring persons taking reports to sign a log, thereby establishing an audit trail of accountability.

With regard to reports that are requested by end users and printed on various isolated and networked printers, typically in unsecured areas throughout the company, controls should be in place so that only authorized persons can request (logical control) and possess (physical control) certain reports and so that printed reports are secured when authorized persons are absent (physical control). A major concern with isolated and network printers is where they are placed (physical control). For instance, if sensitive information, such as payroll information, is printed, the requesting party needs to be physically near the printer so that he can take possession of the report as soon as it is printed. Otherwise, unauthorized persons might read or take the report. The IT auditor should consider where printers are located and who has physical proximity and logical access to the printers.

Another concern with printed reports is their proper disposal. Different reports lead different lives. Some reports are relatively permanent; they are held in company offices for a while and then placed in a secured record retention area for a specified period. For example, certain payroll reports might be held in the payroll office throughout the year and moved to a record retention area for ten years. The length of time in which certain reports are held is sometimes mandated by regulatory agencies, such as the Internal Revenue Service, and other times by company policy. Other reports are relatively temporary; that is, they are printed, immediately used, and quickly discarded. In either the permanent or temporary scenario, the reports must be properly destroyed at the end of their useful lives. This typically involves moving the reports to a secured area where they are shredded and placed into authorized containers. IT auditors need to understand the record retention/destruction policies and determine if such policies are properly established and used.

In conjunction with control concerns over visible output (computer screens and printed reports), other output controls are established to ensure that all input transactions were processed through the computer system. For example, a payroll clerk might batch together 101 payroll cards for processing, create a hash total of all employee numbers in the batch, and calculate batch totals of regular and overtime hours reflected on the cards. When the clerk receives output from the computer system, she will check the timecard count, hash total, and batch totals to make sure that what went into the computer came out on the other end. If an exception is noted—for instance, the clerk finds that one timecard was not processed—there should be documented error handling procedures that allow for tracking, identifying, understanding, and resubmitting the missing timecard transaction. Where such input-output controls are in place, IT auditors need to understand and test such procedures.

Continuity Controls

A major business risk related to the IT function is a disruption of business activity due to computer failures and disasters. The extent to which the company is prepared to effectively deal with such circumstances is paramount to the economic viability of the organization. IT auditors can add considerable value to their clients by fully immersing themselves in all aspects of business continuity risks and controls.

BACKUP CONTROLS   It is imperative that organizations develop and follow a sound backup strategy; otherwise, there would be nothing left to recover after a disaster. The depth and breadth of a backup strategy involves at least two key considerations: downtime and cost. That is, how much downtime can the company afford to lose and how much money is the company willing to pay for its backup strategy? Generally, shorter downtime requirements equate to higher backup costs. The following discussion will examine two types of backup: data and hardware.

DATA BACKUP   Assume that Slow Company can survive for several business days without its computer system. In this scenario, the company might want to perform a *full backup* of all data once each week. This way, if the computer fails on Wednesday afternoon, the company can resort to the latest weekly backup; manually reprocess transactions for Monday, Tuesday, and part of Wednesday (before the system went down); and continue with operations. Next, assume that Medium Company must be up and running within one business day. In this case, the company should consider performing weekly full backups and daily *incremental backups,* in which only daily transaction data are backed up, rather than all files/tables as with full-backups. When a failure occurs, the company can reprocess the daily incremental backups against the latest full backup, reconstructing the files/tables to the end of the last backup day. Any transactions processed during the day of the computer failure would have to be manually reentered into the system. Now, assume that Fast Company must be up and running within hours after a computer disruption. In this event, the company should perform a daily full backup and hourly incremental backups. Accordingly, when a failure occurs, the company can reprocess the hourly incremental backups against the latest daily full backup, and only transactions that occurred within the hour of the failure would have to be manually reentered. Finally, assume that Lightning Company must be up and running within minutes of a computer failure. Now we are in the realm of real-time backup, which involves instantaneous, simultaneous updating of data on the company's computer system and a remote computer system, so that only transactions that were in process within minutes or seconds of the failure would be lost.

These scenarios and their backup solutions are simplified examples for illustrative purposes only, as the particular backup strategy employed by a company depends on a host of additional factors, such as transaction volume, availability of technical support, backup storage location, and hardware redundancy. However, even the real-time backup strategy can be accomplished, given enough resources.

Let's now examine two key issues when designing a backup strategy for an organization—storage location and hardware redundancy. When files/tables are backed up, they are placed on some medium, such as digital tapes, CDs, and magnetic disks. The choice of which media to use depends on such factors as speed, reliability, capacity, and cost. Once the choice is made, the question is where to store the medium on which the backup files/tables are stored. There are two general solutions—physical vaulting and electronic vaulting.

With *physical vaulting,* it is presumed that the medium is removed from the company's computer and taken to an off-site location, such as a bank vault or another company location geographically separated from the processing site. Some companies choose to store one copy of the backup medium on-site (if the computer failure does not destroy the computing environment, the on-site copy is readily accessible) and another copy off-site (if the computer failure is a result of a larger disaster that affects the computing environment, the off-site copy can be retrieved). Of course, this dual strategy involves more time (to copy the backup twice) and money (to purchase and maintain duplicate media).

Electronic vaulting involves sending backup data over a communications network (such as the Internet) to an off-site storage medium, typically another computer. On a shoestring budget, backup data could be sent to the home computer of a trusted employee by using fairly simple, off-the-shelf software. Another option is for the company to send, say, Division A's backup to a computer at Division B and vice versa (assuming, of course, that both divisions are physically separated so that one disaster does not affect both at the same time). This too can be accomplished using shrink-wrapped software that is quite easy to learn and use. Alternatively, the company can engage the services of an Internet business (third-party service provider) that specializes in electronic off-site storage. Some electronic vaulting service providers merely allow the client to periodically send data over the Internet to an electronic storage device connected to a computer. Typically, the monthly charge, which varies depending on the amount of storage space required, also includes backup software. At the high end, other electronic vaulting service providers are designed to handle real-time backup, where the company's data is backed nearly to the last key stroke; however, this strategy requires considerable Internet bandwidth and can consume a great deal of computer processing power. Naturally, there are costs and other considerations involved with various electronic vaulting strategies, but, if the strategy is effective, electronic vaulting provides for ready access to backup files.

HARDWARE BACKUP   Computer downtimes usually do not involve disasters such as fires and floods; instead, one or more hardware components fail and the system is temporarily disabled. Hence, an integral component of a well-rounded backup strategy is the integration of *hardware redundancy* into the computing environment. The hardware components most likely to fail are power supplies and those with moving parts (e.g., disk drives). Accordingly, the company should consider adding redundant power supplies to mission-critical computers. Power supplies are relatively inexpensive and easy to install, and adding such redundancy can avert many downtime situations.

Purchasing extra disk drives for computers is not very expensive either, but backing up data on the redundant drives is more involved than merely plugging the drives into the computer system. There are many ways in which to configure redundant storage devices, depending on the company's computing infrastructure and level of redundancy required. Let's examine three of the more common configurations—redundant array of independent disks (RAID), network attached storage (NAS), and server area network (SAN). It is important to remember that each of these configurations can become quite complicated from a technological perspective; hence, the following discussion is merely an overview of the main points of each configuration.

Redundant array of independent disks (RAID) technology includes many levels of redundancy. One is *disk mirroring,* in which data is simultaneously written to the primary disk and to one or more redundant disks (Figure 5-6, Panel A). Another RAID level is known as *disk striping,* where an array of at least three, but usually five, disks is established (Figure 5-6, Panel B). With disk striping, redundant data is not stored on each disk; rather, a sophisticated scheme of parity checks is used so that if one disk drive in the array

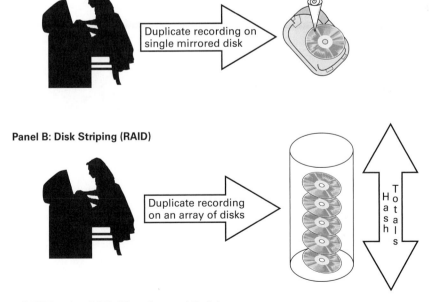

Panel A: Disk Mirroring (RAID)

Duplicate recording on single mirrored disk

Panel B: Disk Striping (RAID)

Duplicate recording on an array of disks

Hash Totals

FIGURE 5-6   RAID Mirroring and Striping

fails, the remaining drives can reconstruct the data on the failed drive and continue processing. Afterward, a technician needs to replace the failed drive and rebuild the data before the array is fully operational once again. Incorporating RAID technology into the computing environment is quite affordable, as most operating systems (e.g., Microsoft NT and XP) are already equipped to handle RAID disks.

Network attached storage (NAS) integrates one or more storage devices, also called NAS appliances, into the company's local area network (LAN). A NAS appliance is typically composed of one or more disk drives and an internal controller to handle input-output operations (which takes the processing load off from the main computer). Most NAS appliances also employ RAID technology to ensure hardware redundancy, and they can be shared by multiple users on the network. NAS appliances can be used as redundant drives only, or they can serve as primary drives (handling live data), especially in a distributed database environment. NAS appliances are relatively affordable and quite scalable, so the company can continue to add NAS appliances to the LAN as storage demands increase. See Figure 5-7 for an example of a NAS configuration.

A *server area network* (SAN) expands the NAS concept to wide area networks (WAN). The primary difference is that a SAN is a dedicated network, which includes storage devices and computers to control/coordinate the devices. A SAN can be linked to multiple LANs throughout the organization via the company's intranet, and multiple SANs can be used simultaneously. Establishing a SAN can be somewhat expensive and technically

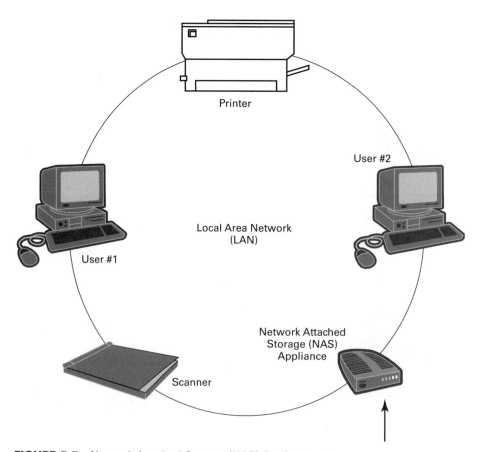

FIGURE 5-7   Network Attached Storage (NAS) Configuration

complicated, but the storage network is capable of handling very high volumes of through-put. Hence, a SAN is a great solution for large companies. As with NAS appliances, a SAN is designed to be *fault tolerant;* redundancy is incorporated throughout the network. See Figure 5-8 for an example of a SAN configuration.

In this section, we examined various strategies for backing up vital company data and computer hardware. After a natural or human-created disaster (e.g., fire, flood, hurricane,

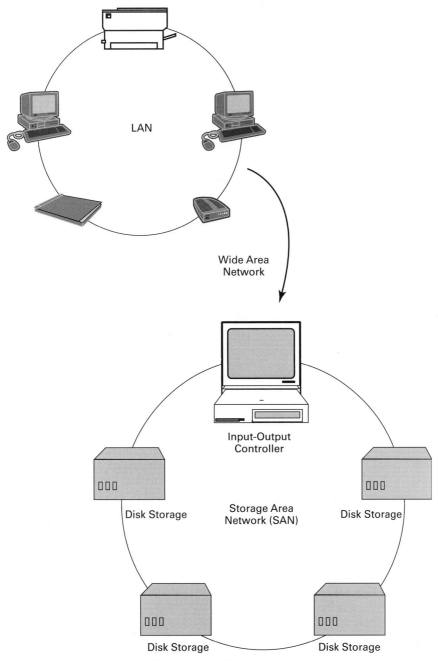

LAN

Wide Area
Network

Input-Output
Controller

Disk Storage

Storage Area
Network (SAN)

Disk Storage

Disk Storage

Disk Storage

FIGURE 5-8   Storage Area Network (SAN) Configuration

or terrorist attack), there are many other things to consider when trying to protect a company from a prolonged period of downtime.

DISASTER RECOVERY CONTROLS   Companies cannot afford to wait for a disaster to happen and then wonder what to do; they must be proactive, not reactive. Toward this end, companies must plan for disasters and periodically test their plans. IT function managers and IT auditors should adopt the attitude of "What are we going to do *when* disaster strikes?" not "What are we going to do *if* disaster strikes?" Think of contingency planning this way: It's a matter of time, not probability!

The first step is to plan for various disaster scenarios. For instance, what are we going to do if a) a single server is damaged, b) an entire company site is demolished, c) multiple company locations are simultaneously struck with disaster, or d) the entire company is destroyed? For each contingent scenario, IT managers and auditors should plan for what, who, when, where, how, which, and why.

After a disaster the company must decide which recovery scenario to evoke. Management must first determine *what* just happened. The plan for that particular scenario should specify *who* to contact, in what order, and what they are expected to do. It is important that everyone involved in the recovery fully understand their roles and responsibilities.

The next decision, *when* to enact the remainder of the contingency plan, now becomes critical. If the computer technicians tell management that they can have the system fully operational in, say, three days, management might decide to wait several hours to a day to see if the forecast holds. If management does wait, it might take as much time to switch the processing load to an alternate site as it would to wait for the technicians to get the system back in operation. Deciding the amount of wait time to see if the technicians are right in their estimate is subjective and potentially costly. If the technicians are wrong, the hold time is forever lost in the recovery cycle.

The next consideration is *where* to transfer the lost computer processing load. For companies with multiple geographically separated locations, it might be possible to shift the processing load to one or more alternate company locations. Naturally, an important consideration is how will the additional load affect business operations at the alternate site(s)? If the company does not have sufficient excess computing capacity, it can establish contractual relationships with peer companies in the same industry or with third-party providers of alternate computing sites.

The first option, using the computers of a peer company, is affordable, as some companies agree to help each other for free in the event a disaster strikes one of the partners. But remember, the healthy partner will likely process its business needs first, leaving the injured partner to wait for slack periods. Plus, it is important to ensure that both companies use the same or compatible operating systems or the software applications might not run. The second option, contracting with a third-party provider, has three general levels— cold site, warm site, and hot site. A *cold site* typically includes a building or office space that contains the basic infrastructure one would expect in an office environment (e.g., lights and climate control), but no computers, phones, or network access. If a cold site is used, the injured company must not only bring its own computing equipment, but must also establish the infrastructure, such as telephone service, Internet connections, specialized computer cooling systems (if needed), and unique power requirements. A *warm site* takes things to a higher level by providing the basic computing infrastructure but not the computers. Finally, a *hot site* is ready to go, complete with computers and (often) a compatible host operating system. As one would expect, recovery times become faster and costs become greater as one moves across the spectrum from cold site to hot site.

The next question to address is "*How* is the company going to get the computer hardware, people, software, and data to the alternate site?" These are logistical issues that might include planes, trains, boats, trucks, automobiles, and even bicycles! It is important to understand that the logistical aspect of a disaster recovery plan is critical, for without considering such matters the plan cannot be enacted.

Last, but not least, the planners of each scenario should establish priorities for the recovery, deciding *which* applications are mission critical and *why* one application or set of applications is more time sensitive than another. For instance, the company might decide that the most important mission-critical applications are the sales ordering, inventory, and purchasing applications. After those are up and running, the next most important set of applications is human resources and payroll. Finally, the third set of applications to recover is general ledger and accounts receivable. Deciding which applications take priority is vitally important to the sustainability of company operations throughout the disaster recovery period, so all potentially affected parties need to be involved in this key planning phase.

Some might think that once the plan is developed, it can be placed on a shelf to collect dust until disaster strikes—wrong! The disaster recovery plan is a living document that must be reviewed and updated on a recurrent basis, and everyone involved in the disaster recovery effort should be initially trained and then required to attend periodic refresher sessions. Additionally, various portions of the recovery plan should be tested without warning. If it can be done without significantly disrupting business operations, it might also be wise to simulate a disaster scenario and set the entire plan into motion. The key point is that people and the organization must continually prepare for unforeseen disasters.

IT auditors can play a key role in helping management to forge a comprehensive and effective disaster recovery plan. IT auditors should obtain an understanding of the disaster recovery plan, evaluate the preparedness of the organization for various scenarios, assess the efficacy of training and preparedness throughout the organization, and determine if the company has sufficiently mitigated business and audit risks associated with the continuity of business operations.

SUMMARY

Effective management of the IT function is a critical success factor in ensuring the economic viability of an organization, for the mismanagement thereof is laden with serious business and audit risks. Key business risks can be categorized as system risks (ensuring the availability, security, integrity, and maintainability of the computing infrastructure) and information risks (ensuring the effectiveness, efficiency, confidentiality, integrity, availability, compliance, and reliability of company information). The IT auditor needs to be satisfied that residual audit risk (inherent risk × control risk × detection risk) is low enough that there is no material misstatement in account assertions related to the IT function.

A theme running throughout this chapter is that IT auditors must evaluate whether the incompatible duties of authorizing transactions, recording transactions, and maintaining custody of assets are properly segregated throughout the IT function. The assets in question can be physical, such as personal computers, power supplies, and computing facilities, and logical, such as software applications, operating systems, and company information. While auditing an IT function might seem overwhelming at first glance, as there are multiple complex facets involved, IT auditors can organize their work by examining the way in which IT management organizes, finances, staffs, directs, and controls the IT function. Using this auditing framework, critical business and audit risks can be evaluated, tested, and controlled in a methodical manner.

DISCUSSION QUESTIONS

5-1 Discuss the business and audit risks of having the IT function improperly located in the company's organizational structure.

5-2 What are some considerations regarding the organizational level at which the IT manager is placed?

5-3 What is the profit center approach to funding IT operations? Discuss the advantages and disadvantages.

5-4 Discuss controls to prevent damage to hardware and software by a terminated employee.

5-5 Discuss what the IT auditor should understand and document regarding the workload administration of the IT department.

5-6 What is a computing infrastructure? What should the IT auditor be looking for with respect to the computing infrastructure?

5-7 What business risks are involved with third-party service providers who support the IT function? What must the IT manager do to minimize these risks?

5-8 What is meant by the term "concurrency control"?

5-9 Explain the concepts of RAID, NAS, and SAN.

5-10 Discuss the considerations of a disaster recovery plan.

EXERCISES

5-11 The Grand Company averages around 200 employees each pay period. It has departments for manufacturing, administration, sales, marketing, customer service, and information systems. Currently the company issues a payroll semimonthly. The company has full-time, part-time, salaried, and hourly employees. Sales people earn commissions based on total sales and bonuses based on meeting budgeted sales goals. For payroll calculations, the company uses 2,030 hours as the number of work hours each year.

The payroll is administered by two full-time employees who earn $30,000 per year plus benefits that average 15 percent of their salary. All employees typically receive a 3 percent increase in pay on January 1 each year.

The payroll software needs updating. The legacy system has the following problems:

- It does not interface with the Human Resources system, so all new hires and employee changes must be entered twice, once into the Human Resources system and once into the payroll system.

- The PR software does not prorate, so all changes must be made at the beginning of a payroll period or manually calculated.

- There is no audit trail of changes from one payroll to the next. A change made in error could go undetected unless the employee notifies the company.

- Tax table changes require an upgrade from a software company, which charges $1,500 each time. The new tax laws indicate there will be changes twice a year for the next five years. The vendor is expected to increase the upgrade fees by 5 percent each year.

- Employees have difficulty understanding their pay stubs. The payroll administrators receive an average of ten inquiries per payroll, mostly from bonus and commission calculations.

- The number of paychecks with errors averages four per payroll.

- Issuing W-2s at the end of the year is always a nightmare. They are never finished until the deadline day, since the payroll administrators are so busy with their regular duties. This overtime activity requires ten total hours, paid at time and one-half.

- Filing federal and state reports and reconciling them to the payroll requires ten hours of overtime (total) per quarter.

- The IT department has one person dedicated to the administrative staff, and about 20 percent of this person's time is devoted to payroll and Human Resources issues. Response to nonemergency requests often takes four weeks. The IT person responsible for payroll-related issues earns $40,000 per year.

The IT department is recommending that the company outsource the payroll function. The Payroll Company claims:

- The Human Resources system would interface with the Payroll system. New hire information and changes would automatically be updated into the Payroll system and salary changes will begin on the effective date.

- The cost would be $1 per paycheck issued, plus $50 per payroll. These fees are expected to increase by 5 percent each year after the first payroll year.

- There would be a one-time setup fee of $2,000.

- The setup would include a commission and bonus calculator. A special report would be generated to show each sales person's calculation and a company summary.

- The timesheets for each department would be online every day for managers to review. A secure report would be issued to them with the payroll, with an electronic signature required for approval.

- The payroll administrator would receive an audit trail report with all changes since the last payroll. This would be issued in time for a final review before the payroll is issued.

- The design of the payroll stub or advice can be customized. The design can include nonpayroll information, such as the number of vacation days available or upcoming company events.

- Direct deposit would be available.

- Tax returns, including W-2s, would be generated after the last payroll of the tax period.

- A free training session would be provided.

- Customer service support would be available at all times, and employee questions are guaranteed to be answered within forty-eight hours.

- Upgrades and tax table changes would be seamless and invisible. The payroll department would be notified when the changes would take place and what changes and features would be included.

In addition to the advantages offered by the Payroll Company, the IS department feels that only one employee will be needed to administer the payroll function, eliminating one full-time position. The IS person dedicated to payroll will be able to devote all of her time to other projects.

Required:

Using the information provided, create a project scorecard for this IS proposal (see the IS Project Scorecard Template that follows). Include goals for each perspective, and show how each goal can be measured. For the Organizational Contribution perspective, detail the net present value cash flow over the next five years for two scenarios: 1) remaining with the current in-house method of administering payroll and 2) outsourcing payroll. Then calculate the net present value gain or loss assuming the company was to outsource payroll. Further assume that the Grand Company will continue to calculate payroll as usual for the remainder of the current year, but that if it decides to outsource payroll, it will do so starting with January 1 of the upcoming year.

IS Project Scorecard Template

REFERENCES AND RECOMMENDED READINGS

Ahituv, N., and S. Neumann. 1990. *Principles of Information Systems for Management*. Dubuque, Iowa: Wm. C. Brown Publishers.

Brown, C. 1999. *IT Management Handbook*. Boca Raton, Fla.: CRC Press-Auerbach Publications.

Doughty, K. 2002. Business Continuity: A Business Survival Strategy. *The Information Systems Control Journal* 1: 28–36.

Gerber, J. A., and Feldman, E. R. 2002. "Is Your Business Prepared for the Worst?" *Journal of Accountancy* 193 (4): 61–64.

Haag, S., M. Cummings, and J. Dawkins. 2000. *Management Information Systems for the Information Age*. New York: Irwin McGraw-Hill.

Hunton, J. E. 2002. "Back Up Your Data to Survive a Disaster." *Journal of Accountancy* 193 (4): 65–69.

IT Governance Institute. 2000. *COBIT Management Guidelines* (3rd Edition). Rolling Meadows, Ill.: Information Systems Audit and Control Foundation.

Krause, M., and H. Tipton. 1999. *Information Security Management Handbook*. Boca Raton, Fla.: CRC Press-Auerbach Publications.

Laudon, K., and J. Price Laudon. 1999. *Management Information Systems: Organizations and Technology in the Networked Enterprise*. New York: Prentice Hall.

McFadden, F. R., J. A. Hoffer, and M. B. Prescott. 1999. *Modern Database Management* (5th Edition). Reading, Mass.: Addison-Wesley Educational Publishers.

Musaji, Y. F. 2002. "Disaster Recovery and Business Continuity Planning: Testing an Organization's Plans." *The Information Systems Control Journal* 1: 49–55.

Simons, R. 2000. *Performance Measurement & Control Systems for Implementing Strategy*. Upper Saddle River, N.J.: Prentice Hall.

NOTES

1. See SysTrust principles and criteria at www.aicpa.org.
2. See CobiT information criteria at www.isaca.org.
3. See AU Section 312.20a, 312.20b and 312.20c.
4. While many titles describe the person responsible for corporate accounting matters, in this chapter we use the term "corporate controller."
5. See the OSHA Web site for more information on workplace safety, www.osha.gov.

CHAPTER 6

IT NETWORKS AND TELECOMMUNICATIONS RISKS

CHAPTER CONTENTS

INTRODUCTION

Attacks against computers and networks have escalated steadily in number and sophistication, to the point where many security experts believe the situation is beyond "out of control."[1]

A stand-alone computer has a limited amount of risk associated with it. Legacy computer systems, often mainframe computers kept in a secure computer room with no remote dial-in access, were fairly easy to protect. Today's distributed systems are quite another matter. Risk increases exponentially as computers are connected to form networks with multiple access points. Imagine a multinational corporation with a variety of networks—including wireless ones—Internet connections, and employee remote network access, and you have a prescription for a major IT auditor headache.

To find the cure, IT auditors first need to know about different kinds of networks. This chapter provides a brief overview of the technologies associated with networks and telecommunications. Next IT auditors must understand the specific risks that threaten an organization's networked telecommunications systems. These threats include attacks via social engineering, compromising a network's physical infrastructure, programmed threats, denial of service attacks, and holes in application and security software.

Finally, since "grinding down" an entity's network can bring business to a halt, IT auditors need to know about the security tools and controls available to protect telecommunications systems against most risks. These include security administration, authentication tools, encryption, firewalls, intrusion detection systems, and penetration testing. They must also know how to audit an organization's network security program.

NETWORK AND TELECOMMUNICATIONS TECHNOLOGIES

A network consists of two or more linked computers. Telecommunications is the transfer of text, audio, video, image, or other data formats across a computer network. Understanding the risks and controls associated with networks and telecommunications systems requires knowledge of their technologies. This section provides a brief overview of this topic.

Network Components

A computer network has several components. In its most basic form, a network consists of multiple computers, a communication link, and users. More complex networks may have thousands of different types of computers, multiple types of communication channels, processors, and switching devices.

COMPUTERS AND TERMINALS Computers process the data in a networked telecommunication system. The networked computers send and receive data to and from terminals, which are input/output devices. A terminal may be dumb or smart. A dumb terminal is an input/output device that can send and/or receive data but has no processing capability. A smart terminal can perform some processing of the data it sends or receives to or from a host computer.

TELECOMMUNICATIONS CHANNELS Data are transmitted from computer to computer via telecommunications channels. These channels use various media, both physical and wireless. Twisted-pair wire, the medium used by telephone systems to transmit voice and data communications, consists of multiple entwined copper wires. There are several standards that specify categories of twisted-pair cabling systems. The categories refer to the speed of the data transmissions. Category 5 (CAT5), for example, is a type of unshielded twisted-pair cable that can handle data transmitted in gigabit Ethernet (common LAN technology) systems. Coaxial network cable, like that which delivers cable television channels, is aluminum or copper wire cable covered by insulation. Fiber optic cables use fine glass strands instead of metal wire to transmit data in the form of light pulses.

Wireless transmissions use microwaves, infrared light, or light pulses to transmit data without using a physical connector. Microwave systems transmit high-frequency radio signals in a straight line. Since they don't curve along the earth, these systems can send messages only short distances without the use of satellites. The protocol, or standard, for wireless technology is wireless application protocol (WAP). This standard allows a variety of devices such as personal digital assistants and cell phones to transmit and receive Web pages.

Wireless networks are increasingly popular, but they have special security issues. Figure 6-1 lists some of the risk indicators for wireless networks. IT auditors need to be particularly watchful for "rogue" wireless networks. Since wireless networks are easy to set up, employees in a large organization might create one without considering the ramifications. For example, a small wireless network that connects to a company's intranet may present a target for *war drivers*. These are hackers who drive around the parking lot of a company's headquarters, looking for wireless network access points, as described in Case-in-Point 6-1.

Case-in-Point 6-1

In October 2002, a number of technology specialists banded together to conduct a global war drive aimed at exposing vulnerable wireless access points. Computer security experts are hoping that the publicity will encourage companies with exposures to purchase security like KPMG's "honeypot." This is a tool that lets network proprietors know when they are being accessed by unauthorized users. Like many hacker efforts, war driving requires little expertise. War drivers can download software such as *NetStumbler* free from the Internet and create an antenna out of a coffee can.[2]

Telecommunications channels vary in terms of speed and capacity. Bandwidth measures the frequency range in a communications channel, and its size determines the maximum rate of transmission. The baud rate measures speed and capacity, typically in terms of bits per second (BPS). Narrow-band channels provide lower speeds, while broadband channels can provide transmission rates of up to several billion BPS.

TELECOMMUNICATIONS PROCESSORS   The most common telecommunication processor is a modem, which is short for modulation/demodulation. A modem transforms

---

Users are not authenticated.
There is no encryption of wireless transmissions.
Some or all wireless LAN security functions are not turned on.
There are weaknesses in the security, such as in wired equivalent privacy (WEP).
The wireless networks are not segregated from the rest of the network.
"Rogue" wireless networks exist.
Communications are vulnerable to interception of transmissions.

FIGURE 6-1   Risk Indicators for Wireless Networks

digital computer signals into analog signals that can travel over telephone lines, and then another modem converts the signals back to digital on the other end. Modems attach to telephone lines and use those lines to transmit data from computer to computer. Modem connection speeds are limited by phone line conditions. Alternatives to traditional telephone lines are integrated services digital network (ISDN) lines, digital subscriber lines (DSL), and cable modems. Both ISDN and DSL use regular telephone lines but allow for high-speed data and voice message transmission. There is an extra charge for both ISDN and DSL, but the higher speeds are often worth the cost. DSL lines are often of the type that are "always on," so users do not need to wait for a connection to be made. The always-on feature is terrific for users but does present an extra security risk, since hackers can connect only to systems that are operational. Cable modems use television cable lines to handle data signals between the cable TV operator and either the television receiver or a personal computer. Cable modems are increasingly popular. T1 and T3 lines also offer high-speed connections. These lines are too costly for individuals and small businesses, but large corporations use them because they can span large distances. T lines carry digital data over a set of wires that may be twisted-pair, coaxial cable, or other media.

The primary difference among alternative modem connections is the data transmission speed. A common telephone line transmits data at perhaps 56 kilobytes per second (Kbps), a DSL line might be as fast as 7 million bytes per second (Mbps), and a T3 line can transmit data at over 40 Mbps.

An increase in digital communications networks reduces the reliance on modems for this function. Multiplexers are communications processors that allow a single communications channel to transmit data simultaneously from multiple terminals. This means that many users can use the same channel at once. There are a variety of methods to allow this sharing. For example, each data channel may be allotted specific times during which it can transmit data, regardless of whether it has data to send at that time.

ROUTERS AND SWITCHING DEVICES   Switches connect network components and ensure that messages are delivered to their appropriate destinations. They work similarly to an old-fashioned phone switchboard. Routers are similar to switches, but they include more intelligent features based on rule sets or protocols.

There are several approaches to switching. In a message switching approach, a complete message is routed to its destination point. With packet switching, a message is broken up into multiple packets or transmittal units. The use of packets maximizes transmission volumes. Yet another approach is circuit switching, which creates a physical communications channel between a specific message sender and recipient, as is the case with phone calls made over telephone lines.

Types of Networks

There are various ways to categorize telecommunications network types. In terms of distance, there are two types. A local area network (LAN) is just as the name implies, a group of connected computers within a short distance of one another. Typically, a LAN is a network within one building or multiple buildings that are geographically close. A wide area network (WAN) connects computers some geographic distance away from one another, perhaps in different countries. A network may consist of one or more LAN systems combined with a WAN.

Another way to classify networks is in terms of their ownership. An intranet is an internal network, perhaps within a company. Extranets are external networks that connect an organization's intranet with outside business partners, such as suppliers. The Internet is, of course, an international network of public and private computers. A virtual private network (VPN) is only "virtually private" because it uses the public Internet as its primary network system to connect remote systems. Therefore, with a VPN, the Internet provides the long-distance connection. Users don't notice the difference from a private point-to-point line. The VPN achieves privacy through encryption and authentication procedures (discussed later in this chapter).

One more type of network is a client/server network. These networks consist of network servers that manage the networks and host applications that they share with client computers. Clients may be characterized as thin or fat, which refers to the strength of the computer's processing capability. Many business and public organizations have traded their legacy centralized mainframe computer systems for client/server networks to obtain greater computing flexibility. A client/server network may be two-tiered or three-tiered. A two-tiered client/server network has two main components: the client, which runs programs, and a database server. The three-tiered client/server architecture includes a thin client, which does little processing, application servers, and database servers.

Figure 6-2 shows the three main types of topologies or network configurations. The star-shaped network is a centralized topology in which computer terminals are each separately connected to a server. In the ring and bus topologies, workstations or clients are connected to one another and also to the server. The ring network provides this connection by connecting each terminal first to a ring network, which links to the server. In the bus structure, the terminals share the same telecommunications channel. Ring and bus networks are most common in LAN systems, although client/server systems may use any of these topologies or a combination of them.

Protocols and Software

Protocols are standardized rule sets that control network communications among hardware and software from different vendors. Computers are said to engage in a handshake (discussed later) when they exchange signals to begin a communications session with each other. These handshakes require protocols so that the sender and receiver speak the same language.

There are several kinds of network standards and protocols. (We've already mentioned WAP, the protocol that allows wireless communications.) The open systems interconnect (OSI) model is a standard architecture for networking with specified protocols that allow different computers to communicate across networks. The OSI model has seven layers, described in Figure 6-3. When one computer in a network sends a message to another computer, the message travels down through the layers in the sending computer (Computer A) and up through the layers in the receiving computer (Computer B). Each layer in Computer A corresponds to the same layer in Computer B. This means that although the data is transmitted vertically (i.e., down and up), layers are programmed as if the transmission were horizontal. For example, when the transport layer in Computer A gets a message from the session layer, it attaches a transport layer header and sends it to Computer B's transport layer. While it isn't really sending it there directly (remember, it's going down layers and up layers), as far as the transport layer knows, it's communicating directly with the transport layer of the other computer. As the message travels down computer A, it picks up a header at each layer and a trailer at the data link layer. As the message goes from the physical layer of Computer A to Computer B and starts ascending, each layer of Computer B begins stripping off the header from Computer A's corresponding layer.

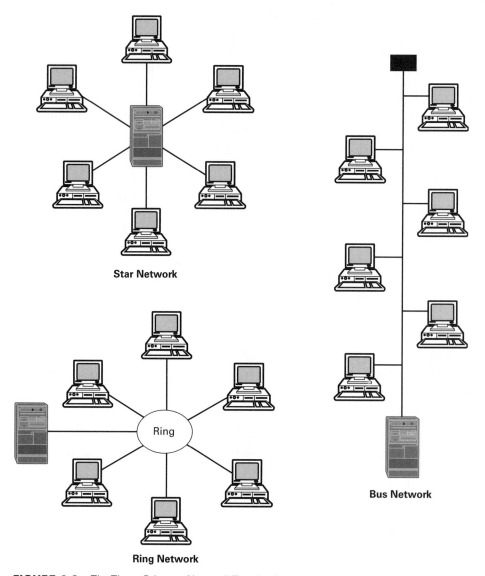

FIGURE 6-2 The Three Primary Network Topologies

The importance of the OSI model to the IT auditor is that many computer attacks involve manipulation of one or more layers in the model. Chapter 7 will discuss this further in the context of TCP/IP, a popular Internet protocol.

Network and telecommunications software includes network operating system software, network management software, middleware, Web browsers, and e-mail software. Network management software manages the server's performance and the communications across the network. It may prioritize communications, record network statistics, manage transmission request queues, detect transmission errors, and provide some security functionality. Middleware may be necessary to facilitate communications from one network to another. Web browsers are a type of telecommunications software that provides a software interface with the Internet. E-mail software allows the exchange of messages in a variety of format across intranets, extranets, and the Internet.

Application	Application layer—converts messages into the format needed by an application, such as a network manager or e-mail application software and identifies communicating computers.
Presentation	Presentation layer—provides the appropriate format and codes for data being transmitted.
Session	Session layer—maintains communication channels to support telecommunication sessions between the applications on different computers.
Transport	Transport layer—performs data reliability and error checks to ensure complete transfer of data between network nodes.
Network	Network layer—provides data routing and delivery.
Data Link	Data link layer—ensures that data is transmitted to the physical layer.
Physical	Physical layer—the physical transmission of data bit streams on the network hardware.

FIGURE 6-3   The Open Systems Interconnect (OSI) Model

RISKS TO IT NETWORK AND TELECOMMUNICATIONS SYSTEMS

Networked computer systems seem to be an irresistible target for intruders. Threats to network security include social engineering, physical infrastructure threats, programmed threats such as viruses and worms, denial of service attacks, and holes in application and security software. We will discuss each type of network security threat separately.

Networks can be attacked by either humans or software. People who attack networked computer systems are frequently referred to as *hackers,* although the term originally referred to an individual who was preoccupied with computers rather than someone who used computers to obtain unauthorized access to information. *Crackers* are hackers who act with malicious intent. A *phreaker* is someone who specializes in computer fraud related to the phone system, such as trading in illegal telephone access codes. A *script kiddie* is someone who uses widely available hacking tools, including preprogrammed code, to break into systems, usually just for the thrill of it. Case-in-Point 6-2 describes some of the activities of one of the world's most famous hackers.

Case-in-Point 6-2

Kevin Mitnick has been described as a cyberpunk who is "dangerous when armed with a keyboard." While quite skilled with computers, Mr. Mitnick also has another skill that is just as important to a computer attacker—social engineering. Some of his network attacks involved him posing as a company employee and talking others into giving him passwords and user information that allowed him to bypass computer security measures.

> Mr. Mitnick is accused of breaking into the North American Air Defense Command computer system, several telephone company offices and phone switching centers, MCI Communications, Digital Equipment Corporation, and Tsutomu Shimomura. The Shimomura attack used flooding and hijacking techniques to create a denial of service attack. Mr. Mitnick served five years in a federal prison on numerous felony convictions. The terms of his parole were unique: he was not allowed to use a computer for three years.

Chapter 10 of this book covers IT fraud in some detail. Case-in-Point 6-2 serves to illustrate some of the vulnerabilities faced by IT telecommunication and network systems.

Social Engineering

Many people credit computer criminals with extraordinarily high technology skill levels. The reality is that most computer frauds or hacking incidents require only a relatively low level of computer adeptness and knowledge, but a high level of acting and persuasion skills, accompanied by persistence. Social engineers use their personalities and social skills to obtain confidential information or unauthorized access by persuading insiders to provide them with assistance. Social engineering or "soc(h)-ing" is a form of manipulation and trickery that relies on behaviors such as fear of getting into trouble or an inclination to help someone. There are several points of particular vulnerability with respect to social engineering. These include security administrators, technical support personnel, security guards, and administrative assistants who either work at physical (e.g., computer room entrance) or logical access points (e.g., assign passwords) or have access to high amounts of private/confidential information.

Social engineering typically begins with the perpetrator learning something about the target organization. For instance, an attacker might start off by learning the name and phone number of a high-level IT staff member. One type of social engineering is the "stranded remote user" attack. The perpetrator pretends to be an IT employee who is out of town on company business and needs to access some files quickly. The help desk can provide information that will allow remote access and can even reset a password. Relatively new or untrained IT staff can be vulnerable to social engineering ploys such as pulling rank. For instance, when a help desk employee receives a call from someone who identifies herself as an upper level manager, the staff member may compromise security in order to be helpful. Someone posing as a high-ranking company officer may at first cajole and ultimately threaten the staff member in order to get the information. Fearing for his job, the lower-level IT staff member may feel he must comply with a request even when he is not sure he should.

While we typically think in terms of person-to-person interactions in social engineering, it does take other forms as well. For example, the Love Bug e-mail virus relied on humans' inclination to believe that someone was sending them a romantic message. Another impersonal way the computer may be used in social engineering is through pop-up windows that ask for passwords.

Figure 6-4 lists control measures that can be used against social engineering. The most important control is awareness. Knowing that social engineering is frequently used by IT network and telecommunications systems hackers is one way to guard against being duped. Authentication can also be important. Network security administrators should train users to ask for one more proof of identity if they are in doubt about imparting information to someone.

Create and monitor a strict authentication policy for use by technical support personnel.
Control public availability of information about employees and their contact information.
Strictly monitor remote access.
Create strict firewall rules regarding outbound traffic.
Train employees in social engineering tactics.
Limit the amount of private/confidential information available to any one employee.
Remind employees to be skeptical in opening unexpected e-mail attachments.
Use penetration to evaluate the effectiveness of other social engineering controls.

FIGURE 6-4 Social Engineering Controls

Physical Infrastructure Threats

Network and telecommunications systems are threatened by many of the same physical infrastructure threats as any other computer system. Chapter 5 discussed several of these, focusing on access controls and backup and contingency plans. However, because these systems involve multiple computers and other equipment, sometimes located across wide geographical areas, they generally have some additional vulnerabilities.

To assess infrastructure threats, the IT auditor must first study the network diagrams. These diagrams show a network's components, including computers, routers, and switching devices, processors, and communications channels. The auditor should consider the appropriateness of the links among these network components and the particular vulnerabilities of the network to threats such as the elements, natural disaster, power supply interruptions, and intentional human attacks through bombs or other means.

THE ELEMENTS   Fire, air, and water all pose threats to network and telecommunications systems infrastructures. To guard against danger from these elements, the IT auditor should make a note of the proximity of network components to dangerous areas. Perhaps this means making sure that computers aren't located close to areas that may face a higher risk of fire, such as restaurants. To protect against water damage, network hardware components should never be housed in a facility built on or near a flood plain, or in a place where water pipes may leak. Air is a threat primarily with respect to temperature. Network equipment generally needs to be kept cool.

Fires are often devastating, and the water that is normally used to suppress them can be as damaging to network hardware components as the flames themselves. Equipment can be protected from fire with smoke detection devices, fire extinguishers, and the use of nonflammable materials in construction. Since water suppression is undesirable, other methods are necessary for putting out a fire in the vicinity. Businesses used to protect their computer rooms with halon systems that release a gas that extinguishes the fire by pulling all the oxygen from the air. Halon systems are now illegal because of the harmful effects of the gas on the environment. Fire suppression systems with carbon dioxide act similarly to halon systems. The problem with these systems is that humans can't breathe in a CO_2 environment. As a result, there are laws controlling its use.

NATURAL DISASTERS   Natural disasters that threaten network and telecommunications system's physical infrastructures include floods, earthquakes, tornadoes, hurricanes, and solar activity such as flares and sunspots. In many instances there is little to be done in terms of protecting against these events. Common sense dictates avoiding locating networks in high-risk areas when possible. If continuous network functionality is particularly important, the network components should be located in as safe an area as practical. For multinational organizations, this could mean avoiding certain geographical areas. The IT auditor's main role here is to inspect insurance policies to ensure that an organization carries appropriate protection against natural disasters, as well as ensuring that the backup and contingency plans discussed in Chapter 5 are in place.

POWER SUPPLY   Severe thunderstorms and other weather conditions or solar activity can create electrical surges that may interrupt network and telecommunications operations. An uninterruptible power supply (UPS) system protects against power spikes by ensuring a constant electrical current. Since electrical power lines may be exposed to various environmental threats, redundant lines may be desirable. Backup power supplies, such as those used at hospitals, are also desirable.

INTENTIONAL HUMAN ATTACKS   The activities of September 11, 2001, reminded us all too well of the threats posed to human life and to computer systems by terrorist attacks. In the wake of September 11, many organizations were able to resume their network and telecommunications operations quickly because they had detailed, tested contingency plans. Another source of human attack, however, may not be taken as seriously. This is the threat of attack by company insiders—most notably disgruntled employees. These vulnerabilities can be guarded against by physical and logical access controls, accompanied by some other controls, such as checking references and monitoring morale. The IT auditor should ensure that an organization has well-documented policies regarding actions to take when an employee is terminated (see Chapter 5).

Programmed Threats

Programmed threats include viruses, worms, Trojan horses, hoaxes, and blended threats—a combination of some or all of these. This classification of security threats gets its name because the attack consists of malicious *program* code developed by hackers or crackers. These threats are on the rise as tools such as virus construction kits become easily available over the Internet. And the costs are high. It's estimated that four large programmed threat epidemics during the past few years have cost $13 billion worldwide in lost productivity and cleanup costs.[3]

A *virus* is a set of program code designed to copy itself from one file to another, just as a human virus might spread from person to person. Viruses *infect* computer systems via the host file, which could be a program or data file. Viruses may be benign, annoying, or destructive. A benign virus spreads without doing harm. These are rare, as most perpetrators of programmed threats want something to show for their efforts. An example of an annoying virus is one that copies your e-mail address book and sends out unwanted e-mail. Destructive viruses destroy data and programs on computer systems. Viruses are transmitted by sharing data, either through exchange of disks or via e-mail systems. E-mail systems spread viruses through attachments and file downloads.

Worms are similar to viruses except that they copy themselves from computer to computer rather than from one file to another. They reproduce over network systems, and they can do it rapidly, sometimes contaminating multiple network servers in just a few minutes. Like viruses, they may or may not be malicious. Worms may be activated by time (e.g., hour or date) or by a specific action such as opening a computer program. Since worms are computer-based versus file-based, the main threat they pose is overloading network resources. The Code Red worm is an example. This particular threat replicated itself on servers and at the same time tampered with Web sites. An interesting, but frightening, feature of the Code Red worm is that computers continued to be infected long after a security patch or fix became available.

Trojan horses are "surprises" embedded in seemingly harmless programs or messages. For example, you may receive an e-mail from a friend with a cartoon attached. Opening the cartoon may activate a worm that modifies your computer in some way. Like other programmed threats, a Trojan horse may erase files on a hard drive each time the computer user enters a certain keystroke pattern.

A *hoax* is an e-mail message that instructs a user to delete certain files as a security precaution against viruses or other programmed threats. It plays upon the fear of virus attacks. Users who are concerned that their computer may be infected might follow the suggestions in the false alert and erase valuable files.

Blended threats are combinations of multiple programmed threats. These can be particularly harmful and difficult to eradicate because of their complexity. In 2002, the Klez worm demonstrated the persistency and longevity of these types of attacks. The Klez worm spread in the same fashion as a virus, but it occasionally acted as a worm, Trojan horse, and a hoax, as described in Case-in-Point 6-3.

Case-in-Point 6-3

The Klez worm has a variety of permutations. The W32/Klez-H spreads itself using an antivirus software vendor's name as its e-mail address. This particular variation can drop itself into the Windows system directory, using a random filename. Infected e-mail could have "Hi," "Re:," or another authentic-seeming message in the subject line. The worm randomly includes a message text, including one that describes the Klez worm as dangerous and offers a free immunity tool to delete it. This message is, of course, a hoax. Since the worm spreads through e-mail and it attaches itself to a randomly chosen file, it may disclose confidential data. Another harmful effect of this Klez variation is that it tries to disable antivirus software. Finally, unlike many other programmed threats, a user can contract W32/Klez-H by simply reading an e-mail, as no attachment download is necessary.[4]

There are many software programs available to help protect users from programmed threats. Antivirus software should be obtained through a subscription service so that it is constantly updated for new viruses. The software should also provide continuous scans of system resources for virus signatures. The security provided by antivirus or worm protection depends largely on human behavior. The network security administrator (described later in the chapter) must consistently scan alerts and apply software patches or fixes in order to be proactive against new threats. In addition, users should be instructed to be cautious in opening suspect e-mail and wary of attachments to e-mail from unknown sources, especially when the attachment contains .exe or .vbs files. The creators of programmed threats often play on human weaknesses, as in the case of the "ILoveYou" virus. By putting such a "teaser" in the subject line of an e-mail message, the virus perpetrator hopes to spread the virus quickly. The security administrator should also caution users against downloading freeware or shareware, which might also contain programmed threats. Finally, security administration should have a plan of action, called an Incident Response Plan, to implement in case a programmed threat outbreak occurs in the network and telecommunications system.

Denial of Service Attacks

A denial of service (DOS) attack occurs when a system is tied up in such a way that it is unable to perform its functions. The perpetrator of a denial of service attack is behaving maliciously but with no hope to gain anything other than embarrassment and financial loss for the target site. And these attacks have done just that to the largest online companies, including eBay, Amazon, Yahoo, and even Microsoft. A widespread attack in 2000 resulted in losses of more than $1 billion for the target companies.

Distributed denial of service (DDOS) attacks occur when a host computer is bombarded with messages from a variety of sources. The source messages may come through innocent computers that have been hijacked through a Trojan horse program, or a hole in the system software. In a Trojan horse attack, the DDOS perpetrators have been able to infect innocent computers with a virus that, when activated, sends a request for data to the target DDOS site. In this three-way handshake (see Figure 6-5), Computer A sends a synchronous (SYN) packet to Computer B. Computer B accepts the packet and acknowledges it with a synchronous/acknowledgement (SYN/ACK). Computer A then returns an acknowledgement of Computer B's SYN/ACK and establishes a connection. A SYN flood is a type of denial of service attack that involves sending multiple messages from Computer A to Computer B, and then leaving the connection open. The target computer then is tied up trying to make continuous ACK connections, all the while receiving a barrage of other messages. This is called a SYN flood, because the target has been flooded with SYN messages.

DOS attacks may involve using the maximum number of network connections so that no new users can obtain access, overloading primary memory, and infecting file systems with unnecessary or incorrect data. To prevent these attacks, auditors can recommend many of the tools and techniques described in the latter section of this chapter, including firewalls, intrusion detection systems, and penetration testing. A few specialized techniques will also control for this risk. One technique involves rate limits that allow transmission of only a limited number of message packets that meet specified criteria. Reverse address look-ups may also help. These entail checking the Internet protocol (IP) address and domain name to ensure the source of a message packet (much as your local pizza delivery service verifies you by phone number before sending a pizza to your home). Yet another control is to establish network connection time-outs that drop inactive connections after a specified period.

Software Vulnerabilities

Many programmed threats and DDOS are enabled by "holes," or weak spots, in application (e.g., sendmail) and operating system (e.g., Unix) software. These holes are frequently programming errors, but they may have been intentionally created to allow programmers quick access for debugging software. Other holes come from errors in configuring software. Two examples of mistakes are keeping unused services open and incorrectly assigning permissions. Case-in-Point 6-4 describes a software vulnerability.

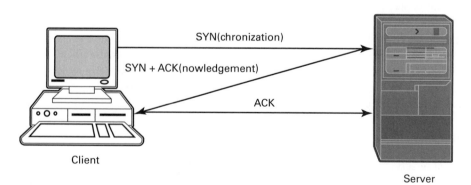

FIGURE 6-5 A Three-Way Computer System Handshake

Case-in-Point 6-4

In 2002, security researchers found a vulnerability in Pretty Good Privacy (PGP) 7.1.1, an e-mail encryption program, that provided hackers with the ability to launch an attack from a remote site. The vulnerability is that this version of PGP didn't check the length of a filename when handling encrypted files. This causes the software to crash if a user chooses a filename that is too long. Hackers can exploit the vulnerability in a number of ways, launching attacks by executing malicious code or retrieving confidential access codes. In the PGP case, the software company quickly issued a patch for the defect.[5]

Hackers can discover security holes by visiting computer security Web sites and noting vulnerabilities.[6] The discovery of such a hole typically is followed quickly by issuance of a patch to plug it. Once again, security boils down to people. Alert security administrators who pay attention to security warnings and install patches and virus updates in a timely fashion can avert attacks from most sources. IT auditors can check a network system for application holes as part of a penetration test (discussed later in the chapter). This begins with identifying the applications running on the network, checking the Internet or other information sources for a list of vulnerabilities associated with that software, and, finally, checking to see if patches have been applied.

IT NETWORK AND TELECOMMUNICATIONS SECURITY

Many security tools are available for preventing or detecting threats to networked systems. We have discussed some of these relative to specific threats. In this section we describe many of the general tools that, taken together, represent a network security defense system. Figure 6-6 presents this defense system as a schema for IT network and telecommunication security. The next sections of this chapter describe each of the components of this security schema in some detail.

Network Security Administration

The network manager is responsible for day-to-day operation of the network. Network security administration is a separate function. The network security administrator reports to the security administration function of an organization.

The network security administrator is responsible for creating a network security plan, developing and communicating a security policy for network resources, and password management. CERT (originally named Computer Emergency Response Team) recommends a set of steps that network security administrators and managers might follow to ensure a comprehensive security plan. These include:

1. Identifying the purpose of each computer on the network;
2. Identifying the service the network will provide to users;
3. Identifying network software, including operating systems, applications, network management software, and network security software;
4. Identifying categories of users and setting user privileges (see the user authorization matrix in Figure 5-4);
5. Planning user and workstation authentication;
6. Determining security procedures over access to network resources;
7. Developing methods of intrusion detection;
8. Documenting backup and contingency plans;

Network Security Administration

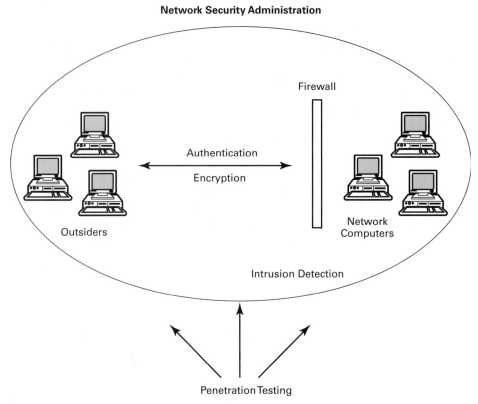

FIGURE 6-6 A Schema for IS Telecommunication and Network Security

9. Determining how to maintain availability of network services;
10. Developing and following plans for acquiring and maintaining systems software;
11. Determining how to connect computers to the network;
12. Identifying day-to-day security concerns by scanning alerts, applying software patches, and monitoring logs and incident reports; and
13. Protecting hardware removed from service.[7]

Network security policies should be developed in conjunction with management and users. These policies describe the responsibilities of each party associated with the network, as well as their privileges regarding network resources. For example, the network security policy should describe whether or not users may install software on their workstations, the organization's policy with regard to sending and receiving e-mail, and virus protection rules (e.g., users should not open e-mail attachments from unknown sources and should update their virus protection weekly).

One of the most important tasks of the network security administrator is managing user identifications and passwords. Internal threats to network security from employees and business partners may pose more risk than threats from external hackers. Managing user access includes making sure that passwords are kept in encrypted files and are highly protected. It also entails removing user identifications and passwords from inside users who are no longer employed. In addition, it includes ensuring that default passwords shipped with vendor hardware and software are changed. One of the easiest ways for an intruder to gain access to internal network systems is by trying these default passwords, which often have maximum user privileges (e.g., SYSADMIN, perhaps the default password for the system administrator).

Authentication

One of the most challenging tasks for network security administrators is making sure of the identity of network resource users. The process of ensuring that users are who they say they are is called authentication.

Users can generally be verified in one of three ways. These are frequently referred to as 1) what you have, 2) what you know, and 3) who you are. *What you have* may be a key or a smart card that allows you physical access, such as to the room where network servers are kept. Since physical authentication can be exchanged, this form of authentication alone does not provide a very high level of user verification.

What you know is a password, the most commonly used type of authentication. Passwords for network access work well when they are carefully constructed (see Figure 6-6) and also when security administrators employ a system that will deny access after a few unsuccessful attempts. When combined with what you have, what you know can provide a fairly high level of authentication. Automated teller machines use this combination, called two-factor authentication, because it requires two types of proof of identity—you need your bank card and your personal identification number (PIN) to withdraw cash. Variations on this combination increase security further. One-time access codes and passwords that change after each use are more secure than those that change relatively infrequently. Security tokens or smart cards with changing access codes can combine with passwords to provide reliable proof of identify. Since the access code changes frequently via a signal bounced off a satellite, no one who observes the access code will be able to use it at a time other than the instant they obtain it. Global positioning satellites can also verify where the person using the access code is located. Token-based log-on systems that plug into a remote user's computer to provide access to company networks are increasing in popularity.

The most sophisticated form of authentication is *who you are*. You can provide who you are only through biometrics, which are measurements of your own biology such as your fingerprint, voice, or retina. While movies like *Entrapment* feature characters bypassing these types of authentication systems, the systems afford a very high level of assurance that access is appropriate to the user obtaining it. Because they're expensive, however, they are not widely used except to the extent that you may need to match a photograph of yourself to obtain access to a physical resource.

Encryption

Encryption involves scrambling, or coding, data so that anyone who views it will not be able to make sense of it without a decoder decryption key. A key in this sense is not a physical one, but rather a data bit string of a set length. The length is directly correlated with the strength of the encryption—a 64-bit key is easier to crack or decode than is a 128-bit key. The encryption key is a mathematical algorithm that transforms plain text messages into ciphertext.

The two main types of encryption are secret key cryptography and public key cryptography. With *secret key cryptography,* the sender and receiver use the same key to code and decode the message. For example, we may both know that in a coded message, the letter M is substituted for the letter A. (Of course, encryption uses complex mathematical encryption techniques, rather than simple letter substitutions.) A problem with secret key cryptography is that the sender and receiver must agree on the key and both need to obtain it, which may require transmitting the key in an insecure manner. Creating, transmitting, and handling keys are all known as key management. IT auditors must ensure that key management is secure, particularly in the case of secret key cryptography.

Public key cryptography uses a private/public key pair. Figure 6-7 illustrates public key cryptography for both privacy and authentication. Public key cryptography is the most commonly used method for encrypting transmitted messages between senders and receivers. With this approach, one key is used for *en*crypting the message and another key is for *de*crypting. The two keys are issued at the same time and are encrypted using an algorithm issued by a trusted third party called a certificate authority. One key is public and the other is private. The public key is widely available and can be transmitted across public networks. The private key is issued to a single party who does not share it or transmit it. A message sender can encrypt plaintext with the message recipient's public key, send it across a network, and only the intended receiver will be able to decrypt it, using the private key.

In addition to providing privacy, public key cryptography can also be used for authentication purposes. In this instance, the message sender (Amanda in Figure 6-7) signs the message with a digital signature, which is an encryption of the message with the sender's *private* key. The digital signature binds the message sender to the message contents. The

Encryption for privacy purposes

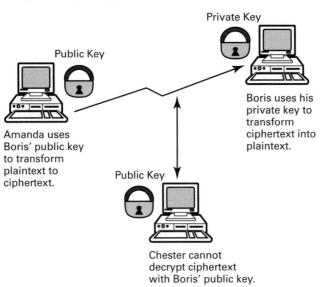

Encryption for authentication purposes

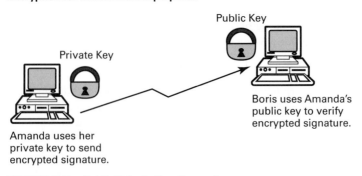

FIGURE 6-7   Public/Private Key Encryption

message recipient verifies the signature through an algorithm that includes the message, the signature, and the sender's *public* key. Public and private keys and digital certificates are all available from certificate authorities (e.g., Verisign and Thawte). A digital certificate may be thought of as an electronic passport. It has the name and public key of the certificate holder, as well as a serial number and expiration date. Certificate authorities are part of a public key infrastructure (PKI), the system of private/public key pairs and digital certification that allows data and dollar exchanges across unsecured public networks. We will discuss encryption as it specifically relates to electronic business in Chapter 7.

Firewalls

A firewall is similar to a guardpost in an upscale residential community. The guard's purpose is to allow access to residents, guests, delivery personnel, and other desirable traffic, while denying entry to through traffic or a *persona non grata.* Similarly, firewalls combine software and hardware to control outside access to an entity's telecommunications networks. The software specifies filters that allow or disallow entry to networks or segments of internal networks. Firewalls can be placed at various levels to block traffic to various internal networks or specific applications. In particular, they protect an organization's internal networks from access via the Internet.

Thieves and paparazzi can get around guardhouses by scaling walls, using false identification, or attacking in a group so large as to overwhelm the guard. The same is true of firewalls. Users can spoof a firewall with a fake IP source address, find holes in the firewall access rules, or overwhelm the firewall with heavy traffic. Firewalls cannot offer foolproof protection against viruses, nor can they provide security against malicious acts by internal network users. As a result, firewalls provide only limited security. Nonetheless they should be part of a solid security policy, and they're particularly important for networks that include Internet access. Figure 6-8 lists some risk indicators for firewall security.

There are several decisions to make when adding a firewall. These include choosing architecture and type of firewall functionality. A single-layered architecture uses just one network host for all firewall functions, and the firewall host is placed between the internal network and the Internet (Figure 6-9). A more secure and costly architecture uses multiple layers. This means that two or more hosts provide the firewall functions. To configure the firewall, the designer will need to select a combination of outer and inner firewall hosts. For example, there may be an outer firewall placed between the Internet and the Web server located on the perimeter network, with an internal firewall between the Web server in the perimeter network and the internal network. A demilitarized zone (DMZ) firewall offers an even higher level of security. The DMZ is a separate network between the Internet and an organization's internal networks. It is protected on both sides by separate firewalls.

There are two main types of firewall functionality. These are packet-filtering routers and application-level firewalls or proxy servers. A packet-filtering router examines

---

The entity has no firewall.

The entity's firewall is poorly configured.

Noone monitors or audits the firewall security.

The entity overrelies on the firewall for access control over internal networks.

The firewall's rules are not updated regularly.

Some internal network users connect via modem directly to the Internet, circumventing the firewall.

FIGURE 6-8   Risk Indicators for Firewall Security

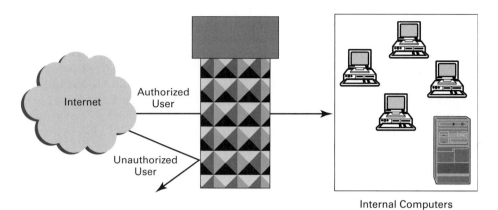

FIGURE 6-9 A Firewall Configuration

incoming IP message packets according to a set of filtering rules. It then forwards or rejects the packet. The filtering rules examine the IP fields and transport headers. The firewall software compares the IP source address to a set of identified addresses. Security administrators will program firewalls with various control settings. For example, the setting for access may often be set to either *Default Deny* or *Default Permit*. The Default Deny setting means that if the firewall does not recognize a user's IP address, the traffic will be turned away. The Default Permit setting allows access to the network, unless the IP address is specifically designated to be blocked. To set the default to deny most traffic is to provide a higher level of security. Firewalls may be static, which means they are set to either deny or permit. Other firewalls are dynamic and can change defaults. Packet filters require continual updating. Since they rely on specifications about the traffic to permit or deny, addresses to be included or kept out must be specified in the firewall rules.

Stateful inspection is a more advanced type of packet filtering that is particularly useful in organizations that have a lot of inbound communications from the Internet to the internal network. With stateful inspection, the firewall software tracks the destination IP address for each outbound message packet. It then checks each incoming message packet address with the outbound destination list to make sure that it's a legitimate response. An advantage over a regular packet-filtering system is that the firewall administrator is not doing the updating of the acceptable IP address file, but rather the file is updated automatically each time there's an outbound message.

An application-level firewall is also known as a proxy server. These systems offer more security than packet filters because there is never a real connection between the sender and the receiver. Instead, the firewall acts as a proxy, or substitute, for the receiver. The sender connects to the firewall proxy, which in turn connects to the receiver. The firewall can recognize any attacks before they reach a target. In an application-level firewall, the rules are configured to accept or reject traffic from various parts of the network trying to access hosts in other parts of the network. That is to say, it segments the network and controls the traffic flow throughout it. Proxies are secure, but they are expensive and typically do not have the same performance level as packet-filtering firewalls.

Intrusion Detection Systems

Many firewalls maintain logs of access activity. The system may record data about unsuccessful access attempts and other anomalies. These records may indicate a pattern of activity that will alert the firewall administrator that an intruder is trying to obtain unauthorized access to internal network systems. This logging and associated monitoring activity constitutes an intrusion detection system (IDS). The IDS may be included in a firewall package or it can be a stand-alone system. The IDS is trying to monitor any unusual scanning activities or features in access that might fit an attack profile.

To be effective, the IDS must be correctly configured and the security administrator must know how to interpret the messages and reports the system provides. All the IDS can do is *report* an attack, and by itself it's powerless to stop one. Organizations that lack the expertise to maintain an IDS might purchase IDS managed services from a third party.

An attacker can bypass the IDS with certain kinds of probes and coordinated attacks. A signature-based IDS studies groups of message packets and profiles them against known attack patterns. An intruder can get around this detection by sending the packets over a longer period of time.

There are many types of IDS, with varying levels of sophistication. At its simplest, the IDS is a log. More advanced IDS programs may use artificial intelligence such as neural networks and data mining techniques to identify intrusion patterns. They also look for anomalies, such as traffic patterns that are out of the ordinary. While IDS programs are helpful, they cannot keep attackers out if there are weaknesses in policies and authentication procedures or if there are access holes in applications.

Penetration Testing

Penetration testing, which might also be called "hacking for hire," or ethical hacking, is just what it sounds like. IT auditors use it to test their ability to penetrate an information system. By trying to get into a system, penetration testers are able to learn about the logical access vulnerabilities in an information system. A comprehensive network security test checks for access from both the standpoint of remote and internal access. Since IT auditors take on the roles of hackers in penetration testing, they often use hacker tools and techniques. A number of such tools are available, many of which are for specific operation systems or network software. We will discuss four general penetration testing tools: war dialing, port scanning, sniffing, and password cracking.

WAR DIALING War dialing is one of the older approaches employed by hackers and penetration testers to gain remote access to network and telecommunications systems. War dialing requires only a phone line, a modem, and war dialing software. The software, available for purchase or on the Internet as freeware, will randomly dial phone numbers until it locates an open modem connection. These open connections to telephone lines exist to provide remote access convenience for legitimate employees and IT vendors, but they present a significant network system vulnerability if not properly secured. Once the war dialer makes a connection, the penetration tester will attempt to access the network through password cracking (discussed later in this section). An IT auditor may use war dialing to make sure remote connections are secured. The process may reveal that employees are using software tools such as pcAnywhere for remote connectivity to the office network without properly securing it. Penetration testing using war dialing could also find that vendors haven't changed easily learned default passwords.

PORT SCANNING Computer ports provide hardware or software connections. You are probably familiar with the physical serial and parallel ports in the back of your PC. These ports allow for data transmission; for example, a user who connects a cable to a computer's parallel port can send data to a printer. A logical software port similarly provides a connection—such as one between a PC and the Internet. The port number designates how the Internet message should be handled during transmission. The port number appears in the message header and gets passed from the server to its eventual destination. Many software applications (such as Web browsers using Internet protocols such as TCP/IP and HTTP) will use ports with numbers that have been pre-assigned by the U.S. Internet Assigned Numbers Authority or the international Internet Corporation for Assigned Names and Numbers. Other applications receive port numbers dynamically as they establish connections.

Hackers and penetration testers scan ports to find out which network services a particular system provides. This is possible due to their association with known port numbers. To scan ports, a hacker "pings" a system by sending separate messages to each port. The message response will tell the potential intruder which ports are used and which are open and therefore vulnerable to penetration. There are a variety of kinds of port scanning techniques. For instance, in a *Strobe* scan, the hacker tries to connect only to a limited set of ports. Since many port numbers are well known, hackers can choose their targets (e.g., Port #110 is reserved for POP, or post office protocol). IT auditors may use intrusion detection systems or port scanning software to find out which ports are open and not being used. Once they identify these ports, they should ask the network administrator to disable them if possible. The following example describes one type of port scanner that potentially provides access to hackers.

> **EXAMPLE** Network Mapper (nmap) is a freely available port scanning tool that operates on UNIX and Windows NT. Nmap can perform stealth scans, so called because these scans are able to avoid detection by the target host without one of the newer IDS software programs. They do this because they don't allow the three-way handshake (discussed earlier in the chapter) to be completed. To use nmap, the hacker customizes the attack with a set of commands. For example, you might use the command "-sS TCP SYN stealth port scan" if you were going to do a TCP scan. The command "-P0" configures the scan so that it will not ping host computers. This instruction may be necessary, depending on the systems being scanned.

SNIFFERS   A sniffer (sometimes called spy software) is a program that hackers and IT auditors use to capture data as it is transmitted across networks. As with port scanners, sniffer programs are available as freeware at Internet sites. Sniffers can be very damaging because they may attach themselves to a host computer and capture data from every system sending messages to the compromised computer system—without being detected. The most common use of sniffers is for capturing user IDs and passwords, but they can also copy any unencrypted text, such as that in e-mail messages.

PASSWORD CRACKERS   Password crackers are, as the name implies, software tools that guess passwords. Some of this software will use a dictionary approach in which the software tries to match the password against all the terms in a standard dictionary. A hybrid method is a modification of the dictionary approach. The hybrid attack modifies dictionary words in the same ways people might do when trying to disguise a word as a password. Another approach is a brute force attack, in which the hacker tries increasingly complex sequences of letter and number combinations to obtain access to systems. The more complex the password (i.e., longer and mixed alphanumeric characters), the more difficult is the job of the password cracking software. IT auditors conducting penetration tests may use password cracking software to identify poor or insecure passwords. They then help users select better ones. Figure 6-10 lists characteristics of secure passwords that are less vulnerable to cracking. Conventional wisdom

Easy to remember but difficult to guess
    (Because you should never write a password down)
Not a dictionary word
    (Because hackers often use dictionaries to crack passwords)
Not a name of a person
    (Because hackers can use name lists to crack passwords)
More than six characters long
    (Because brute force attacks will take more time to guess longer passwords)
Mix of upper- and lower-case letters and numbers
    (Because a dictionary cracking approach will not guess these)
Try putting a symbol in the middle of a word, such as an exclamation point
    (Because this will make it more difficult to guess)
Try using the first character of each word in a phrase you can remember
    (This makes for a nonword password that is easy to remember)

FIGURE 6-10 Characteristics of Secure Passwords

has been that IT auditors should require users to switch out their passwords on a regular basis, such as every sixty days. Recent research, however, suggests that requiring such password changes actually decreases security because it encourages users to record their password somewhere.[8]

AUDITING NETWORK SECURITY

In addition to penetration testing, auditors may use other auditing approaches to ensure that an organization's network and telecommunications security incorporates appropriate controls. To date, there is no universal benchmarking standard for network security. IT auditors generally need to employ either the types of risk assessment discussed in Chapter 3 or the observed best practices to evaluate whether the controls in place are sufficient protection against the threats identified in this chapter. Tools such as the Windows 2000 Benchmark, for the Windows 2000 operating system, are likely to become increasingly available. Windows 2000 Benchmark lets users evaluate their security settings against the Center for Internet Security (CIS) benchmarks. The three security areas that the benchmark software evaluates are: hot fixes (patches) and service packs (bundles of hot fixes), user account (e.g., password standards) and auditing policies (monitors and logs), and security settings (system configurations).[9] An IT auditor evaluating network and telecommunication systems will typically examine controls in each of these areas.

An IT audit program for network security will include the tools described in this chapter. The program will have components similar to those for auditing any IT application area. Figure 6-11 describes some of the components and specific steps that would be included in an audit program for network security.[10]

SUMMARY

Network and telecommunications systems pose extra risks for management and IT auditors. This chapter began with a discussion of network technologies, including network hardware components, various network architectures and configurations, and standards and software. We described some of the more recent developments in network and telecommunications technologies, including wireless systems and virtual private networks (VPNs). (Many of the newest developments are related to the Internet, and Chapter 7 will explore these in more detail.)

There are numerous risks to network systems. Many of these are the same threats faced by all information systems. However, the additional access provided by networked systems and distributed

---

Obtain an understanding of network configuration and network security administration

Audit steps include obtaining and reviewing documents such as network diagrams, organization charts, and network security policies

Evaluate logical access security

Audit steps include evaluating policies and procedures for user ID and password management, remote access, firewalls (and examining firewall configurations and rules), intrusion detection systems, and encryption techniques

Evaluate physical security

Audit steps include ensuring that network assets are protected from the natural elements, reasonably shielded from natural disasters, inspecting insurance policies to evaluate appropriateness of coverage, evaluating physical access controls, and using techniques that ensure uninterrupted power supplies

Evaluate programmed threat security

Audit steps include examining virus software agreements and update procedures, policies over user ability to download software, e-mail filters, e-mail policies, practices regarding scanning security alerts, and applying software patches

Examine backup and contingency plans

Audit steps include ensuring that appropriate procedures exist for backing up network data regularly (i.e., backup rotations and retention schedules), that appropriate contingency plans exist (i.e., arrangements to bring the network up within twenty-four hours in the case of an emergency) and have been tested, that an incident response team is in place, and that procedures are in place for addressing a denial of service attack

---

FIGURE 6-11 Audit Program Components for an IT Audit of Network Security

---

processing increase risk significantly. The greatest risk to any IS is likely to be human behavior, and social engineering is one type of behavior practiced by crackers that can do much harm to network and telecommunications systems. The physical infrastructure of networked systems is at risk from natural elements, natural disasters, interruptions in power supply, and intentional human acts, such as terrorist attacks. Another category of risks is programmed threats, which includes viruses, worms, Trojan horses, hoaxes, and a combination of these, called blended threats. Denial of service attacks can cost companies millions of dollars in lost revenues and customer base. Finally, holes in application and security software allow a variety of network attacks to occur.

Fortunately managers and IT auditors have tool sets to help them cope with the network and telecommunications systems threats identified in this chapter. These begin with the creation of a security administration function that is responsible for planning network security and creating a security policy. Authentication tools, such as passwords, key cards, and biometrics ensure appropriate physical and logical access to network and telecommunications system resources. Encryption is a tool that can provide both authentication and privacy. Firewalls and intrusion detection systems (IDS) are tools to keep unauthorized visitors from accessing an organization's internal networked systems. Penetration testing is an approach used by IT auditors and others to test the vulnerability of a networked system to attack. It is accomplished by using many of the same techniques a hacker would use to identify system vulnerabilities. These include war dialers, port scanners, sniffers, and password crackers. IT auditors may also use benchmarking tools, best practices, and risk analysis to evaluate network security.

DISCUSSION QUESTIONS

6-1 This chapter discussed a variety of network configurations. How many clients and servers do you think are on the networks of a Fortune 500 company?

6-2 Just about every business has been affected by a programmed threat. What are the costs associated with a threat such as Code Red?

6-3   Suppose you work for a company that is the object of a Denial of Service attack. Describe the steps managers and auditors should take during and immediately after the attack to control it and prevent future attacks.

6-4   Some people think Kevin Mitnick is a hero, and others see him as a criminal. What do you think? What is he doing now?

6-5   Describe five ways a hacker might use social engineering to penetrate a business network system.

6-6   Network and telecommunications systems are even more vulnerable to attack from insiders than from outside hackers. Describe three things an IT auditor can do to verify controls over these systems specifically related to employees.

6-7   Using the Internet, find two examples of software vulnerabilities. Discuss how security administrators and auditors can protect themselves from these types of threats.

6-8   Discuss the level of security afforded by firewalls. What are some of the protections offered by personal firewalls?

6-9   Discuss the level of security afforded by intrusion detection systems. How do these systems use artificial intelligence techniques such as pattern recognition to detect network intrusions?

6-10 Describe the benefits to a company of hiring an IT audit consultant to conduct a penetration test of a network system.

EXERCISES

6-11 Amanda and Chris McDermott own a small business, Plastic Dollars, that produces and maintains stored value cards for retailers. Most of the cards they sell are gift cards, such as those available in various restaurants and stores. They just started their business two years ago, but this year they hope to sell about four million dollars worth of cards. Depending on the arrangement with the business, they may or may not maintain the database that contains the card owner's name and the current value on the card. Their revenue comes from the percentage of retail value they charge businesses for the cards. Therefore, although the business is doing well, money is still tight.

Plastic Dollars employs five people, including Chris and Amanda. Two of the employees are full-time, and the other is a part-time worker who is also a college student. The business has two servers and three client computer work stations. They also have three phone lines that allow them to communicate with various retail and restaurant establishments in real time. The company has been "hit" a few times by various programmed threats. Chris and Amanda use anti-virus software, but they aren't always careful about keeping it up to date. They know they should do more but they don't think the cost is worth it. Although they have no disaster recovery plan, they do back up their files every three hours, by encrypting and compressing their data and uploading it to a remote location.

Required:

a. Evaluate the risks to Plastic Dollars of programmed threats. What are the potential direct and indirect costs associated with these risks?

b. Develop a security plan for Plastic Dollars that will protect them against blended and other programmed threats.

6-12 Figure 6-11 describes the components of an IT audit program to evaluate network security. The first step an IT auditor must take in conducting a review of this security area is to obtain an understanding of network configuration and network security administration.

Required:

a. Describe in some detail the specific steps you would take to obtain such an understanding.

b. What is the purpose of this portion of the audit?

REFERENCES AND RECOMMENDED READINGS

Allen, Julia H. 2001. *The CERT Guide to System and Network Security Practices.* Boston: Addison-Wesley.

Bigler, Mark. 2000. "Defeating the Cyber Criminal: Defense Tactics for Denial of Service Attacks." *Information Systems Control Journal* 3: 49–51.

Burnette, Mark. 2001 "When Code Red Attacks: Addressing Vulnerabilities Behind Virus Hysteria." *Information Systems Control Journal* 6: 30–32.

Damle, Pramod. 2002. "Social Engineering: A Tip of the Iceberg." *Information Systems Control Journal,* 2.

Garfinkel, Simson. 1997. *Web Security and Commerce.* Cambridge, Mass.: O'Reilly.

Glover, Steven M., Stephen W. Liddle, and Douglas F. Prawitt. 2002. *E-Business Principles and Strategies for Accountants,* 2nd ed. Upper Saddle River, N.J.: Prentice Hall.

Hall, James A. 2000. *Information Systems Auditing and Assurance.* Cincinnati, Ohio: South-Western College Publishing.

Hunton, James E. 1998. "Facts and Fables About Computer Viruses." *Journal of Accountancy.* May: 39–44.

Information Systems Audit and Control Association. *2002 CISA Review Manual.* Rolling Meadows, Ill.: Information Systems Audit and Control Association.

Klevinsky, T. J., Scott Laliberte, and Ajay Gupta. 2002. *Hack I.T.* Boston: Addison-Wesley.

Laudon, Kenneth C., and Jane P. Laudon. 1998. *Management Information Systems* (5th ed.). Upper Saddle River, N.J.: Prentice Hall.

Louw, Aldora, and William A. Yarberry, Jr. 2002. "Wireless Security: Here We Go Again." *Information Strategy: The Executive's Journal.* May: 6–12.

Mahadevan, Chidambaram. 2001. "Intrusion, Attack, Penetration—Some Issues," *Information Systems Control Journal,* 6: 52–57.

McClure, Stuart, Joel Scambray, and George Kurtz. 2001. *Hacking Exposed,* 3rd ed. New York: Osborne/McGraw-Hill.

Moody, Robert. 2001. "Ports and Port Scanning: An Introduction." *Information Systems Control Journal,* 5: 34–39.

Northcutt, Stephen, and Judy Novak. 2001. *Network Intrusion Detection: An Analyst's Handbook,* 2nd ed. Indianapolis: New Riders.

O'Brien, James A. 2001. *Introduction to Information Systems,* 10th ed. Boston: McGraw-Hill Irwin.

Piscitello, David. 2002. "Intrusion Detection … Or Prevention?" *Business Communications Review.* May: 42–45.

Scalet, Sarah D. 2002. "Cheap, Cool, and Dangerous." *CIO.* July 1: 80–86. www.cio.com/archive/040102/chap_content.html.

Spindel, Brian. 2002. "Benchmarking System Security." *Internal Auditor.* February: 23–25.

Stallings, William. 2000. *Network Security Essentials.* Upper Saddle River, N.J.: Prentice-Hall.

Web Sites

A resource for definitions of technical terms related to security is www.toptentechs.com. The site includes white papers on top technologies, applications, issues, and emerging technologies of interest to accounting professionals.

The Computer Security Institute (CSI), www.gocsi.com, is a member organization that provides education and information to computer and network security professionals. The Web site for *SC Magazine* (Information Security News), another source for information about the latest security tools, is www.scmagazine.com.

The Forum of Incident Response and Security Teams (FIRST), www.first.org, is a group of computer security incident response teams representing government, business, and educational institutions. Their purpose is to share information and coordinate the prevention of disruption to computer networks.

The Computer Emergency Response Team (CERT), www.cert.org, is a center for Internet security information. This group, located at Carnegie Mellon University, works to control computer security incidents. The Web site provides security alerts and discussion forums.

Several vendors provide antivirus software and maintain virus advisories at their Web sites. Two software vendor sites are www.mcafee.com and www.symantec.com.

Many Web sites allow you to download port scanners, sniffers, and other hacker software tools. Two of these are www.insecure.org and www.packetstormsecurity.org.

Black Hat is a company that sponsors a heavily attended annual computer security convention each year in Las Vegas, Nevada. Information about the meeting is available at www.blackhat.com.

NOTES

1. Piscitello, David. "Intrusion Detection … Or Prevention?" *Business Communications Review*. May 2002: 42.
2. William M. Bulkeley, "Hacker Assault on Networks Is Chance for Security Sales." *The Wall Street Journal Online*. October 23, 2002.
3. These four epidemics were Nimda, Code Red, Sircam, and ILoveYou. Source: "Hacks and Attacks: A Complex Infestation," *SC Magazine,* September 2002: 27.
4. Information about the W32/Klez-H worm is adapted from www.sophos.com/virusinfo/analyses /w32klezh.html. (September 6, 2002).
5. "PGP Vulnerability Opens Door to Remote Attacks," Dennis Fisher, *eWeek,* September 6, 2002. www.eweek.com/article2/0,3959,518907,00.asp
6. Several security Web sites listed at the end of this chapter provide updates on vulnerabilities in software. www.ntbugtraq.com specifically tracks vulnerabilities for Microsoft NT.
7. These steps are adapted from *The CERT Guide to System and Network Security Practices*. Julia H. Allen. Boston: Addison-Wesley. 2001.
8. "Golden Business Ideas," *Journal of Accountancy*, September 2002: 120.
9. The software is available at www.cisecurity.org.
10. An excellent source for detailed guidance in constructing an audit program over network security is *Networking Audit Program & Internal Control Questionnaire* (2001), available in CobiT's audit guidelines.

CHAPTER 7

E-BUSINESS RISKS

CHAPTER CONTENTS

INTRODUCTION

On the Internet there are totally new ways to get taken.[1]

As this quotation indicates, e-business brings with it a new set of risks. For example, businesses connecting to the Internet run the risk that outsiders will access their internal network systems. As a result, the development of the Internet and e-business pose many challenges for IT auditors beyond those they face in securing traditional network systems.

This chapter describes e-business models, ranging from electronic data interchange (EDI) to collaborative commerce. The levels of risk and the need for controls vary along the continuum. These risks include threats to privacy and confidentiality, security and information system availability, and transaction integrity. Not only do risks and controls vary across the spectrum of e-business models, but there are also special risk and control issues associated with specialized e-business technologies like EDI, collaborative commerce, and e-mail. This chapter discusses all these risks, as well as the controls over them.

Apart from new sets of risks and controls, e-business also creates more third-party services and reliance on these services by others. IT auditors may find themselves in the position of validating the work of other auditors and of offering additional e-business risk and assurance services themselves.

E-BUSINESS MODELS

We frequently use the terms "e-business" and "e-commerce" interchangeably, but they don't really mean the same thing. E-commerce means using IT to buy and sell goods and services electronically. E-business is a broader term, covering not just goods and services exchanges, but also all forms of business conducted using electronic transmission of data and information. For example, e-business includes using the Internet or intranets for employee training or customer support.

While it may seem that e-business just suddenly appeared, in reality it has developed over some time. Figure 7-1 shows this evolution. Various entities and individuals may be at any point along the spectrum.

E-business began when customers and suppliers recognized the advantages of exchanging documents such as purchase orders and invoices electronically, rather than through the postal service. This electronic data interchange (EDI) could speed ordering and fulfillment dramatically. The advent of the Internet allowed businesses, organizations, and individuals to publish World Wide Web pages and communicate to broader audiences. At first, Web pages were mirrors of paper documents. But as they increased in sophistication, users recognized that there were things they could do with Web pages that weren't possible with paper media. For instance, they could capture information about the number of times someone accessed a Web page (number of hits). They could also ask for information from those perusing a Web page. As Internet usage and Web page development evolved, managers learned to take advantage of the Internet's unique nature in many ways. For example, retailers realized changing the price of an item required a few keystrokes on the Internet versus reprinting promotional materials and price lists in an offline environment. The transparency of the Internet, or the ability for mass instantaneous sharing of information, also created an almost perfectly efficient marketplace for goods and services. The next stage in the evolution of e-business was to distribute its use throughout an organization. This came in the form of intranets. Businesses created these internal Internets to allow employees to communicate with one another and exchange information. Employee self-service is an example of intranet functionality. Through internal networks,

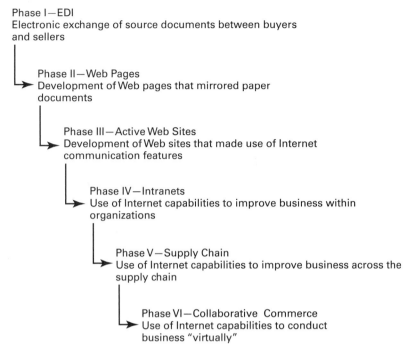

FIGURE 7-1 The Evolution of E-business

employees can complete expense forms, change their tax deduction information, apply for insurance, request vacation time, and so on.

Once enterprises mastered internal communications through their intranets, they turned outward. The link to customers occurred early on—with the first Web pages. The rest of the supply chain linkage took place in the next stage of the evolution as businesses began expanding on their connections to suppliers, customers, and distributors. These included adding supply chain management (SCM) and customer relationship management (CRM) functionality. Portals allowed customers and suppliers to link more closely with an enterprise.

The current state of e-business is really c-business, where the "c" stands for collaborative. In c-business, the boundaries among enterprises become blurred. Businesses up and down the supply chain work together to achieve objectives that maximize profitability for all of them. For example, in the "real" world, Customer C places an order with Enterprise B. Enterprise B then requests supplies from Supplier A. Supplier A provides the goods to B, which distributes them to C. In the "virtual" c-commerce world, Customer C may see it this way, but in reality Customer C's order is going right through B into A in real time. B is involved only to the extent that it adds value to Supplier A's materials or for helping A and C to get together.

THE TECHNOLOGY OF E-BUSINESS

The Internet is a network of hardware, software, and communications systems with many of the network features described in general in Chapter 6. In fact, the Internet is the world's biggest network, connecting thousands of other networked computer systems Doing business over the Internet requires a variety of specialized protocols, software, and browsers and servers. In addition, e-business requires specialized software languages.

Protocols, Software, and Hardware

One of the most widely used of all protocols is the Transmission Control Protocol/Internet Protocol (TCP/IP), shown in Figure 7-2. The Internet is an international network of local area networks (LANs) and computers with no single controlling site. TCP/IP allows communication among Internet nodes, and each computer or network connected to the Internet must support it. Each message transmission over the Internet requires an IP address for both the sender and receiver.

The IP address is the numerical translation of the text address. The IP address includes both source and destination information. Each address is unique and consists of a network and host address. The length of an IP address varies, depending on the classification. For example, a Class A IPv4 address is for very large organizations that need to identify many networks and host computers; in fact, this class can accommodate more than sixteen million host computers. An example of an IP address would be 251.36.220.5. The first group of numbers identifies a geographic region, the next group is for a specific organizational entity, the third set is the group of computers or network identification, and the last number references a specific computer. Finally, IP addresses may be static or dynamic. Static IP addresses are assigned and stay the same from one computing session to another. With a dynamic addressing approach, a computer, typically a client, receives a new IP address for each computing session. A server may maintain a set of dynamic addresses for this purpose.

Based on TCP/IP, the Internet supports other protocols for specialized tasks. Hypertext Transmission Protocol (HTTP) is one of these. HTTP is the standardized rule set that governs data transmission over the World Wide Web, the graphical component of the Internet.

The main hardware component in e-commerce is the Web server, which hosts an organization's Web pages and the program that gets network requests and sends back HTML files in response. These pages are in hypertext markup language (HTML) format. The Web server sends and receives messages from users in HTTP message format.

Two basic client/server architectures support e-business systems. A two-tiered system includes a client browser and a Web server. The three-tiered configuration consists of a client browser, a Web server, and a database server. Network routers can be either hardware devices or software, and they control the flow of traffic across the Internet network. Routers, located at various points across the network, determine where to forward a packet or data file.

Application Layer	Translates messages into the host's computer application software for screen presentation.
Presentation Transport Layer	Breaks messages into TCP packets called datagrams and attaches header plus information on reassembling, and ensures data delivery.
Internet Protocol (IP) Layer	Breaks down packets further and routes them from sender to receiver.
Network Interface Layer	Handles addressing and the interface between requesting and receiving computers.

FIGURE 7-2   The TCP/IP Model

Users connect to the Internet via Web browser software and a modem or other form of high-speed connection. An Internet service provider (ISP) allows individual user computers to have Internet access without maintaining a point-of-presence (POP) on the Internet. Each POP is an Internet access point and requires a unique IP address. The high-speed connections maintained by ISPs also provide their clients with faster communications.

HTML and XML

HTML is a formatting language that specifies the presentation of information over the World Wide Web. There is no question that HTML has been fundamental to the development of the Internet. However, e-business needs another language to enable the transmission and manipulation of information across the Internet network. This language is extensible markup language (XML).

Because application systems store data in a variety of formats, the Internet requires a common language for communicating and manipulating information. By converting data to a common XML format, different computer systems can exchange data more easily than would be possible otherwise. Databases can also store data in XML format, which allows disparate applications to easily retrieve and exchange data.

Like HTML, XML is a *markup language.* It uses tags to describe data elements. Unlike HTML, these tags describe the data rather than describing just how the data should be presented. For example, an HTML tag for September 30, 2003, might read <body>, showing that the date is to be presented in the body of text that a Web browser will view. HTML describes how the data are *displayed.* An XML tag for the same date might read <date>, describing what the data *mean.*

Another way that XML differs from HTML is that it is extensible, another word for expandable. There is a fixed set of markup tags for HTML, but users and software designers can create new tags for XML. Of course, if each software developer or user creates a separate set of tags, there goes the common standard. As a result, user groups are working to create specialized sets of industry tags, which, in a sense, represent that industry's proprietary language. The accounting and finance industry is developing extensible business reporting language (XBRL), which is to be used for business reporting over the Internet. Most businesses report some type of financial information over the Internet, but as yet there is no way of retrieving that data easily for comparison and manipulation purposes. For example, if you wanted to find the 2003 revenues for a particular retail chain, a search using the store's name and "revenue" would not likely yield the result you wanted. Further, if you did manage to find the data, you would not have it in a form that would allow you to compare it with similar data for another company. XBRL tags would ensure retrieval of similar data and allow for manipulation of the information so that comparisons would be possible. An advantage of XBRL will be that business entities can store the data once in XBRL format and extract it as needed for a variety of reporting purposes.

Another industry-specific language under development is e-business XML or ebXML. The mission of the developers working on this specification is

> To provide an open XML-based infrastructure enabling the global use of
> electronic business information in an interoperable, secure and consistent
> manner by all parties. (www.ebxml.org)

It's hoped that this standard will facilitate the exchange of business data across an Internet supply chain in a fashion similar to the way EDI standard languages (e.g., EDI-FACT and X12) facilitated the communication of business source document data among trading partners.

UNDERSTANDING E-BUSINESS RISK

E-business requires allowing access to some part of an organization's information system, so at any stage there is the threat of unauthorized access. The use of dedicated Web servers should restrict that access, although, as we discussed in Chapter 6, hackers can often find their way into even highly secure networks. Other risks vary more with the stage of e-business evolution. For instance, when organizations engage simply in publishing marketing materials on a Web site, the risk is that the site might be altered. An active Web page where customers and suppliers buy and sell online is subject to the threat of service interruption. In c-commerce, an interruption in service could literally bring business to a halt.

This section of the chapter discusses specific risks and controls associated with several categories of risk related to e-business. These are privacy and confidentiality, security and availability, transaction integrity, and business policies.

Privacy and Confidentiality

Privacy concerns the protection afforded to proprietary information, including personal information and information related to an exchange or transaction. The protection may be against unauthorized access, or it may be policies ensuring that users who access information do not use it for any purpose other than what is allowed by the information provider. *Confidentiality* is similar to privacy, except that it focuses on information that is specifically designated to be confidential or secret.

Privacy and confidentiality are extremely important in e-business for three reasons. First, e-business provides an opportunity to collect more data about buyers and sellers than is possible in a brick and mortar world. Second, the Internet allows for dissemination of information to more people more easily than through any other communication channel. Finally, the information obtained in e-business exchanges may be captured without the information provider's knowledge. For example, in making an online purchase, customers provide sellers with demographic and credit card information. This is overt, and customers are aware they are parting with personal information. However, customers also provide information subconsciously. For instance, the pages the customer peruses at the retailer's Web site provide some information about that customer's shopping pattern. Each time a Web browser accesses a page, the Web server's log files record the access. Case-in-Point 7-1 describes one privacy issue stemming from e-business.

Case-in-Point 7-1

Citibank, in looking to improve its electronic communications with customers, hired Acxiom Corp. to collect its credit-card customers' e-mail addresses. The bank then engaged Touchwood Technologies, Inc. to send e-mails to these customers, inviting them to access their own account information either online or by e-mail. The initiative led to privacy concerns because it was possible that some of the e-mail addresses did not belong to account holders, thus risking disclosure of sensitive financial data to the wrong parties.[2]

Many individuals wrongly think they don't need to be concerned about privacy because they "have no secrets." Unfortunately, that is not likely the case. Even those who are careful in crafting their e-mail would likely not want the text of those e-mails exposed to the world. Nor would they necessarily want others to know how they spend their time online—that is, what sites they access.

Many transactions require giving up some privacy, and there is a trade-off between privacy and personalization. By ceding information about ourselves, we allow businesses to better understand our needs. Where to draw the line on this may be a matter of individual preference. You may like it that an online bookstore is able to suggest books to you based on its record of your prior purchases. On the other hand, a somewhat spooky world of the year 2054 is suggested in the movie *Minority Report.* It is a future in which sales clerks greet customers personally and display a level of familiarity with the customers' personal history that brings home the idea that maybe personalization isn't worth a loss of privacy at some level.

There are also trade-offs between privacy and security. Government agencies and police forces argue that they need information in order to provide security. For instance, in order to track terrorists the Bureau of Immigration and Customs Enforcement needs to carefully monitor the movements of visitors to this country. Following the terrorist acts of September 11, many Americans expressed greater willingness to give up some of their privacy for security.

For individuals, the privacy risks faced by engaging in e-commerce range from simple embarrassment to identity theft. For business entities, privacy risks may be in the form of litigation for unauthorized disclosure of confidential information or loss of competitive proprietary information. Figure 7-3 describes some of the risk indicators related to privacy and confidentiality. The remainder of this section discusses two important topics related to privacy: privacy policies and Internet tracking.

PRIVACY POLICIES   Most entities engaged in e-business have privacy policies. The policies serve two main purposes. First, they protect the entity because they clearly spell out how they will treat proprietary information. Second, they provide assurance to business partners about how their information will be used. IT auditors are frequently involved either in crafting such a policy or in evaluating one.

There are several elements of a sound privacy policy. These include a general statement, a description of the information collected at the site, and the use of the collected information. We will discuss each of these using General Electric's privacy policy as an example.[3]

The first part of a privacy policy generally describes the entity's philosophy toward privacy. Note that GE's policy conveys a concern about privacy and provides some assurance about the use of personal information.

> **EXAMPLE**   "The General Electric Company (GE) is committed to protecting any personal information that you may provide to us. In particular, we believe it is important for you to know how we treat information about you that we may receive from this Web site."

The entity has no privacy policy.
The entity captures data not needed to process transactions.
The degree of protection afforded by the privacy policy is minimal.
The entity uses primary cookies.
The entity allows third-party cookies.
Transmissions to and from the entity are not encrypted.
The entity does not promise not to share data with third parties.

FIGURE 7-3   Risk Indicators for E-business Privacy and Confidentiality

Another section of a privacy policy describes the information collected from those accessing the site. Note several features in this section of GE's policy. The policy explicitly explains that the Web server does not obtain individual personal information without permission. It also provides a statement regarding access to the site by children.

EXAMPLE "In general, you can visit this Web site without telling us who you are or revealing any information about yourself. Our web servers collect the domain names, not the e-mail addresses, of visitors. In addition, there are portions of this Web site where we may need to collect personal information from you for a specific purpose, such as to provide you with certain information you request....

... For our supplier diversity site, we necessarily collect information about gender and ethnicity, such as whether your business is female-owned. This Web site is not intended for persons under 13 years of age. We do not knowingly solicit or collect personal information from or about children, and we do not knowingly market our products or services to children."

Privacy policies not only need to describe what information is collected, but they also should explain how the information will be used. GE's policy explains the general use of information as well as how the company may share the information. The final portion of this section explains that parts of the business require registration.

EXAMPLE "Domain name information that we collect is not used to personally identify you and instead is aggregated to measure the number of visits, average time spent on the site, pages viewed, etc. We use this information to measure the use of our site and to improve the content of our site.... Usually, we use the personal information you provide only to respond to your inquiry or to process your request (such as to receive electronic annual reports or to be added to our supplier diversity database). This information may be shared with other GE businesses, but only if necessary to fulfill your request or for related purposes. We may share the personal information you provide with other companies we have hired to provide services for us. These companies—our vendors—are contractually bound to use personal information we share with them only to perform the services we have hired them to provide. We do not share, sell, or lease personal information about you to any third parties for their marketing use.... You should review the privacy policy associated with that GE business' Web site for further information about that GE business' privacy practices."

A privacy policy may include several other sections in addition to the three main segments described here. For GE, these include a statement about cookies (discussed in the next section), how the site links to other sites (e.g., business partner sites), security of collected information, your ability to access the information provided to the site, contact information, and a notice about the frequency of changes to the privacy policy statement.

INTERNET TRACKING TOOLS Businesses and software applications may use Internet tracking tools to monitor behavior over the Internet. Two of these devices are logs and cookies.

Web servers make a record each time a user's Web browser views an Internet page. These records, called log files, are key to the fact that "someone is always watching" when a user is on the Internet. Most of the time, no one really cares and the log files have no value. Sometimes, however, the information may be useful for a variety of purposes. For example, some employees have been reprimanded or fired after their log files revealed they had been visiting recreational Web sites during business hours. Log files are legal documents, and they may be used against an individual in court.

The data in a log file typically includes the name and IP address of the user's computer, the time of the request, the address requested, and the uniform resource locator (URL) of the previous page visited. The URL of the current or launch page provides a refer link. Advertisers are very interested in these links because they indicate behavior patterns of Web users.

Another Internet tracking tool is a cookie. Cookies are pieces of data (strings of text) placed in a browser's memory. The text contains both the identity of the server leaving the cookie (the site visited) and the identity of the user's computer. While cookies have been the subject of much controversy because of their privacy infringement, they do serve many useful purposes. Cookies can store preferences and personal data that make browsing easier for users. For example, Internet shoppers may be greeted by name at some sites, and as they move from page to page the information on previous pages can be accumulated—perhaps into a shopping cart. While many online users have become somewhat comfortable with cookies used by a primary site, they may prefer not to have their cookies shared with third parties. Third-party cookies come from a source other than the page being viewed. An example is a pop-up advertisement that appears when you access a primary site. The advertiser may use a cookie to track your travel through Web pages for marketing purposes.

Web tracking tools are controls in that they provide audit trails of activity. They infringe on privacy. Online users have some power over this monitoring, at least with respect to cookies. A user or user group may choose to disable cookies on a personal computer. This can be done quite easily in any major Web browser. For example, Figure 7-4 shows the Internet Explorer 6.0 screen that allows a user to choose a setting or level of control over cookies (available by clicking on Tools | Internet Options | Privacy). Users may also delete cookies at any time from their computer.

Spyware is another type of Internet tracking tool. It operates by installing applets or other software programs on a user's computer that transmit usage information to a third party. Spyware may be used for marketing purposes or by hackers to obtain confidential or private information.

Securing Information and Maintaining System Availability

Since the Internet is a network, all the general network and telecommunications systems risks and controls apply to it. E-business, however, poses security risks beyond those of other networks for several reasons. The first is that the network is public—accessible to any user with a Web browser and an Internet service provider (ISP)—and therefore cannot be protected in the same ways a private network might be. A second reason is that e-commerce by definition involves the exchange of monetary and other liquid assets, in addition to information assets. The transmission of these assets, such as credit card numbers, over a public network creates additional vulnerabilities. Another increased risk for the Internet versus other networks is its sheer size and its increasing importance to the functioning of the economy. Case-in-Point 7-2 emphasizes concerns about secure e-business.

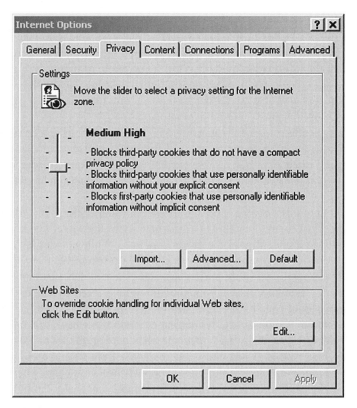

FIGURE 7-4   Internet Explorer's Privacy Settings Screen

Case-in-Point 7-2

The risks associated with e-commerce, specifically with credit card numbers transmitted over the Internet, led Visa to establish a list of security requirements for its business partners. Merchants who do business with Visa now must annually demonstrate compliance with a dozen security requirements, including a documented security policy, secure application development practices, access control and user authentication, encryption, firewalls, plans for attack response, segmented systems architectures, background checks on employees, and periodic security compliance audits.

Many of the controls mandated by Visa were discussed in Chapter 6. In this section of the chapter, we describe in greater detail a few controls that relate specifically to the Internet and e-business.

SECURING E-BUSINESS INFORMATION WITH ENCRYPTION

Encryption, a part of any network security system, is particularly important in e-business. The information transmitted during an exchange of goods or services is frequently confidential or sensitive. Offering customers a secure way to purchase goods over the Internet is critical to the success of online retailers.

The Internet basically uses the public/private key encryption discussed in Chapter 6. Parties conducting business over the Internet are concerned about establishing a secure connection. Secure Sockets Layer (SSL) technology, an encryption protocol developed by

Netscape, provides for this. With SSL, a customer's browser locates the merchant's public key, which is stored at the retail Web site. The customer's browser uses the public key to encrypt the message so that only the merchant can read it. Note that this process ensures that any data sent by the customer to the vendor can't be read by anyone but the merchant, but it does not authenticate anyone. It only protects against someone listening in. But what if the merchant is dishonest? Then the merchant could use the customer's information to pretend to be the customer and purchase items in his name. As a result of this weakness, SSL can be enhanced with digital certificates to authenticate transaction parties.

SSL is used when a browser and server communicate. Other encryption protocols applicable to specific Open Systems Interconnect (OSI) layers are Secure Socket Shell (SSH), Secure Electronic Transmission (SET), Secure-HTTP (S-HTTP), and IP security. SSH uses strong cryptography to open a secure session from a remote terminal. It provides both confidentiality and authentication. The SET protocol was jointly developed by Visa and MasterCard to ensure secure credit card payments over the Internet. SET is similar to SSL but includes authentication through the use of digital certificates associated with the financial institutions of buyers and merchants. SET uses two common types of cryptography algorithms. Rivest, Shamir, Adelman (RSA) is used to encrypt public keys, and the Data Encryption Standard (DES) encrypts private keys. These algorithms are complex mathematical formulas that use prime numbers. S-HTTP is also similar to SSL. But whereas SSL uses private key encryption, S-HTTP uses a complex encryption algorithm to encrypt HTTP requests and responses. IP security (IPSec) is a low-level protocol used to encrypt IP packets. It primarily provides confidentiality.

SECURING ELECTRONIC PAYMENTS   Most parties in business-to-consumer e-business transactions pay for goods and services with credit cards. Businesses engaged in e-commerce use either credit cards or the same types of accounts payable invoicing and payment systems for offline transactions. There are, however, many transactions online that require specialized payment systems. For example, an individual making a purchase on eBay is unlikely to be willing to share credit card information with the anonymous party from whom a purchase is being made. That individual would, however, be willing to convey credit card information to eBay itself, or a representative company, which could then make the payment to the individual seller. This type of payment system, using a third party as the credit card intermediary, is common for business-to-consumer payments. It has created a demand for a new type of business—that of credit card intermediary.

Electronic checks are another type of online payment system. These are similar to paper checks, bearing information about payee, payer, date, amount, and account number. The difference is that there is no paper involved. The payer creates the electronic check and sends it to the payee electronically, through e-mail. The payee deposits the check by sending it to the bank online. The bank clears the check and credits the payee's account. Electronic checks bearing digital signatures are actually more secure than paper checks.

Individuals and businesses are increasingly paying bills online. This is done through an electronic bill presentment and payment (EBPP) system. Users can do this by making arrangements either directly with each creditor or through a banking service. This business is expected to grow exponentially over the next few years. Consumers will find that the ability to pay bills electronically and view their account status online provides them convenience and time savings. Businesses should also save as the transaction costs for setting up individual customer accounts and processing payments decreases. Case-in-Point 7-3 describes how CheckFree facilitates EBPP.

Case-in-Point 7-3

CheckFree has partnered with hundreds of billing enterprises so that consumers can make all their online bill payments at a personalized Web site called MyCheckFree. Users log onto the site to pay their bills or look at their billing and payment information. The service is free to the bill-payers. CheckFree collects service fees from the billing companies, which benefit through more timely bill paying and lower transaction costs.

Of course, cash payments aren't possible over the Internet. Cash is a stored value payment system in which the value comes from the currency and coins themselves, or at least the belief in what those coins and currency represent. An advantage of cash payments is their anonymity. Cash exchanges leave no footprints. Buyers and sellers on the Internet, wishing for the same anonymity, need a form of virtual cash. This may take the form of digital tokens or stored value cards with predetermined values, but a widely used virtual cash system has yet to be developed.

SECURING THE WEB SERVER   The purposes of securing the Web server are to ensure privacy and confidentiality, prevent downloads of programmed threats, and resist attacks from intruders both outside and inside the organization. While many users may be authorized to interact with the Web server, the server security should ensure that only a limited set of authorized users can actually shut down the server, maintain it, log onto it, and control the job accounting data associated with it (e.g., logs and usage statistics).

To ensure Web server security, a network should be configured to minimize the services provided by the host computer. For example, there should be separate servers for e-mail versus Web access. The location of the Web server with respect to the firewall is another security issue. Web servers are frequently the subject of attacks from intruders. For this reason, the Web server should not be located *inside* the firewall. If the Web server is inside the firewall, an attacker who gains access through it will then have access to the entire network. There are two other options, shown in Figure 7-5. One is to locate the Web server outside the firewall, and the other choice is to locate the Web server between external and internal firewalls, in the DMZ (discussed in Chapter 6). Then, if the Web server is compromised, access is limited to the resources located in the DMZ.

SYSTEM AVAILABILITY AND RELIABILITY   Business-to-consumer e-commerce is big, but international business-to-business e-commerce is bigger and could reach $8 trillion annually by 2004. As the dollar amount of transactions over the Internet increases, so does concern about the availability and reliability of online business processes. Availability refers to an Internet site and its associated processes being "on" at any time, and reliability means that the site and processes are performing as expected.

There are many threats to e-business availability and reliability. The most common one is the distributed denial of service (DDOS) attack described in Chapter 6 and illustrated in Case-in-Point 7-4.

Case-in-Point 7-4

On October 22, 2002, the Internet was hit by a DDOS attack that targeted the thirteen root servers that provide a domain directory for almost all Internet communications. The attack went on for about an hour, during which most Internet users were oblivious because of built-in safeguards. Had more servers been affected or if the attack had gone on longer, there would have been delays and connection failures.[4]

The Web server is located outside the firewall.

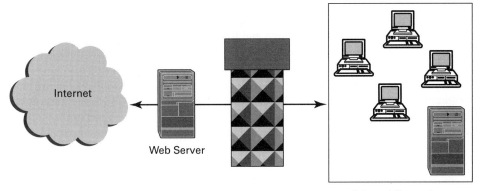

Internal Computers

The Web server is located inside an external firewall and outside the internal firewall.

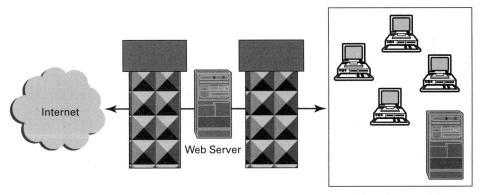

Internal Computers

FIGURE 7-5   Alternative Firewall Configurations for Web Server

In 2001, several of the most popular Web sites went down. The cost of such "time-outs" is far beyond the lost sales for the time period of the outage. Because an interruption in availability or reliability creates loss of confidence, the risk may be business survival. An attack that brought down the entire Internet infrastructure could have ramifications for the global economy.

Ensuring availability and reliability of online services requires maintaining all of the security precautions described in this chapter and the previous one. It is difficult, if not impossible, to protect servers from DOS attacks, which increases the importance of the backup and recovery plans and procedures described in Chapter 5.

Transaction Integrity and Business Policies

The integrity of e-business transactions and comprehensive e-business policies are important components of these systems' reliability. The nature of e-business creates additional transaction risks with respect to repudiation, or the ability to deny an aspect of the transaction. In addition, e-business transactions create electronic rather than paper audit trails and electronic evidence.

TRANSACTION INTEGRITY The AICPA's *Systrust* practice principles defined transaction integrity to mean that "system processing is complete, accurate, timely, and authorized."[5] Completeness and, to some degree, accuracy are ensured primarily by maintaining manual or automated transaction and transmission error logs, regularly inspecting the logs, and resolving errors. Accuracy and completeness also require appropriate input and output controls, such as program edit checks that ensure complete and error-free data input. Timeliness of transactions is assured in part by maintaining system availability and communicating timing needs. Transaction authorization relies on policies and procedures that guarantee that appropriate personnel and automated systems initiate and complete transactions in accordance with specified policies and levels of authorization. In addition to these controls, complete, accurate, timely, and authorized transaction processing in an e-business scenario may rely on some specialized control areas. Two of these are controls to ensure nonrepudiation of e-business transactions and electronic audit trails.

Repudiation Repudiation is the ability of a party engaged in a transaction to deny either their participation or certain characteristics of the transaction itself. Repudiation is a problem whenever the parties to a transaction are not physically present during an exchange. For example, a pizza delivery service must make sure that it delivers the right pizzas to the right parties for the right price. In this case the word "right" means "agreed to." Since the person doing the ordering can give a false delivery address, the pizza business needs some way to associate a phone call with an address. It must also have a way to prove the nature of the merchandise ordered (i.e., large pepperoni versus small mushroom) and the price the ordering party agreed to pay.

In many ways, integrity issues for online transactions aren't all that different from the ones faced by the pizza delivery business. There is a need to ensure origin nonrepudiation (that the sender did transmit a message or asset) and reception nonrepudiation (that the receiver got the message or asset). In addition, repudiation calls for proof of delivery of goods for agreed upon amounts. Tools that can provide for nonrepudiation include digital signatures and other authentication techniques, and electronic evidence and audit trails.

Repudiation in an e-business world does carry an added level of risk because it's easier to "spoof" an identity in a virtual environment than in a physical one. For example, customers who want to buy products online may be enticed by a well-designed Web page that's a lot cheaper to create than a fancy office. Business and end consumers may think they're doing business with a multinational conglomerate when the reality is that the "business" behind a Web site might be just one individual with a PC. Case-in-Point 7-5 highlights this issue.

Case-in-Point 7-5

The Securities and Exchange Commission (SEC) is concerned about investors being scammed by individuals who create business Web sites to lure investors. To help make the public aware of the dangers of believing that all business Web sites are bona fide, the SEC created its own set of false business sites. An example is the site for McWhortle (www.mcwhortle.com). The site purports to be that of a biotech company with soaring profits. Interested investors are directed to a page where they find a surprise—a warning from the SEC that if they fall for deals like this one they could get scammed.

Digital signatures are one means of ensuring against repudiation because they "bind" the message sender to the communicated document. In 2000, Congress passed the

Electronic Signature in Global and National Commerce Act, which gave documents signed with electronic signatures the same legal status as signed paper documents. The law allows for several types of electronic signatures that provide varying degrees of security and authentication. Digital signatures are at the high end of the spectrum in this regard. An individual "signs" a document with a digital signature by encrypting the message content with a private key. This encrypted message digest becomes a unique digital signature. The message can't be separated from the key. The signer sends both the digital signature and the message itself to a recipient. The sender may also forward the public key that corresponds to the private key. The recipient of this electronic document decrypts the message with the public key. If the key works and the decrypted message matches the sent message, the recipient is assured that the document originated with the digital signee; the document is authenticated because the public key is part of the private/public key pair for that document signer. Any attempt to alter a message attached to a digital signature will result in decryption failure. The message recipient can verify the public key with the issuing certificate authority for additional assurance. This use of a digital signature ensures nonrepudiation of origin and content. Including a time stamp in the message content provides additional control over transaction repudiation.

A digital certificate is a statement of authentication issued by a trusted third party. These third parties are called certificate authorities (e.g., Verisign or Thawte). Certificate authorities essentially issue ID cards to online users. They typically require several forms of authentication before they issue these certificates. Digital certificates include identification information about the certified party, public key information, and the signature of the certificate authority. The public key is sent by your browser when you send an e-mail message. The certified party keeps its private key confidential.

Electronic Audit Trails   E-business transactions generate data in bytes, not paper. Electronic evidence includes logs, audit trails, source documents, e-mail messages, and other communications. Transaction logs capture data such as user log ins, passwords, and time and date. Audit trails show the history of a transaction—from its inception to the point where it gets published in a financial statement. Transaction logs show who did what, when, and where. Audit trails allow IT auditors to trace transactions to their origins, showing who initiated a transaction, when they did it, and what information was modified, added, or deleted as a result.

IT auditors in an e-business environment need to review logs and other records as in any audit, but the nature of e-business necessitates a few extra steps. For example, auditors need to look for failed attempts to access networks, unreasonably long log-on sessions, dual log-ons (two or more computers logged on with the same ID at the same time), and attempts to make unauthorized changes to data. Electronic versus paper audit trails can be harder or easier to follow, depending on the care with which they are created. IT auditors need to make sure that audit trails exist in all e-business applications and that there are adequate internal controls to preserve them.

Electronic evidence is different from paper documentation in several respects. For one thing, electronic documents may exist only for a certain period of time. This may mean that the auditor needs to select audit samples on a periodic basis. In the absence of exhaustive backups or without proper access tools and skills, auditors may have difficulty retrieving electronic data. In 1996 and 1997, the Auditing Standards Board of the American Institute of Certified Public Accountants (AICPA) issued Statement on Auditing Standards (SAS) No. 80, *Amendment to SAS No. 31, Evidential Matter* and an *Auditing Procedures Study (APS), The Information Technology Age: Evidential Matter in the Electronic Environment,* to provide guidance to auditors regarding electronic evidence.

The APS provides practical guidance for implementing the auditing standard and describes some of the attributes of electronic evidence to be considered, including the difficulty of alteration, *prima facie* credibility, completeness of documents, evidence of approvals, ease of use, and clarity. SAS No. 94, discussed in detail in Chapter 3, also requires auditors to understand automated procedures used by organizations to prepare financial statements and other disclosures.

E-BUSINESS POLICIES   Effective e-business policies are evolving as organizations learn what constitutes best practices. The lack of business policies for activities such as processing returns of merchandise purchased online is a risk indicator for e-business. There should be a business policy for each event within a business process. For example, for the sales process, there will be policies governing sales orders, order fulfillment, and payment activities.

The IT auditor's responsibility with respect to e-business policies is to first ensure that the established policies meet organizational objectives and, second, to assess the degree to which these policies are observed.

SPECIALIZED E-BUSINESS APPLICATIONS

E-business and e-commerce include some application areas that pose unique control risks. For example, an early form of e-commerce, EDI, involves third parties and therefore adds an additional element of risk. Collaborative commerce also involves third parties. Business entities engaged in collaborative or c-commerce frequently provide information system access to other entities in their supply chain. Finally, e-mail is a unique e-business aspect that is especially risky. E-mail systems pose special security and privacy risks because they are, by nature, open systems. This section of the chapter examines each of these specialized applications.

EDI

Electronic data interchange (EDI) is the computer-to-computer exchange of business documents. EDI evolved from a desire to decrease the time involved in customer/supplier transactions. For example, when a manufacturing customer needs raw material, the customer creates a purchase order and then does what with it? Before EDI, the customer would put it in an envelope and mail it. The supplier might receive it a few days later and then start the process rolling. Order acknowledgements, shipping notices, invoices, and payments all traveled through the "snail mail" system. With EDI, orders and other source documents can be exchanged almost instantly. As shown in Figure 7-6, a computer translates

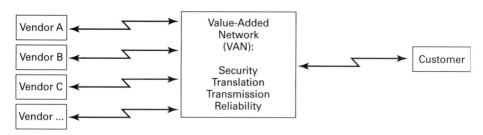

FIGURE 7-6   A VAN-Based EDI System
Source: *Core Concepts of Accounting Information Systems* 8th ed. Stephen A. Moscove, Mark G. Simkin, and Nancy A. Bagranoff. John Wiley and Sons, Inc. 2003. (Used with permission.)

an order to a common format (X12 or EDIFACT) and forwards it to an electronic post office, called a value-added network (VAN). The VAN collects mail, adds value by checking for errors, sorting, and providing some security, and then forwards the electronic documents to their recipients. The recipient computer translates the document from the EDI standard used for transmission into a format compatible with its own order management software, and processes the order.

EDI is expensive because it requires its users to install special software and requires either a dedicated communication channel or a third-party VAN. As a result, it has been adopted primarily by large manufacturers and their suppliers, who sometimes were forced to use it if they wished to do business with customers requiring it. Until e-commerce began affording computer-to-computer information exchange opportunities to smaller businesses, these entities sometimes resorted to phone calls and faxes to obtain some of the same efficiencies of EDI.

The Internet and World Wide Web offer customers and suppliers an alternative to EDI. Business partners can send encrypted EDI data back and forth over the Internet. The Internet becomes the communication channel and eliminates the need for a VAN. Encryption creates a virtual private network (discussed in Chapter 6). Internet EDI, however, requires that business trading partners use the same software, unless the data is in a standard format that each partner can upload or download. The standard emerging for the exchange of EDI business data across the Internet is ebXML, a version of XML. As this standard matures, businesses are likely to change their traditional EDI document exchanges to Web-based systems. Another alternative to EDI is the extended intranet, where customers are given password access to a supplier's intranet so they can check inventories and prices and place their orders.

The concern of IT auditors with respect to EDI and emerging forms of computerized data sharing between trading partners varies with the approach used. In the case of a VAN, IT auditors will need to conduct third-party assurance audits (discussed later in this chapter). For a Web-based EDI, the same network security issues exist as with any e-business transactions. Finally, where customers have access to intranets, access controls assume additional importance.

Collaborative Commerce

In the Internet age it's getting difficult to say where one enterprise stops and another begins. Businesses are using all of the "net" technologies—Internet, intranet, and extranet—to extend their information systems to customers, suppliers, and other business partners. The strategy is to create alliances and partnerships that provide competitive advantages. For example, airlines have partnered to create Orbitz, an online travel service that searches the partner airline databases for flights. The site also allows users to purchase hotel rooms, rental cars, and other services. This requires cooperation or partnerships among competing businesses, as well as complementary industry organizations.

Collaborative commerce means that any two or more entities with shared interest may partner to accomplish a specific goal. This partnering is likely to entail sharing information, which creates additional risk. When Orbitz brings partner companies together, these businesses become privy to information about one another that they are not likely to have had before. Ensuring that the shared information is confined to "need to know" may be the task of the IT auditor. Privacy also becomes a more important issue in collaborative e-business, because data shared with one entity might be shared with that entity's business partners.

E-mail Security and Privacy

It is hard to imagine that there was ever a time when e-mail didn't exist. Today, e-mail and instant messaging are the preferred mode of communication for many businesses and individuals.

E-MAIL RISKS   The benefits of electronic communication, unfortunately, bring with them some additional privacy and security risks. Because an e-mail system is likely to be a company's biggest network application, a security issue at one point can have a pervasive impact. E-mails can carry viruses or worms. Virus screeners and common sense in opening attachments are fairly effective against this threat, but most people get burnt a time or two before they catch on. There are other risks, too, such as e-mail spam, bombs, and electronic eavesdropping or sniffing. (See Figure 7-7 for a listing of e-mail threats.) In addition, there are threats that we may not have even thought of yet. Case-in-Point 7-6 describes a different kind of e-mail threat.

Case-in-Point 7-6

Starbucks seemed to be having a run on its crème frappuccino coffee drinks one day in summer 2002. Customers bought the drinks with coupons that they had received in an e-mail. Unfortunately, the e-mail didn't come from Starbucks, but rather from a hacker playing a hoax. Store managers redeemed the coupons for some time before they got the message from headquarters that the coupons were counterfeit.[6]

Spamming involves sending multiple unwanted e-mails. This may just be a nuisance, or it may create a more severe effect by overloading servers and communication channels or by launching a virus or DDOS attack. Sometimes spamming is unintentional. Your worst nightmare may be accidentally sending a personal message to a list serve—for this

---

E-Mail Security Threats

Viruses/worms—E-mail messages and attachments may contain malicious code. In some cases, the code will replicate and send itself to all addresses in the mail recipient's address book.

Spam—This involves sending unrequested e-mail to multiple users.

Bombs—This involves sending unwanted e-mail repeatedly to the same e-mail address.

Sniffing—During transmission, an unauthorized user can read a plain text e-mail message.

Session hijacking—An unauthorized user can take over a communications session by sending a forged message to an e-mail user following the user's authentication.

Spoofing—The source address of an e-mail may be forged.

E-Mail Privacy Threats

Sexual or racial harassment—An e-mail user can send salacious or inappropriate e-mail messages.

Privacy leaks—There are many ways that privacy can be compromised through e-mail. For example, private messages may be forwarded, shared, or sniffed by hackers.

E-mail paper trail—E-mail messages are somewhat permanent and can be used as evidence in legal proceedings. Deleting e-mails that could be subpoenaed may be viewed as obstruction of justice.

Corporate espionage—An insider may leak corporate trade secrets through e-mails. Electronic eavesdroppers may also obtain proprietary data sent through an e-mail system.

FIGURE 7-7   E-mail System Threats

reason it's a good idea to think before hitting the reply button. It is also good policy to avoid sending anything personal or controversial as an e-mail in any case, because e-mail messages can be permanent.

Another e-mail issue is spoofing. It is quite easy to "hide" identities in e-mails. There was a case at one university in which a male student sent an e-mail to a female student he liked, using her boyfriend's e-mail address as the message source and breaking up with her. Changing the e-mail source address is relatively easy and allows e-mail spoofers to pretend e-mails come from different locations.

Employers need to create and communicate an e-mail policy to all employees so that there are no misunderstandings regarding the privacy of these communications. The e-mail policy should explain that the e-mail system is the property of the company, that the company maintains the right to audit and monitor it, and that it has the right to disclose e-mail information. The policy should further state that employees may not assume confidentiality of their e-mail, that e-mails should be sent and received only for business purposes, and that employees should never send or accept offensive e-mails. Finally, the e-mail policy should state an e-mail retention policy. This is important in case supporting e-mails are needed in litigation. IT auditors need to make sure these policies exist and are thorough, broadly communicated, and enforced.

CONTROLLING E-MAIL SYSTEMS The e-mail policy is arguably the most important component of effective e-mail security, but there are many specialized security products available that can help manage and secure e-mail applications. Features of these products include encryption, file compression, authentication, content scanning, tracking, automatic expiration, digital shredding, filtering and blocking (e.g., blocking all executable attachments), and anti-virus protection. Some of the software available that provides this security are Genidocs Server, GLWebMail XT Professional, enRole, and CAMEO Recon.

The best way to ensure e-mail privacy is through encryption. Two encryption standards used for e-mail are Pretty Good Privacy (PGP) and Secure Multipurpose Internet Mail Extensions (S/MIME). PGP has a public and private key and you need both. Potential e-mail recipients can obtain the pubic key through e-mail, a Web site, or a digital certificate authority.[7] The following describes how to use PGP for encryption.

There are two ways to encrypt an e-mail message with PGP. One way is to compose a text message and then encrypt the text file using the appropriate PGP command. It is also possible to write, encrypt, and send the message all at once, using the PGP command for this function, and including the appropriate public key and e-mail address of the recipient along with the command. The second approach provides additional security because the unencrypted message is never stored. PGP users share a directory of public keys called a key ring—you can't send an encrypted message to anybody who doesn't have access to the key ring.

S/MIME is free and comes with Netscape Navigator and Microsoft Internet Explorer browsers. It is also available as a plug-in.[8] It uses a shorter encryption code than PGP and, as a result, the code is easier to break. Even with encryption, sniffers and hackers can tamper with messages during transmission, but PGP and S/MIME can detect tampering by inspecting the digital signature. If they are able to decrypt the signature, the message is authentic. Individuals may use personal e-mail digital certificates to digitally sign their e-mail messages. These signatures provide the recipients with authentication that the communications are from the signer. These certificates also allow individuals to encrypt their messages in order to keep unauthorized users from viewing them.

MANAGING THIRD-PARTY PROVIDERS

CobiT, discussed in Chapter 3, considers control over third-party services as part of its Delivery and Support (DS2) dimension. Businesses have been relying on third parties to provide services for some time. The advent of e-business, however, brings increased reliance on outsiders in the form of Internet service providers (ISP), application service providers (ASP), certificate authorities, and electronic payment providers. Many organizations outsource much of their e-business functionality, including Web site development and maintenance. The degree of influence a third party has on an entity's own internal control system varies with the extent of services provided.

IT auditors, in evaluating controls over third-party services, need to first understand the relationship between the entity under review and the third party. This begins with a review of organizational policies and procedures that should be in line with the engagement of the third-party service provider. It also includes reviewing and monitoring service-level agreements and contracts. The IT auditors also need to review and document the third party's processes and controls as they relate to the client organization. IT auditors should confirm their understanding of the third party's processes and controls through surveys, conversations, and observation. They should also evaluate the risks of the relationship, test the controls, and develop conclusions regarding the effectiveness of the controls. Figure 7-8 describes several specific steps that would be incorporated in an audit plan for third-party services.

It is not unusual for a third party to produce an internal control report containing an evaluation by an independent evaluator. Businesses that provide such services for clients frequently obtain these reports and may use them to provide assurance to potential customers. An IT auditor who accepts such a report will need to consider the professional qualifications and independence of the party providing the report, the sufficiency of the report, and the period of time covered by the report.

Third-party service audits are sometimes referred to as SAS 70 reviews. Statement on Auditing Standards (SAS) 70, *Reports on the Processing of Transactions by Service Organizations,* was issued by the AICPA Auditing Standards Board in 1992. The purpose of the standard was to provide financial auditors with some guidance in auditing the financial statements of organizations that rely on third-party service organizations to process some of their transactions. The standard also offers guidance to auditors providing a SAS 70 review or report on the transaction processing of a service organization that will be used by other auditors. IT auditors have frequently found themselves engaged in these types of audits because it is generally an information system that generates the transactions.

Evaluate whether or not contracting for third-party services meets organizational objectives.

Inspect service-level agreements and evaluate compliance with these agreements.

Evaluate the scope of services being offered by the third party and determine whether it is in line with the service-level agreement.

Inspect contracts and determine whether contract terms are being complied with by both parties.

Ensure that contracts include provisions for contingencies, confidentiality, security, duration, costs, term, and contract violation and dissolution terms.

Ensure that all third-party services are performed by pre-approved vendors and that contracts are awarded competitively.

Determine whether the contracts include performance metrics and the degree to which those are observed and evaluated.

FIGURE 7-8 Sample Audit Steps for Evaluating Third-Party Services

THIRD-PARTY ASSURANCE SERVICES

The objective of third-party assurance services is to address the privacy and security concerns of end consumers and companies conducting business over the Internet. Third parties, such as IT auditors, can evaluate a business in terms of its online privacy, security, transaction integrity, systems reliability, and business policies. They then demonstrate to the public, typically by displaying a certification seal at the business Web site, that the organization has obtained this assurance. Figure 7-9 shows sample assurance seals.

Many types of organizations offer third-party assurance services to clients and, as a result, the levels of assurance vary. For example, CPA WebTrust, a joint initiative of the American Institute of Certified Public Accountants (AICPA) and the Canadian Institute of Chartered Accountants (CICA), offers a full spectrum of e-business assurance, and clients can purchase all or pieces of it. One client may wish to obtain assurance only over online privacy, while another might be interested in showing business partners that it has been evaluated in terms of its privacy, security, and availability.

As online business grew in the 1990s, accountants and others saw opportunities to provide assurance services. CPAs viewed themselves as natural candidates for this type of work because of their assurance expertise. The AICPA and CICA believed that consumers would feel more secure trading with a business that displayed a certificate of assurance issued by a CPA. As a result, they created two "trust" services: WebTrust and SysTrust. WebTrust is directed primarily at e-commerce transactions and is a subset of SysTrust, which is for any information system.

Both WebTrust and SysTrust embody a set of principles and criteria. The principles are: security, availability, processing integrity, online privacy, and confidentiality.[9] In a WebTrust engagement, the auditor evaluates any or all of these principles against a set of criteria. The four categories of criteria are policies, communications, procedures, and monitoring. Within each category are specific criteria that are common for each principle. For example, the three criteria for policies are policy creation and approval, policy requirements, and assignment of responsibility for policies and any changes to them. Finally, each specific criteria may be accompanied by specific illustrative controls.

The AICPA/CICA framework of trust principles and criteria provides very specific guidance for a WebTrust or SysTrust engagement. For instance, an auditor evaluating the processing integrity principle would be directed to examine specific authorized user

The Good
Housekeeping
Institute
Website

Certification

FIGURE 7-9   Third Party Assurance Seals

access policies when examining an organization's policies over system processing integrity. After evaluating the client organization against the criteria for each principle selected, the auditor awards an electronic seal to the Web site. Clicking on the seal reveals the CPA's report and other information about the level of assurance provided.

An important aspect of assurance is that it be granted by a "brand" that consumers and businesses will recognize. The CPA is one such brand, but some public accounting firms have invested heavily in creating and marketing their own name brand. As a result a CPA firm may offer online assurance and provide a stamp of approval that has its own signature on it. PricewaterhouseCooper's BetterWeb is an example. The BetterWeb program is directed at consumers and provides assurance about sales terms, privacy, security, and customer complaints. The section on sales terms concerns information about prices, payments, cancellations, and returns. The privacy principle concerns the use of personal information collected at a Web site, and security shows how information and assets are protected. The customer complaint principle ensures that consumers will have a contact for complaints and that the online business is able to confirm receipt of complaints within a short time. As with WebTrust, a Web site visitor can click on the seal to view a statement describing the standards and policies applied by the third-party assurance service.

Another brand that the public knows well is the Better Business Bureau (BBB). The Council of BBBs has been providing assurance to consumers about business practices since 1912. The Internet created an opportunity for the BBB to expand its assurance to online, as well as brick and mortar, companies. The e-business subsidiary of BBB, BBB Online, offers several kinds of certification, including a reliability seal program and a privacy seal. To obtain a reliability seal, a business must be a member of the local BBB and must meet the program eligibility criteria. These require a company to have been in business for a certain length of time, to have a satisfactory complaint-handling record, and to agree to comply with the BBB's Code of Online Business Practices. To obtain the BBB Privacy seal, a business must adopt and post a privacy policy at its Web site and complete a compliance assessment questionnaire.

TRUSTe, like the BBB, is a nonprofit organization providing third-party e-business assurance services. Unlike BBB Online, however, TRUSTe offers assurance only over privacy. The TRUSTe certification requires approval of a company's privacy statement. TRUSTe offers a resource guide to help organizations create them. Both BBB Online and TRUSTe charge licensing fees for their certifications, based on company revenues.

Verisign, Inc., is another specialized third-party assurance service provider. This company offers a variety of digital trust services, including a security seal. The security seal has quickly become one of the most recognized on the Internet. It provides assurance that the Web site is authentic and that data transmission uses SSL encryption.

SUMMARY

Because e-business risk varies with the type of e-business model, this chapter began with a discussion of the evolution of e-business models. E-business in its earliest form consisted of EDI and electronic transfer-of-funds technologies. As the Internet developed, businesses began moving paper content to it in the form of Web pages. Today many enterprises are using the Internet along with intranets and extranets to work collaboratively with their business partners.

E-business technologies are similar to other network protocols, hardware, and software. Special protocols associated with e-business are TCP/IP and HTTP. Various software languages used in e-business include HTML and XML. Specialized forms of XML for e-business are likely to be XBRL and ebXML.

E-business creates new risks, apart from those associated with traditional networks. These risks may be categorized as privacy issues, security and availability concerns, or transaction processing and business policy issues. One of the greatest concerns of individuals and businesses involved in online transactions is privacy. This chapter described privacy issues and provided guidance in creating a privacy policy. Secure e-business requires the use of many of the controls and tools described in Chapter 6. These include firewalls, encryption, intrusion detection systems, security administration, authentication tools, and penetration testing. In addition, there are special e-business security issues, such as special encryption standards, electronic payment mechanisms, Web server protection, and system availability and reliability. Transaction integrity and business policies ensure successful e-business.

Certain specialized e-business applications carry with them unique risks and controls. This chapter described three of these application areas—EDI, collaborative commerce, and e-mail—in some detail.

E-business creates opportunities for many third-party services. IT auditors may be called on to evaluate third-party services, and they may also find themselves providing assurances as third parties themselves. The last two sections of this chapter discussed both of these options.

DISCUSSION QUESTIONS

7-1   What would be the differences in risks faced by an organization that used the Internet primarily to display content versus a business that conducted collaborative e-business?

7-2   What are the differences between the OSI protocol described in Chapter 6 and the TCP/IP protocol described in this chapter?

7-3   XML is developing as a language to facilitate the extraction and manipulation of data on the Internet. Discuss some of the obstacles likely in the development of a common language for communicating and manipulating e-business data.

7-4   Privacy is considered to be one of the biggest concerns in conducting consumer-to-business transactions across the Internet. Find the privacy policy for a popular online retailer and compare it with that of GE.

7-5   Discuss the difference between privacy and confidentiality issues for two businesses engaged in e-commerce.

7-6   Discuss the advantages and disadvantages of cookie files from an end consumer standpoint.

7-7   SSL is the most common encryption form used for e-business. Discuss its shortcomings and explain how it compares with SET.

7-8   Discuss the advantages to both an end consumer and to banks and billing companies of EBPP systems.

7-9   Why is the issue of repudiation so important in e-business?

7-10   Explain how you would go about obtaining a digital signature. Also explain why a digital signature might carry less risk than a paper signature.

7-11   Describe at least four implications of electronic versus paper evidence for IT auditors.

7-12   E-business conducted over the Internet may supplant traditional EDI systems. Why would a company choose to continue using EDI for exchange of business documents versus the Internet?

7-13   If you were an IT auditor who learned that the company for which you work is planning to engage in collaborative commerce over the Internet, what would be your concerns regarding risk?

7-14   Describe four specific topics that should be included in an organization's e-mail policy.

7-15   Businesses have long been using the services of third parties. Why does the Internet make management of third-party providers an increasingly important issue?

7-16   The AICPA introduced its WebTrust assurance service several years ago. It has been slow to catch on, and its seal is on only a few Internet sites. Why do you think this service has not been more popular?

EXERCISES

7-17 Equip-Your-Office, Inc., is a Chicago-based company that sells office equipment to end consumers and retail stores, primarily throughout the midwestern United States. Pierce Bennett, the
CIO, is directing a project to develop an online sales operation. He has many concerns about
security and privacy. The CFO, Halle Banks, is recommending that the company obtain third-
party assurance at the Web site. She feels that it will be important to customers to see a seal or
other form of guarantee that will give them some comfort about doing business with Equip-
Your-Office online.

Required:

a. Discuss the advantages and need for third-party assurance in this scenario.

b. Which third-party assurance type would you recommend?

7-18 Extensible business reporting language (XBRL) is an XML-based standard for business
reporting on the Internet, being developed by a consortium of more than 170 organizations.
Ideally, XBRL will allow easy comparison, exchange, and analysis of financial reports. More
than 80 percent of U.S.-based companies publish some financial information on the Internet,
but this data is in a variety of formats that makes it difficult to use the information.

Required:

a. Explain the likely benefits of XBRL to each of the following groups:

- Investors
- Accountants
- Reporting entities
- Lenders

b. While XBRL holds a lot of promise, there are many impediments to its development
and usage. Discuss the problems in creating this standard.

REFERENCES AND RECOMMENDED READINGS

Adam, Nabil R., Oktay Dogramaci, Aryya Gangopadhyay, and Yelena Yesha. 1999. *Electronic
Commerce: Technical, Business, and Legal Issues.* Upper Saddle River, N.J.: Prentice Hall.

Armstrong, Illena. 2002. "Email Security: Juggling the Risks." *SC Info Security Magazine.* May:
26–32.

Berkman, Eric. 2002. "How to Practice Safe B2B." *CIO Magazine.* June 15: 52–58.

Blanco, Louis. 2002. "Audit Trails in an E-commerce Environment." *Information Systems Control
Journal* 5: 32–35.

Cuningham, Patrick J. 2002. "Are Cookies Hazardous to Your Privacy?" *The Information
Management Journal.* (May/June): 52–54.

Dwan, Berni. 2002. "A Clean Sweep." *SC Info Security Magazine.* May: 54–69.

Garfinkel, Simson, and Gene Spafford. 1997. *Web Security and Commerce.* Cambridge, Mass.:
O'Reilly & Associates.

Glover, Steven M., Stephen W. Liddle, and Douglas F. Prewitt. 2001. *e-Business: Principles &
Strategies for Accountants.* Upper Saddle River, N.J.: Prentice Hall.

Greenstein, Marilyn, and Miklos Vasarhelyi. 2002. *Electronic Commerce: Security, Risk
Management, and Control.* Boston: McGraw-Hill Irwin.

Halpern, Marcelo. 2001. "Not All E-Signatures Are Equal." *CIO Magazine.* January 15: 54–56.

Hoffman, Charles, and Carolyn Strand. 2001. *XBRL Essentials.* New York: American Institute of
Certified Public Accountants.

Information Systems Audit and Control Association. *2002 CISA Review Manual.* Rolling
Meadows, Ill.: Information Systems Audit and Control Association.

Martin, Chuck. 1999. *netFuture.* New York: McGraw-Hill.

ISACA Standards Board. 2002. "Effect of Third Parties on an Organization's IT Controls." *Information Systems Control Journal* 4: 28–31.

Mascha, Maureen Francis, and Cathleen L. Miller. 2002. "Stop E-Mail SNOOPS." *Journal of Accountancy.* July: 61–63.

Mehta, Raj. 2000. "Secure E-Business." *Information Systems Control Journal* 1: 32–37.

Parker, Xenia Ley. 2001. *An e-Risk Primer.* Altamonte Springs Fla.: Institute of Internal Auditors Research Foundation.

Pathak, J. P. 2000. "Are E-mails Boon or Bane for Organisations?" *Information Systems Control Journal* 1: 27–29.

Williamson, Louise A. 1997. "The Implications of Electronic Evidence. *Journal of Accountancy.* February: 69–71.

Zarowin, Stanley, and Wayne E. Harding. 2000. "Finally, Business Talks the Same Language." *Journal of Accountancy.* August: 24–30.

Web Sites

The Internet Engineering Task Force, www.ietf.org, is an international group of IT professionals concerned with the evolution of the Internet.

For more information about XBRL, visit www.xbrl.org or www.xbrlsolutions.com. Information about ebXML is available at www.ebxml.org.

NOTES

1. Piturro, Marlene. "Internet Success." *Strategic Finance* (October 2001): 32.
2. "Citibank Mails Raise Privacy Concern," Yochi J. Dreazen. *The Wall Street Journal*, 3 September 2002.
3. General Electric's privacy policy is available at its Web site: www.ge.com. We use it with permission from Nate Kirtman, content manager, ge.com.
4. David McGuire and Brian Krebs, "Attack on Internet Called Largest Ever," www.washingtonpost.com, 22 October 2002.
5. SysTrust Principles and Criteria, Version 2.0. (www.aicpa.org/assurance/systrust/princip.htm—24 September 2002)
6. ElBoghdady, Dina, "Starbucks: Coupons Are Fake." *Washington Post.* 18 July 2002, p. E1.
7. For more information about PGP, see www.nal.com/products/security/pgpfreeware.asp.
8. For more information about S/MIME see www.baltimore.ie/products/mailsecure/index/asp.
9. These principles are identified in *Exposure Draft—AICPA/CICA Trust Services, Principles, and Criteria.* July 1, 2002. Version 1.0. The new exposure draft took effect 1 January 2003.

CHAPTER *8*

USING COMPUTER ASSISTED AUDIT TOOLS AND TECHNIQUES (CAATTS)

CHAPTER CONTENTS

INTRODUCTION TO CAATTS

If you spend much time reading audit books, articles, or other professional literature, you undoubtedly have come across the term "CAATTs." Sometimes there is one "T," and other times there are two "Ts." In case you're wondering what the difference is, let's begin this chapter by clearing that up.

Definition of CAATTs

CAATTs (with two "T"s) refers to "computer assisted audit tools and techniques." CAATs (with one "T") refers to "computer assisted audit techniques." Professionals use both terms, but they mean slightly different things. CAATTs is a broader umbrella whose subcomponents can be grouped into two categories: 1) software used to increase an auditor's personal productivity and software used to perform data extraction and analysis, and 2) techniques to increase the efficiency and effectiveness of the audit function. CAATs, on the other hand, usually refers to only the second part, or techniques used to increase the efficiency and effectiveness of the audit function.[1] In this chapter (and in the entire book), we adopt the convention of using "CAATTs" when we discuss IT audit tools or when we are collectively referring to *both* audit tools and techniques, and "CAATs" when we discuss IT audit techniques. Figure 8-1 provides a graphic to help you understand the framework for classifying CAATTs.

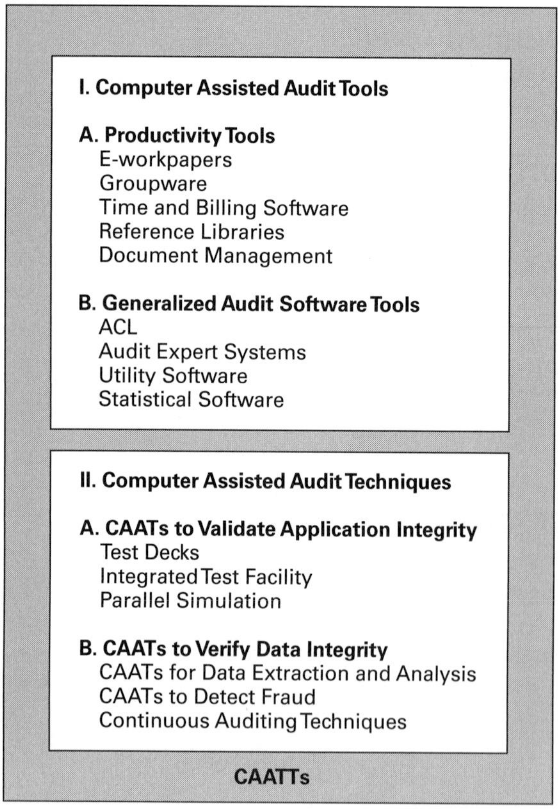

I. Computer Assisted Audit Tools

A. Productivity Tools
E-workpapers
Groupware
Time and Billing Software
Reference Libraries
Document Management

B. Generalized Audit Software Tools
ACL
Audit Expert Systems
Utility Software
Statistical Software

II. Computer Assisted Audit Techniques

A. CAATs to Validate Application Integrity
Test Decks
Integrated Test Facility
Parallel Simulation

B. CAATs to Verify Data Integrity
CAATs for Data Extraction and Analysis
CAATs to Detect Fraud
Continuous Auditing Techniques

CAATTs

FIGURE 8-1 Categories of Computer Assisted Audit Tools and Techniques (CAATTS)

Types of CAATTs

Productivity tools include any software that assists the auditor in performing administrative tasks more efficiently. For example, the audit firm might use Lotus Notes to update and exchange electronic information regarding a client. They might use electronic workpapers to document the work performed during the audit. And they might use software to manage the audit engagement and time and billing software to streamline the billing process. These CAATTs would all be considered productivity tools because they are designed to increase the auditor's efficiency at managing the hundreds of administrative details incumbent in an audit.

Myriad software tools also help auditors extract data from client records and perform various quality assurance tests on that underlying client data. These tools are collectively referred to as "generalized audit software." The best-known software tool is Audit Command Language, or ACL for short. Other software within this category includes audit expert systems, various types of utility software programs, and software that performs statistical analysis.

Beyond productivity and generalized audit software tools, CAATTs also include computerized audit techniques that auditors can perform on data once it has been extracted from the client's computer system. These techniques include, for example, generating test decks of data, writing and embedding automated audit modules, and performing digital analysis and linear regression on a client's data. Specialized techniques can also be used to detect suspected fraud in a client's financial statements.

This chapter discusses all of these computer-assisted tools and techniques used by auditors. IT auditors, in particular, should be intimately familiar with the computerized techniques highlighted in this chapter.

AUDIT PRODUCTIVITY SOFTWARE

Any software that facilitates the auditor's personal productivity would be classified as "audit productivity software." This section discusses electronic working papers (including electronic audit programs and questionnaires), groupware, engagement management, reference libraries, and document management.

Electronic Working Papers

The "paperless" office has been touted over the past decade as the way of the future for CPAs and other accountants. While most accounting firms have not gone totally paperless, most have implemented varying degrees of paperless technology.

The move toward the use of electronic working papers is one trend that has been especially beneficial in increasing productivity. In the not-so-distant past, auditors expended a great deal of time and effort on creating manual audit workpapers, including lead schedules, detail schedules, and supporting schedules. They generated audit programs and internal control questionnaires manually during the planning phase of the audit. Today, however, e-workpapers can automate that process and thus greatly increase an individual auditor's efficiency. For example, e-working papers can import a client's trial balance, map accounts back to the client system, and allow the auditor to input audit adjustments electronically. After the auditor completes the audit, the auditor can automatically generate GAAP-compliant financial statements.

Many e-working papers are compatible with Windows-based data processing and spreadsheet programs such as Word, Excel, and PowerPoint, allowing auditors to use familiar tools and provide client-compatible documents. Additionally, audit supervisors can edit workpapers and reports while leaving an audit trail that allows staff to easily learn from these changes. We describe several popular electronic working paper software programs in Figure 8-2. Case-in-Point 8-1 discusses how one firm saves money by using electronic working papers.

Case-in-Point 8-1

Efficiency translates directly into dollars saved. Just ask Habif, Arogeti, and Wynne, a two-hundred-employee accounting firm using CaseWare's Working Papers. The firm operates on a 100 percent paperless engagement system in which employees are sent to clients with laptops. Audit workpapers are kept electronically, and files are backed up digitally. Altogether, the firm has saved hundreds of thousands of dollars by going paperless.[2]

Figure 8-3 shows the importing of a client's financials into CaseWare's Working Papers, a popular e-working paper software program.

Name of Software	Manufacturer	Notes
Intacct Audit	Intacct Corporation and Deloitte & Touche	Web-based system Monthly subscription required Designed to work integrate with Intacct accounting package Over 150 customizable e-workpapers Includes audit programs
Working Papers	CaseWare International, Inc.	Allows import and export of client data from legacy systems Drill-down capability Intelligent document generator generates GAAP-based financial statements Built-in mapping to client's system
ProSystem fx Trial Balance and Prosystem fx Engagement	CCH, Inc.	These systems were formerly known as "ProSystem fx Audit" and "ePaceEngagement" Offers fully integrated audit engagement practice Simultaneous reviewer approval Remote access with file sharing and updating Allows more than 32,000 line accounts
TeamMate	PriceWaterhouseCoopers	A data base-driven system used by over 20,000 auditors in 375 firms worldwide Files can be used concurrently by several auditors Compatible with multiple operating systems and third-party software Incorporates an "Auditor Toolset" for use in review notes, tick marks, and other traditional audit references Incorporates state-of-the-art imaging software to enable inclusion of scanned documents in the workpapers

FIGURE 8-2 Audit Productivity Tools: Electronic Workpapers

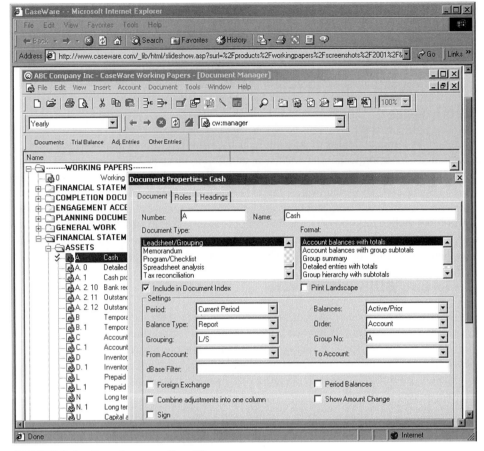

FIGURE 8-3   E-workpapers: CaseWare

Common features of electronic working paper software programs include the ability to:

- Import client's raw data from legacy systems;
- Automatically generate working papers and their references (i.e., lead and detail schedules);
- Export to Excel and other file formats to facilitate sharing of information with the client and others;
- Drill down and see underlying transactions from financial statements;
- Enter adjusting journal entries;
- Break down accounts into subcomponents;
- Create consolidated financial statements;
- Map accounts from lead and detail schedules to the client's general ledger accounts;
- Populate report templates and risk assessments from findings sheets;
- Calculate predefined ratios and other performance measures such as the Balanced Score Card;
- Compare versions of a document and highlight differences or changes;
- Generate risk analysis and business cycle analysis;

- Conduct file interrogation;
- Share files among other members of the audit engagement anytime both locally and remotely;
- Generate audit programs from predetermined audit objectives; and
- Generate internal control questionnaires.

Groupware

To maintain competitiveness in the audit industry, firms are finding more ways to increase productivity by using technology better. In addition to electronic working papers, groupware can facilitate sharing of information across firms and between the auditor and the client. Some common groupware programs are Lotus Notes, Novell GroupWise, and Microsoft Exchange. These programs are collaborative tools that allow multi-user calendaring, scheduling, and file sharing. These tools are particularly useful for the IT auditor in planning the audit. Because multiple schedules can be considered simultaneously, engagement staffing and planning can be streamlined.

Time and Billing Software

As anyone who has worked in public accounting can attest, managing time and billing are necessary evils. If billing is not attended to on a timely basis, the audit firm's cash flow will quickly suffer. Time and billing software can ease the formerly onerous process of accounting for chargeable hours and compiling and preparing bills accordingly. Examples of time and billing software are ProSystem's fx Practice, Timeslips, Bill Central Time and Billing, among many others.

Reference Libraries

Auditors use internal reference libraries for two main reasons: to locate company-specific policies and procedures, and to search for authority when researching a particularly thorny problem. Company-specific policies and procedures will contain guidance on issues such as creating workpapers, staffing audit engagements, communicating with the client, and a multitude of other audit issues. Auditors cannot keep thousands of company-specific policies and procedures in their head. After all, they're only human! Most companies recognize the importance of maintaining a database of such rules. Auditors can access this database remotely via the Web. Even easier, often companies will maintain CDs for portability and ease of access.

Auditors can easily become overwhelmed when faced with the daunting task of searching for authority while researching a problem. Once again, an auditor can't be expected to keep every audit, tax, and consulting rule in her head. Instead, the auditor will access the company database of such information. Search and retrieval capabilities also increase the auditor's efficiency. Additionally, the auditor doesn't need to copy down the authority once it's located. Rather, she can cut and paste the authority as needed into the workpapers.

Document Management

Software that has made online document storage readily available and practical has greatly enhanced the auditor's productivity. For example, software that allows the scanning and storing of tax returns means not only more efficient use of storage space, but also quick access to prior year tax returns. Information can be stored locally on a firm's own network hard drive using programs like CSI's FileCabinet. Alternatively, software such as Intuit's WorkSpace Pro allows online document management through the use of the Internet. For example, a firm that wants to share its financial statements with a potential lender can allow the banker access to a password-protected Web site holding the information.

Taken together, these productivity tools can create huge economies of efficiency for IT auditors. The next section looks at audit software tools that increase the efficiency of the audit function itself.

GENERALIZED AUDIT SOFTWARE TOOLS

One of the most powerful tools in the IT auditor's toolkit is generalized audit software (GAS). GAS includes several tools, including software that enables extraction of data from a client's system and analysis of that data, statistical software, and audit expert systems.

Data Extraction and Analysis

Before the advent of this type of audit software tool, auditors spent countless hours performing mundane (but necessary!) tasks such as recalculating client totals, verifying data integrity, calculating sample sizes, inputting data into spreadsheets, preparing confirmations, etc. With the technology revolution, however, audit software such as ACL can quickly and easily perform these kinds of tasks. The biggest advantage of using software to perform these routine tasks is that the auditor has considerably more time to concentrate on analytical thinking. Additionally, it significantly reduces auditor error and the likelihood of spreadsheet formula errors.

SAS 94, *The Effect of Information Technology on the Auditor's Consideration of Internal Controls in a Financial Statement Audit,* amends SAS No. 55, *Consideration of Internal Control in a Financial Statement Audit.* It is effective for financial statement audits for periods beginning on or after June 1, 2001. This standard addresses the auditor's responsibility to fully understand the client's technology as part of gaining an understanding about the client's internal controls in the conduct of a financial statement audit. It also assists auditors in determining whether IT auditors and their specialized skill set should be called on to assist in the financial audit. If the external auditor believes it is necessary, an IT auditor will be called in to provide expertise and the assurance that detection risk is restricted to an acceptable level.

SAS 94 also mandates that the auditor understand the client's process for recording all types of transactions into the general ledger, including regular journal entries, special journal entries, and recurring and nonrecurring adjusting journal entries. The auditor must also understand what types of material misstatements might be likely to occur.

While ACL enjoys substantial popularity, there are other audit software tools that perform similar tasks, including Computer Associates' Advantage CA-Easytrieve and Interactive Data Extraction and Analysis (IDEA).

Statistical Analysis

A second type of GAS tool is one that enables auditors to perform statistical analysis on a client's data file. For example, the auditor may wish to calculate averages or standard deviations or perform linear regression to determine if there is an underlying relationship between certain variables of interest. ACL can perform simple statistical analysis like this, or the auditor may choose a more sophisticated statistical package such as Statistical Analysis System (SAS) or SPSS.

Audit Expert Systems

Expert systems are still another type of audit software tool that can be useful in making routine, structured decisions. They have been used in audits since the late 1980s for everything from audit planning, setting materiality, and performing risk analysis to evaluating internal controls. Expert systems are most often based on a series of if-then production rules, which in turn access a knowledge base consisting of information relevant to the topic. An "inference engine" runs the system, and based on a user's answers to relevant questions, returns an answer.

Expert systems have many advantages and disadvantages. Advantages include:

1. Unbiased decision-making;
2. Incorporation of expertise of multiple experts; and
3. Constant availability (i.e., expert systems don't get sick or "have a bad day" or any of the other frailties from which humans suffer).

The disadvantages of expert systems include:

1. Difficulty in eliciting the decision-making process and criteria from the expert(s);
2. Difficulty in updating the knowledge base and rules contained therein;
3. Time required to develop and test the system;
4. Expense to develop and maintain the system;
5. Difficulty in modeling uncertainty in decisions; and
6. Mechanical adherence to the process—no room for intuition or human reasoning.

In spite of these disadvantages, all of the Big Four accounting firms use expert systems for audit and/or tax applications. Case-in-Point 8-2 discusses one popular system.

Case-in-Point 8-2

In 1996, PricewaterhouseCoopers won the Innovative Applications in Artificial Intelligence award for its audit expert system, Comet. Comet provides a unique approach to systems assurance in its analysis of internal controls, including the strength of compensating controls and weaknesses in internal control.[3]

Generalized audit software such as ACL (and its counterparts) and statistical software tools such as SAS require specialized training. While menu-driven interfaces have simplified the use of these tools, the IT auditor will need to spend some time either in self-study courses or in formal courses to acquire a full appreciation of the strengths and weaknesses of these tools. The appendix of this book provides an introduction to Audit Command Language through the use of the ACL workbook provided with the text. We also use ACL in the following section to demonstrate various audit techniques.

COMPUTER ASSISTED IT AUDIT TECHNIQUES

Now that we've seen various audit software *tools,* we're ready to move on to computer assisted audit *techniques.* These are procedures that assist IT auditors in obtaining sufficient, reliable, relevant, and useful evidence to support predefined audit objectives.

IT auditors are fortunate to have guidelines provided for the conduct of CAATs by the Standards Board of the Information Systems Audit and Control Association (ISACA).

Professional Standards and Guidelines

In 1998, the ISACA Standards Board issued Guideline 060.020.070 (hereafter "Guideline 70") governing the use of CAATs. Note that this guideline is specific to the use of computer assisted audit techniques (hence the use of one "T" here). The guideline provides guidance in the areas of CAATs planning, execution, documentation, and reporting. The highlights of Guideline 70 are shown in Figure 8-4. Students should study Figure 8-4 carefully to understand what the IT auditor's responsibilities are with respect to using CAATs. Students can view the entire text of the guideline at www.isaca.org/standard/guide8.htm.

---

2. Planning

2.1.1 When planning the audit, the IS Auditor should consider an appropriate combination of manual techniques and CAATs. In determining whether to use CAATs, the factors to be considered include:

- Computer knowledge, expertise, and experience of the IS Auditor
- Availability of suitable CAATs and IS facilities
- Efficiency and effectiveness of using CAATs over manual techniques
- Time constraints
- Integrity of the information system and IT environment
- Level of audit risk

2.2.1 The major steps to be undertaken by the IS Auditor in preparing for the application of the selected CAATs are:

- Set the audit objectives of the CAATs
- Determine the accessibility and availability of the organization's IS facilities, programs/system, and data
- Define the procedures to be undertaken (e.g., statistical sampling, recalculation, confirmation, etc.)
- Define output requirements
- Determine resource requirements, i.e., personnel, CAATs, processing environment (organization's IS facilities or audit IS facilities)
- Obtain access to the organization's IS facilities, programs/system, and data, including file definitions
- Document CAATs to be used, including objectives, high-level flowcharts, and run instructions

3. Performance of Audit Work

3.1.1 The use of CAATs should be controlled by the IS Auditor to provide reasonable assurance that the audit objectives and the detailed specifications of the CAATs have been met. The IS Auditor should:

- Perform a reconciliation of control totals if appropriate
- Review output for reasonableness
- Perform a review of the logic, parameters, or other characteristics of the CAATs
- Review the organization's general IS controls which may contribute to the integrity of the CAATs (e.g., program change controls and access to system, program, and/or data files)

(continued)

FIGURE 8-4   Summary of ISACA Guideline 060.020.070 Use of Computer Assisted Audit Techniques (1 of 2)

4. Documentation

4.1.1 The step-by-step CAATs process should be sufficiently documented to provide adequate audit evidence.

4.1.2 Specifically, the audit workpapers should contain sufficient documentation to describe the CAATs application, including the details set out in the following sections.

4.2 Planning

- CAATs objectives
- CAATs to be used
- Controls to be exercised
- Staffing and timing

4.3 Execution

- CAATs preparation and testing procedures and controls
- Details of the tests performed by the CAATs
- Details of inputs (e.g., data used, file layouts), processing (e.g., CAATs high-level flowcharts, logic) and outputs (e.g., log files, reports)
- Listing of relevant parameters or source code

4.4 Audit Evidence

- CAATs preparation and testing procedures and controls
- Details of the tests performed by the CAATs
- Details of inputs (e.g., data used, file layouts), processing (e.g., CAATs high-level flowcharts, logic) and outputs (e.g., log files, reports)
- Listing of relevant parameters or source code

5. Reporting

5.1.1 The objectives, scope and methodology section of the report should contain a clear description of the CAATs used. This description should not be overly detailed, but it should provide a good overview for the reader.

5.1.2 The description of the CAATs used should also be included in the body of the report, where the specific finding relating to the use of the CAATs is discussed.

5.1.3 If the description of the CAATs used is applicable to several findings, or is too detailed, it should be discussed briefly in the objectives, scope and methodology section of the report and the reader referred to an appendix with a more detailed description.

FIGURE 8-4 Summary of ISACA Guideline 060.020.070 Use of Computer Assisted Audit Techniques (2 of 2)

Ten Steps to Using CAATs

The IT auditor typically follows an identifiable process in deciding when and how to incorporate CAATs into the audit. Figure 8-5 shows how IT auditors can view this process as a framework consisting of ten steps.

In step 1, the auditor sets key audit objectives during audit planning, based on risk assessment. Areas that the auditor determines to be high risk are areas where CAATs will likely be heavily used to verify data integrity.

In step 2, the auditor identifies which specific CAATs will provide sufficient, relevant, useful evidence to achieve key audit objectives. Experience plays a strong role in helping the auditor determine which CAATs the auditor will choose to perform. It's important to be as thorough as possible in this step, because a later decision to add another CAAT to the audit program could mean having to go back to the client for another round of data extraction, which the client may not be happy about having to repeat.

In step 3, the auditor must identify which files, records, and fields are needed from the client. Frequently this is done through a meeting with the client's IT personnel.

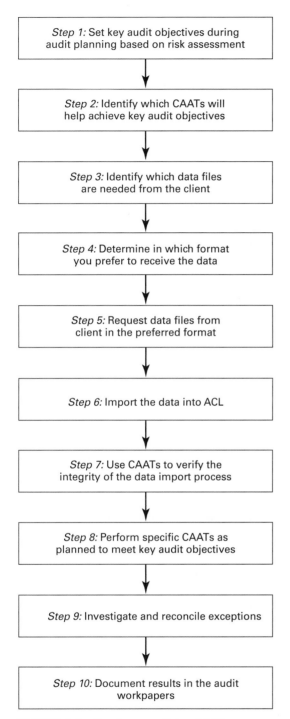

FIGURE 8-5   Ten Steps to Using CAATs

Sometimes the client is reluctant to allow the auditor access to sensitive data such as customer information and payroll information. The auditor may need to reassure the client that their data will remain secure and confidential.

In step 4, the auditor will determine which method of data extraction is most convenient for both parties. Tape is an inexpensive medium for extracting and storing the data. If the client does not have access to tape, the auditor and client will agree on another format such as CD or Zip disk. Alternatively, the client may allow the auditor to access its system directly through ODBC connectivity, or they can send the files via e-mail or secure FTP Web site.

In step 5, the auditor will formally request data from the client, specifying the preferred format for the extracted data. Often the audit firm sends a letter of request so that there is formal documentation for the audit workpapers of what was requested, what was subsequently received, and what media the client used. The auditor should also request control totals such as record counts, key field totals, hash totals, and other similar controls in order to verify the integrity of the data import process.

Once the auditor has the client data, step 6 involves importing that data into ACL. ACL provides a wizard that will guide the auditor through the process. The wizard identifies the type of data being imported, the field lengths, and other properties of the data files.

In step 7, the auditor verifies the integrity of the data import process using ACL commands such as Count, Verify, Total, and Stratify to ensure the data were not compromised during the importing process.

In step 8, the auditor performs the specific CAATs that the audit team earlier identified for risk assessment. The auditor may use interactive batches for standard fraud detection or analytical procedures to increase efficiency. Data output options may include tables, graphs, or additional files for further analysis.

In step 9, the auditor will investigate and reconcile any exceptions uncovered in the execution of the CAATs.

Finally, in step 10 the auditor documents the CAATs performed, the exceptions reconciled, and the overall conclusion with respect to the tests the audit firm performed in the audit workpapers.

Now that we've seen the framework for conducting CAATs, let's look more closely at the two categories of techniques: CAATs to validate application integrity and CAATs to verify overall data integrity. All computer assisted audit techniques fall into one of these two categories.

CAATs to Validate Application Integrity

The first category of techniques are tests that validate client applications, the objective being to determine whether the source code has been compromised, either intentionally or unintentionally. Applications are typically validated through the use of test data, integrated test facilities, and parallel simulation.

TEST DATA   Suppose an auditor wishes to verify the integrity of the payroll program. To do so, he will create a set of fabricated data, in this case, employee hours worked, and determine what the gross pay, deductions, and net pay should be, assuming the payroll program is working properly. Finally, he will run the test data through the application and compare the results with the results he expected to obtain. He will also validate that the employee master files were updated properly.

Test decks are an effective means for testing application logic and processing, but there are certain caveats. This method depends on the auditor's anticipating and capturing all possible deviations and exceptions. For example, how would the program handle negative hours worked? How would it handle hours input for a salaried employee or a salary input for an hourly employee? What if the auditor tried to generate a paycheck for a previously terminated employee? Experienced auditors will think of most deviations. However, even the most experienced auditor will miss some situations. This is the main disadvantage of the test deck method. At the same time, the auditor must be careful in analysis of the results so that errors and deviations in the test deck output aren't overlooked.

INTEGRATED TEST FACILITY (ITF)   A variation on the test deck method is the integrated test facility method of validating the integrity of an application. One of the disadvantages of the test deck method is that it does not allow for testing of "live" data through the client's system. In other words, what we'd really like to do is test the client's application as it is being used daily. This is the purpose of the integrated test facility (ITF) approach. As its name implies, the ITF approach integrates the auditor's contrived test data through the client's system along with normal transaction processing.

To continue with the payroll example, an auditor using the ITF method would first create dummy employees against whom the test data would be run. Then the auditor would merge the dummy test data into a regular payroll run and subsequently compare the results with the expected results.

As previously stated, the method provides added assurance as to the integrity of the client's application. The auditor must be careful, however, that the client's data are not inadvertently corrupted in the testing process. Typically, the auditor makes adjusting entries to remove the effects of the test transactions from the client's records. An accounting urban legend that makes the rounds in accounting recounts how a novice auditor using ITF forgot to remove the test transactions before the payroll checks were cut. The paymaster was undoubtedly surprised to see checks made out to Donald Duck and Mickey Mouse!

PARALLEL SIMULATION   Like the test deck and ITF methods of testing application integrity, the objective of the parallel simulation method is to test the integrity of a client's application. To do so, the auditor uses audit software to reproduce a module of an application, or sometimes an entire application. While this might sound like a daunting undertaking, today's audit software makes this task much easier than it was in the past. Client transactions that were recently run are then input into the program written by the auditor. The output is compared with what was obtained when the transactions were originally run through the client's system. Any discrepancies or errors are flagged and investigated.

CAATs to Verify Data Integrity

The second category of computer assisted audit technique includes tests that verify data integrity. This category includes techniques for data extraction and analysis, digital analysis and Benford's Law, data query models, continuous auditing techniques, ACL batches, and embedded audit modules. These techniques are performed both to verify data were imported properly into ACL (step 7 in Figure 8-5) and to uncover anomalies in the data from either unintentional (i.e., errors) or intentional (i.e., fraud) acts (step 8 in Figure 8-5).

CAATS TO EXTRACT AND ANALYZE DATA   In the past, auditors relied heavily on sampling techniques to obtain a representative sample that was then examined for exceptions. For example, an audit of payroll would involve randomly selecting a number of payroll records and manually examining each record for discrepancies or anomalies. With today's audit tools, auditors have the luxury of testing 100 percent of the transactions.

Continuing with our payroll example, today's auditor can extract all of the payroll data from the client's system and use ACL or any other similar tool to quickly determine if there are any anomalies in the audit population. No longer is it an issue of sampling; instead we can quickly and easily examine the entire population. Vendor transaction files can be downloaded to the auditor's system and examined 100 percent, as can customer files. These innovations in technology have virtually transformed the audit process. Because auditors can now focus on identification and investigation of anomalies, the emphasis shifts more to a risk assessment focus. In addition, data used in other client applications can be used to identify high-risk transactions. For example, an auditor interested in identifying possible conflicts of interest or vendor fraud can use vendor files to identify employee-owned companies.

You might wonder if it's safe to import client data into ACL and perform these audit techniques. The short answer is that for the most part it is safe, since ACL is a read-only application. It does not change the underlying data in any way. One way to think about it is that the auditor is working with a copy of the client's data as it existed at the time it was imported into ACL. The auditor generally does not export the data back into the client's system. For other procedures that involve entering live transactions into the client's system, corruption of data is a real danger against which the auditor must guard.

Important note to the students: At this point, we urge you to load the Workbook.ACL file on the CD and follow along with the material in this next section in order to get the most from the discussion and examples. We have provided ample figures for you to easily replicate the CAATs described in this section. You will not need to actually import the data into ACL, because this step has already been done for you.

IMPORTING THE DATA INTO ACL   Once you have obtained the client's data files, you must import them into ACL. The method of data transfer is dependent on the size of the data files being extracted. For example, Zip disks can generally store up to 250 megabytes of data, CD-ROMs can store up to 650 megabytes, and tape can store up to 2.1 gigabytes. If tape is used, the auditor will use a tape reader to retrieve the data. Once the data are extracted and retrieved into ACL, ACL uses what it terms an Input File Definition (IFD) to determine the record layout and identify the fields. ACL identifies the type of data stored in each of the fields (i.e., character or numeric) and whether the fields are fixed or variable length. For example, the ACL file Workbook.ACL contains the data with which you will be working in the ACL workbook CD that accompanies this text. The data included in the Workbook.ACL file has been imported and stored in ACL as a "project."

This project includes 13 data files. An IFD, as well as a default view, is generated for each of these files. The default view contains all of the fields imported into ACL based on the IFD. A view is simply one way to view the data. If you rearrange data field order, change record lengths, or remove fields from a view, you can save it as a separate view. Thus, there can be multiple views for each of the thirteen data files. Figure 8-6 shows the default view for the Trans file, which is a file of sales invoices.

Once the data have been imported into ACL, some of the data verification procedures that can be performed on the data include counting, totaling, verifying, classifying, and stratifying. ACL retains the results of these procedures in a command log. Printouts of the command log showing the results of all procedures performed would be included in the audit workpapers as evidence that the procedures were performed. Comments can be added to the log to explain why tests were performed or to interpret the results obtained.

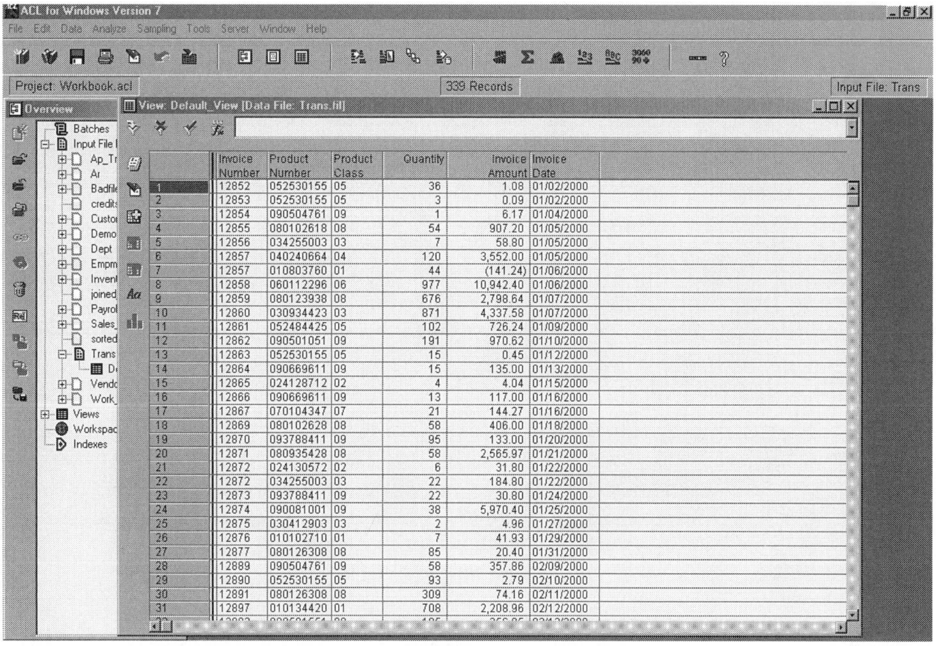

FIGURE 8-6 The "Trans" File after Being Imported into ACL
Source: Reproduced with permission of ACL Services Ltd.

COUNTING Counting the number of records is almost always the first step after a client's data is imported into ACL. The record count is then checked against the control total provided by the client to ensure that the data were not compromised in the importing process. Figure 8-7 shows the results of the "Count" command, with 339 records counted.

You can also count records for a specific criteria. This is called a "conditional count." For example, if you wanted to count the number of records for which the Amount field was negative, you would enter the criteria "Amount<0" in the If box. As shown in Figure 8-8, eleven records have negative amounts.

The "Count" command is a completeness test, as is the "Total" command, which we'll look at now. The "Total" command sums a specified numeric field. The auditor then compares this total with the known control totals to verify the data import was successful. Figure 8-9 shows the total of the Invoice Amount field is $300,682.04. Just as you can perform conditional counts, you can perform conditional totals. For example, we could use the criteria "Amount<0" in conjunction with the "Total" command to determine the total for the 11 records identified in the previous step that have negative invoice amounts.

VERIFYING Another important step in validating the data is checking to be sure the data types conform to the description in the input file definition created when you imported the file into ACL. For example, data identified as numeric should not contain any alphabetic characters within the field. Conversely, fields specified as alphabetic should not contain any numeric data. Figure 8-10 shows the input file definition and field types for the Trans file.

The results of the "Verify" command are shown in Figure 8-11. As shown in the command log, there were no errors in data definitions in this file; if there had been any data type mismatches, the error would have been reported in the command log and the auditor would then investigate to determine the source of the error. Data verification errors can be

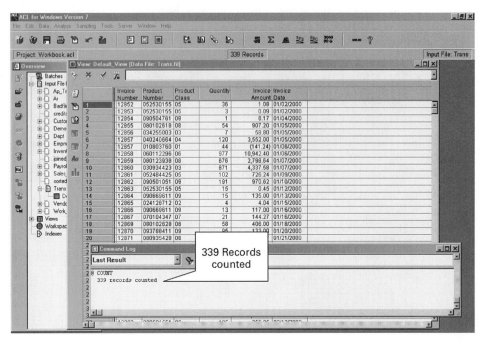

FIGURE 8-7 Results of the "Count" Command in ACL
Source: Reproduced with permission of ACL Services Ltd.

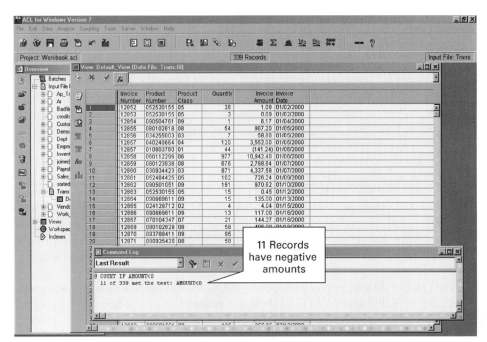

FIGURE 8-8 Results of a "Conditional" Count to Determine the Number of Negative Amounts
Source: Reproduced with permission of ACL Services Ltd.

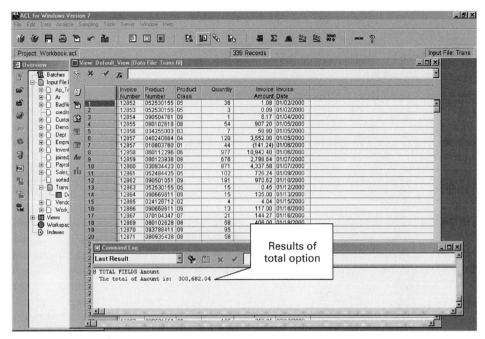

FIGURE 8-9   Results of the "Total" Option
Source: Reproduced with permission of ACL Services Ltd.

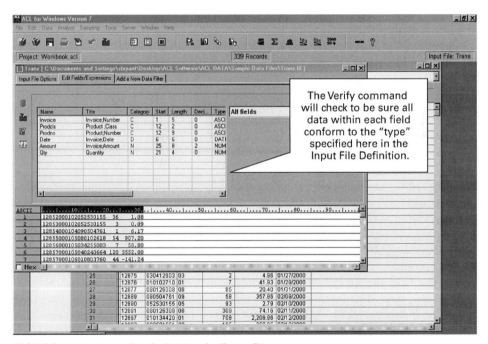

FIGURE 8-10   Input File Definition for Trans File
Source: Reproduced with permission of ACL Services Ltd.

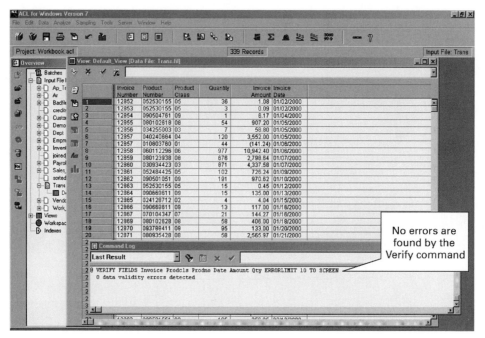

FIGURE 8-11   Results of the "Verify" Command
Source: Reproduced with permission of ACL Services Ltd.

due to data errors in the client's database, ACL conversion errors, or data incompleteness. Case-in-Point 8-3 looks at one kind of error.

Case-in-Point 8-3

Though Y2K didn't result in the feared worldwide catastrophe of computer network crashes, it did cause a significant number of verification errors in date fields that were in an incompatible format of MMDDYY instead of MMDDYYYY.

STATISTICS   Another useful data analysis tool is "Statistics." This command from the Analyze menu will identify statistical properties of any date or numeric data elements you identify. Figure 8-12 shows how to select the Statistics command in ACL. For example, suppose you wanted to analyze the Amount, Date, and Quantity fields from the Trans file. Executing the "Statistics" command from the Analyze menu will result in ACL displaying the maximum and minimum values in each field, the number of records with a value of 0 in that field, the number of records with negative values for that field, and the average for each field. This information allows the auditor to perform analytical review to determine if any records lie outside reasonable ranges. Figure 8-12 shows the results of running the Statistics command on the Trans file.

STRATIFY   Stratifying is an ACL tool that auditors often use to determine ranges for numeric data. For example, if the auditor wanted to divide the records in the Amount field into ten equal groups, the Stratify command can do that in a flash. Figure 8-13 shows the results of the "Stratify" command on the Trans file.

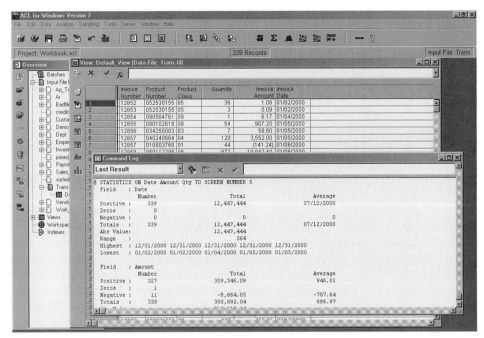

FIGURE 8-12   Results of the "Statistics" Command
Source: Reproduced with permission of ACL Services Ltd.

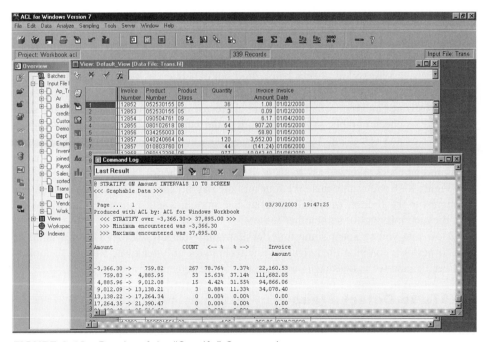

FIGURE 8-13   Results of the "Stratify" Command
Source: Reproduced with permission of ACL Services Ltd.

The auditor could again perform analytical review to determine the reasonableness of the numbers in each of the ten strata. ACL permits the auditor to customize the strata ranges as needed. Case-in-Point 8-4 gives an example of stratifying vendor data.

> ### Case-in-Point 8-4
>
> Suppose you are auditing accounts payable for vendor purchases. The client requires one signature for purchases less than $5,000 and two signatures for purchases between $5,001 and $25,000. Additionally, the client requires purchases greater than $25,000 to go through a bidding process. To test these controls, you can use ACL to stratify vendor purchases into three categories: $0–$5,000; $5,001–$25,000; and $25,000 up.

AGE   Aging accounts receivable and accounts payable is a task auditors commonly perform. Perhaps you want to verify the aged accounts receivable schedule provided by the client. You can use Data, Age to display an aged accounts receivable, based on 30-day (or any other interval you wish to specify) intervals. In Figure 8-14, we have used the AR file from the Workbook.fil project provided on the CD that accompanies this book. You will note that invoice dates range over the year 2000. We have requested ACL show us the aging of receivables as of December 31, 2000. Figure 8-14 shows the results. You can also click on Graphable Data to have ACL show you the results graphically, which is a handy analytical review tool as well.

GAPS AND DUPLICATES   Auditors also find it useful to examine records for gaps and duplicates. For example, suppose you wanted to examine the payroll file and determine if there were any gaps in payroll checks. This would indicate a missing check or series of checks, as well as checks being used out of sequence. You can also ask ACL to show you any duplicate check numbers. In either of these cases, exceptions would need to be investigated and reconciled. If you are interested in gaps and duplicates on the same field, such as check number, you can do both at the same time. From the Analyze menu, choose Gaps and select the "duplicates" checkbox, as shown in Figure 8-15. You can choose to have ACL show you the missing check numbers either in a range or a list of each missing check. We will ask to see a list of missing checks.

Figure 8-16 shows that there are four missing payroll checks. This would certainly be of interest to the auditor, who will set about determining whether these checks were void or if they are missing for some other reason.

Now that you've spent some time familiarizing yourself with ACL, you should be able to perform common analytical review techniques on your own. Next, let's look at data verification techniques designed specifically for detecting fraud.

CAATs to Detect Fraud

All of the above data verification techniques can uncover fraud. After all, the only difference between fraud and error is an intention to deceive. However, there are CAATs whose specific purpose is fraud detection. We'll look at two special CAATs: digital analysis and data query models.

DIGITAL ANALYSIS   Digital analysis uses the statistical properties of a series of naturally occurring numbers through the use of Benford's Law, named for an American physicist who discovered these properties in 1938. Most people believe that the first digit

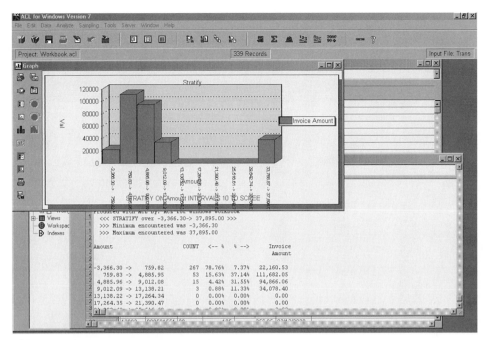

FIGURE 8-14   Results of the "Age" Command
Source: Reproduced with permission of ACL Services Ltd.

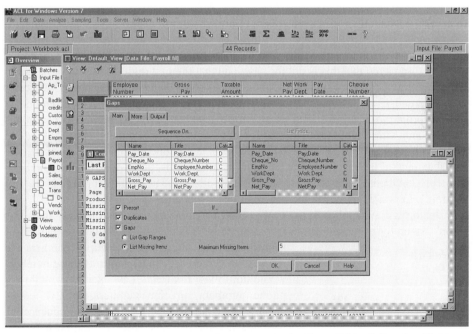

FIGURE 8-15   Searching for Gaps and Duplicates in the Payroll Check Number Field
Source: Reproduced with permission of ACL Services Ltd.

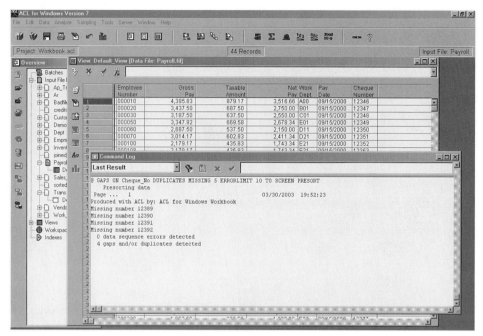

FIGURE 8-16 Results of Duplicate and Gap Search in Payroll Check Number Field
Source: Reproduced with permission of ACL Services Ltd.

of a series of naturally occurring numbers follows a uniform distribution, where each digit has an equal probability of occurring. If this were true, the numbers 1, 2, and 3 as first digits would have the same probability of occurring as first digits as the numbers 7, 8, and 9. Benford discovered that this is not the case, and that the first digit of a series of naturally occurring numbers follows a distribution that has since come to be known as Benford's Law. Figure 8-17 shows this distribution, which in fact is an *exponential* distribution.

According to Benford's Law, in a series of 100,000 invoices, 30,100 invoice totals would begin with the number 1; 17,600 would begin with the number 2; 12,500 would begin with the number 3; 9,700 would begin with the number 4; and so on. Note that the actual amount of the invoice is not relevant. In other words, the invoice totals could be in the tens, hundreds, thousands, or higher, of dollars. In searching for fraud, we use Benford's Law as it applies to the first digit of the amount.[4]

Benford's Law applies to naturally occurring numbers, but what exactly does this mean? Naturally occurring numbers are numbers that do not occur in a set pattern or sequence. For example, social security numbers are issued in a certain sequence, and thus these numbers would not follow Benford's Law. Neither would telephone numbers, invoice numbers, or ZIP codes because they all follow a pattern or sequence of issuance. Invoice amounts, however, don't usually follow a set pattern since invoices can be for any amount. Thus, invoice amounts and other dollar figures such as compound interest are good candidates for the application of Benford's Law.

The auditor must be careful to determine if artificial barriers have been placed into the population

Left-Most Digit	Frequency %
1	30.1
2	17.6
3	12.5
4	9.7
5	7.9
6	6.7
7	5.8
8	5.1
9	4.6

FIGURE 8-17 Expected Frequencies Using Benford's Law

which affect its "naturalness." For example, college students may be charged a per credit tuition fee up to a maximum of fifteen hours of credit. This system of fees would result in an "unnatural" distribution of invoice amounts, and thus Benford's Law would not be effective in detecting fraud.

Another consideration of Benford's Law is that the population on which digital analysis is being performed must be sufficiently large enough to support the test. A test population of one hundred or more will usually be large enough to yield results.

To help you understand the practical significance of how Benford's Law can help IT auditors detect fraud, consider the following scenario. A midlevel manager at a large company is vested with the authority to sign checks up to $10,000. In an attempt to cover large gambling losses, over the year he forges numerous checks to fictitious vendors and mails them to a post office box he rents. He makes most of the checks for somewhere in between $9,000 and $9,999 to avoid having to obtain a second signature on the check. He then endorses the checks and deposits them into his personal bank account.

How might this manager be caught? Certainly a strong system of internal control would go a long way. However, because all of the checks were within his authorization level, no one else ever sees the checks. But digital analysis would quite possibly uncover this fraud, depending on how many fraudulent checks he wrote to himself. If he wrote enough to cause the observed frequency distributions to be significantly different from the expected frequency distribution (based on Benford's Law), these checks would be flagged for further investigation and the manager's fraud revealed.

While many accounting numbers do exhibit distributions that follow Benford's Law closely, not all sets of accounting data will adhere exactly to Benford's Law. However, if the auditor has a set of data known to be valid data, the auditor can generate the exact distribution for that set of data and use that distribution as the expected frequency distribution. Note that this alternative expected frequency distribution will be similar, but not exactly the same as, Benford's Law of first digits expected frequency distribution.

Accounting numbers (or any other numbers) that involve exponential growth will follow Benford's Law exactly because Benford's Law follows an exponential distribution. That's why, for example, compound interest numbers follow Benford's Law exactly.

ACL can calculate the frequency distribution of first digits of a series of numbers using the "Benford" menu item. Again using the Trans file of 339 sales invoice transactions in the Workbook file on the CD, ACL will calculate how many of the invoice amounts start with the number 1, how many start with the number 2, and so on. These "observed" frequencies will be compared to the "expected" frequency using Benford's Law. The observed numbers will almost never be exactly equal to the expected numbers. ACL uses a z-statistic to identify statistically significant differences, which the auditor would then investigate and reconcile. A z-statistic of 1.0 or less is considered insignificant (i.e., no fraud detected). Figures 8-18 and 8-19 show digital analysis run on the Amount field in the Trans file. Clicking on Graphable Data in the results, you can see that the invoice amounts conform closely to Benford's Law. None of the digits' observed frequencies is statistically significantly different than what Benford's Law would expect to occur.

The results of the digital analysis doesn't mean fraud might not still be present in this very file. In our previous example, if the manager had spread the forged checks out in amounts, quite likely the fraud would not be detected through digital analysis.

DATA QUERY MODELS   In performing various CAATs, auditors must go beyond simply extracting the data and casually viewing the results. It is vital that the auditor maintain a keen sense of critical analysis. This means that after the CAAT is run, the results

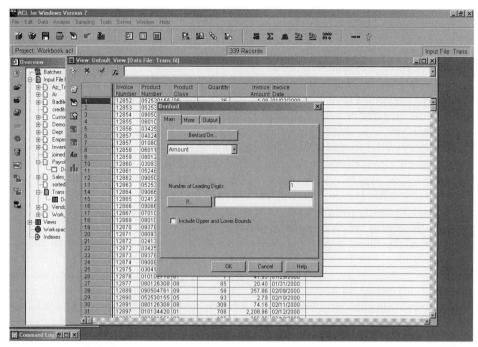

FIGURE 8-18 The Application of Digital Analysis Using Benford's Law to the Sales Invoice File ("Trans.fil")
Source: Courtesy of ACL

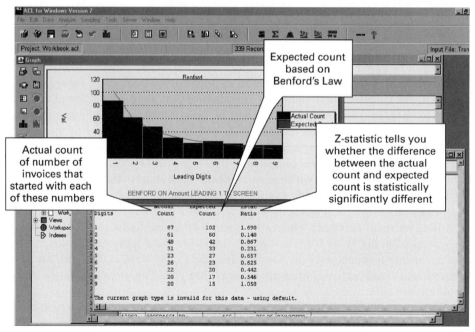

FIGURE 8-19 Results of the Digital Analysis
Source: Courtesy of ACL

should be viewed globally, in context with other relevant information about the client or the situation under review. A data query model (DQM) is a useful framework for doing this.

The auditor develops a DQM using audit software such as ACL, or in some cases spreadsheet tools. The purpose of the DQM is to determine if the evidence obtained from the CAAT fits within the *context* of other evidence obtained during the course of the audit, including tests of controls, substantive testing, interviews with client personnel, risk assessment performed during audit planning, and the environment in which the business operates. The auditor should consider, for example:

- Does the evidence make sense when other relevant trends are considered?
- Does the evidence support assertions made by management or employees?
- Does the CAAT pertain to an area identified as high risk?

To answer these questions, the auditor will develop a model that can help identify fraud.

Travel expenditures are one area particularly ripe for DQMs. For example, let's say that you are auditing a company that has had some difficulty in monitoring travel expenditures in the past. Based on this knowledge, you assess risk as high in this area and decide to spend extra time on auditing the travel expense accounts of the company's ten salesmen. Preliminary analysis shows that travel amounts seem to be within reasonable amounts. The average travel per salesman seems reasonable and the maximum and minimum travel expense vouchers pass muster. However, you decide to investigate a little closer. You might compute travel as a percentage of sales or review travel locations to see if they are outside the salesman's geographical regions. Another test might be to calculate the average travel days per trip. To proceed, you pull all of the vouchers of one randomly chosen salesman. You see that he has attended several out-of-town conferences for several days. You decide to verify the dates of the conference and discover that the salesman routinely stayed at least two extra days beyond the conference date—time which should have been charged as personal time. However, the employee charged all expenses for the extra days to the company. All together, you estimate the company was overcharged about $5,000 for this padded expense account.

Obviously, this kind of analysis comes at a cost. This kind of extended detail work is done when risk is high and, for whatever reason, the auditor regards the additional time as necessary. Whether or not $5,000 is material, we can't tell from the facts provided. However, we do know that there are ten salesmen. If each of them padded their expense accounts to the tune of $5,000, the company would then be looking at a $50,000 fraud. Again, the specific circumstances will help the auditor decide whether or not additional work through the use of a DQM would be cost beneficial.

CAATS BY FUNCTIONAL AREA TO DETECT FRAUD   Auditors who need to design CAATs to detect fraud often "re-create the wheel" for different clients in different industries. However, the CAATs performed to detect fraud have several commonalities and can be grouped according to functional area. Figure 8-20 provides a guide for fraud testing in three areas: payroll, expenditures/payables, and revenue/receivables.

CONTINUOUS AUDITING TECHNIQUES

As the business environment moves towards a model of increased reliability and more timely information, continuous auditing techniques will become commonplace. Continuous auditing refers to the auditor's daily online access to client data. Embedded audit routines screen data and run batch programs to detect anomalous data as they occur, as opposed to perhaps several months after the transaction has been entered into the

PAYROLL

Ghost Employees

1) No taxes or benefits
2) Invalid Social Security Number
3) More than one employee with same address and/or phone number but different last name
4) Frequent employee address changes
5) More than two paychecks to the same bank account
6) P.O. Box, Drop Box Address, Organization's Address, or no home address
7) Unusual work location, no work phone or location
8) No annual or sick leave used over a reasonable period
9) No evaluations, raises, or promotion over an extended period
10) Terminated employees still on the payroll
    a. Paycheck issued after the termination/last worked date
    b. Match paycheck file with active employee file

Excessive Pay Rates

1) Non-market pay rates or pay rates in excess of authorized
2) More than one pay increase/change without a position change in the last year
3) Employees with the same address in the same unit (preferential hiring/nepotism)
4) Excess pay rates or comparison of pay rates by unit/location
5) Excess overtime or continual pattern of overtime
6) Commissions or bonuses are excessive or don't agree to performance factors

Nepotism

1) Same department, same address

EXPENDITURES/PAYABLES

Duplicate Claims

1) Duplicate invoices paid

Conflict of Interest

1) Vendor address same as employee address
2) Vendor phone same as employee phone

Fraudulent Vendor

1) More than one vendor with the same address
2) Vendors with P.O. Boxes, Drop Boxes, or no address
3) Vendors with no phone numbers
4) Sequentially numbered invoice
5) Numerous invoices just below approval thresholds
6) Invoices with same dates and amounts
7) Invoices significantly greater than purchase order
8) Vendor names that SOUND LIKE well known vendors
9) Invalid FEID numbers
10) Deliver to address not entity address

Vendor Kickbacks/Bid Rigging

1) Contract award date precedes proposal due date (bid rigging)
2) Bid received date of awarded contract is always latest bid (bid rigging)
3) Contracts just below bid limits (preferential buys)
4) Splitting contracts to avoid bid limits (preferential buys)
5) Purchase quantities exceed contract quantities (excess purchases)
6) Purchases do not result in a related increase in inventory levels (merchandise never shipped or under-shipped)
7) Inventory levels continue to rise (excess purchases)
8) Duplicate invoice numbers (duplicate pays)

(continued)

FIGURE 8-20 CAATS by Functional Area to Detect Fraud (1 of 2)
Source: Courtesy of Kate Head, Office of Inspector General, University of South Florida. Used with permission.

9) Duplicate date and invoice amounts (duplicate billings)
10) Increase in production costs due to increase in supply costs (inflated prices)
11) Increase in returned merchandise/credits (inferior supplies)
12) Unusually high discounts or credit terms (preferential treatment)
13) Inventory write-off for obsolete goods then additional purchase of these items

Theft of Services

1) Use of phone system for personal or outside business calls (excess activity)
2) Use of postage, express mail services (ship to same last name as approver, excess activity)
3) Use of 800 calling system (frequent call from numbers)

REVENUE/RECEIVABLES

Skimming

1) Reduction of sales yet inventory levels falling
2) Increase in inventory shortages
3) Cashier overages or shortages
4) Increase in customers returning merchandise without receipts (duplicate returns)
5) High number of cashier no sales, voids, corrections, or overrides
6) Duplicate credit memos or gift certificate numbers redeemed

Lapping Receivables

1) Increase in A/R aging
2) Amounts paid don't agree to amounts owed
3) No collection letters being mailed on outstanding debt (no bill flag)
4) Increase in average time from billing to collection
5) Increase in small dollar write-offs

Borrowing

1) Lags from receipt dates to deposit dates

Writing Off Debts Collected (funds retained)

1) Increase in write-offs
2) Increase in adjustments (customer complaints)
3) High value credit, adjustments
4) Gaps in invoice sequence (invoices not recorded in A/R System)
5) Duplicate credit memo numbers (processing credit memos twice)

Kickbacks/Conflict of Interest

1) Unusually high sales discounts
2) Unusual credit terms, credit limits
3) Gaps in invoice numbers
4) Frequent credit memos to the same customer
5) Ship to address same as employee address
6) High damages items rate
7) Increase in inventory markdowns

FIGURE 8-20   CAATS by Functional Area to Detect Fraud (2 of 2)

accounting records. One can think of embedded audit modules much like a virus-scanning program. They run in the background looking for unusual or high-risk transactions based on models the auditor has provided. These models are often based on "red flags" for fraud.

Corporate accounting scandals have also contributed to the clamor for current information. Technological innovations such as extensible markup language (XML) will also aid in standardizing the form of continuous auditing. XML provides a standard for publishing Web-based data and has greatly advanced the continuous auditing paradigm.

SUMMARY

CAATTs can be broken down into two broad categories: computer assisted audit tools and computer assisted audit techniques. Tools encompass software used to manage the audit engagement and boost auditors' productivity, as well as software used to gather evidence to support key audit objectives. Techniques include two main types: techniques to validate client applications, and techniques to verify data integrity. This chapter has also introduced the student to ACL and different types of tests that might be performed using ACL to gather audit evidence. We also discuss audit techniques specifically to detect fraud, including digital analysis and data query models. These techniques highlight exceptions that the auditor will then investigate and reconcile. The chapter also provides a detailed listing of audit techniques to detect fraud within the payroll, expenditures/payables, and revenue/receivables functional areas.

The next chapter will introduce the student to the actual performance of an IT audit, where some of the techniques discussed here will be incorporated.

DISCUSSION QUESTIONS

8-1   Electronic working papers have many advantages. What are the disadvantages of using electronic working papers?

8-2   What kinds of tasks would be good candidates for an audit expert system?

8-3   Do you think there would be any liability on the auditor's part for relying on an expert system that provided a bad recommendation? Discuss.

8-4   What are some of the methods for obtaining a client's data in electronic form?

8-5   What are some of the problems that auditors must be careful to avoid in using test decks and integrated test facilities?

8-6   Explain what an "input file definition" in ACL is. How is this different from a "view" in ACL?

8-7   What kinds of data can the Statistics command yield in ACL? Can this command be run on any field?

8-8   Explain the concept of digital analysis. Does digital analysis work with any numeric data?

8-9   What is a data query model? How does it help an auditor uncover fraud? When should this method not be used?

8-10   What is an embedded audit module? Who generates an embedded audit module?

EXERCISES

8-11   Included with this book is a CD with an education version of ACL v. 7.2. The files needed for the following exercises are on the CD. Load ACL and open the project called "Workbook.acl." You are now ready to do any or all of the following exercises.

Open the Accounts Receivable file ("Ar"). Perform the appropriate tests to answer the following questions:

   a.   How many customers are there?

   b.   How many customers have negative balances, and what do these negative balances total? What do the negative balances mean?

   c.   How many customers have individual receivables for more than $1,000?

   d.   What is the average amount of accounts receivable?

   e.   Stratify the receivables into ten strata. Click on Graphable Data to see the graph. Which strata has the highest number of receivables?

   f.   Perform Benford analysis on the accounts receivable amounts. What are some possible explanations for these results? How would you as an auditor proceed?

   g.   Open the Accounts Payable transaction file (Ap_trans). Perform the appropriate tests to answer the following questions:

   h.   How many transactions are there in this file?

    i. How many vendors are represented in this file?

    j. Determine if there are any gaps in invoice numbers. Would this be of concern to you as an auditor? What would you do to reconcile the differences.

    k. Are there any duplicate invoice numbers? How would you resolve this discrepancy?

    l. Which vendors purchase inventory items of more than $100 each?

    m. Age the accounts payable file as of December 31, 2000. Click on Graphable Data to see a visual of the results. If you were auditing this company and got these results, would you be concerned? Explain.

    n. Do any vendors have post office boxes as their street address?

    o. Perform Benford analysis on the accounts payable invoice amounts. Is there any evidence of fraud in payables? How would you as an auditor proceed?

8-12 Open the Inventory file. Perform the appropriate tests to answer the following questions.

    a. How many different inventory items are maintained by this company?

    b. How many inventory items are sold at Location 3?

    c. What is the average cost of an inventory item? What is the most expensive and least expensive inventory item?

    d. What is the profit on inventory item # 034255003?

    e. How many products have a status of "U"?

    f. Are there any products for which the sales price is less than the unit cost? Would you be concerned about this as an auditor?

    g. Are there any products on hand for which the quantity on hand is less than the reorder point, but which do not have any quantity on order? Is this a problem? Why or why not?

    h. What is the total market value of the inventory?

8-13 Open the employee master file (Empmast). Perform the appropriate tests to answer the following questions.

    a. How many total employees are there?

    b. How many male and how many female employees are there?

    c. How many employees have a college degree? Assume an education level of sixteen years is equivalent to a college degree.

    d. What is the average employee annual salary? What are the highest and lowest salary amounts?

    e. Do any employees appear to be grossly over- or underpaid? How would you investigate this?

    f. Have any employees received unusually large bonuses or commissions?

    g. Are there any employees with the same address? Would this be of concern to you as an auditor?

    h. Do any employees appear to be related? Do any work in the same department? Explain how you tested this.

8-14 Open the Payroll file. Perform the following tests.

    a. Are there any duplicate check numbers?

    b. Are there any gaps in payroll check numbers?

    c. Does gross pay less taxes equal net pay in all cases?

REFERENCES AND RECOMMENDED READINGS

Coderre, D. G. 1999. *Fraud Detection: Using Data Analysis Techniques to Detect Fraud.* Vancouver, Canada: Global Audit Publications.

———. 1998. *CAATTS and Other BEASTS*. Vancouver, Canada: Global Audit Publications.

———. 1994. "Seven Easy CAATTs." *Internal Auditor*. (August): 28–32.

———. 1993. "Computer Assisted Audit Tools and Techniques." *Internal Auditor*. (February): 24–27.

Goldsmith, J. 2000. "Using Audit Tools, Part 3, Applications." *IT Audit Forum* 3, January 1, 2000. www.theiia.org/itaudit/index.cfm?fuseaction=forum&fid=61.

———. 1999. "Using Audit Tools, Part 2, Applications." *IT Audit Forum* 2, October 15, 1999. www.theiia.org/itaudit/index.cfm?fuseaction=forum&fid=60.

———. 1999. "Using Audit Tools, Part 1, Audit Software Packages." *IT Audit Forum* 2, 15 August 1999. www.theiia.org/itaudit/index.cfm?fuseaction=forum&fid=59.

LeGrand, Charles. 2001. "Use of Computer-Assisted Audit Tools and Techniques, Part 1." *IT Audit Forum* 4, 1 October 2001. www.theiia.org/itaudit/index.cfm?fuseaction=forum&fid=320.

———. 2001. "Use of Computer-Assisted Audit Tools and Techniques, Part 2." *IT Audit Forum* 4, 15 October 2001. www.theiia.org/itaudit/index.cfm?fuseaction=formum&fid=380.

Web Sites

E-Workpapers
Intacct Audit: www.intacct.com/solutions_CPAs_system_audit_overview.html
CaseWare Working Papers: www.caseware.com/home.asp
ProSystem fx Trial Balance (formerly ProSystem fx Audit): www.epacesoftware.com/products/
TeamMate: www.pwcglobal.com

Groupware
IBM's Lotus Notes: www.lotus.com
Novell GroupWise: www.novell.com/products/groupwise/
Microsoft Exchange: www.microsoft.com/exchange/default.asp

Time and Billing
ProSystem *fx* Practice: www.epacesoftware.com/products/practice/default.asp
Timeslips (now owned by Peachtree): www.timeslips.com
Bill Central Time and Billing: www.integsoft.com/bc.htm

Document Management
IntuitAdvisor WorkSpace Pro: www.intuitadvisor.com/
Creative Solution's File Cabinet: www.csisolutions.com/products/fcs/

Generalized Audit Software Tools
ACL: www.acl.com/en/
Advantage CA-Easytrieve: www3.ca.com/Solutions/ProductFamily.asp?ID=122
SAS Institute, Inc.: www.sas.com

NOTES

1. Coderre, David. 1998. *CAATTS and Other BEASTS*. Vancouver, Canada: Global Audit Publications.
2. Lombardo, Carly. 2001. "Winning the War on Paper?" *Accounting Technology*. www.electronicaccountant.com/AccountingToday/.
3. www.pwcglobal.com
4. Benford's Law could be used to derive the distributions for the second and subsequent digits, but this is not particularly useful for fraud detection.

CHAPTER 9

CONDUCTING THE IT AUDIT

CHAPTER CONTENTS

INTRODUCTION

The previous chapter focused on providing the tools and techniques IT auditors most commonly use as tools of the trade. Many textbooks discuss internal controls and other topics germane to IT audit, but fail to deliver the essentials of just *how* an IT audit is conducted. Now that you have the tools, this chapter gets down to basics, that is, how an IT audit takes place.

Many people refer to an "IT audit" as though there were only one type of IT audit. Actually, IT auditors engage in a variety of types of audits. But regardless of the type of audit, there is a definable life cycle through which the IT audit progresses. We refer to this process as the "IT audit life cycle," in which the basic procedures are the same for any IT audit.

This chapter begins by detailing the IT audit life cycle applicable for any type of IT audit. We then give an overview of four primary types of IT audits. We include audit programs as needed to convey the practical nature of this chapter. Because there are so many types of IT audits, it is impossible for us to lay out particulars on *every* type of IT audit within the limited scope of this book. Additionally, topics such as network security audits and application audits are highly technical, and audit procedures depend on the hardware and software used by the client. However, our ultimate goal in this chapter is to leave you with the feeling that you have a broad understanding of the logistics of conducting IT audits.

AUDIT STANDARDS

As discussed in Chapters 1 and 3, there are myriad audit standards that the IT auditor must consider. These include Statements of Auditing Standards (SASs), issued by the American Institute of Certified Public Accountants (AICPA); the IS Audit Standards, Guidelines, and Procedures of the Information Systems Audit and Control Association (ISACA); the AICPA's Statement on Standards for Attestation Engagements (SSAE); the International Auditing Standards of the International Federation of Accountants (IFAC); and ISACA's Control Objectives for Information and Related Technology (CobiT). The IT auditor must discern which standards are appropriate for which audit. For more information on the various types of audit standards, see Chapters 1 and 3.

THE IT AUDIT LIFE CYCLE

All IT audits go through a cyclical process that we call the "IT audit life cycle." These processes include: planning, risk assessment, development of the audit program, gathering evidence, forming conclusions, preparing the audit opinion, and following up. Figure 9-1 shows the IT audit life cycle. Let's see what's involved in each of these steps.

Planning

Step one involves planning the IT audit project. This means determining what the risks are inherent in the audit, familiarizing yourself with the audit client and the environment in which the client operates, and laying out a plan for conducting the audit, including who will staff the audit and how the audit will generally be conducted.

ISACA Standard 050.010, "Audit Planning," states: "The information systems auditor is to plan the information systems audit work to address the audit objectives and to comply with applicable professional auditing standards." ISACA Guideline 050.010.020 provides more specific guidance on planning. Per the guideline, the auditor should perform the following tasks during the planning phase:

- Establish the scope and control objectives of the work the auditor will perform;
- Perform a preliminary assessment of controls relevant to the process that the auditor will be auditing;
- Gain an understanding of the organization and its business, financial, and inherent risks, as well as environmental issues germane to the industry or client;
- Identify the extent to which the client relies on outsourcing;
- Develop the audit program containing specific audit procedures the auditor will conduct during the audit fieldwork;
- Develop the audit plan for the conduct of the overall audit; and
- Document the audit workpapers with the audit plan and audit program and other documentation necessary to substantiate an understanding of the client's business operations and operating environment.

FIGURE 9-1 The IT Audit Life Cycle

SCOPE AND CONTROL OBJECTIVES   The scope of the audit determines the nature and extent of testing to be performed in the audit. For example, if the purpose of an IT audit is to evaluate program change controls, the scope is specified accordingly, and all audit work is planned and performed within that scope. The control objectives, in turn, are specified to provide support for the scope of the audit.

MATERIALITY   As in a financial audit, setting the level of materiality is done during the planning phase. The level of materiality establishes the benchmark by which the auditor gauges the importance of exceptions. In financial audits, auditors usually set materiality as a percentage of total sales or total assets. In an IT audit, Guideline 050.010.010 instructs auditors to consider 1) the aggregate level of error tolerable by management and the audit team, and 2) the potential for small errors and weaknesses in control to become material.

Guideline 050.010.010 instructs auditors to set materiality using the following criteria:

- The auditor selects controls to examine based on materiality. A control is material if its absence prevents control objectives from being met;
- The auditor determines materiality for an information system or operation that processes financial transactions by assessing the value of the assets controlled by the system or the volume of transactions processed through the system.

The auditor determines materiality for an information system or operation that processes nonfinancial transactions by considering the cost of the system, the criticality of the information processed, and the potential costs of errors, among other items listed in the Guideline.

OUTSOURCING   During planning, the IT auditor must consider the extent to which the client relies on outsourcing of services to third parties. Guideline 010.010.020 requires the auditor to gain an understanding of the nature, scope, and timing of such services by reviewing the existing service agreements. Additionally, the auditor reviews controls in place relative to the outsourced service. If the third party has had a SAS 70 audit performed, the IT auditor should obtain a copy of the audit opinion, ensure that it is an unqualified opinion, and add the opinion to the audit workpapers. SAS 70 engagements will be described in more detail later in the chapter.

Risk Assessment, or "What Can Go Wrong?"

Because risk assessment is such an important topic in IT audit, we have devoted an entire chapter (see Chapter 3) to a discussion of risk. For that reason, we will keep the discussion of risk assessment brief here.

Many auditors today use a *risk-based audit approach* to conducting in audit. In this type of audit, risk assessment revolves around the question of "What can go wrong?" That is, IT auditors focus on first determining what the critical support processes are for a given audit process. Next, they ask themselves what can possibly go wrong within those support processes. This helps the auditor identify the controls that should be in place to safeguard the integrity of the process under audit. The auditor includes controls that she deems material as items to be tested in the audit program.

A risk-based approach requires the auditor to have a thorough understanding of the client, the industry and environment in which the client operates, and the nature of the client's business processes. Without a thorough understanding, the auditor may fail to correctly identify the critical business processes and corresponding internal controls that he should evaluate. Materiality also plays an important part in risk assessment. If a control is absent, how material is that control? If it is a minor process, the auditor may not test the control, as the benefit of doing so will not outweigh the cost.

Of course, internal control is the responsibility of management. Some companies, recognizing and embracing this responsibility, perform self-assessment of their internal controls. This type of control environment can assist the auditor greatly in assessing the effectiveness of controls.

The Audit Program

There is no standard audit program for IT audit since the audit procedures must be customized to the client's hardware and software, the network's architecture and topology, and a host of environmental and industry-specific considerations. The audit programs we provide later in this chapter are *generic* audit programs, the details of which auditors would customize as needed.

A generic audit program includes the following components:

- The audit scope;
- The audit objectives;
- The audit procedures; and
- Administrative details such as planning and reporting.

The audit program, which should be documented in the workpapers, serves as a template for the work to be performed. After the audit is completed, the audit program provides documentation as to who performed individual audit procedures and references to the workpapers where the results of each test and audit step can be viewed.

Gathering Evidence

The purpose of field work is to gather "... sufficient, reliable, relevant and useful evidence to achieve the audit objectives effectively. The audit findings and conclusions are to be supported by appropriate analysis and interpretation of this evidence" (ISACA Standard 060.020, "Evidence"). Gathering evidential matter is the heart of the audit, as it provides the basis for the audit opinion that is eventually rendered.

ISACA Guideline 060.020.030 identifies several types of evidence IT auditors will gather as part of fieldwork, including:

- Observed processes and existence of physical items such as computer operations or data backup procedures;
- Documentary evidence such as program change logs, system access logs, and authorization tables;
- Representations such as client-provided flowcharts, narratives, and written policies and procedures; and
- Analysis such as CAATs procedures run on client-provided data files.

If the auditor does not obtain sufficient evidence, he may need to request more from the client in order to satisfy a given objective. If sufficient evidence cannot be obtained, the auditor must consider the materiality of the evidence and the effect on the scope of the audit.

Not all evidence is created equal. Rather, auditors must discern the quality, or reliability, of evidence they collect during the audit fieldwork. For example, evidence provided independently from outside sources is considered more reliable than evidence obtained from inside the client company. That's why, for example, auditors obtain cutoff statements directly from the bank and accounts receivable confirmations directly from the client's customers instead of simply taking the client's word for these numbers. Furthermore, evidence that is objectively obtained is considered more reliable than the contrary. For example, an inventory of a client's tape library is more reliable than an auditor's interpretation of controls around the tape library based on discussion with the client's personnel.

SAMPLING ISSUES   ISACA Guideline 060.020.040 defines sampling as "… the application of audit procedures to less than 100% of the population to enable the [IT] Auditor to evaluate audit evidence about some characteristic of the items selected in order to form or assist in forming a conclusion concerning the population." As mentioned in Chapter 8, IT auditors using software such as ACL can perform analytics and recalculations on entire populations when the file exists in an electronic format. Sampling is necessary when it is not possible or practical to perform audit procedures on the entire population of interest.

There are two types of sampling approaches: attribute sampling and variable sampling. *Attribute sampling* is the approach used by most IT auditors, as it involves testing internal controls around processes deemed critical during audit planning. The auditor will select for testing items that are relevant to the control objective being assessed according to the scope of the audit. After testing the controls, the auditor determines that the control objective is either achieved or not achieved. Thus, the IT auditor can count the number of deviations from the control and include that count (percent) as evidence. *Variable sampling* is most relevant to financial statement audits, as it involves substantive testing of population characteristics that vary (i.e., dollars or weights).

Forming Conclusions

After all the audit evidence is gathered, it is the auditor's job to evaluate the evidence and form conclusions about whether the audit objectives were met and the sufficiency of audit procedures performed in arriving at an overall audit opinion. The auditor will also identify any *reportable conditions*. This refers to any situation that comes to the attention of the auditor that represents a substantial control weakness. Reportable conditions are usually compiled in a Management Letter, which is discussed with the audit committee and client management in an exit interview at the conclusion of the audit.

The auditor conclusions should never be a surprise to management personnel. If the auditor uncovers substantial weaknesses in internal control and/or material misstatements in the financial statements, the auditor should bring these anomalies to the attention of management when they are discovered. At the conclusion of the audit, management should have reconciled and discharged these problems. If not, the auditor may need to qualify the audit opinion.

The Audit Opinion

Just as there is no standard IT audit program, there is no standard audit report. Some types of IT audits have special criteria for what is to be included in those audit reports. Audit reports for attestations, findings and recommendations, SAS 70 audits, and SAS 94 audits are discussed later in the chapter.

Guidance for the general items to be included in the audit report is provided by ISACA Guideline 070.010.010. The following items should be included in the audit report:

- The name of the organization audited;
- A title, signature, and date;
- A statement of the objectives of the audit and whether the audit met these objectives;
- The scope of the audit, including "the functional audit area, the audit period covered and the information systems, applications or processing environments audited;"
- Acknowledgement of a scope limitation where the auditor could not perform audit work adequately to achieve a particular audit objective;
- The intended audience for the report, including any restrictions on distribution of the report;
- The standards and criteria under which the auditor performed the audit work;
- A detailed explanation of all significant findings;
- A conclusion on the areas the audit evaluated, including any significant reservations or qualifications;
- Suggestions for corrective action or improvement where appropriate; and
- Significant subsequent events occurring after the fieldwork for the audit was completed.

Following Up

The final stage of the IT audit life cycle is follow-up. After the auditor communicates audit results to the client and delivers the audit opinion to the client, the auditor will make provisions to follow up with the client on any reportable conditions or deficiencies the audit uncovered during the course of the audit. For example, if a significant control deficiency is noted, the auditor may plan to revisit the issue with the client in thirty days to determine if the deficiency has been corrected.

Of course, some deficiencies may take significantly longer for the client to reconcile. During the exit interview, the auditor and client will agree on the extent and timing of follow-up procedures. Follow-up may take the form of a telephone call to management and subsequent documentation of the conversation, or the auditor may schedule additional audit procedures to satisfy all parties that management has corrected a material internal control weakness.

FOUR MAIN TYPES OF IT AUDITS

As we first discussed in Chapter 1, there are four main types of IT audits: 1) attestation; 2) findings and recommendations; 3) a SAS 70 audit; and 4) a SAS 94 audit. We'll examine each of these in turn.

Attestation

In an attest engagement, the auditor provides assurance on something for which the client is responsible. For example, the client is responsible for maintaining an effective internal control structure. The client's representative—say, the corporate controller in this case—is termed the *responsible party.* The responsible party makes an assertion using some criteria. In this example, the controller makes an assertion in the form of a *representation letter* that the company's internal control structure is effective using the standards of COSO. The auditor then performs an examination, review, or agreed-upon procedure (AUP) and provides a written report, often called a "Report to Management," on the findings. Typically an AUP is a negative assurance report. That is, the auditor states what it was asked to do and any findings—or lack of findings—to provide feedback to the user of the report.

Attestation guidance is provided by the Auditing Standards Board (ASB)'s Statement on Standards for Attestation Engagements (SSAE) No. 10, *Attestation Standards: Revision and Recodification,* effective June 1, 2001. SSAE 10 consists of seven chapters that provide guidance on various attest services and supersedes and replaces all prior SSAEs. Figure 9-2 shows the components of SSAE 10.

According to SSAE 10, the criteria, or standards, against which the auditor performs the attestation must be *suitable* and *available* to users of the attestation report. SSAE 10 specifically identifies as suitable some criteria, such as COSO. If not specifically listed, a criteria will be deemed to be suitable if it is objective, measurable, complete, and relevant.[1]

It's easy to confuse an attestation engagement and a findings and recommendations (often referred to as "consulting") engagements. One of the purposes of SSAE 10 is to clarify the distinction between the two. Figure 9-3 shows the primary differences. In general, in an attest engagement, the client specifically agrees to the procedures to be applied, while in a findings and recommendations engagement, the client states in general terms

Chapter Number	Chapter Title
1	Attest Engagements
2	Agreed-Upon Procedures Engagements
3	Financial Forecasts and Projections
4	Reporting on Pro Forma FInancial Information
5	Reporting on an Entity's Internal Control Over Financial Reporting
6	Compliance Attestation
7	Management's Discussion and Analysis

FIGURE 9-2   Statement on Standards for Attestation Engagements (SSAE) No. 10 Attestation Standards: Revision and Recodification

	Attest Engagement	Consulting Engagement
Written report providing assurance	Yes	No
Representation letter	Not required on every attest engagement, but often used	No
Written assertation	Required only for an agreed-upon procedures engagement on compliance or internal control over compliance	No

FIGURE 9-3 Differences between Attest vs. Findings and Recommendations ("Consulting") Engagements

what he wants done, but specific line items are not agreed to by auditor and client. Additionally, a written report is not required in a consulting engagement, whereas it is required for an attestation engagement.

Examples of attest procedures in which IT auditors are most likely to engage include data analytic reviews, commission agreement reviews, WebTrust and SysTrust engagements, financial projections, and compliance reviews. Additionally, Section 404 of the Sarbanes-Oxley Act will likely be a significant source of attestation engagements for auditors as clients seek to comply with internal control requirements of the Act.

DATA ANALYTIC REVIEWS In a data analytic review, the IT auditor makes significant use of software such as ACL to determine whether the financial statement numbers are reasonable. Typically, this involves ratio analysis, recalculations, verifying, and summarizing financial statement numbers to ensure they are reasonable. This type of analytical review is always performed in a typical financial statement audit. However, if the client wishes additional analysis, perhaps based on suspicions of errors or irregularities, the client may contract with the audit firm to perform this type of additional analysis as an agreed-upon procedure.

COMMISSION AGREEMENT REVIEWS In a commission agreement review, the IT auditor's job is to verify that a client's commission agreement is being properly accounted for. For example, a company with a commission agreement with a third party may engage the auditor to perform this type of analysis. Sometimes this review is required in the contract between the client and third party. Alternatively, a company that pays commissions to its employees as an integral part of the compensation plan may have the commission process audited for integrity.

> **EXAMPLE** ABC Sales Company wishes to have a commission review audit performed. Specifically, they want assurance on the integrity of their commission payment system. They have hired XYZ External Auditors to obtain this assurance. This engagement is an agreed-upon procedures engagement where the auditor and client specifically agree to what will be attested. The audit program might look something like Figure 9-4.

The IT auditor would likely be involved in parts of this audit, but not all steps. In the audit program above, the IT auditor would be involved in planning, in downloading the client files, in analytics, and in recalculation of commissions. The IT auditor would use ACL or a similar tool to extract the population of commissions paid to the third party and recalculate what the paid commissions should be.

The audit opinion in an agreed-upon procedures attestation notes the nature of the work performed by the auditor and states that the work is not an audit. The audit opinion for our example would look something like Figure 9-5.

Audit Scope	W/P Ref	Completed By
Review of the commission payment system		

Audit Objectives

1. To ensure the integrity of the commission payment system.
2. To evaluate the effectiveness of the internal controls around the commission payment system.

Audit Step

Planning

1. Meet with client management and obtain an understanding of the engagement.
2. Review similar prior engagements performed for client, if any, to determine any past problems.
3. Perform preliminary risk assessment to determine risks and vulnerabilities.
4. Write detailed audit program.
5. Staff the audit depending on technical skills needed.
6. Set the audit budget.

Field Work

1. Interview client key personnel involved in the commission process.
2. Obtain an understanding of the client's business environment and organizational structure and document this understanding in the audit workpapers.
3. Request electronic copies of relevant client files.
4. Recalculate commission amounts and compare to historical records.
5. Test general and application controls around the commission payment process. (This section would include detailed audit procedures for the testing of general and application controls.)
6. Perform analytics to determine the reasonableness, timeliness, and payee verification of commission payments.
7. Ensure proper documentation is included in the audit workpapers for all evidence gathered.

Conclusions and Reporting

1. Formulate conclusions as to the integrity of the commission payment system and the effectiveness of the internal controls around the commission payment system.
2. Review findings with client management and audit committee.
3. Prepare the audit report.
4. Follow up on reportable conditions with client at agreed time.

FIGURE 9-4 Sample Audit Program for Commission Review Agreed-Upon Procedure

WEBTRUST ENGAGEMENTS   Both WebTrust and SysTrust are covered in detail in Chapter 7, so we'll keep the discussion here brief. A WebTrust engagement is part of a larger set of assurance services that CPAs can provide. While still considered an attest service, WebTrust guidelines are provided separately by the AICPA and the Canadian Institute of Chartered Accountants (CICA) (see www.aicpa.org/assurance/webtrust/index.htm and www.aicpa.org/assurance/systrust/index.htm).

Independent Accountant's Report on
Applying Agreed-Upon Procedures

Date

To the Board of Directors of [Client's Name]
[Address]

You have requested that we apply the agreed-upon procedures enumerated below. Management has determined that these procedures are necessary and sufficient to achieve their purposes. As such, we make no representations about the sufficiency of these procedures in obtaining management's goals. This engagement was performed in accordance with standards established by the American Institute of Certified Public Accountants.

Enumerate Agreed-Upon Procedures Individually
[Findings for each AUP]

Performance of these agreed-upon procedures does not constitute an audit, and thus, we do not express an opinion herein. We have performed only those procedures that were agreed-upon, and have no obligation to perform any other procedures not specifically agreed to prior to the conduct of the engagement.

This report is intended solely for the use of [Client name or client-identified third parties] and should not be used by others.

Manual or Printed Signature of Accounting Firm
Date of Completion

FIGURE 9-5 Sample Audit Opinion for Agreed-Upon Procedures

The objective of a WebTrust engagement is to evaluate a company's Web site according to AICPA/CICA standards. IT auditors are often involved due to the technical nature of the engagement. In particular, evaluating transaction integrity as required by WebTrust standards means the auditor must ensure that transactions are correctly processed through the Web site, and this requires special expertise.

SYSTRUST ENGAGEMENT The purpose of a SysTrust engagement is to evaluate the reliability of a company's business information system. The AICPA/CICA standards define reliability along four dimensions: availability, security, integrity, and maintainability. The technology proficiency needed is high for a SysTrust engagement. Due to the complex nature of a SysTrust engagement, the AICPA provides a competency model that provides a framework for identifying particular IT specialties an auditor needs to conduct a SysTrust engagement (www.aicpa.org/assurance/systrust/comp.htm). By virtue of their training, IT auditors are often tapped to conduct the security and integrity tests necessary to verify the system's reliability.

FINANCIAL PROJECTIONS Financial projections include financial statement forecasts and pro forma financial information. This analysis is often performed in conjunction with seeking loans or issuing stock. IT auditors are less involved with this type of attest service. They are usually only involved to the extent the auditor needs to use special software to perform the projections.

COMPLIANCE REVIEWS Compliance reviews usually involve verifying a company's compliance with business regulations. For example, a company might engage an audit firm to determine whether the company is in compliance with environmental regulations applicable for their industry. A manufacturing plant might be interested in determining whether they are in compliance with Occupational Safety and Health Administration (OSHA) regulations.

Compliance reviews might use IT auditors, but usually only to the extent they are needed to access the technology used by the client company. For example, IT auditors may be involved in a PIN (personal identification number) encryption security review. A PIN encryption review is a special type of AUP whereby the auditor tests the integrity of the client's encryption process for personal identification numbers. For example, a bank may hire an auditor to test the integrity of its encryption scheme for its ATM PINs. This type of engagement requires special expertise on the part of the auditor, who will need to have received special training on PIN key management.[2] Chapter 6 of SSAE 10 covers compliance reviews.

Findings and Recommendations

A findings and recommendations report includes most reviews that would be considered "consulting" or "advisory" services. Examples of engagements that fall under this category include systems implementations, including enterprise resource planning (ERP) implementations (for example, an SAP, Oracle, or PeopleSoft implementation engagement); security reviews; database application reviews; IT infrastructure and improvements needed engagement; project management; and IT internal audit services.

A findings and recommendations report does not produce an opinion. Rather, it is a summary of the work performed in connection with the engagement. IT auditors are often used on these types of engagements, again due to the complexity of the project undertaken. For example, an ERP implementation will require knowledge of specific hardware and software systems requirements. To the extent IT auditors can provide the needed technical expertise, they are the logical choice to staff such engagements.

SAS 70 Audit

As technology becomes increasingly complex and expensive, companies often outsource applications such as accounting, payroll, e-commerce, and other computer services to third-party service providers. Many companies have been doing so for years. For example, a company that doesn't have the expertise to manage payroll in-house might outsource this task to ADP, a widely used payroll service provider. The company hiring ADP is referred to as the "user organization." When the company undergoes its annual audit, its external auditor (the "user auditor") may want assurance as to the controls in place at ADP relative to its payroll services. If ADP has undergone a SAS 70 audit, ADP can provide its auditor's report (called a Service Auditor's Report) to this company and all of their other clients. The primary users of a SAS 70 report are management of the service provider, its customers, and the independent auditors of the users of the service provider.

The SAS 70 report is also an effective tool for management to use when considering how the service organization affects its internal control environment. Further, it helps identify any additional controls the organization should have in addition to the service organization's controls or to compensate for its lack of controls.

A SAS 70 audit is applicable to any service organization that wishes to assure its clients of the existence and effectiveness of its internal controls. Examples of service organizations that often obtain annual SAS 70 opinions include application service providers, banks, claims processing centers, Internet service providers, and data processing service bureaus.[3]

The service organization benefits from this type of audit because it enables the organization to provide valuable information on its internal control system and, in certain cases, the effectiveness of the controls at the service organization relative to the service provided. (Note that the SAS 70 opinion does not cover the *entire* internal control structure of the service organization, but is limited to the controls around the service provided.[4]) Without such assurance, user organizations would likely have to pay for their own auditors to check out the controls of the service provider. And think how time consuming and disruptive it would be for the service provider to endure this from multiple users! See Case-in-Point 9-1 for an example.

Case-in-Point 9-1

TSI, Inc., a division of Verizon telephone services, notes that it would have 130 auditors on site from 130 customers if it had to accommodate its customers' external auditors individually. Instead, TSI has a SAS 70 audit performed annually, and the results are made available to all of its customers' external auditors.[5]

The SAS 70 audit is opinion-based and includes two main type of reports: a *Type I* report describes a company's internal controls, but does not perform detailed testing of these controls. Instead, the auditor performs a "walkthrough" of controls, in which the auditor validates his understanding of the controls in place. An unqualified Type I report is equivalent to deeming the controls in place "effective, but not tested beyond a walkthrough." A *Type II* report goes a step further in that the service organization's controls are reviewed *and* tested over a minimum of six months (though the industry standard is a one-year period.) An unqualified Type II report is the equivalent of deeming that controls are "effective and tested beyond a walkthrough." External auditors ("user auditors") can rely on both a Type I and Type II SAS 70 report to reduce their substantive testing; however, substantive testing is not reduced as much with a Type I SAS 70 report since controls are not tested beyond a walkthrough. Figures 9-6 and 9-7 show what an auditor should include in a SAS 70 Type I and Type II report.

The SAS 70 audit employs IT auditors when the technology to be audited is complex enough to require specialized expertise. For example, an audit of an application service provider would require obtaining an understanding of how the system works, how data flow through the system, and where the control points are. It will also be necessary to

---

1. A description of the service organization's process for which the internal controls are being evaluated;
2. A description of the scope, nature, and timing of the audit procedures performed;
3. A statement of purpose of the engagement and opinion as to whether:

   a. The service organization has presented fairly in all material respects, the internal control policies and procedures relevant to their internal control structure, and the process or service for which the audit is being conducted;

   b. Whether the internal control policies and procedures were operational on a specific date;

   c. Whether those internal control policies were adequately designed to meet specific control objectives;

4. A disclaimer of opinion as to operating effectiveness;
5. Statement of the risk of projecting to future periods the current findings on internal controls;
6. A statement restricting the use of the report to the appropriate parties (ordinarily the company, its clients and the auditors of its clients).

FIGURE 9-6   What to Include in a SAS 70 Type I Report

1. A description of the service organization's process for which the internal controls are being evaluated;
2. A description of the scope, nature, and timing of the audit procedures performed, including a description of all tests of controls and operating effectiveness performed;
3. A statement of the time period covered by the independent auditor's report (must be a minimum of six months);
4. A statement of purpose of the engagement and opinion as to whether:
   a. The service organization has presented fairly in all material respects, the internal control policies and procedures relevant to their internal control structure and the process or service for which the audit is being conducted;
   b. Whether those internal control policies were operating with sufficient effectiveness to provide *reasonable* assurance that the company's control objectives were achieved during the period specified.
5. Statement of the risk of projecting to future periods the current findings on internal controls,
6. A statement restricting the use of the report to the appropriate parties (ordinarily the company, its clients, and the auditors of its clients);
7. A statement that no work was performed at individual user organizations.

FIGURE 9-7   What to Include in a SAS Type II Report

obtain an understanding of the application's environment, including the platform on which the application resides and the hardware supporting the application. IT auditors often provide this type of technical expertise.

SAS 94 Audit

SAS 94, *The Effect of Information Technology on the Auditor's Consideration of Internal Controls in a Financial Statement Audit,* amends SAS No. 55, *Consideration of Internal Control in a Financial Statement Audit.* It is effective for financial statement audits for periods beginning on or after June 1, 2001.

This standard addresses the auditor's responsibility to fully understand the client's technology as part of gaining an understanding about the client's internal controls in the conduct of a financial statement audit. It also assists auditors in determining whether IT auditors and their specialized skill set should be called on to assist in the financial audit. If necessary, the external auditor should use an IT auditor to provide expertise and assurance that detection risk is restricted to an acceptable level.

When a company undergoes a financial audit, SAS 94 requires the auditor to consider the effect of the company's information technology on its assessment of control risk. Specifically, when a company has such a significant amount of transactions processed electronically that the auditor cannot restrict detection risk to an acceptable level by performing only substantive tests, SAS 94 requires the auditor to:

- Consider how a client's IT processes affect internal control, evidential matter, and the assessment of control risk;
- Gain an understanding of how transactions are initiated, entered, and processed through the client's information system; and
- Gain an understanding of how recurring and nonrecurring journal entries are initiated, entered, and processed through the company's information system.

Although SAS 94 is applicable only for companies that have a significant amount of transactions processed electronically, practically speaking, this usually includes most companies that would be undergoing an audit. Audits in which both the financial and IT components are evaluated are referred to as *integrated* or *comprehensive* audits. SAS 94 audits make up the majority of IT audits performed.

A SAS 94 audit may involve any or all of the following six steps, identified by Sayana (2002): 1) physical and environmental review; 2) systems administration review; 3) application software review; 4) network security review; 5) business continuity review; and 6) data integrity review.[6] The auditor's selection of areas to review depends on which areas they identified during the risk assessment stage as having the most risks and vulnerabilities. Let's look at what's involved in each of these six areas.

PHYSICAL AND ENVIRONMENTAL REVIEW   In a physical and environmental review, the IT auditor is concerned with the physical security of the data center itself. For example, is the system in a secure location and in a clean, dust-free environment? Is the room properly ventilated and cooled? Many computer systems require strict environmental controls to function properly. Is the system supported by an uninterruptible power supply? This device will maintain power for up to an hour after a power outage, buying users time to shut down programs. Are smoke detectors and fire suppression systems installed? Is the cabling and wiring marked and identifiable?

The IT auditor also examines access controls relevant to the data center and information system. For example, is access to the computer facility governed by a security policy? Are there security guards, if deemed necessary? Is identification required for gaining access to the data center (such as badges, swipe cards, electronic keypads, or biometric devices)? All of these questions would be incorporated as audit procedures in a review of general controls.

SYSTEMS ADMINISTRATION REVIEW   A systems administration review involves a review of the operating systems, database management systems, and compliance with system administration procedures. Work in this area is highly technical because it requires intimate knowledge of various systems such as UNIX, IBM AS/400, and Windows NT. The IT auditor will gather an inventory of all hardware and software and a schematic for the particular platform and will evaluate password and other access controls. The auditor may use a program such as Crack to determine whether any ineffective passwords exist.[7] The auditor will also review who has access to the *root password,* which grants access to all files and applications running on the system and to see what types of access controls are in place. Note that many hackers seek to obtain root access. In the UNIX environment, root access is referred to as *super user* access. The IT auditor will also review user profiles to determine what privileges the user has and whether users' access rights are appropriate for their job responsibilities.

APPLICATION SOFTWARE REVIEW   In this step, the auditor will review any applications identified in the risk assessment stage as vulnerable, including accounting applications, payroll, time and billing software, inventory, or applications that are outsourced to third parties. An application software review focuses on validation of data inputs, processing, and output, access control and authorization, error handling, and system log procedures.

Input data validation consists of a number of error checks designed to ensure that only accurate and complete data can be entered. A computer operator who attempts to enter invalid or incomplete data into a field for which this type of data validation has been set up will usually be met with an obnoxious beep. There are numerous input data validation checks. A few of the more common ones include:

- *Limit check.* Establishes an upper boundary for acceptable data. Example: no hourly employee earns more than $15 per hour.

- *Range check.* Similar to a limit check except that the check for valid data applies to both an upper and lower boundary. Example: hours worked should be between 0 and 40 (assuming no overtime).

- *Validity check.* Specifies allowable numbers or characters as valid. For example, if a company does business only in Florida and Louisiana, a state field might have FL and LA set up as the only allowable entries.

- *Completeness check.* Prevents zeros or blanks from being accepted in a field for which those values are invalid.

If an error makes it past an input validation control, controls over processing may catch the error. Some of the more common processing controls include:

- Run-to-run totals, which the computer automatically computes to verify the data were processed correctly;

- Operator recalculation of batch control totals to computer generated totals;

- Limit checks on fields that were calculated during processing (such as gross pay); and

- Programmed controls that run in the background and detects processing errors and, in some cases, initiate corrective action.

Output controls ensure that whatever output an information system generates is adequately controlled. For example, procedures should be in place to govern the distribution of sensitive reports, including who receives the report and whether they must sign for the report. Proper disposal of reports is also important. More than one company has been known to engage in "dumpster diving" in an effort to obtain information on a competitor. Controls should govern how long and where organizations keep reports, and how they secure the reports during storage.

The auditor is also concerned with verifying that an organization handles errors appropriately. To this end, the auditor will need to determine how errors are handled. The objective is to determine whether there is a systematic process to appropriately identify and deal with errors. If an error log is available, the auditor will examine it to become familiar with the types of errors that appear to be most common and to identify any patterns that may be undetected.

The auditor usually tests the application through the use of several audit tools and techniques. We discuss these techniques, such as test desks and integrated test facilities, in detail in the next chapter.

Audit programs for application software review are highly specific to the client. The fieldwork and audit procedures the auditor chooses to conduct will depend on such issues as the operating system the application is run under, the complexity of the process, whether the application is "canned" (off-the-shelf) software or a customized application, and whether the application runs over a database or ERP environment. Typically, an IT auditor will start with a generic industry-specific audit program and tailor the program to the client as needed. A generic program for an application review might include the audit procedures shown in Figure 9-8.

NETWORK SECURITY REVIEW   We cover network security and controls that should protect the network in detail in Chapter 6. A network security review focuses on verification and validation of these control procedures around the information system network, including firewalls, router access controls, intrusion detection systems, incident response plans, port scanning, penetration testing, and virus/worm protection. The IT auditor will

Audit Scope	W/P Ref	Completed By

Review payroll system

Audit Objectives

1. Ensure the integrity of the payroll system.
2. Examine internal controls around the payroll system.

Audit Step

Planning *(Same as Figure 9-4)*

Field Work

1. Identify key personnel involved in the payroll process and the application software used.
2. Review all existing documentation for the payroll system to obtain an understanding of the physical and logical flow of data through the payroll system. This will include system, program, and analytic flowcharts, narratives, data flow diagrams, decision tables, etc.
3. Familiarize yourself with the payroll program used.
4. Interview key payroll personnel.
5. Document your understanding of the payroll process.
6. Prepare test data to test input and processing validation controls. (This section would include detailed audit procedures for testing input and processing controls.)
7. Run input validation controls and document results.
8. Identify and reconcile exceptions.
9. Prepare and run controls over processing. (This section would include detailed audit procedures for processing controls.)
10. Examine the process in place for handling errors.
11. Evaluate access controls, including all password controls.
12. Evaluate program change controls.
13. Evaluate the operating system environment under which the application runs, including backup and restore procedures.

Reporting *(Same as Figure 9-4)*

FIGURE 9-8   Generic Audit Program for Application Software Review

evaluate the existence of the necessary controls and test the controls deemed to be material to ensure that they work. Again, the IT auditor will usually start with a generic audit program and customize the procedures to fit the client's operating environment and network. A generic audit program for network security review might look like Figure 9-9.

BUSINESS CONTINUITY REVIEW   A business continuity review focuses on the auditor testing whether the information system can continue to function even if an event disrupts normal business operations. These procedures include backup procedures, disaster recovery plans, and the maintenance of fault tolerant systems. Some of these procedures are also covered in a network security review. Consequently, if the auditor is engaged to conduct both a network security review, there will be some overlap.

Audit Scope	**W/P Ref**	**Completed By**

Review information system network

Audit Objectives

1. Ensure the security of the client's network.
2. Ensure client's disaster recovery and backup procedures are adequate.

Audit Steps

Planning *(Same as Figure 9-4)*

Field Work

1. Identify and document key network personnel such as network administrator, programmers, database administrator, librarian, and operators.
2. Request a complete network diagram from the client that includes configuration for servers, workstations, bridges, repeaters, etc.
3. Determine the network topology.
4. Identify operating system and platform-specific hardware and software.
5. Obtain system and program flowcharts for applications running on the network.
6. Obtain the client's disaster recovery plan and review, noting when and how often the plan is tested.
7. Obtain the client's incident recovery plan, if one exists.
8. Obtain backup logs and determine adequacy of backups, including recovery procedures and off-site storage.
9. Verify that virus protection is maintained at the network, workstation, and application levels.
10. Identify and document network access controls, including the existence of security guards, swipe cards, biometrics, electronic keypad access, etc.
11. Identify and test firewalls.
12. Test authorization controls (detailed procedures here).
13. Test access controls (detailed procedures here).
14. Identify open ports such as port 80 and the existence of super user passwords.

Reporting *(Same as Figure 9-4)*

FIGURE 9-9   Generic Audit Program for Network Security Review

The IT auditor will obtain documentation from the client on its backup procedures. For example, are written procedures routinely tested? Is there a provision for off-site backup? The World Trade Center attacks highlighted the need for off-site backup, as some of the companies in one of the WTC towers had their information system backups stored in one of the other buildings. The IT auditors, who will visit the off-site storage facility, will verify that off-site backup procedures are adequate.

Unfortunately, many companies spend a great deal of money hiring consultants to help them draft a disaster recovery plan, only to fail to update it as their technology and companies grow and change. Like virus protection, a disaster recovery plan is effective only if the organization regularly maintains and tests the plan. The disaster recovery plan will be examined as part of the audit procedures. The organization should have a written plan, and it should be tested, *unannounced,* periodically.

The auditor will also investigate the existence of business interruption insurance. Such insurance protects a company against loss of operating income due to a catastrophic event such as riots, weather-related business closures, or other unforeseen events that can interrupt business operations.

DATA INTEGRITY REVIEW   In a data integrity review, the IT auditor verifies and validates the client's data using computer assisted audit techniques such as those discussed in Chapter 8. For example, preliminary risk assessment procedures might have indicated the accounts receivable program suffered from some exposures. The IT auditor would use a program such as ACL to perform recalculations and other analytics as needed.

USING COBIT TO PERFORM AN AUDIT

We introduced the reader to CobiT in Chapter 1 as an integrated control framework for information technology. The CobiT framework was developed by the Information Systems Audit and Control Association (ISACA) and is intended to bridge several technical and internal control models. Thus, CobiT is designed to be used by several parties, including management, internal, and external auditors. This section assumes an internal or external auditor wishes to conduct an IT audit and plans to use CobiT as the control framework.

The CobiT framework consists of six interrelated components:

- Executive summary;
- Framework;
- Control objectives;
- Management guidelines;
- Implementation toolset; and
- Audit guidelines.

Auditors will use the *Framework, Control Objectives,* and *Audit Guidelines* to formulate the audit program. CobiT is an "open standard," which means that most of the six components are available on the Internet. The only component that is not freely available is the *Audit Guidelines* component, which provides specific audit procedures to achieve identified control objectives. The *Audit Guidelines* are, however, available at no charge to ISACA members.

CobiT defines IT processes within four domains: Planning & Organization, Acquisition & Implementation, Delivery & Support, and Monitoring. The four domains contain a total of thirty-four high-level control objectives. Each high-level control objective contains several detailed control objectives, for a total of 318 detailed control objectives. Figure 9-10 shows the CobiT framework.

An audit conducted using CobiT does not vary from the IT audit life cycle we presented at the beginning of this chapter. The only difference is the development of the audit program. Auditors must first determine if there is an existing audit program. If so, the IT auditor can map CobiT audit procedures back to the audit objectives and audit procedures already in place. Additionally, the auditor can use CobiT's *Audit Guidelines* to identify any areas not covered sufficiently in the existing audit program. If there is no audit program with which to start, the *Audit Guidelines* can be used to build an audit program. Figure 9-11 shows the steps in developing an audit program using CobiT.

Domain	High Level Control Objectives	
Planning and Organization	PO1	Define a strategic IT plan
	PO2	Define the information architecture
	PO3	Determine the technological direction
	PO4	Define the IT organization and relationships
	PO5	Manage the IT investment
	PO6	Communicate management aims and direction
	PO7	Manage human resource
	PO8	Ensure compliance with external requirements
	PO9	Assess risks
	PO10	Manage projects
	PO11	Manage quality
Acquisition and Implementation	AI1	Identify automated solutions
	AI2	Acquire and maintain application software
	AI3	Acquire and maintain technology infrastructure
	AI4	Develop and maintain procedures
	AI5	Install and accredit systems
	AI6	Manage change
Delivery and Support	DS1	Define and manage service levels
	DS2	Manage third-party services
	DS3	Manage performance and capacity
	DS4	Ensure continuous service
	DS5	Ensure systems security
	DS6	Identify and allocate costs
	DS7	Educate and train users
	DS8	Assist and advise customers
	DS9	Manage the configuration
	DS10	Manage problems and incidents
	DS11	Manage data
	DS12	Manage facilities
	DS13	Manage operations
Monitoring	M1	Monitor the processes
	M2	Assess internal control adequacy
	M3	Obtain independent assurance
	M4	Provide for independent audit

FIGURE 9-10 CobiT's Framework
Copyright 1996, 1998, 2000. Information Systems Audit and Control Foundation. Reprinted with the permission of the Information Systems Audit and Control Foundation and IT Governance Institute

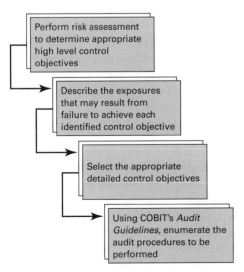

FIGURE 9-11 Using COBIT to Develop an Audit Program

SUMMARY

All IT audits follow a certain progression, which we have called the "IT audit life cycle." These steps include strategic planning, risk assessment, preparing the audit program, gathering audit evidence, forming conclusions based on the evidence obtained, preparing the audit opinion, and following up. We also identified four main types of IT audits, including attestation, findings and recommendations ("consulting"), a SAS 70 audit, and a SAS 94 report. While there are other types of audits, these are the primary audits in which IT auditors are generally involved. Attestation and findings and recommendations engagements are similar, the main difference being whether specific, enumerated procedures are agreed upon between the client and the auditor or whether the client simply wants general, broad advice. A SAS 70 audit is designed to provide assurance of a company's internal controls around a service provided to others. A SAS 94 audit takes place as a part of a regular financial audit. This type of audit is applicable when a company has a significant number of transactions processed electronically, and the auditor must gain a knowledge and understanding of the information system and the processing of those transactions through the system in order to reduce control risk. Finally, the chapter discussed how ISACA's CobiT *Framework, Control Objectives,* and *Audit Guidelines* can be used to design an audit program.

DISCUSSION QUESTIONS

9-1 Discuss how an IT audit is different from a financial statement audit.

9-2 Several audit standards are listed in the chapter. Who is bound by the ISACA audit standards and guidelines? What happens if the standards or guidelines are not followed?

9-3 Go to www.ifac.org. What is the purpose of IFAC? What is its role in IT audit?

9-4 Describe what the IT audit does during planning the audit.

9-5 How is materiality different in a financial audit than in an IT audit?

9-6 What is risk-based auditing? What is the alternative to risk-based auditing? Why have IT auditors moved to a risk-based approach?

9-7 What are the components of an audit program? How does an IT auditor go about constructing an audit program?

9-8 Describe the types of evidence an IT auditor might gather. Is all evidence equally reliable? Why or why not?

9-9 Discuss the difference between attribute and variable sampling. Give an example of each sampling approach.

9-10 Briefly describe the four primary types of audits as discussed in the chapter. Which type is performed most often?

9-11 A SAS 70 audit opinion is the only authorized auditor-to-auditor communication. What does this mean?

9-12 Describe the difference between a Type I and a Type II SAS 70 report. Do both allow the reduction of substantive testing?

9-13 How does an audit performed using CobiT methodology differ from an audit that does not?

EXERCISES

9-14 Several generic audit programs were presented in this chapter. Review those audit programs. Then develop a generic audit program for a network security review.

Identify the type of IT audit that would be employed for each of the following scenarios:

a. A company wishes to have management's assertions regarding its internal control under Section 404 of Sarbanes-Oxley audited.

b. A company hires a firm to maintain their application source code in escrow.

c. A company outsources its backup procedures to an online backup specialist.

> **d.** A company wishes to have its tape library procedures audited.
>
> **e.** A company wishes to have its Oracle implementation process audited.

9-15 CobiT can be accessed online at www.isaca.org. Visit this Web site and read the Executive Summary, which provides an overview of the CobiT process. Write a short summary of the audit methodology employed in CobiT.

REFERENCES AND RECOMMENDED READINGS

Bayuk, J. L. 2000. *Stepping through the IS Audit.* Rolling Meadows, Ill.: Information Systems Audit and Control Association.

Certified Information Systems Auditor Review Manual 2003. 2002. Rolling Meadows, Ill.: Information Systems Audit and Control Association.

Control Objectives for Information and related Technology (CobiT). 2002. Rolling Meadows, Ill.: Information Systems Audit and Control Association.

Gallegos, F. "Due Professional Care." 2002. *Information Systems Control Journal* 2.

———. 2002. "The Audit Report and Follow-up: Methods and Techniques for Communicating Audit Findings and Recommendations." *Information Systems Control Journal* 4, pp. 17–20.

Ernst & Young Assurance and Advisory Business Services. "Preparing for Internal Control Reporting: A Guide for Management's Assessment Under Section 404 of the Sarbanes-Oxley Act." 2002.

Sayana, A. S. 2002. "The IS Audit Process." *Information Systems Control Journal,* Vol. 1.

———. 2002. "The Necessity for Documentation." *Information Systems Control Journal* 3.

———. 2002. "Auditing General and Application Controls." *Information Systems Control Journal* 5, pp. 16–18.

NOTES

1. Mancino, J., and C. Landes, "A New Look at the Attestation Standards," *Journal of Accountancy*, July 2001.
2. See, for example, Delap White Caldwell & Croy LLP seminars on PIN and symmetric key management at www.yourcpas.com/security.asp.
3. See www.sas70.com.about.htm.
4. See the AICPA Audit Guide, *Service Organizations: Applying SAS No. 70*, for further information.
5. "What's Behind the Growing Popularity of SAS 70," knowledgespace.arthurandersen.com.
6. "The IS Audit Process," Anantha Sayana, *Information Systems Control Journal*, Vol. 1, 2002.
7. The Crack program is available at ftp://ftp.auscert.org.au/pub/cert/tools/crack/*.

CHAPTER 10

FRAUD AND FORENSIC AUDITING

CHAPTER CONTENTS

UNDERSTANDING FRAUD

Fraud is broadly defined as "any act involving the use of deception to obtain an illegal advantage" (ISACA Irregularities and Illegal Acts Guideline 30.010.010). Fraud is a hot topic today, primarily due to the spotlight on recent massive corporate failures such as Enron, Global Crossing, Adelphia, WorldCom, Tyco, and numerous other high-profile fraud cases. Legislation such as the Sarbanes-Oxley Act of 2002 is the direct result of a crackdown on corporations and executives responsible for committing corporate fraud. Furthermore, the auditor's responsibility to detect fraud has been broadened by new audit standards that require auditors to extend their efforts to detect fraud. The implications for the IT auditor are immense. Not only must IT auditors be knowledgeable of all types of fraud, but they must also know how to conduct the audit to provide reasonable assurance of detecting fraud.

In this chapter, you will learn about various types of fraud, what the auditor's responsibility is in detecting fraud, and how forensic auditors use electronic tools to uncover the nature and extent of fraud that has already occurred.

Why Fraud Occurs

Experts agree that fraud occurs as a result of the interplay between three factors: opportunity, incentive or pressure, and attitude or rationalization. These factors are collectively referred to as the "Fraud Triangle."[1] See Figure 10-1.

Opportunity exists when internal controls are not sufficient or when collusion exists so that perpetrators can circumvent the controls. Opportunity is the most important of the three factors, simply because even the greediest or neediest employee cannot carry out a fraud without opportunity.

Incentive or pressure typically comes from personal circumstances. For example, let's suppose a long-term faithful employee suddenly has a personal financial crisis. Perhaps a child is sick and the employee doesn't have insurance to cover medical care. Under normal circumstances, the employee might not be tempted to steal from the employer. But under these extraordinary circumstances, even a scrupulously honest employee might fall victim to situational pressures.

The final factor that is usually present when fraud is committed is attitude or rationalization. This means the employee finds a way within his or her conscience to justify the theft. Perhaps the employee believes he or she is underpaid. The employee might then rationalize that he or she is simply getting money owed anyway. This has been referred

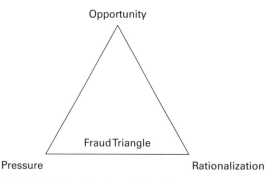

FIGURE 10-1 The Fraud Triangle
Source: Reprinted from "Occupational Fraud and Abuse," by Joseph T. Wells, Obsidian Publishing Co. 1997.

to in fraud studies as "wages in kind."[2] Such an attitude of rationalization will contribute to the employee's ultimate decision to steal from the employer. Case-in-Point 10-1 discusses motivation.

Case-in-Point 10-1

We usually associate fraud with greedy or needy employees. Occasionally, however, employees will steal for other reasons. Take the case of Jacqueline McTair, a forty-year employee of J. P. Morgan Chase & Co. By all accounts Ms. McTair was a well-liked and respected employee. Bank officials discovered, however, that Ms. McTair had embezzled $4.5 million from the bank. Interestingly, Ms. McTair didn't steal the money for herself. Indeed, she didn't keep a cent. She mistakenly thought that the money she was embezzling and depositing in various accounts was going to funds that compensated Holocaust victims. Ms. McTair, who is 70 years old, recently received a sentence of seven years and three months jail, and must pay four million dollars in restitution.[3]

Major Fraud Studies

Researchers have conducted many studies and surveys to determine the nature and extent of fraud. Of course we can only study fraud that has been detected and is therefore known about. The true nature of fraud is unknown, since much fraud goes undetected. Researchers estimate that only about 20 percent of fraud has been detected and is known about publicly.[4]

Major fraud studies include the landmark 1987 Committee of Sponsoring Organizations (COSO) fraud study, the 1996 study published by the Association of Certified Fraud Examiners, the 1998 KPMG fraud study,[5] the 1999 follow-up COSO fraud study, and the 2002 follow-up to the Association of Certified Fraud Examiners 1996 fraud report. Additionally, the Computer Security Institute, in conjunction with the FBI, has published a computer crime survey annually since 1996.[6] All of these studies attempt to discover trends in occupational (i.e., committed in the workplace) fraud, such as what kinds of fraud are most likely to be perpetrated, who the most likely perpetrators are, what methods are used, and so on. Let's take a closer look at two major studies, the 1999 COSO study, and the 2002 Association of Certified Fraud Examiners study.

THE COSO STUDY: "FRAUDULENT FINANCIAL REPORTING: 1987–1997, AN ANALYSIS OF U.S. PUBLIC COMPANIES" The 1999 COSO study focuses mainly on financial statement fraud committed over an eleven-year period. This study revealed three hundred cases of alleged fraudulent reporting by Securities and Exchange Commission (SEC) registrants and analyzed two hundred randomly selected cases. In the cases analyzed, the most common method used to commit financial statement fraud was some type of improper revenue recognition (50 percent). Other methods included overstatement of assets (50 percent), understatement of expenses/liabilities (18 percent), asset misappropriation (12 percent), and improper or inappropriate financial statement disclosures (8 percent).[7] Some cases involved more than one kind of fraud.

Other interesting characteristics of these fraud cases came to light. For instance, the companies analyzed in the COSO study were found to be relatively small, with less than $100 million in assets in the year immediately preceding the occurrence of the fraud.[8] The COSO study also highlighted a problem that has received increasing attention with the current rash of corporate frauds: governance. That is, what are the qualifications of the individuals who serve (often receiving tens of thousands of dollars in compensation) on corporate boards? The study found that board members were typically individuals with family or fraternal ties to the owners and, in many cases, were people who had little experience as corporate directors. Further, in more than 20 percent of the companies involved in fraudulent financial reporting, officers held incompatible job functions, such as serving as both the CEO and CFO.[9]

Of the balance sheet accounts that were frequently involved in fraudulent financial reporting, inventory was the most commonly misstated account. Accounts receivable was not far behind, followed by properly, plant and equipment, and loans/notes receivable.[10]

One might be curious to know which industries were more prevalent in fraud cases. Figure 10-2 shows that computer companies and manufacturing companies had the highest incidence of fraudulent financial reporting

THE "2002 REPORT TO THE NATION ON OCCUPATIONAL FRAUD AND ABUSE," ALSO KNOWN AS THE "2002 WELLS REPORT" While the COSO study focuses on fraudulent financial reporting, the National Association of Certified Fraud Examiners fraud report is not limited to one type of fraud. Instead, it is based on 663 known occupational fraud cases reported by certified fraud examiners who investigated those cases. This report is particularly instructive in noting trends in fraud because it compares the 1996 reported statistics with the 2002 statistics. The report discusses five main areas relevant to fraud: the costs associated with fraud, the methods for committing the frauds, who the victims are, who the perpetrators are, and the legal aspects and outcomes of the 663 cases.

Costs Associated with Fraud Fraud in 2002 was estimated at $600 billion, compared with $400 billion in 1996. Over half of the frauds in the study resulted in a loss of at least $100,000. Sixteen percent resulted in a loss of at least $1 million, and 3.2 percent (or twenty frauds out of 620) were more than $10 million. The largest category of fraud in terms of number committed was the $100,000 to $500,000 category, with over 27 percent of frauds falling into this category. See Figure 10-3.

Methods for Committing Fraud The 1996 and 2002 Association of Certified Fraud Examiners "Report to the Nation on Occupational Fraud and Abuse" identified three categories of fraud: asset misappropriation, corruption, and fraudulent statements.

Industry	Percent of Companies Where Fraud Occurred
Computer	15%
Manufacturing	15%
Financial services	14%
Health care	11%
Other service providers	8%
Retailers and wholesalers	8%
Oil and gas	8%
Telecommunications	6%
Insurance	4%
Real Estate	3%
Other	8%

FIGURE 10-2 Fraudulent Financial Reporting by Industry
Source: "Shedding Light on Fraud," *Journal of Accountancy*, September 1999.

Dollar Loss Range/ Percent of Cases	Number of Cases out of 620 Frauds Identified by CFEs
$1–999 (2.3%)	14
$1,000–$9,999 (10.2%)	63
$10,000–$49,000 (22.9%)	142
$50,000–$99,000 (12.1%)	75
$100,000–$499,000 (27.6%)	171
$500,000–$999,999 (8.5%)	53
$1,000,000–$9,999,999 (13.2%)	82
$10,000 + (3.2%)	20

FIGURE 10-3 Distribution of Dollar Losses of Occupational Fraud
Source: "Association of Certified Fraud Examiners (Austin, Texas) 2002 Report to the Nation
Occupational Fraud and Abuse" page 5; www.cfenet.com/media/2002RttN/; Used with permission.

All fraud falls into one of these three categories. Figure 10-4 shows the three categories of fraud, along with their subcomponents.

Asset misappropriation involves the theft or misuse of a company's assets, such as stealing cash, inventory, or fixed assets. Within the cash category, embezzlement can occur through skimming schemes such as lapping of accounts receivable or under-recording or understating sales. The theft of cash also involves myriad fraudulent disbursement schemes such as billing schemes, payroll fraud, expense reimbursement schemes, check tampering, and cash register fraud. Asset misappropriation is by far the largest category of occupational fraud in terms of the number of frauds committed, comprising nearly 86 percent of fraud covered in the study. However, fraudulent financial reporting was the category with the largest dollar value. These numbers are comparable to statistics reported in the 1996 study. Figure 10-5 shows the median loss by category of fraud.

Within asset misappropriation schemes, misappropriation of cash accounted for 90.1 percent of the frauds. Within cash fraud, fraudulent disbursements accounted for 71.1 percent of the fraud cases.

Corruption involves misuse of personal power or position for personal gain, ignoring the fiduciary duty to an employer. Examples of corruption include giving or receiving bribes, taking kickbacks to influence a business decision, or engaging in activities in which a conflict of interest exists. Corruption comprised 12.8 percent of fraud in the study.

Fraudulent statements consist of both financial and nonfinancial fraud. Financial fraud involves misrepresenting an organization's assets and revenues or expenses and liabilities. Nonfinancial fraud involves items such as misrepresentation of credentials in applying for a job and falsification of internal and external documents. While financial statement fraud has received the lion's share of press attention with high-profile failures such as Enron and WorldCom, this study reported that only 5.1 percent of frauds fell into this category. However, frauds tend to be significantly larger in value in this category.

Regarding the duration of fraud schemes, the median time frame from inception to detection was eighteen months. The report further states that nearly two-thirds of fraud schemes continued undetected for more than a year. Figure 10-6 shows the duration of fraud scheme by type of fraud.

With respect to *how* frauds are initially detected, the average person on the street would probably guess that frauds are detected by an audit. However, of the 532 responses to this question in the study, a whopping 46.2 percent were detected by some type of tip (either employee, customer, anonymous, or vendor), while 18.8 percent were detected by accident. Only 18.6 percent were detected by an internal audit, while 11.5 percent were detected by external audit. A strong system of internal control was helpful in fraud detection, with 15.4 percent of frauds being detected this way. The remaining 1.7 percent of

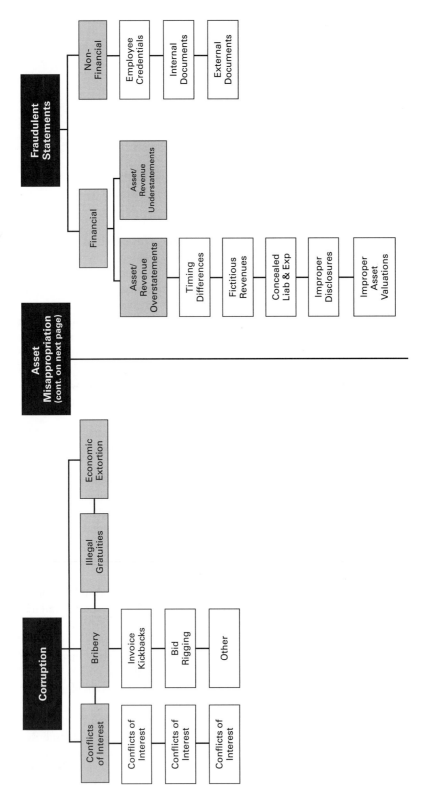

FIGURE 10-4 Occupational Fraud and Abuse Classification System (1 of 3)

Source: "Association of Certified Fraud Examiners (Austin, Texas) 2002 Report to the Nation Occupational Fraud and Abuse," page iii; www.cfenet.com/media/2002RttN/; Used with permission.

(continued)

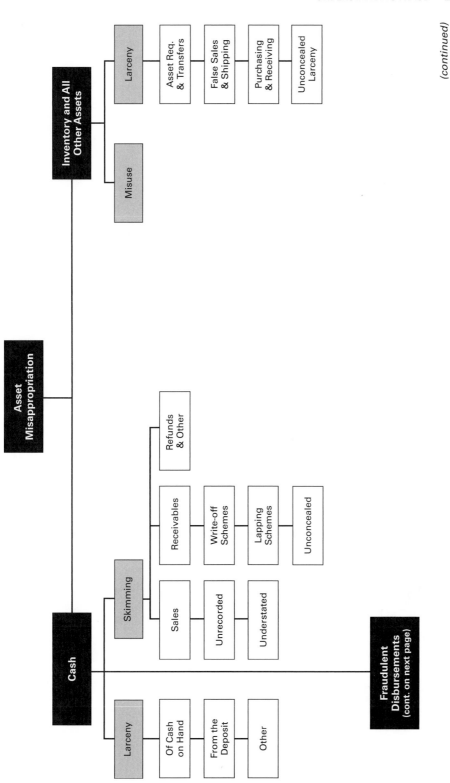

FIGURE 10-4 Occupational Fraud and Abuse Classification System (2 of 3)

(continued)

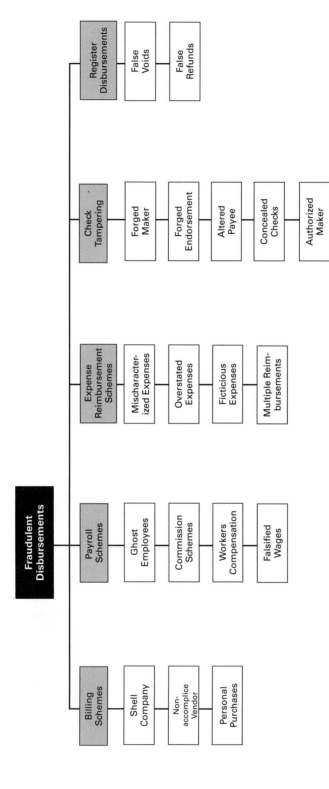

FIGURE 10-4 Occupational Fraud and Abuse Classification System (3 of 3)

Method of Fraud (Percent Cases)	Median Loss
Asset misappropriation (85.7%)	$ 80,000
Corruption (12.8%)	530,000
Fraudulent Statements (5.1%)	4,250,000

FIGURE 10-5   Methods of Occupational Fraud
Source: "Association of Certified Fraud Examiners (Austin, Texas) 2002 Report to the Nation Occupational Fraud and Abuse," page 6; www.cfenet.com/media/2002RttN/; Used with permission.

Method of Fraud	Median Length Before Detection (in Months)
Fraudulent statements	25
Expense reimbursments	24
Check tampering	24
Billing schemes	23
Corruption schemes	22
Payroll schemes	19
Skimming	17
Register disbursements	17
Asset misappropriations	17
Non-cash misappropriations	12
Cash larceny	8

FIGURE 10-6   Duration of Fraud Scheme by Type
Source: "Association of Certified Fraud Examiners (Austin, Texas) 2002 Report to the Nation Occupational Fraud and Abuse," page 10; www.cfenet.com/media/2002RttN/; Used with permission.

frauds were detected by law enforcement. Note that the percentages add to more than 100 percent because some participants cited more than one method of how a fraud was initially detected.

With respect to which measures are most helpful in *preventing* fraud, survey respondents viewed a strong system of internal controls as the most effective anti-fraud measure by a wide margin, followed by background checks on new employees, regular fraud audit, established fraud policies, willingness of companies to prosecute, ethics training for employees, anonymous fraud reporting mechanisms, and workplace surveillance.

Who the Perpetrators Are   Within an organization two categories of fraud perpetrators exist: employees and managers/executives. The survey found that, of the occupational fraud that was committed, 58.1 percent was committed by employees, 35.9 percent was committed by managers/executives, and 6 percent was committed by managers/executives in collusion with employees. Interestingly, while employees were more likely to perpetrate fraud, fraud committed by managers or executives resulted in a significantly greater dollar loss ($250,000 median cost as compared with $70,000 median per fraud for employee fraud.

Other characteristics of fraud perpetrators are shown in Figure 10-7. Those who commit smaller frauds tend to be middle-aged individuals with less higher education. Big-dollar frauds are more likely to be committed by middle-aged or older individuals with college degrees. For example, while only 2.5 percent of frauds were committed by individuals over the age of 60, the median loss was $500,000. Almost 70 percent of frauds were committed by individuals who had never been charged with or convicted of prior crimes.

Who the Victims Are   The report indicates that, of the companies found to have fraud, the incidence of fraud was highest in privately held companies (31.9 percent), with

Characteristic	Percent of Occurrance
Gender	
Male	53.3%
Female	46.5%
Age (in years)	
>60	2.5%
41–59	44.8%
26–40	50.7%
<26	5.0%
Education	
Bachelor's degree	32.7%
Postgraduate degree	10.4%
High school or less	56.9%
Criminal History	
Never charged or convicted	68.6%
Don't know	21.3%
Had prior convictions	6.9%
Charged but not convicted	2.9%

FIGURE 10-7 Characteristics of Fraud Perpetrators
Source: "Association of Certified Fraud Examiners (Austin, Texas) 2002 Report to the Nation Occupational Fraud and Abuse," page 14–16; www.cfenet.com/media/2002RttN/; Used with permission.

publicly traded companies victims 30.0 percent of the time. Not-for-profit organizations suffered 13.4 percent of the losses, while government agencies were fraud victims in 24.7 percent of the cases. Companies with less than one hundred employees suffered higher median losses than the largest organizations (those with more than ten thousand employees). The report speculates that this may be because many small companies often have a single individual in charge of the entire bookkeeping process. In these situations, the absence of segregation of duties creates opportunity that when combined with situational pressures and rationalization on the part of the perpetrator may be impossible to resist. Figure 10-8 shows losses by size of organization (e.g., number of employees).

Legal Aspects and Outcomes This section of the study examined whether an organization's anti-fraud measures were effective in deterring fraud, whether internal controls could have prevented the fraud, and whether the companies pursued legal action against the perpetrators.

Four basic anti-fraud measures included background checks, anonymous reporting mechanisms, internal audits, and external audits. Figure 10-9 shows that all of these measures, when present, deterred fraud to some degree. Further, companies with a given anti-fraud device in all cases suffered lower median losses.

One of the most significant findings of the study is that 46.2 percent of respondents indicated that insufficient internal controls contributed to the ability to perpetrate the

Number of Employees/ Percent of Cases	Median Loss
1–99 (39.0)	$127,500
100–999 (20.1%)	135,000
1,000–9,999 (23.4%)	53,000
10,000+ (17.5%)	97,000

FIGURE 10-8 Losses by Number of Employees
Source: "Association of Certified Fraud Examiners (Austin, Texas) 2002 Report to the Nation Occupational Fraud and Abuse," page 18; www.cfenet.com/media/2002RttN/; Used with permission.

Anti-Fraud Measure	Percent of Cases (Median Loss)
Background checks	
Yes	47.9% ($90,000)
No	52.1% ($130,000)
Anonymous reporting mechanism	
Yes	35.2% ($77,500)
No	64.8% ($150,000)
Internal audit/fraud exam	
Yes	57.7% ($87,000)
No	42.3% ($153,000)
External audit	
Yes	73.0% ($100,000)
No	27.0% ($140,000)

FIGURE 10-9 The Impact of Anti-Fraud Measures
Source: "Association of Certified Fraud Examiners (Austin, Texas) 2002 Report to the Nation Occupational Fraud and Abuse," page 19; www.cfenet.com/media/2002RttN/; Used with permission.

fraud, while 39.9 percent indicated that controls existed but were ignored. Thus, in over 86 percent of cases, internal controls either did not exist or were not followed.

Finally, with respect to disposition of the fraud cases, in most cases (61.1 percent) victims were insured. In 47 percent of the cases in the study, insurance paid for at least half of the loss. Contrary to the popular myth that victim organizations rarely prosecute dishonest employees, approximately 75 percent of cases were referred for criminal prosecution, and in 75 percent of these cases the perpetrator was convicted, either through a plea bargain (64 percent) or at trial (14 percent). For those cases where no legal action was taken against the offender, the fear of negative publicity (cited 30.6 percent of the time) was the primary reason for taking no legal action, followed by a private settlement being reached between the employer and dishonest employee (cited 26.6 percent of the time).

IT Fraud

The discussion so far has focused on fraud in a broad sense, while the focus of this book is on IT audit. Thus, one might wonder how IT fraud fits into the picture.

IT fraud can be defined as fraud committed through the use of computerized technology. Thus, almost any of the categories of fraud outlined in the "2002 Wells Report" can be committed as an IT fraud. That's why it's important for IT auditors to understand all types of fraud. Additionally, IT auditors must be proficient at using sophisticated technology to detect fraud. Chapter 8 covers this topic and presents specific types of computer assisted auditing techniques (CAATs) that can be used to detect frauds by functional area.

Cybercrime

Cybercrime is discussed in Chapter 2. Broadly speaking, cybercrime can refer to any type of crime committed through the use of a computer network and the Internet. Typically, cybercrime comes down to obtaining unauthorized and/or illegal access to a third party's computer network. The third party can be a government agency, a not-for-profit company, or a public or private company. Once the cyber criminal gains access, he or she may engage in a multitude of malicious or nonmalicious activities such as espionage, e-shoplifting, embezzlement, and the planting of viruses or worms. Methods for gaining access to networks are discussed in Chapter 6. Specific types of cybercrime are discussed in detail in Chapter 2.

RESPONSIBILITIES TO DETECT FRAUD

Ask any ordinary individual off the street, "Whose job is it to detect fraud?" and chances are he or she will say, "The auditor, of course." However, the auditor will beg to differ! The primary responsibility to detect fraud lies with the company. From an audit profession standpoint, the auditor must design the audit with the reasonable assurance of detecting fraud, but the purpose of an audit is not to detect fraud (unless of course it is a special fraud engagement). Rather, the purpose of an audit is to determine whether the company has followed generally accepted accounting principles (GAAP) in the preparation of its financial statements.

This difference between what the *public* thinks and what the *auditor* thinks regarding the responsibility to detect fraud has been referred to as the "expectations gap." In the late 1980s the audit profession sought to narrow the expectation gap with a series of audit standards. However, more needs to be done. With the large number of fraud cases coming to light recently, lawmakers are working with the audit profession to narrow the expectations gap even more. Let's look a little closer at what the company's responsibility is, and then what the auditor's responsibility is regarding fraud deterrence and detection.

Corporate Responsibility

POSITIVE VERSUS NEGATIVE SECURITY MODEL First and foremost, companies should strive to maintain a positive, proactive security model. This means they understand the risks and threats and seek proactively to identify their vulnerabilities where information technology is concerned. They don't wait until something happens to jump on the security bandwagon. In contrast, a negative security model is a reactionary model. Problems, including security breaches, are handled as they arise. Little attempt is made to formulate a broad, forward-looking plan for security. The positive security model includes fostering an ethical atmosphere, maintaining corporate policies on computer use and misuse, protecting the computer system through appropriate security measures, and maintaining a corporate security incident response plan.

ETHICS Ethics, covered in detail in Chapter 2, is probably the most important factor in the corporate realm where fraud is concerned. Management's "tone at the top" sets the standard for the entire company. If management takes the issue of ethics lightly, you can be assured that employees will be quick to follow management's lead. Therefore, it is incumbent upon management to lead by example.

A written, dispersed, and adhered-to corporate code of ethics is one way management can demonstrate a commitment to ethics. Many corporations publish their code of ethics on the Internet to demonstrate to customers and employees that they are fully committed to running an ethical business. The Center for the Study of Ethics in the Professions (CSEP) at the Illinois Institute of Technology has developed an extensive database of more than 850 companies that maintain codes of conduct on the Internet.[11] Figure 10-10 shows the Better Business Bureau of Canada's code of conduct, which can be viewed on the Internet at www.bbbvan.org/aboutbbb/prog_services/codeethics.html.

COMPUTER USE AND ABUSE Companies also should have policies governing the proper and improper use of company technology, including computers. Some examples of issues that should be specifically addressed include:

1. Whether or not employees can take laptops home or on vacation;
2. The lending of laptops to others;

Better Business Bureau of Mainland British Columbia

Equality: We shall recognize the individual rights of all members of the community in accordance with the Canadian Charter of Rights and Freedoms, and display a fair sense of justice.

Truth: We shall make accurate claims to our customers, use only competent testimonials, and strive to be open about all aspects of the products or services we offer.

Honesty: We shall uphold the principle of fair play and be vigilant against conduct which has the intent, capability, or effect of being deceptive towards our customers.

Integrity: We shall not merely abide by the law in a technical way but will strive to serve our customers with honest values, avoiding all devices and schemes which prey on human ignorance or gullibility.

Cooperativeness: We shall support a healthy marketplace for all through cooperation with customer, other businesses, and every person who would benefit from an ethical, free-market system.

Self Regulation: We shall be self regulating, we will honor all commitments including any guarantees we offer, ensure that the normal use of our merchandise or services will not be hazardous to public health or safety, and seek to resolve, in a fair and expeditious manner, any disputes which may rise.

FIGURE 10-10   Sample Code of Ethics
Source: www.bbbvan.org/aboutbbb/prog_services/codeethics.html. Used with permission.

3. Copying software owned by the company;

4. The use of unauthorized software on an employee's desktop computer;

5. The use of company time to surf the Internet or conduct personal business on the Internet (for example, making plane reservations for a vacation);

6. E-mail dos and don'ts;

7. Password protocols such as requiring passwords to be changed at regular intervals;

8. Virus protection updating; and

9. Sharing of files and disks.

POLICIES ON SECURING THE CORPORATE NETWORK   The company also has a responsibility to maintain appropriate security measures to protect the corporate network. This includes internal controls both at the network level and the application level to control who has access to the corporate network (i.e., authentication), and to which applications he or she has access. Firewall protection should be in place, and a system of intrusion detection should be constantly in use. Encryption of documents and e-mail should be used where appropriate and where cost-beneficial. Virus protection should be in place and constantly updated. Security patches should be downloaded daily by network administrators. All of these controls should be stated explicitly as a matter of policy.

CORPORATE FRAUD POLICY   One policy that is typically separated from a general policy statement concerns fraud. Many companies maintain a separate corporate fraud policy. This policy specifically states what constitutes fraud, to whom the policies apply, how the perpetrator(s) will be dealt with, and possibly any whistle-blower protection afforded by the company. The fraud policy for the City of Toronto, as shown in Figure 10-11, contains most of these provisions.

As part of the corporate fraud policy, it is vital that the company engage in incident response planning. This plan is a written document that details what procedures are appropriate when a breach of security has been encountered. Much like a national defense operation has written step-by-step instructions on what to do in the event of a security breach,

POLICY
Fraud and Other Similar Irregularities
Statement of Policy Principles

The City of Toronto is committed to protecting its revenue, property, information and other assets from any attempt, either by members of the public, contractors, sub contractors, agents, intermediaries or its own employees, to gain by deceit, financial or other benefits.

This policy sets out specific guidelines and responsibilities regarding appropriate actions that must be followed for the investigation of fraud and other similar irregularities.

Definitions

Fraud and other similar irregularities includes, but is not limited to:

1. Forgery or alteration of cheques, drafts, promissory notes and securities.
2. Any misappropriation of funds, securities, supplies or any other asset.
3. Any irregularity in the handling or reporting of money transactions.
4. Misappropriation of furniture, fixtures and equipment.
5. Seeking or accepting anything of material value from vendors, consultants or contractors doing business with the City in violation of the City's Conflict of Interest policy.
6. Unauthorized use or misuse of City property, equipment, materials or records.
7. Any computer related activity involving the alteration, destruction, forgery or manipulation of data for fraudulent purposes or misappropriation of City-owned software.
8. Any claim for reimbursement of expenses that are not made for the exclusive benefit of the City.
9. Any similar or related irregularity.

Applicability

This policy applies to Council Members, all employees of the City of Toronto and to employees of local Boards, Agencies and Commissions over which Council has authority to require general policies to be followed.

General Policy and Responsibilities

1. It is the City's intent to fully investigate any suspected acts of fraud, misappropriation or other similar irregularity. An objective and impartial investigation will be conducted regardless of the position, title, length of service or relationship with the City of any party who might be or becomes involved in or becomes/is the subject of such investigation.
2. Each Commissioner is responsible for instituting and maintaining a system of internal control to provide reasonable assurance for the prevention and detection of fraud, misappropriations and other irregularities. Management should be familiar with the types of improprieties that might occur within their area of responsibility and be alert for any indications of such conduct.
3. The City Auditor, in consultation with the City Solicitor, has the primary responsibility for the investigation of all activity as defined in this policy.
4. The City Auditor will notify the Chair of the Audit Committee and the Chief Administrative Officer of a reported allegation of fraudulent or irregular conduct upon the commencement of the investigation to the extent practical. Throughout the investigation these officials should be informed of pertinent investigative findings.
5. In all circumstances, where there are reasonable grounds to indicate that a fraud may have occurred, the City Auditor, subject to the advice of the City Solicitor, will contact the Toronto Police Service.
6. Upon conclusion of the investigation, the results will be reported to the Chair of the Audit Committee, the Chief Administrative Officer and the Commissioner.
7. The City will pursue every reasonable effort, including court ordered restitution, to obtain recovery of the City losses from the offender, or other appropriate source(s).

Procedures

1. All Employees

Any employee who has knowledge of an occurrence of irregular conduct, or has reason to suspect that a fraud has occurred, shall immediately notify his/her supervisor. If the employee has reason to believe that the employee's supervisor may be involved, the employee shall immediately notify the Commissioner and the City Auditor.

(continued)

FIGURE 10-11   Sample Corporate Fraud Policy, City of Toronto (1 of 3)
Source: www.city.toronto.on.ca/audit/fraud_policy_page.htm; Used with permission.

The employee shall not discuss the matter with anyone other than his/her supervisor, the Commissioner, the City Auditor and the police. Employees who knowingly make false allegations will be subject to discipline up to and including dismissal.

2. Managers

Upon notification from an employee of suspected fraud, or if the manager has reason to suspect that a fraud has occurred, the manager shall immediately notify the Commissioner and the City Auditor. The manager shall not attempt to investigate the suspected fraud or to discuss the matter with anyone other than the person to whom the fraud was reported, the City Auditor and the police.

3. Commissioner

Upon notification from an employee or manager of suspected fraud, or if the Commissioner has reason to suspect that a fraud has occurred, the Commissioner shall immediately contact the City Auditor. The Commissioner shall not attempt to investigate the suspected fraud or to discuss the matter with anyone other than the City Auditor, City Solicitor and the police.

4. City Auditor

Upon notification or discovery of a suspected fraud, the City Auditor will promptly investigate the fraud. In all circumstances where there appears to be reasonable grounds for suspecting that a fraud has taken place, the City Auditor, in consultation with the City Solicitor, will contact the Toronto Police Service.

5. Contacts/Protocols

After an initial review and a determination that the suspected fraud warrants additional investigation, the City Auditor will notify the Chief Administrative Officer, the City Solicitor and the Chair of the Audit Committee of the allegations. The City Auditor shall coordinate the investigation with the appropriate law enforcement officials.

6. Security of Evidence

Once a suspected fraud is reported, the City Auditor, in consultation with the City Solicitor, shall take immediate action to prevent the theft, alteration, or destruction of relevant records. Such actions include, but are not necessarily limited to, removing the records and placing them in a secure location, limiting access to the location where the records currently exist, and preventing the individual suspected of committing the fraud from having access to the records. The records must be adequately secured until the City Auditor obtains the records to begin the audit investigation.

7. Confidentiality

All participants in a fraud investigation shall keep the details and results of the investigation confidential. However, the City Auditor, in consultation with the Corporate Access and Privacy Office of the City and the Toronto Police Service, may disclose particulars of the investigation with potential witnesses if such disclosure would further the investigation.

8. Personnel Actions

If a suspicion of fraud is substantiated by the investigation, disciplinary action, up to and including dismissal, shall be taken by the appropriate level of management, in consultation with the Human Resources Division, the City Auditor and the City Solicitor, in conformance with the City's Personnel Policies and Procedures.

Unless exceptional circumstances exist, a person under investigation for fraud shall be given notice in writing of the essential particulars of the allegations following the conclusion of the audit investigation and prior to final disciplinary action being taken. Where notice is given, the person against whom allegations are being made may submit a written explanation to the City Auditor no later than seven calendar days after the notice is received. This requirement is subject to any collective agreement provisions respecting the rights of employees during disciplinary proceedings.

9. Whistle-Blower Protection

No employer or person acting on behalf of an employer shall:
- dismiss or threaten to dismiss an employee;
- discipline or suspend or threaten to discipline or suspend an employee;

(continued)

FIGURE 10-11 Sample Corporate Fraud Policy, City of Toronto (2 of 3)

- impose any penalty upon an employee; or
- intimidate or coerce an employee,

because the employee has acted in accordance with the requirements of the policy. The violation of this section will result in discipline up to and including dismissal.

10. Media Issues

Any staff person or elected official contacted by the media with respect to an audit investigation shall refer the media to the Director of Corporate Communications or designate. The alleged fraud or audit investigation shall not be discussed with the media by any person other than through the Director of Corporate Communications or designate, in consultation with the City Auditor.

If the City Auditor's office is contacted by the media regarding an alleged fraud or audit investigation, the City Auditor or designate will consult with the Director of Corporate Communications or designate, as appropriate, before responding to a media request for information or interview.

The City Auditor and Director of Corporate Communications will determine media messages and identify an appropriate City spokesperson, as required.

11. Documentation

At the conclusion of the investigation, the City Auditor will document the results in a confidential memorandum report to the Chair of the Audit Committee with a copy to the Chief Administrative Officer and the Commissioner. If the report concludes that the allegations are founded, the report will be forwarded to the Toronto Police Service.

The City Auditor will also be required to make recommendations to the appropriate Commissioner which will assist in the prevention of future similar occurrences.

12. Completion of Investigation

Upon completion of the investigation including all legal and personnel actions, any records, documents and other evidentiary material will be returned by the City Auditor to the appropriate department.

13. Reporting to External Auditors

The City Auditor will report to the external auditors of the City all information relating to investigations.

14. Annual Report

As directed by Council, the City Auditor will report, on an annual basis, information related to investigations conducted during the year.

Approved by City Council at the meeting of May 21, 2002.

FIGURE 10-11   Sample Corporate Fraud Policy, City of Toronto (3 of 3)

the company should have a similar action plan. It also involves documenting incidents as they occur, including:

1. How the incident was brought to light;
2. Which systems were penetrated and specifically how they were accessed;
3. When (date and time) the fraud occurred;
4. Who the perpetrators were (or as much information as is known);
5. How the incident was resolved;
6. Costs attributable to the incident; and
7. Modifications to existing security needed to prevent similar incidences in the future.

The Auditor's Responsibility—Professional Guidance

Professional guidance in the area of fraud detection stems from the AICPA's *Professional Standards,* including SAS No. 1 and SAS No. 99. Additional guidance is provided by

Guideline 30, "Irregularities and Illegal Acts," promulgated by the Information Systems Audit and Control Association (ISACA). Chapter 2 summarizes Guideline 30. Therefore, we refer the reader to that chapter for a complete summary of this standard and how it applies to IT auditors.

SAS NO. 1, "CODIFICATION OF AUDITING STANDARDS AND PROCEDURES"   SAS No. 1 (as amended by SAS 82) states:

> The auditor has a responsibility to plan and perform the audit to obtain reasonable assurance about whether the financial statements are free of material misstatement, whether caused by error or fraud. Because of the nature of audit evidence and the characteristics of fraud, the auditor is able to obtain reasonable, but not absolute assurance that material misstatements are detected. The auditor has no responsibility to plan and perform the audit to obtain reasonable assurance that misstatements, whether caused by errors or fraud, that are not material to the financial statement are detected.[12]

The concepts of "reasonable assurance" and "material misstatement" are not used by accident. The only way auditors could be certain there is not material misstatement is to audit every single transaction, which, of course, is not a cost-beneficial solution to attacking fraud. And even if every single transaction is audited, there is still the possibility that fraud through collusion would go undetected. Instead, auditors rely on sampling procedures to provide reasonable assurance that the financial statements are free from material misstatement. The audit opinion reflects these concepts of reasonable assurance and material misstatement.

Having said that the auditor cannot audit every single transaction, we should point out that in a sense, computer assisted audit tools such as ACL allow for "virtual" examination of whole populations of transactions. For example, the IT auditor might be interested in determining whether there is nepotism in the company. He or she might initiate a test using ACL to search for all employees with the same address. This test might or might not be successful in exposing nepotism in the company, as some addresses might be apartment complexes, etc. The point is, that in this example, every employee record can be examined through the use of ACL.

SAS NO. 99, "CONSIDERATION OF FRAUD IN A FINANCIAL STATEMENT AUDIT"   The Auditing Standards Board recently issued SAS 99,[13] which supersedes SAS 82. The standard is effective for audits performed after December 15, 2002. This new standard provides enhanced guidance to auditors on fraud topics including an expanded definition of fraud, guidance on team discussions, professional skepticism, expanded inquiries of management, a broader range of risk factors to consider, revenue recognition, evaluation of internal controls, and the auditor's response to the risk factors identified during the risk assessment process.

Fraud Definition and Characteristics   SAS 82 recognized two main categories of fraud: asset misappropriation and fraudulent financial statements. The new standard enhances the definitions provided in SAS 82 and incorporates the Fraud Triangle (see Figure 10-1) in recognition of the importance of considering opportunity, incentive/pressure, and attitude/rationalization in the conduct of an audit. Research has consistently shown that the consideration of these factors is instrumental in identifying environments where fraud might be more likely to occur.

SAS 99 requires the auditor to assess the risk of material misstatement due to fraud and to design the audit procedures accordingly. In assessing the risk of material misstatement, auditors were required to specifically consider "risk factors" as outlined in the standard. Additionally, auditors are required to exercise professional judgment when considering what risk factors may be present and to maintain an attitude of professional skepticism. These risk factors, characterized using the Fraud Triangle, are divided into risk factors for fraudulent financial reporting and risk factors for misappropriation of assets. The following risk factors continue to be important:

1. Management's attitude toward control;
2. Industry conditions; and
3. Operating characteristics and financial stability of the company.

Management's Attitude toward Control   As previously mentioned, management's attitude toward control is often referred to as the "tone at the top." It means looking at how management perceives security and control. Are there policies such as a code of ethics, a mission statement and statement of values, and a corporate fraud policy? The presence of such policies is indicative of a management team that cares about ethics and propriety of behavior.

Specific Industry Conditions   Companies that operate in difficult economic and regulatory environments are susceptible to external pressures that may create opportunity for fraud. The telecommunications industry, for example, has experienced many of the recent high-profile business failures. An auditor working in this industry should be aware of this situation and consider how a current engagement may be affected.

Operating Characteristics and Financial Stability   Operating characteristics and financial stability refer to company-specific items. Has the company experienced several years of declining profits? Has there been a significant turnover of key employees? Is there a large loan coming due for which cash is not available? Items such as these would usually be red flags to an auditor, who may or may not modify the audit procedures, depending on his or her professional judgment.

SAS 99 also requires the auditor to ask management directly if he or she is aware of any type of fraud within the company. Interestingly, some frauds that have later come to light were known or suspected by company employees. In many cases employees who are stealing from the company arouse suspicion by noticeable lifestyle changes and the appearance of living beyond their means. When asked why the employees didn't report the suspected fraud, they responded, "Because no one asked!"

Further Risk Assessment   SAS 99 requires extensive documentation of the auditor's risk assessment, understanding of the controls, and how risk factors were considered in the conduct of the audit. The auditor is charged with continually monitoring and assessing the risk of material misstatement due to fraud throughout the audit. The auditor's risk assessment may affect the following elements of the audit:

1. *Professional skepticism.* In assessing risk, the auditor should maintain an attitude of professional skepticism. That is, the auditor should not assume management is dishonest, nor does the auditor assume unquestioned honesty; rather, the auditor should keep in mind that fraud is always a possibility and he should conduct the audit accordingly.
2. *Assignment of personnel.* The auditor's assessment of the risk of material misstatement should also affect how the audit company decides to staff an audit

engagement. Highly complex environments and businesses require highly trained auditors. (See Case-in-Point 10-2.)

3. *Accounting principles and policies.* To the extent management's choice of accounting policies may be questionable, the auditor may need to further examine these choices. (See Case-in-Point 10-3.)

4. *Controls.* If a company's internal controls appear to be deficient and thus a contributing factor to the possibility of fraud, the auditor must, of course, lower his or her reliance on controls, or perhaps not rely on those controls at all and instead perform more substantive testing.

Case-in-Point 10-2

The importance of the assignment of qualified personnel to an audit team was borne out by the Enron fraud. Undoubtedly, one of the contributing factors to the success of the management fraud at Enron was the technical nature of the special purpose entities (SPEs) used to hide much of Enron's debt. It is unlikely that a first-year auditor with a bachelor's (or even master's) degree in accounting would understand the complexities inherent in such a technical series of transactions. One might argue that even a fairly experienced auditor may not grasp the intricacies of transactions like these. Only an auditor with specialized experience and training in SPEs would be likely to have a full understanding of this complex topic.

Case-in-Point 10-3

One of the contributing factors to WorldCom's recent bankruptcy was its choice to capitalize expenditures that should have rightfully been expensed. When the corrections were eventually made, WorldCom's assets and equities were so significantly affected that bankruptcy was the only alternative.[14]

Team Discussions   While SAS 82 required a consideration of the possibility of material misstatement due to fraud, SAS 99 expands that consideration to include audit team discussions during planning to discuss the possibility of fraud. Experienced audit team members are expected to share their opinions as to the likelihood of fraud, based on their experience both with that client and with other clients.

Expanded Inquiries of Management and Others   The new standard requires auditors to specifically inquire of management and others within the company as to the possibility of fraud in the company. Additionally, the auditor is to query the audit committee as to its understanding of the risk for fraud within the company. For those companies with internal audit functions, the external auditor is charged with querying the internal auditors as to their procedures in place to detect and deter fraud, including asking them directly whether they are aware of any fraud within the company.

Revenue Recognition   You may remember from earlier in the chapter that the 1999 COSO study on fraudulent financial reporting found that revenue recognition was at the root of 50 percent of such frauds examined over the 1987–1998 period. This trend appears to be continuing, with many financial fraud cases involving improper revenue recognition. See Case-in-Point 10-4.

> ### Case-in-Point 10-4
>
> Recently Qwest Communications came under fire for improperly recognizing over two billion dollars in revenue. As a result, the company expects to restate 2000 and 2001 earnings accordingly.[15]

The new standard requires auditors to specifically consider risks related to revenue recognition, including performing analytical procedures to identify any potential problem areas in how the client recognizes revenue.

Evaluation of Management's Programs and Controls   SAS 82 required the auditor to consider management's programs and controls in place to prevent, deter, or detect fraud. The new standard enhances this requirement by mandating that auditors consider whether these programs have been adequately designed and placed in operation.

The existence of management override is explicitly stated as a consideration in the auditor's risk assessment. As even a novice accounting student or auditor knows, the best of controls become essentially worthless if a member of management exercises his or her authority to circumvent those controls. (See Case-in-Point 10-5.)

> ### Case-in-Point 10-5
>
> Two middle-level executives at WorldCom were not comfortable with their boss' instructions to capitalize certain expenditures that they knew should be expensed according to GAAP. In fact, one of them gave serious consideration to resigning over the issue. But they did it anyway. After all, their boss was the CFO of a major multinational corporation! As a result, these two midlevel executives are facing substantial jail time and millions of dollars in fines. If only the external auditors had asked these two employees about the existence of management override, perhaps the employees would not be facing jail today.[16]

Technology Implications   The new standard also notes the importance of technology in the conduct of an audit, including the appropriate use of computer assisted audit tools and techniques (covered in the detail in Chapter 8). The standard also provides examples and commentary to guide the auditor in this area.

Evaluation of Audit Tests   Once the audit has been conducted, the auditor must evaluate the test results again and consider whether the evidence gathered in aggregate affects the initial assessment of the risk of material misstatement. According to the standard, the procedure is:

1. Determine whether any misstatements identified in the conduct of the audit are likely to be a result of fraud.
2. Determine whether the misstatement is material. If so, or if the auditor cannot make this determination, he or she should:
    a. Consider the implications for the audit as a whole;
    b. Discuss the situation with senior management and with management at least one level above those suspected to be involved and with senior management and the audit committee. If the fraud involves senior management, it should be reported directly to the audit committee;

c. Try to gather additional evidence as to determine if material fraud has occurred, or is likely to have occurred, and the effect on the financial statements and the audit opinion; and

d. If appropriate, suggest that the client consult with legal counsel.

3. If the misstatement is *not* material, the auditor should still consider whether a systematic problem may exist. In particular, the auditor should consider the position of the employee(s) suspected to be involved in the fraud.

4. Consider withdrawing from the engagement if the fraud is pervasive and the auditor cannot satisfy himself or herself as to overall audit risk. If this happens, the auditor should tell the audit committee why the withdrawal was necessary. The auditor may seek legal advice when considering withdrawing from an engagement.

The auditor does not normally disclose the existence of fraud to others outside the company. However, in cases where a successor auditor makes inquiries in accordance with SAS 84, *Communications Between Predecessor and Successor Auditors,* the auditor has a duty to disclose the reasons for withdrawing. Additionally, an auditor responding to a subpoena may disclose the circumstances of the withdrawal.

Future Plans by the Accounting Profession Regarding Fraud

The AICPA is eager to help the accounting profession regain some of its lost credibility and restore its reputation. To this end, AICPA president Barry Melancon in late 2002 announced the creation of the Institute for Fraud Studies, to be established in conjunction with the University of Texas at Austin and the Association of Certified Fraud Examiners. The institute will assist investors in protecting themselves against fraud. The AICPA also has a number of other initiatives on the forefront, including the design of anti-fraud criteria and controls for public corporations, and training for students and professionals (both accountants and corporate America) on anti-fraud measures.[17]

The Corporate and Auditing Accountability, Responsibility, and Transparency Act of 2002 (Sarbanes-Oxley Act)

The Sarbanes-Oxley Act was signed into law by President George W. Bush on July 30, 2002.[18] The law instituted sweeping changes in the accounting profession, which, until that point, had been largely a self-regulating profession. This law created new responsibilities for both the accounting profession and corporate America.

PUBLIC OVERSIGHT BOARD Under Sarbanes-Oxley, the Public Company Accounting Oversight Board was created to regulate the accounting profession. Public companies and their auditors are required to register with the board and pay registration and annual fees to fund the board's operations. The board, composed of five independent members, will issue or adopt standards set by the AICPA and other standard-setting bodies. It is also empowered to investigate members and discipline those found to be in violation of securities laws, ethics breaches, or competency considerations.

INCREASED AUDIT COMMITTEE RESPONSIBILITIES Audit committees in the past have been criticized for being too detached from the audit process. Under the new law, audit committees will directly oversee the auditors' work as opposed to the auditor reporting to management. Additionally, audit committees must preapprove all audit and nonaudit services provided by the auditor, and the auditor must report disagreements between the auditor and management and other relevant communications to the audit committee.

SPECIFICALLY PROHIBITED ACTIVITIES   Independence has long been a contentious issue for the accounting profession. The law lists eight nonaudit services that audit firms are specifically prohibited from providing, plus one additional generic service:

1. Bookkeeping services;
2. Information systems design and implementation;
3. Appraisals or valuation services, fairness opinions, or contribution-in-kind reports;
4. Actuarial services;
5. Internal audits;
6. Management and human resources services;
7. Broker, dealer, or investment advisor;
8. Legal or expert services unrelated to audit services; and
9. Any other services the Public Company Accounting Oversight Board deems to be unallowable.

There's some question as to what "expert services" exactly refers to in item number 8. Does it include the preparation of the client's tax return? Such work has been standard in many audits, and in fact it has been considered part of the audit engagement in many cases. Because the law is so new, these nuances will be worked out over time.

CONDUCT AND ADMINISTRATION OF THE AUDIT   Many audit failures have been attributed to a failure of the auditor to maintain professional skepticism. This happens when the same audit team is in charge year after year and establishes an almost familial relationship with the client. Under these circumstances, the auditor's objectivity can be surreptitiously compromised. The new law is designed to prevent this type of relationship from occurring by requiring mandatory lead audit partner rotation every five years. Further, in addition to a lead audit partner, audits will require a thorough review by a second audit partner.

Management is also now required to assess the company's system of internal control prior to the conduct of the audit. The auditor attests to the accuracy of management's assertions on internal control. The auditor is required to thoroughly document testing done in attesting to management's assertions on the effectiveness of the company's internal control system.

CRIMINAL SANCTIONS AND WHISTLE-BLOWER PROTECTION
Largely as fallout from the Enron fraud and subsequent collapse of its auditor, Arthur Andersen, auditors now face criminal penalties including up to ten years in prison for willfully failing to maintain audit workpapers for a minimum of five years. Likewise, destroying documents relevant to a federal investigation can cost the perpetrator twenty years in prison. Personal loans to executives, such as the $400 million in personal loans Tyco made to its CEO, Dennis Kozlowski, are now prohibited. And the statute of limitations on securities fraud claims will now run the lesser of five years from the fraud occurrence or two years after the fraud was discovered. Finally, whistle-blowers such as Sherron Watkins at Enron are extended protection against companies

that may want to retaliate against them; additionally, they are granted special damages and attorney's fees.

Now that we've seen why fraud is committed and what the auditor and corporate responsibilities are with respect to fraud prevention, deterrence, and detection, let's turn our attention to a special area of auditing called "forensic auditing."

FORENSIC AUDITING

What Is Computer Forensics?

Suppose you are the owner of a small hardware store. You have a trusted bookkeeper who has been employed for over ten years. The problem is, while the inventory balance is growing, the cash balance is shrinking. You hate to think the bookkeeper might be dishonest, but she *is* driving a new BMW while collecting a modest salary.

Suspicions like these might lead you to contact a specialist in forensic auditing to see just how honest the bookkeeper is. A forensic accountant is hired by a company that either suspects a fraud has occurred but doesn't have proof or that knows a fraud has been perpetrated but doesn't know how extensive the loss is. Thus, the forensic accountant functions much like a detective. It is his or her goal to find out who perpetrated the fraud, how the fraud was perpetrated, and how much money or other assets the company has lost as a result of the fraud.

Forensic accountants actually do many other types of services, including reviewing a company's internal controls, conducting penetration testing, performing background checks on current or prospective employees, or providing litigation support such as serving as expert witnesses in criminal or civil court proceedings. Because this book is written mainly for IT auditors, we will focus on computer forensics.

What Can Computer Forensics Do?

Computer forensics involves the discovery and retrieval of electronic data on a computer or electronic media such as tape, CD, DVD, or disks. Many times these files have been deleted. In the case of fraud, they are usually purposefully deleted. What the individual usually doesn't know, however, is that deleted files are not really deleted. They are stored intact in a different place on the computer's hard drive (or other electronic media). They can stay there for several years, assuming the computer's hard drive doesn't fill up and overwrite the files. Even if the hard drive is reformatted, the information can be retrieved. Most forensic experts say that a disk wiping utility would need to wipe the hard drive clean seven times before one could be assured that no data is retrievable.

In addition to recovering deleted files, a forensic accountant can recover works in progress. For example, let's say that an individual is constructing a phony invoice. Perhaps this process requires several steps, including making the invoice template, copying and pasting the company logo, and filling in the invoice. Each of these steps might be captured separately and retrieved as evidence in a criminal investigation.

Forensic accountants are often called in to investigate an employee's inappropriate use of the Internet. For example, e-mail is a source of great interest in many criminal investigations. Recovering deleted e-mail is similar to recovering deleted files. Most deleted e-mail can be recovered intact, along with files that might have been originally attached. Forensic accountants can also discover which Internet sites the employee has visited, what information was downloaded, and to whom the information was disseminated.

Conducting the Forensic Investigation

DEVELOPING A FRAUD THEORY Usually the forensic accountant walks into a company of which he or she has no prior knowledge. The first order of business is to become intimately familiar with the company—from the employees to the jobs they perform. If one particular employee is under suspicion, the accountant has a starting point. If not, the accountant must start from square one—the Fraud Triangle.

You will remember from earlier in the chapter that the Fraud Triangle involves considering opportunity, pressure, and rationalization. Opportunity is the most important piece of the fraud triangle. Without opportunity, fraud cannot occur. So, who has the opportunity within the company? Once you identify the possible perpetrators, who might be under financial pressure? And third, who might be prone to justifying or rationalizing a theft?

Putting these three pieces together will often lead the forensic accountant to one or more suspects and the formation of a working hypothesis. The hypothesis is then tested by gathering evidence and refined as needed.

GATHERING EVIDENCE When a suspect is identified and a working hypothesis has been developed, the next step is to begin the arduous process of obtaining evidence. However, this process doesn't happen without extremely careful planning and execution of that plan. This is because evidence is the foundation of the legal case against the perpetrator. Any tainting of the evidence either as it is collected or while it is in custody can render a case inadmissible in court. The Rules of Evidence require that a strict chain of custody be maintained for the forensic investigator. This means a written log is kept of each piece of evidence gathered. Figure 10-12 shows a sample chain of custody form. In a court proceeding, this form will be subpoenaed and come under scrutiny, so the investigator must take great pains to comply meticulously with this requirement. Evidence is inadmissible otherwise. The investigator must be able to explain where the evidence was at any time, why it changed hands, who authorized the change in custody, and what types of procedures were performed on the evidence.

When a forensic investigation begins, it is essential for the auditor to "freeze" the audit logs. This includes system logs, access logs, firewall logs, backup logs, and any other logs the company uses to monitor its systems. Freezing the logs means making an immediate copy as evidence. This ensures that a clear record exists up to the moment the investigation begins.

Nature of Evidence Gathered:				
Date Gathered:				
Gathered by:				
Name of custodian	Purpose for change in custody	Date and time of change in custody	Tests or procedures performed	Change in custody authorized by:

FIGURE 10-12 Sample Chain of Custody Record

If necessary, the forensic investigator may be empowered to seize the computer of the suspected fraudster, assuming the computer is on company premises. If it is, this seizure would not violate a person's Fourth Amendment rights against unlawful search and seizure. A search warrant is not needed since the company, and not the employee, owns the computer. Note, however, that a person working at home on a company computer would be protected under the Fourth Amendment, and a search warrant would be needed.

INTERVIEWING   During the evidence-gathering phase, the investigator will likely interview many people in the company. These include perhaps someone suspected of fraud, but also many people peripheral to the suspect. The value of a "tip" cannot be underestimated. Estimates are that about 80 percent of all frauds are discovered through tips.[19]

There is a definite skill involved in approaching this interview. For example, the investigator should try to project a nonthreatening image. The more relaxed the suspect is, the more likely he or she is to let their guard down. An icebreaker is a good way to proceed. The investigator should have a planned list of questions, tailored to the individual being interviewed. Questions such as, "Do you know of anyone in the company who might be committing fraud?" seem almost too direct to work, but they often do. Many times employees are just waiting to be asked!

Interviewing the suspect requires a great deal of finesse and patience. And it requires knowing what kinds of verbal and nonverbal cues to look for. Verbal cues include changes in speech pattern, using oaths or swearing, sudden selective memory, and feigned unconcern (a classic symptom of dishonesty). Nonverbal cues include breaking eye contact, shifting body positions, crossing and recrossing arms and legs, and removing eyeglasses.[20] Experts also note other interesting characteristics of dishonesty. For example, people who are being dishonest don't use contractions in their speech. They tend to speak very adamantly. Further, someone under a great deal of stress will often keep their arms and legs crossed for long periods. In other words, they will maintain a very closed body position. Experts note that confessions rarely, if ever, come from an individual in this body position.

INVIGILATION   Another technique for gathering evidence is *invigilation*. This technique involves imposing such strict internal controls as to completely eliminate any chance for fraud to occur. The purpose of invigilation is to eliminate fraud for a period of time and then compare that period with a time when the controls were not in effect. The key question: What's different?

INDIRECT METHODS OF PROOF   The evidence that has been mentioned so far has been concerned with direct methods of proof. That is, you're seizing computers, making copies of hard drives, interviewing employees, and perhaps employing techniques such as surveillance and invigilation. There are indirect methods of gathering evidence as well. These include looking at the suspect's financial profile, including his or her assets, debts, salary and other revenue sources, and expenses and expenditures. A credit report will often turn up financial information such as liens or judgments against an individual.

Looking at the individual's lifestyle is also an easy and useful technique. Like the bookkeeper earlier, is the suspect earning $20,000 per year and driving a new BMW? Does the individual take expensive vacations and wear expensive clothes and jewelry? Does he or she own an expensive home that appears beyond his or her financial means? Of course, just because someone makes $20,000 per year and drives a BMW and lives in a mansion doesn't mean he or she is a crook. There are other legitimate reasons this person might be able to afford that lifestyle. But it certainly is worth looking at.

Prosecution

It is the client's decision whether or not to prosecute an employee who has committed occupational fraud. While some companies do not prosecute out of fear of embarrassment or negative publicity, most (about 75 percent) do prosecute the person suspected of fraud. A criminal case has the heaviest burden of proof: beyond a reasonable doubt. This is often practically translated into a 95 percent assurance standard. If that burden is not met, the company may seek judicial relief in a civil proceeding. Here the burden of proof is considerably less. Guilt must be proved by a reasonable "preponderance of the evidence." Practically speaking, this translates into a 51 percent standard.

For a fraud conviction to occur, the common-law "fraud statute" requires the presence of four elements:

1. *Misrepresentation of a material fact.* What is "material" is often decided by the "reasonable man" standard. That is, if a reasonable man would have acted differently had the fact been correctly known, it will be deemed to be material.

2. *Intent to defraud.* This is often the most difficult component of the fraud statute to prove. The "it was an accident" defense is vitiated by repetition of the act.

3. *Justifiable reliance.* The victim must have relied on the misrepresentation.

4. *Resulting in an injury.* The injury must be quantifiable in economic terms; for example, lost wages or lost revenue.

The Forensic Auditor's Tool Kit

Obtaining electronic evidence will involve the use of special forensic tools and utility programs to either recover data from the hard drive or make an image of the suspect's hard drive. Figure 10-13 shows a list of the tools that might be considered the essential toolkit for a forensic auditor.[21]

A screwdriver and pliers are needed if the computer case must be disassembled. Once you have access to the computer's hard drive, you must use some type of archive media to dump the contents of the drives being copied. Another hard drive is an option, but this can become expensive quickly. Tape is a practical medium due to its affordability. A recordable CD-ROM doesn't have the high capacity usually needed. A recordable DVD has the highest capacity, at 4.7 gigabytes.

A digital camera is a must for photographing the exact condition of the computer, in case the computer must be reassembled in exactly the same way. You also want to photograph what's on the monitor.

The other items listed in Figure 10-13 are mostly applications that forensic auditors use to gather electronic evidence, including disk wiping, disk imaging, hash calculating, search, file and data recovery, and password-cracking utilities.

Disk wiping is used to ensure that the hard drives and removable media are thoroughly cleaned prior to processing evidence. The wiping process overwrites all data with binary information. *Disk imaging* is a read-only process used to create an image of the computer's hard drive. The operating system is not involved in disk imaging. The process creates a bitstream backup that preserves every bit of information on the source computer's hard drive. To verify that the source and destination files are exactly the same, hash calculations are used. A hashing algorithm calculates a 32-bit hash value for both the source and destination computers. If even a single bit is changed, the two hash values will not match. *Search utilities* allow forensic auditors to search for text strings of information on hard drives.

File and data recovery is accomplished through a program such as EnCase. EnCase, made by Guidance Software, has gained significant respectability in the forensic accounting

Tools	Example Utilities	Manufacturer
Screwdriver and pliers		
Disk wiping utility/clean hard drive	Pretty Good Privacy (PGP)	Network Associates, Inc.
	Disk Scrub	New Technologies, Inc.
	SecureClean	New Technologies, Inc.
Disk imaging application	SafeBack	New Technologies, Inc.
	EnCase	Guidance Software
Hash calculation utility	SafeBack	New Technologies, Inc.
	EnCase	Guidance Software
	DiskSig	New Technologies, Inc.
	CRCMDS	New Technologies, Inc.
Search utilities	EnCase	Guidance Software
	DiskSearch Pro	New Technologies, Inc.
	TextSearch Plus	New Technologies, Inc.
File and data recovery tools	EnCase	Guidance Software
	RecoverNT	LC Technology
	Recover98	LC Technology
	GetSlack	New Technologies, Inc.
	GetFree	New Technologies, Inc.
	Linux Extractor	WetStone Technologies
	Norton Utilities	Symantec Corporation
File viewing utilities	Thumbs Plus	Cerious Software
	Quick View Plus	Jasc Software
	EnCase	Guidance Software
	Hex Workshop	BreakPoint Software, Inc.
Password cracking software	Advanced Password Recovery Software Kit	New Technologies, Inc.
	Password Recovery Toolkit	AccessData
	123 Password Recovery	Iopus
Archive media	Hard drive, tape backup, recordable CD-ROM, recordable DVD	
Digital camera		

FIGURE 10-13   The Forensic Auditor's Essential Toolkit
Source: Information Provided by JANUS Associates, Inc. Used with permission.

world, mainly because the software has repeatedly held up under rigorous court scrutiny. EnCase can also handle the needs of most routine forensic accountants, some of whom will say that EnCase is the only forensic tool one really needs.

Computer assisted audit tools such as ACL can be invaluable in helping the IT auditor detect fraud. This topic is covered in detail in Chapter 8.

SUMMARY

Occupational fraud is a serious problem. This chapter has presented statistics showing the nature and extent of fraud in corporate America. Both corporate America and the auditing profession have responsibilities for fraud prevention, deterrence, and detection. Recent legislation, the Sarbanes-Oxley Act of 2002, is the direct result of numerous high-profile fraud cases over the recent past. This law has far-reaching implications for both corporate America and the auditing profession. Forensic auditing allows auditors to retrieve deleted data and files, even after those files have been deleted. The rules for evidence must be followed, including the chain of custody requirements. Tools for the essential toolkit were presented and discussed. The IT auditor should be aware of the various types of tools discussed in this chapter.

DISCUSSION QUESTIONS

10-1   Explain the concept of the Fraud Triangle.

10-2 The "2002 Wells Report" is the most recent comprehensive fraud report. Describe some of the major findings of the report, including: who is most likely to perpetrate fraud and who the victims are.

10-3 Describe the three categories of fraud according to the "Wells Report." Give examples of frauds that fall into each category. In which category do the majority of frauds occur?

10-4 What is a company's responsibility to detect fraud? Describe some of the ways a company can fulfill its responsibility.

10-5 What does SAS 99 require of the auditor with respect to fraud detection and the conduct of the audit?

10-6 Identify the major components of the Sarbanes-Oxley Act of 2002. How will this change the auditor's responsibility to detect fraud?

10-7 What is computer forensics?

10-8 What is meant by "freezing the audit logs"? When is this done, and why is this so important?

10-9 What are some interviewing techniques IT auditors can employ to determine if a fraud suspect is telling the truth?

10-10 Identify the four elements that under common law must be present for a fraud conviction to occur.

10-11 Describe some of the tools a forensic auditor can use in a forensic audit.

EXERCISES

10-12 The year 2002 might be called "The Year of the Whistleblower." Sherron Watkins, Cynthia Cooper, and Coleen Rowley were named "Persons of the Year" for their roles in high-profile frauds. Read the article at www.time.com/time/personoftheyear/2002/poyintro.html. Describe how each of these individuals exposed fraud at their respective institutions. Can their companies legally retaliate against them?

10-13 Guidance Software's EnCase program is one of the most comprehensive tools available for forensic auditing. A demo of EnCase is available at www.guidancesoftware.com. Obtain a copy of the demo and familiarize yourself with some of the capabilities of the software. Prepare a short report on the capabilities of EnCase.

REFERENCES AND RECOMMENDED READINGS

Albrecht, W. S. 2003. *Fraud Examination.* Mason, Ohio: Southwestern.

Association of Certified Fraud Examiners. 2002. *Report to the Nation on Occupational Fraud and Abuse*. Austin, Tex.: ACFE.

Certified Information Systems Auditor Review Manual 2003. 2002. Rolling Meadows, Ill.: Information Systems Audit and Control Association.

Coderre, D. 1999. *Fraud Detection: Using Data Analysis Techniques to Detect Fraud.* Vancouver, Canada: Global Audit Publications.

Davia, H. 2000. *Fraud 101: Techniques and Strategies for Detection.* New York: John Wiley & Sons.

Pickett, K., and J. Pickett. 2002. *Financial Crime Investigation and Control.* New York: John Wiley & Sons.

Rezaee, Z. 2002. *Financial Statement Fraud: Prevention and Detection.* New York: John Wiley & Sons.

Stephenson, P. 2000. *Investigating Computer-Related Crime.* Washington, D.C.: CRC Press.

Wells, J. 1997. *Occupational Fraud and Abuse.* Obsidian Publishing.

Web Sites

Sarbanes-Oxley Act of 2002
www.aicpa.org/info/sarbanes_oxley_summary.htm

Ethics
EthicsLine: www.ethicsline.com/
Illinois Institute of Technology Center for Study of Ethics in the Professions:
    www.iit.edu/departments/csep/PublicWWW/codes/index.html

Fraud
Association of Certified Fraud Examiners: www.acfe.org
www.cfenet.com/resources/fraud.asp
marketplace.cfenet.com/products/products.asp
National Fraud Center: www.nationalfraud.com/

Fraud Interviewing Techniques—The Reid Seminar Series
www.reid.com/training-hosting.html

Fraud survey statistics
1998 KPMG Fraud Survey: www.us.kpmg.com/microsite/fraud/

Association of Certified Fraud Examiners "2002 Report to the Nation Occupational Fraud and Abuse"
www.cfenet.com/media/2002RttN/
"2002 Computer Crime and Security Survey" www.gocsi.com/pdfs/fbi/FBI2002.pdf

Cybercrime
Cyber stalking: www.ccmostwanted.com/cyberstalk.htm

> *Cybercrime Laws in the United States*
> www.usdoj.gov/criminal/cybercrime/1030_anal.html
> State cyber crime laws: www.ccmostwanted.com/stateagencies.htm

Professional Guidance
The Institute of Internal Auditors' IT audit Web site www.theiia.org/itaudit
The American Institute of Certified Public Accountants www.aicpa.org
Computer Emergency Response Team (CERT), at Carnegie Mellon University. This center provides guidance on a host of computer security topics, including intrusion detection, incidence response planning, and viruses and worms: www.cert.org

> *Professional Services Firms*
> JANUS Associates, Inc., Stamford, CT. www.janusassociates.com/default.html

NOTES

1.   Wells, J. 1997. *Occupational Fraud and Abuse,* Obsidian Publishing.
2.   Wells, Joseph T. 2001. "Why Employees Commit Fraud." *Journal of Accountancy*. February, pp. 89–91.
3.   "Former J.P. Morgan Official Admits to $4.5 Million Fraud." 2002. *The Wall Street Journal.* September 5; and "Ex-J.P. Morgan Exec Gets 7-Year Sentence For Embezzlement" 2003. *The Wall Street Journal.* March 26, 2003.
4.   Davia, Howard. 2000. *Fraud 101.* New York: John Wiley & Sons.
5.   Available at www.us.kpmg.com/microsite/fraud/.
6.   For the 2002 CSI/FBI "Computer Crime and Security Survey," see www.gocsi.com/pdfs/fbi/FBI2002.pdf. The survey is free, but requesters are required to provide some personal information before downloading the survey.

7.   "COSO's New Fraud Study: What it Means for CPAs." 1999. *Journal of Accountancy.* May, pp. 12–13.

8.   Ibid.

9.   Ibid.

10.   Ibid

11.   See www.iit.edu/departments/csep/PublicWWW/codes/index.html.

12.   AICPA *Professional Standards.* Vol. 1, AU Sec. 110.

13.   This section summarizes SAS 99. The reader is urged to read the entire SAS to gain a complete understanding of the standard.

14.   "U.S., Pushing WorldCom Case, Indicts Ex-CFO and His Aide." 2002. *The Wall Street Journal.* August 29, p. A1.

15.   "Taking the Pledge: Restatements Trickle In." 2002. *The Wall Street Journal.* August 15, p. A7. Also "Latest Restatement From Qwest Is to Clip $357 Million in Revenue." 2003. *The Wall Street Journal.* February 12, 2003, p. B3.

16.   "U.S., Pushing WorldCom Case, Indicts Ex-CFO and His Aide," *The Wall Street Journal*, August 29, 2002, p. A1.

17.   See www.aicpa.org/news/2002/p020904b.htm.

18.   The AICPA provides the "Summary of Sarbanes-Oxley Act of 2002" on its Web site, www.aicpa.org/info/sarbanes_oxley_summary.htm.

19.   Well, Joseph T., 2001. "Why Ask?" You Ask, *Journal of Accountancy.* September.

20.   Buckhoff, Thomas, "Fraud Auditing and Interviewing Techniques," Presented at the 2001 American Accounting Association Annual Meeting, Atlanta, Ga. Used with permission.

21.   This information was provided courtesy of JANUS Associates, Inc., of Stamford, Conn., and is used with permission.

attestation   A service provided by an auditor whereby the auditor provides assurance on something for which the client is responsible.

agreed-upon procedure (AUP)   An attestation engagement in which the client requests that the auditor examine very specific items.

American Institute of Certified Public Accountants (AICPA)   The professional accounting association that certifies public accountants. This organization, through its Auditing Standards Board (ASB), issues Generally Accepted Auditing Standards (GAAS) and interpretations of these standards, known as Statements on Auditing Standards, that guide CPAs in their auditing work.

application service provider (ASP)   A vendor who implements, hosts, and maintains a software application for a customer.

asset misappropriation   Involves the theft or misuse of a company's assets.

Association of Certified Fraud Examiners (ACFE)   The organization that issues the certified fraud examiner (CFE) credential to professionals specializing in fraud auditing.

audit command language (ACL)   A generalized audit software program used for data access, analysis, and reporting functions.

audit risk   The likelihood that an organization's external auditor makes a mistake when issuing an opinion on financial statements or that an IT auditor fails to uncover a major fraud or error. Audit risk is a combination of inherent, control, and detection risk.

authentication   Ensuring the identity of network resource users.

availability   Criteria indicating that an Internet site and its processes are on or available for use at any time.

Benford's Law   In a large sample of naturally occurring numbers, such as invoice amounts, the left-most digit will follow an exponential distribution wherein the number 1 will appear approximately 30.1 percent of the time, the number 2 will appear approximately 17.6 percent of the time, and so on. The number 9 will appear approximately 4.6 percent of the time. Benford's Law is used to examine the possibility of fraud in a sample of financial data.

big bang implementation strategy   A strategy for deployment of a new IT application. An organization ceases using the old system and immediately begins operating the new one.

blended threats   Combinations of multiple programmed threats—for example, a virus, worm, and hoax.

business risk   The likelihood that an organization will not achieve its business goals and objectives.

Cadbury   An internal control model developed by the United Kingdom's Cadbury Commission.

certificate authority   A trusted third party that issues various types of authentication to online users.

certified fraud examiner (CFE)   A credential granted by the Association of Certified Fraud Examiners to candidates who have accumulated sufficient points based on their educational and professional experience. Certification also requires successful completion of a proficiency examination.

certified information security manager (CISM)   A credential given by the Information Systems Audit and Control Association for non–audit information system security professionals.

certified information systems auditor (CISA)   The most widely respected and known certification credential for an IT auditor. The certification is awarded by the Information Systems

Audit and Control Association (ISACA) and requires a combination of work experience and proficiency evidenced by successfully completing an examination.

certified information technology professional (CITP)   A professional certification that a CPA can acquire to evidence specialized IT expertise.

certified internal auditor (CIA)   A certification granted by the Institute of Internal Auditors indicating that an internal auditor has met educational standards and work requirements and has passed a proficiency examination.

chain of custody   Requirement in a forensic audit that all evidence obtained is accounted for from the point the evidence is gathered and for the entire time it is in custody.

client/server network   A network consisting of servers that manage the networks and host applications that they share with client computers.

CoCo   An internal control model developed by the Canadian Criteria of Control Committee.

cold site   A contract arrangement with a third-party provider that provides for the availability of a building or office space in case of a disaster.

collaborative (c-) business   A network of business enterprises with blurred boundaries.

computer assisted audit tools and techniques (CAATTs)   Refers collectively to two categories: 1) software used to increase an auditor's personal productivity and to perform data extraction and analysis; and 2) techniques used to increase the efficiency and effectiveness of the audit, such as routines used to analyze data once it has been extracted.

computer assisted audit techniques (CAATs)   Routines used to increase the efficiency and effectiveness of the audit, such as routines used to analyze data once it has been extracted.

Computer Crime and Intellectual Property Section (CCIPS)   A section of the U.S. Department of Justice that consists of a group of lawyers who focus exclusively on the issues raised by computer and intellectual property crime.

Computer Fraud and Abuse Act of 1986   A federal statute that clarified definitions of criminal fraud and abuse for federal computer crimes and removed legal ambiguities and obstacles to prosecuting these crimes.

concurrency control   A control over problems that occur when multiple users attempt to update the same data item simultaneously or when one user updates while another reads the same data item.

confidentiality   Protection afforded to information specifically designated to be kept secret.

continuity risk   Risks associated with an information system's availability and backup and recovery processes.

continuous audit   Using embedded audit modules to audit client data continually.

Control Objectives of Business Information Technology (CobiT)   An internal control model that integrates internal control with information and information technology. CobiT was first issued by the Information Systems Audit and Control Association.

cookies   Pieces of data placed in a Web browser's memory that contain both the identity of the Web server leaving the cookie and the identity of the user's computer.

corruption   Misuse of personal power or position for personal gain.

COSO framework   COSO stands for the Committee of Sponsoring Organizations, the group of accounting and finance professional organizations that developed this internal control framework. The framework consists of a definition of internal control, internal control objectives, and five interrelated components of internal control.

crackers   Hackers who act with malicious intent.

cybercrime   Any crime committed through the use of a computer.

cyber criminal   An individual who engages in crime through the use of the computer.

data analytic review   An IT audit in which the auditor extracts data from the client system and uses software such as ACL to analyze the quality and integrity of the data.

data query model   An analytical tool in which data is examined to determine if the evidence obtained fits within the context of other data obtained in the course of the audit.

data scrubbing   Cleaning data via data conversion programs that check for missing information, incorrect formats, duplicate postings, and so on.

denial of service (DOS) attack   An attack against a network system that occurs when a system is tied up in such a way that it is unable to perform its functions.

development library   A secured area of the computer where programmers develop and store source code while creating software programs or making program changes.

digital analysis   Analyzing the pattern of first digits in a large sample of financial data to see if the distribution conforms to Benford's Law, an exponential distribution.

digital certificate   A statement of authentication issued by a trusted third party, such as a certificate authority.

digital signature   A use of encryption that binds a message sender to a communicated document.

disk imaging   Process used to create an exact image of the hard drive.

disk wiping   The process of overwriting a computer hard drive and removable media to ensure that data cannot be recovered later.

distributed denial of service (DDOS) attack   A type of DOS in which the attack message comes from a variety of sources.

dumb terminal   An input/output device that can send and/or receive data but has no processing capability.

electronic audit trails   Electronic evidence (e.g., e-mail messages, logs, and electronic source documents) showing the history of a transaction.

electronic bill presentment and payment (EBPP) system   An approach to paying bills over the Internet. This is done either by making arrangements with individual creditors or through a banking service.

electronic business extensible markup language (ebXML)   An industry-specific language of XML under development to enhance the use of global electronic business information.

Electronic Communications Privacy Act of 1986 (ECPA)   Legislation enacted to address legal privacy issues surrounding the use of computers.

electronic data interchange (EDI)   The computer-to-computer exchange of business documents.

electronic working papers   Software that automates the audit workpaper process.

electronic vaulting   Sending backup data over a communications network.

encryption   Scrambling or coding data so that anyone who views it will not be able to make sense of it without a decoder or decryption key.

enterprise systems   Enterprise resource planning (ERP) information systems that integrate an organization's systems for distribution, accounting and finance, manufacturing, and human resources.

expected value of risk   The product of the estimated loss from a specific risk times the percentage likelihood of the loss.

expert systems   Software based on a series of if–then rules that assists auditors in making structured decisions.

extensible business reporting language (XBRL)   A specialized set of XML tags for the accounting and finance industry to facilitate business reporting on the Internet.

extensible markup language (XML)   A tagging or markup language that facilitates the transmission and manipulation of information across the Internet. Unlike HTML, XML tags are expandable and describe the data rather than the data format.

extranet External networks that connect an organization's intranet with outside business partners.

feasibility study A recommendation to the IT steering committee concerning a proposed project's technical, financial, and cultural feasibility.

financial auditors Auditors whose objective is to attest to the reliability and fairness of an entity's financial statements.

firewall A filter that screens and monitors network traffic.

focused implementation strategy A strategy for deployment of a new application system in which an organization identifies a relatively small group of users to first use the system before wide-spread use.

forensic auditing Using software and other tools to determine the nature and extent of a fraud; often involves recovering deleted files.

Fourth Amendment Protects citizens from unlawful search and seizure of personal property.

fraud triangle The three factors present when fraud occurs—opportunity, incentive or pressure, and attitude or rationalization.

generalized audit software (GAS) Software used to increase the efficiency of the audit, such as ACL, expert systems, utility software, and statistical software.

groupware Software that facilitates sharing of information across firms and between the auditor and the client, including multi-user calendaring, scheduling, and file sharing.

hackers People who attack networked computer systems or individuals who are simply preoccupied with computers.

hoax An e-mail message instructing a user to delete certain files as a security precaution against viruses or other programmed threats.

hot site Contract arrangement with a third party that provides for the availability of a building or office space, complete with computers and perhaps a compatible host operating system, in case of a disaster.

hypertext mark-up language (HTML) A formatting language that specifies the presentation of information over the World Wide Web.

Hypertext Transmission Protocol (HTTP) The standardized rule set that governs data transmission over the World Wide Web.

illegal acts Acts representing a willful violation of law.

Information Systems Audit and Control Association (ISACA) The professional organization for IT auditors. ISACA licenses certified information systems auditors. The professional association also established the IT Governance Institute, which recently published the third edition of CobiT.

Institute of Internal Auditors An international organization of internal auditing professionals that promotes the practice of internal auditing through quality assurance; issuance of standards, guidelines, and best practices; certification of professionals; and publication of a journal and other resources.

integrated test facility (ITF) A method for testing fabricated data (test data) through the client's live system along with normal data processing.

intellectual property Valuable creations of the mind. Two general categories of intellectual property are industrial and individual property.

internal control flowcharts Graphic descriptions of internal controls associated with a specific risk or process.

internal control narratives Text descriptions of internal controls associated with a specific risk or process.

internal control questionnaires   A data-gathering tool for collecting information concerning strengths and weaknesses of a system of internal controls.

International Federation of Accountants (IFAC)   An international umbrella organization of national professional accountancy member groups. The mission of IFAC is to develop harmonized international accounting standards and guidelines.

Internet log files   The record that Web servers make each time a user's Web browser views an Internet page.

Internet Protocol (IP) address   The numerical translation of a text address, including both source and destination information.

Internet service provider (ISP)   A service that provides a point-of-presence (POP) on the Internet to individual user computers. The service provides clients with high-speed Internet connectivity.

Internet tracking tools   Software applications and features designed to monitor user behavior on the Internet.

intranet   An internal computer network with resource access limited to authorized users.

intrusion detection systems (IDS)   Software consisting of logging and monitoring activities to detect unauthorized attempts to access network resources.

invigilation   A method of detecting fraud in which strict internal controls are imposed for a short time to completely eliminate any chance for fraud to occur.

irregular acts   Acts that reflect an intentional violation of corporate policies or regulatory requirements, or an unintentional breach of law.

ISO 9000   A series of quality control standards developed by the International Organization for Standardization. These standards can lead to certification that an organization complies with quality control standards that contribute to high quality products and processes.

IT Function Scorecard   Based on the Balanced Scorecard concept of financial and nonfinancial performance measurement, an approach to evaluating the IT function.

IT governance   The process for controlling an organization's IT resources. The objectives of IT governance are to use IT to promote organizational objectives and enable business processes and also to manage and control IT-related risks.

legal contracts   Agreements among two or more persons or entities to do, or abstain from doing, something in return for an exchange of consideration.

local area network (LAN)   A group of connected computers within a limited geographical area.

monitoring   Continuous checking and evaluation of a process or system.

network attached storage (NAS)   An approach to configuring redundant storage devices that integrates one or more storage devices into the company's LAN.

network management software   Manages the server's performance and communications across the network.

network security administration   The functional group in an organization responsible for creating a network security plan, developing and communicating a security policy for network resources, and managing passwords.

network topologies   Network computer configurations such as star, ring, and bus topologies.

networked computer systems   Two or more computers linked by a communication channel.

open systems interconnect (OSI)   A standard architecture for networking with specified protocols that allow different computers to communicate across networks.

parallel implementation   A strategy for deployment of a new software application in which the new one is placed into production alongside the existing application and both are used to simultaneously process live data.

parallel simulation Creating a replica of the client's application, running live data through the system, and comparing the results with data actually run through the client's system in normal data processing.

partial implementation A strategy for deployment of a new software application in which a new system is phased in one piece at a time.

password crackers Software tools used for guessing passwords.

penetration testing A technique employed by ethical hackers and auditors to access network resources in order to determine system vulnerabilities.

penetration testing Attempting to gain access to information resources in order to discover security weaknesses.

phreaker A hacker who specializes in computer fraud related to the phone system.

physical infrastructure threats Threats to computer systems associated with the physical hardware—for example, threats from the elements, natural disasters, power supplies, and intentional human attacks.

physical vaulting Moving a data storage medium to an off-site location for backup and recovery purposes.

port scanning A technique used by hackers and penetration testers to survey network ports to determine the network services provided by a particular system.

Pretty Good Privacy (PGP) An encryption standard used for e-mail systems.

privacy The protection afforded to proprietary information such as personal information and information related to exchanges or transactions.

production library A secured area of the computer where live data and applications are housed.

programmed threats Attacks to computer systems consisting of malicious program code developed by hackers or crackers.

project life cycle The various phases in managing a project, which include planning, scheduling, monitoring, controlling, and closing.

protocols Standardized rule sets that control network communications among hardware and software from different vendors.

Redundant Array of Independent Disks (RAID) An approach to configuring redundant storage devices that provides for multiple levels of redundancy, including disk mirroring and striping.

reliability Criteria indicating that an Internet site and its associated processes or an information system are performing as expected.

repudiation The ability of a party engaged in a transaction to deny either its participation or particular aspects of the transaction itself.

risk indicators Indications of increased levels of risk associated with the IT deployed. Risk indicators point to need for internal controls. Similar to *vulnerabilities*.

roll-back procedure A procedure in which uncompleted transactions are placed back into a processing queue after an interruption in processing.

routers and switches Devices that connect network components and ensure that messages reach their appropriate destinations.

SAS 70 audit An audit provided to a service organization (for example, an application service provider) who provides services to a large number of users. The audit focuses on the internal controls around that business process for a period of at least six months.

SAS 94 audit Examines the role of technology in a client organization and how technology affects the auditor's assessment of control risk within the financial statement audit. Part of a regular financial statement audit.

Sarbanes-Oxley Act of 2002   Legislation enacted to improve the reliability of financial reporting for public companies. The act requires management to assess and make representations concerning internal controls.

script kiddies   Hackers who use widely available tools to break into computer systems. These hackers have a relatively low skill level with respect to computers and software.

secure electronic transmission (SET)   An encryption protocol using strong cryptography to open a secure Internet session from a remote terminal. SET has some similarity to SSL but it includes authentication through the use of digital certificates.

Secure Multipurpose Internet Mail Extensions (S/MIME)   An encryption standard used for e-mail systems.

Secure Sockets Layer (SSL)   An encryption protocol developed by Netscape that uses public/private key encryption to provide for secure business transactions on the Internet.

security risk   IT security risks associated with data access and integrity.

server area network   An approach to configuring redundant storage devices that expands the network attached storage (NAS) concept to wide area networks (WAN).

Six Sigma   A standardized approach to process improvement through reducing defects to less than 3.4 per million.

smart terminal   A computer terminal that can perform some processing of the data it sends or receives to or from a host computer.

sniffer   A type of spy software that hackers and IT auditors use to capture data as it is transmitted across networks.

social engineering   A form of manipulation and trickery that relies on human behaviors.

software vulnerabilities   Holes or weak spots in application and operating system software caused by programming errors or left by programmers for debugging purposes.

spamming   Sending multiple unwanted e-mails.

spoofing   Purposefully hiding one's true identity on the Internet.

spyware   Software used to capture, or "listen in" on, data transmitted across networks.

Statements on Auditing Standards (SAS)   Standards issued by the Auditing Standards Board of the American Institute of Certified Public Accountants. Several have implications for IT auditors, such as SAS No. 94, *The Effect of Information Technology on the Auditor's Consideration of Internal Control in a Financial Statement Audit.*

Statements on Standards for Attestation Engagements (SSAE)   Guidelines for work by a CPA on an engagement requiring the auditor to issue a report stating a conclusion about the reliability of subject matter that is the responsibility of another party.

stress testing   Testing a newly developed application system under extreme conditions to determine if it can handle peak loads and to ascertain the point at which the system can no longer handle the load.

string or module testing   Testing a module or group of related computer programs.

SYN flood   A type of denial of service (DOS) attack that involves sending multiple messages from one computer to another and leaving the connection open.

systems reliability assurance   Assurance or increased comfort that information systems are reliable against specified principles and criteria. Includes trust services developed by the American Institute of Certified Public Accountants, such as WebTrust and SysTrust.

telecommunications   The transfer of text, audio, video, image, or other data formats across a computer network.

telecommunications channels   Transfer communications among networked computers. These channels use various media, including twisted pair wire, coaxial network cable, fiber optic cable, and wireless.

telecommunications processors   Processors that transform computer signals and transfer them across telecommunications channels. Examples are modems, ISDN, T1, T3, and DSL lines.

test data   Fabricated data used to test the integrity of application software.

test library   A secured area of the computer where applications reside during testing, without compromising live data and applications.

third-party assurance services   The use of an independent third party to evaluate a business' information systems with respect to online privacy, security, transaction integrity, systems reliability, and business policies (e.g., AICPA trust services).

threats   Areas in which IT is exposed to various risks. Risk assessment includes an analysis of threats.

Title 18 crimes and criminal procedure   Part of the U.S. Code representing the most comprehensive legal guidance from the federal government regarding cybercrime.

transaction integrity   Criteria that indicate that an information system processes transactions that are accurate, authorized, complete, and timely.

Trojan horse   Malicious program code embedded in seemingly harmless programs or messages.

Type I audit opinion   Report produced after a SAS 70 audit in which internal controls are examined only on a "walkthrough" basis, but the controls are not tested.

Type II audit opinion   Report produced after a SAS 70 audit in which the internal controls are tested over a period of at least six months.

unit testing   Testing an individual software program or unit of code.

U.S. Patriot Act of 2001   A federal statute that provides law enforcement agencies with sweeping powers with respect to their ability to monitor and arrest suspected terrorists.

value-added network (VAN)   A third-party intermediary in EDI transactions that acts as an electronic post office.

virtual private network (VPN)   A network that uses the public Internet as its primary network system to connect remote computer systems.

virus   A set of malicious program code designed to copy itself from one file to another.

vulnerabilities   Increased levels of exposure resulting from the IT that is deployed. Risk assessment includes an analysis of vulnerabilities to specified threats.

war dialing   A technique used by hackers to repeatedly dial random phone numbers to try to access network systems.

war drivers   Hackers who drive around parking lots or other business areas searching for wireless network access points.

warm site   A contract arrangement with a third-party provider that provides a building or office space and basic computing infrastructure in case of a disaster.

Web browser   Telecommunications software that provides an interface with the Internet.

wide area network (WAN)   A network connecting computers some geographic distance away from each other.

wireless application protocol (WAP)   A set of standardized rules that allow wireless communications.

worm   A set of malicious program code designed to copy itself from computer to computer.

APPENDIX B: PEOPLE STATE UNIVERSITY—AUDITING PAYROLL USING ACL

INSTRUCTIONS

You are in charge of the Payroll Audit for People State University (PSU). The audit consists of four steps: 1) ACL administration, 2) analytical review procedures, 3) fraud tests, and 4) other procedures. As you progress through the audit outline, there are questions about the procedures and outcomes. Include your answers to the questions, as well as relevant output from the ACL tests, as support in your workpapers.

SCOPE AND OBJECTIVES

Scope

Conduct an audit of the Peoplesoft payroll module for payroll period ending 10–26–2000.

Objectives

1. Ensure that payroll information is accurate and reliable.
2. Assess the extent to which People State University complies with policies and procedures, plans, laws, and regulations.

ACL ADMINISTRATION

Identify and obtain access to all database records necessary to conduct the following computer-assisted audit procedures.

Download the following databases from John Wiley & Sons and import the databases into ACL:

EMPLOYEE_FILE.DBF (www.wiley.com/college/hunton)
EMPLOYEE_PAY.DBF (www.wiley.com/college/hunton)

Save your ACL project as "PSU."

Refer to the dictionary of codes used by these databases when appropriate (see Attachments One and Two).

Be sure to include documentation of each of the following tests in your workpapers.

Open EMPLOYEE_PAY.

How many records are there in the database?

How many data validity errors are there in the database?

What are the following totals?

Gross pay (TOTAL_GROS)
Taxes withheld (TOTAL_TAXE)
Deductions withheld (TOTAL_DEDU)
Net pay (NET_PAY)

Open EMPLOYEE_FILE
How many records are there in the database?
How many data validity errors are there in the non–date fields?
What are the total annual salaries? (ANNUAL_RT)

Analytical Review Procedures

Be sure to include documentation of each of the following tests and related questions in your workpapers.

Using the EMPLOYEE_FILE database, classify on PAY GROUP and accumulate on ANNUAL_RATE.

Review this report. What are you verifying? Explain by giving an example.

Using the EMPLOYEE_PAY database, confirm that total gross pay amount less total taxes withheld less total deductions withheld equals the net pay amount by recalculating another net pay field. Call your new field "Computed_Net."

What are the totals of Computed_Net and Net_pay?

When you tested that total gross less total taxes less total deductions equals net pay, were there differences between the Computed_Net and Net_Pay fields? If so, obtain a report of all records where differences exist and explain what is probably causing the differences.

Fraud Tests

Be sure to include documentation of each of the following tests and related questions in your workpapers.

INVALID EMPLOYEES TEST
Use EMPLOYEE_PAY database.

Determine if there are duplicate social security numbers in the EMPLOYEE_PAY database.

What could be the possible reasons for the duplicate social security numbers?
What would you do to find out the actual reason for these duplicates?

ADDRESS TEST
Review addresses for the following unusual items:

How many blank addresses are in the database?
Why might these blank addresses exist?
How many instances are there of multiple employees using the same address?
Describe the probable causes for the duplicate addresses.
How many post office box numbers are listed as addresses?
How many out-of-state addresses are listed?
Assuming PSU operates only in Florida, why would there be non-Florida addresses?

DUPLICATE APPOINTMENTS TEST IN EMPLOYEE MASTER FILE
Use EMPLOYEE_FILE.

Determine if there are duplicate employee numbers (EMPLID), and save the results to a separate file. Call this file "Duplicates." Count the records and duplicates. List: Employee ID, name, department ID, full-time or part-time, pay group, employee status, effective date, action reason, and annual rate on the report.

What were some of the causes of the duplicate numbers? Do not list actual employees, just describe the general causes. (You will need to use the code list here. Duplicates include changes of status and terminated employees.)

INACTIVE EMPLOYEE TEST

Test to verify that all employees who received paychecks were also in the current EMPLOYEE_FILE. Count the number of records that do not. (Hint: You will need to join the files to identify unmatched records.) Call the joined file "UNMATCHED."

First, we must ensure that the primary key used to match (EMPLID) is a character field of the same length in both files (EMPLOYEE_FILE and EMPLOYEE_PAY).

Open EMPLOYEE_FILE. Using edit input file definition, open the field named EMPLID by double clicking on the field name. Change the type to ASCII and verify that the length is 12.

Open EMPLOYEE_PAY. Using edit input file definition, open the field named EMPLID by double clicking on the field name. Change the type to ASCII and verify that the length is 12.

With the EMPLOYEE_PAY file open, join the two files using DATA, JOIN.

The Primary key is EMPLID. Click on Primary fields and select add all.

The Secondary file is EMPLOYEE_FILE. The Secondary key is EMPLID. Since we are looking for unmatched records, there are no secondary fields.

In the TO box enter file name UNMATCHED.

Click on the MORE tab, then click the box marked UNMATCHED Primary RECORDS. Click on OK.

Open the file called UNMATCHED.

How many unmatched records are there?

Why would these employees receive paychecks when they are no longer active per the Master File?

What would you do to verify the reasons?

Other Procedures

Be sure to include documentation of each of the following tests in your workpapers.

Identify three additional audit tests to be performed using ACL and the two data files (EMPLOYEE_FILE and EMPLOYEE_PAY).

What is the audit objective of each test?

Perform each of the three tests identified above.

Describe and analyze your findings.

ATTACHMENT ONE: DICTIONARY OF DATABASE CODES FOR EMPLOYEE_FILE

Field Codes

EMPLID—Employee ID number
NAME—Employee name
DEPTID—Department ID
JOBCODE—Job code
U STUDENT—Student union employee (All-Times, Graduation-Periods, Holiday-Only)
REG TEMP—Regular or Temporary employee
PAYGROUP—Pay group

PEU	Exceptional hourly USPS
POP	Salaried and hourly OPS
PS3	3-month salaried faculty
PS9	9-month salaried faculty
PSA	Salaried A&P (Administrative and Professional)
PSF	Salaried faculty
PSU	Salaried USPS

ACTION—Payroll action

EMPL STATU—Employee status (active or terminated)

FULL PART—Full-time (F) or Part-time (P)

STD HOURS—Standard hours

ACTION DT—Payroll action date

EFFDT—Payroll action effective date

EFFSQ—Effective payroll sequence number

ACTION REA—Payroll action reason

EMPL TYPE—Employee type

COMP FREQ—Compensation frequency (Biweekly or Hourly)

HOURLY RT—Hourly rate

MONTHLY RT—Monthly rate

COMPRATE—Compensatory time rate

ANNL BENEF—Annual benefits

ANNUAL RT—Annual benefit rate

CHANGE AMT—Change amount

CHANGE PCT—Change percentage

CMPNY SENI—Company seniority date

EE06CODE—Equal Employment Opportunity code

1	Executive
2	Faculty
3	Prof nonfaculty
4	Secretarial/clerical
5	Technical/paraprofessional
6	Skilled craft
7	Service maintenance

EMPL RCD—Employment record

FICA STATU—FICA status (Exempt, Nonexempt)

HIRE DT—Hire date

JOB ENTRY—Job entry date

LAST INCRE—Last increase date

REHIRE DT—Rehire date

SAL ADMIN—Salary administrative code

SERVICE DT—Service date

TERMINATIO—Termination date

U DUAL COM—Union dual compensation

U OVERLAP—Union overlap

ATTACHMENT TWO: DICTIONARY OF DATABASE CODES FOR EMPLOYEE_PAY

Field Codes

EMPLID—Employee ID number
SSN—Social security number
PAYCHECK N—Paycheck name
BENEFIT RC—Benefits reclassification code
ADDRESS1—Check address
CITY—Check city
STATE—Check state
ZIP—Check ZIP code
COUNTRY—Check country
CHECK DT—Check date
PAY END DT—Payroll ending date
EMPL TYPE—Employee type (Exempt, Salary, Hourly)
DEPTID—Department ID number
NET PAY—Net pay amount
PAY GROUP—Pay group

PEU	Exceptional hourly USPS
POP	Salaried and hourly OPS
PS3	3-month salaried faculty
PS9	9-month salaried faculty
PSA	Salaried A&P
PSF	Salaried faculty
PSU	Salaried USPS

TOTAL DEDU—Total deductions amount
TOTAL GROS—Total gross pay amount
TOTAL TAXE—Total taxes amount

INDEX

A

American Institute of Certified
Public Accountants
(AICPA), 8, 10, 11, 56, 249
assurance service of, 59–60,
171
audit standards and guidelines, 11, 12, 208; *see
also* Statements on
auditing standards
on electronic evidence, 165
Institute for Fraud Studies
and, 249
International Federation of
Accountants and, 12
privacy rights and, 43
SysTrust of, 59–60, 164,
171, 216
WebTrust of, 171, 172, 215,
216
application service provider
(ASP), 104, 166, 170
assessing risks, 51–53, 210
approach example, 51
calculating value of risk, 52
for fraud, 246–247
indications and measure-
ment of risk, 52–53
steps application example,
53
threats and vulnerabilities,
51–53
Association of Certified Fraud
Examiners (ACFE), 8,
10–11, 232, 233–239, 249
attestation, 12, 213–217
agreed–upon procedure
(AUP), 213, 214, 215
commission agreement
reviews, 214–215, 216
Committee of Sponsoring
Organizations and, 213
compliance reviews,
216–217
data analytic reviews, 214
financial projections, 216

findings and recommenda-
tion versus, 213, 214
representation letter, 213
Statement on Standards for
Attestation Engagements
(SSAE), 12, 208, 213
SysTrust engagements, 216
WebTrust engagements,
215, 216
audit overview, 1–18
audit program generic components, 210
audit report, 212
audit risks, 49–50, 92, 94
controlling information and,
110
infrastructure compromise
and, 106
learning opportunities and,
102
rewarding employees and,
101
staffing and, 99–100
audit skills, 7–8
educational background, 7
general, 8
technical, 7–8
auditing standards, statement
on. *See* Statements on auditing standards
Auditing Standards Board
(ASB), 56
auditor organizations and certifications, professional, 7,
8–11
auditors, IT
educational background of, 7
internal, 10
responsibilities with respect
to irregular and illegal
acts, 22–23
skills of, 7–8
work of, 4–5
authentication, 139
authorized identification, 108,
109, 111, 114
availability breach, 33

B

backup controls, 110, 115; *see
also* data backup; hardware
backup
balanced scorecard, 74–75
Benford's Law, 8, 196, 198, 199
business continuity review,
222, 223–224
business process analysis, 81
business risk, 48–49, 92, 93;
see also e-business risks
controlling information and,
110
infrastructure compromise
and, 106
learning opportunities and,
102
rewarding employees and,
101
staffing and, 99, 100

C

Canadian Criteria of Control
Committee (CoCo), 55
Canadian Institute of Charter
Accountants (CICA), 59,
171, 215, 216
Certified Fraud Examiner
(CFE), 7, 10–11
Certified Information Security
Manager (CISM), 9, 10
Certified Information Systems
Auditor (CISA), 7, 9, 11,
13, 21
Certified Information
Technology Professional
(CITP), 11
Certified Internal Auditor
(CIA), 7, 9, 10
Certified Public Accountant
(CPA), 7, 10, 11, 179
assurance services, 171,
172, 215
attestation and, 12
generally accepted auditing
standards and, 12

273